THE HAYS HOUSE

Ghosts Are People Too!

Keith Evans (signature)

Keith Evans

outskirts press

Outskirts Press, Inc.
http://www.outskirtspress.com

ISBN: 978-1-9772-0105-8

Library of Congress Control Number: 2018907942

Outskirts Press and the "OP" logo are trademarks belonging to Outskirts Press, Inc.

PRINTED IN THE UNITED STATES OF AMERICA

determined that a virgin pine forests would proof resident within the first three years.

d turpentine farms on the Panhandle of Florida,
arms in Sanford and Lakeland Florida. Jeff Buck
Id purchase virgin pineland in Franklin County,
. Buck was 14 years old, his father, Jeff Buck
ast Bay, Florida along Doyle's Creek. While the
being built to include a distillery, barns, commis-
nd barrel producing buildings. His family lived in
hen the turpentine farm was completed. Jeff Buck
th black and white families from South Carolina
on his turpentine farm.

00 James F. Buck had leased close to 5000 acres of
ty. James F. Buck also purchased land near Whiskey
vas unable to purchase the land in Whiskey George
nto West Bayou and is part of East Bay, he would
as not for sale. In one lease with Nick Hays, James
tems of a well-established naval store business that
ted for number many years. Here is a list of the fol-
es F. Buck leased: 125 barrels still, four mules, one
agons, one pump 24,976 virgin huty, 29,700 year-
y cups, miscellaneous tools, 4 crops of turpentine
buildings, one commissary, one barn, one outfit of
r items on location. This lease included a complete
ion. This operation was primarily a naval store busi-
roduction of spirits of turpentine and resin. These
turned into more than just making spirits of turpen-
d into a variety of businesses.

00s Apalachicola went through an increase in
mboat business at its peak and the Apalachicola
ming into Apalachicola in 1905. This brought an
als who needed buildings to work in and places
increase need for lumber in Apalachicola in the
. Buck saw the opportunity and began different

Table of Contents

The Buck
House, G

This is a history o
F. Buck built and v
House. He, his w
Hays House. Jame
had six children: |
Vincent Kern, and
1907 and the Hay
have seen it spell
member who was
middle name wa
James Buck's fami
South Carolina. H
rice. Tobacco wa
tine. Jeff Buck lo\
farming, but that'

Jeff Buck's motiva
had a virgin pine
amount of turpen
produce as much
Buck planned to
word still is deriv
turpentine farm fe

still. Jeff Buck had
duce the best flow

Before Jeff Buck ha
he had turpentine 1
learned that he cou
Florida. When L. (
purchased land at
turpentine farm was
sary, copper shop, a
Hosford, Florida. W
arranged to move b
to East Bay to work

By September 5th 19
land in Franklin Cour
George Creek. If he v
Creek, which flows
lease the land that w
F. Buck lease all the
Nick Hays had opera
lowing items that Jan
horse, 2 two horse w
ling huty, 18,000 hu
boxes, 26 shanty or
still fixtures and othe
turpentine still operat
ness, which is the p
naval stores business
tine and resin. It turn

During the early 19
growth with the stea
Northern Railroad c
increase of individu
to live. There was ar
early 1900's. James

types of businesses such as the saw mill named the East Bay Lumber Company. The East Bay Lumber Company: furnished the railroad with crossties, furnished the steamboats with firewood, and furnished the steam engine trains with firewood. James F. Buck saw the need to build the Franklin Hotel to accommodate the influx of travelers to Apalachicola. Some of these businesses were more lucrative than James F. Buck's turpentine farms.

James F. Buck had a company launch, (boat), to travel back and forth between Apalachicola and his naval stores business on whiskey George Creek. Also, the company launch and some barges were used to transport the barrels of turpentine and resin between Whiskey George Creek and Apalachicola. James F. Buck also used freight boats to transport shipments of turpentine and resin to Apalachicola to be loaded onto such steamboats as the Tarpon, Oceangoing ships, and the trains of the Apalachicola Northern Railroad. In 1910 James F. Buck had an ideal to save money on shipping costs. He was able to convince the railroad officials at the Port St. Joe office to sign a contract to build a 1500-foot spur. A spur is just a side railroad track. This spur was built close to Whiskey George Creek. This spur became known as Buck's Siding. At the end of Buck's siding there was a long dock like platform, the same height as the floor of a freight car. There was a long open shed on the side of the platform which was used to place items for shipment until they could be loaded onto the train car. One end of the platform was closed in and used as an office. This room had wooden windows which were propped open only when it was being used. From one end of the platform to the other were 6-foot-long poles extending up from the platform with a single strand of wire between each pole. This was used to connect lanterns to light the area for working after the Sun went down. Buck's siding was 8 miles from the still on Whiskey George Creek and only 5 miles from the still that James F. Buck had leased from Nick Hays. Today, there is nothing left of Buck's Siding except for the name. On the 7th December 1904 James F. Buck sold one half interest of his turpentine still to J. V. Creel and his brother, J. F. Creel. On May 28, 1910 James F. Buck sold the remaining one-half interest of his turpentine still to J. V. Creel and his brother, J. F. Creel.

A large part of the Apalachicola business section was destroyed by the fire of 1900. I feel that in 1900 there was a structure on the property where the Hays House is today, but it was destroyed in the 1900 Fire. In 1907 Jeff Buck saw the need and potential for Apalachicola to have a hotel to accommodate the visitors that arrived in Apalachicola. After all Apalachicola was a major hub for the riverboats from Columbus, Georgia, ocean going ships from European nations, and passenger travel by ships to other American ports. In addition to ships and boats bringing people and goods to and from Apalachicola, soon people and goods would be traveling to and from Apalachicola by train. In 1907 the railroad was extended to Apalachicola.

In 1907 Jeff Buck purchase the land for the Franklin Hotel and his home, soon to be located at 48 Avenue D, Apalachicola. Jeff Buck handpicked and purchase the best timber for the Franklin Hotel and his family home from all of the lumber mills that were operating in Apalachicola. At that time there was the Kimball Mill, Porters, Shingles, Mill, the Bluff Mill, the two Mills at Bay City, Loxley Lumber Company in the Cypress Lumber Company. The Franklin Hotel and the Buck's family home now known as the Hays house, were built from Pine, Cypress, and Black Cypress. It took a total of two years to construct the two buildings. The first train arrived in Apalachicola in 1907 and the Franklin Hotel was completed and ready to greet the travelers. In 1908, Jeff Buck moved his family from East Bay into their new home at 48 Avenue D. His new home was directly west and to the rear of the Franklin Hotel.

After 1909 Jeff Buck started another turpentine farm called Buck's Siding, near Sumatra, Florida. When L. G. Buck became 18 years old he started school at the Meridian Military Institute in Meridian, Mississippi. When L. G. Buck was 19 years old, his father became ill and he had to return home to manage Buck's Siding. During this time Jeff Buck's sister Pearl's husband, William Duffy was managing the Franklin Hotel for about two years. When L. G. Buck was 21 years old, his Aunt Pearl and her husband moved to Birmingham, Alabama. L. G. Buck became the manager of the Franklin Hotel that year. The Franklin Cafe had a reputation as an upscale restaurant with snowy white table cloths and finger bowls. Sophia Carter was in charge of the kitchen. The menu was meticulously planned to meet the appetite of the patrons. This menu also included the new invention called Jell-O. The Franklin Cafe's customers were very excited and enjoy eating Jell-O.

L. G. Buck was married to Terry McBride from, Bainbridge, Georgia in 1914. In 1918 Jeff Buck deeded the Franklin Hotel to L. G. Buck. Jeff Buck had built the third floor of the Franklin Hotel to resemble a boat with very low ceilings just like the cabin on a boat. Jeff Buck liked boats. On the other hand, L. G. Buck wanted to raise the ceilings on the third floor and he completed this in 1918 or 1919. L. G. Buck and Terry McBride Buck lived in a suite of rooms on the second floor of the Franklin Hotel. L. G. Buck and Terry Buck's only child was a daughter, Doris. She was born at the Franklin Hotel. Doris Buck, L. G. Buck, and Terry Buck lived at the Franklin Hotel until their daughter was three years old.

Mrs. Terry Buck was a member of the 500-card club. 500 was a popular card game back during 1918 through the 1920s. Mrs. Terry Buck would have 500 club parties at the Franklin Hotel and she would obtain imported crystal violets to decorate the dessert table. Dances were held at the Franklin Hotel, where the present lobby and the bar are today. Back in the early 1900's and 1920's, there was just one large open lobby in this area. This area had large comfortable chairs and other furniture that would be moved out of the lobby area so that the couples would have room to dance. In the 1930's and 1940's Terry Buck would play bridge every Tuesday afternoon with the No Trump Bridge Club. It is believed that back in the 1930's and 1940's that bridge was a card game played by females only. It is believed that L. G. Buck may have been a Poker Card player during the same time period.

In 1920 Jeff Buck's health was not good, even though he had started another turpentine farm. In 1922, Jeff Buck passed away in the Hays House. Jeff Buck's wife Lillian Maude Huggins Buck moved to Deland, Florida. Sometime after his father death, L. G. Buck gave the Hays House and the Franklin Hotel back to the Apalachicola State Bank, so that he could spend all of his efforts in managing the turpentine business. In

1923, L. G. Buck and his family moved from the Franklin Hotel to High Bluff on Graham Creek. In 1923 the bank sold the Franklin Hotel to Mrs. Annie Gibson Hays and her sister Mary Ella, (Sunshine), Gibson. In 1924 Lillian Maude Huggins Buck passed away.

L. G. Buck loved Base Ball and help to financially support the Apalachicola City semi-pro Baseball team. This team played at Porter Field which was an entire block in Apalachicola, located between 10th and 11th St. and Ave. B and Ave. C. The City of Apalachicola had the Baseball team as early as the 1920's and up until World War II.

James Fulton or Fulion Buck was born James F. Belin Jr. James F. Belin Jr. and his wife change their last names to Buck. This happened after an angry, and unpleasant court case that last for many years between James F. Belin Jr. and his two half-brothers Cleland and Jacob Belin and his two half-sisters Mary Belin Davis and Sarah Jane Elizabeth Stuckey. When James F. Belin Jr.'s father James Fulton Belin (1796-1862) was 63 years old, he decided to settled his estate before his fourth marriage to Miss Laura Jane Stone. There were two children were born as a result of this marriage, Virginia Ellen Belin and James F. Belin Jr. At the conclusion of this court case James F. Belin Jr. and his mother Laura Jane Stone Belin were awarded their share of the estate that was settled by their father before his death and prior to his marriage to his fourth wife. So, James F. Belin Jr's. two half-brothers Cleland and Jacob and two half-sisters Mary Belin Davis and Sarah Jane Elizabeth Stuckey had to give back part of their inheritance. As a result of this court case in 1899, James F. Belin Jr. changed his, his wife's, and his children's last name to Buck. In 1900 James F. Buck, his wife, Lillian Maude Huggins Buck and their children moved from South Carolina to Apalachicola, Florida.

There is a similar connection between the property where Franklin Hotel was and the Hays House is, James F. Buck, L. G. Buck, Pat Hays, Kathleen Hays, Annie Gibson Hays Palmer, and Sunshine Gibson, all had been either or employed, managed, lived, and or owned both the Franklin Hotel and the Hays House. Did the Ghosts and Spirits manage to manipulate the individuals who they thought or knew would take good care of their treasured properties.

CHAPTER **2**

Den Room, Hays House, Ghosts are People too.

A brief description of the Den Room, Saturday, 21st May 2016, Hays House.

On Saturday, 21 May 2016, I arrived at the Hays House at about 4:45 PM. I parked westbound on Fourth Street, about the second parking space from the corner of Fourth Street and Avenue D. I met Molly and she showed me around the common areas of the Hays House. Molly also showed me the room I would be staying in, the Den Room. Molly introduced me to the cat Jilly. Jilly is a female cat who seems to be sensitive to the paranormal. I like to call her Jill and she does not mind. Jill seemed to stare in certain areas and crouched down like she was watching something on a couple occasions. The first occasion was in the First Floor Front Stairway Room. I did not see anything on the stairway that she could have been attracted to. The second occasion occurred in the Living Room. Jill was looking at something near the fire place, but I could not see anything. That was the first and last day that I noticed her looking intensely into the thin air for any long periods of time. Due to the severe pain that I was having in both of my knees, I decided to stop obtaining all back-ground information for the paranormal investigating and my book writing activities at 9 PM on Saturday, 21 May 2016. I have only taken 70 pictures of the Den Room. I have not had time to review any of the pictures that I've taken today. I will start tomorrow with a description of the Den Room and complete the Mel Meter based readings for this room and then start a Paranormal Investigations with the Ovilus IV & Mel Meter Session 1 on Sunday, 22 May 2016.

The dimensions of the Den Room are 12 feet by 15 feet and this does not include the bathroom. The bathroom's dimensions are 7' x 8'. The bathroom was added on to the house sometimes later and it takes up a portion of what use to be the southeast area of the back porch. The entrance to this bathroom is located on the Den Room's east wall. This bathroom door is original, it is painted white, and has five sunken panels. This door also has the original decorative brass doorknob and matching skeleton key baseplate. The threshold board between the Den Room and the bathroom is 7 inches wide. When this house was first built, the door that now leads into the bathroom was an exterior door that led to the back porch. At one time the back porch extended across the entire exterior east side of the Hays House. In the past having an exterior door where the bathroom door is today, would allow for excellent cross ventilation during the hot summer months in Florida. The side of the bathroom door facing the Den Room shows some areas of missing paint down to the wooden grain. The next layer is olive green, the next layer is an off-white. This door has five 1' x 2.5' decorative sunken wooden panels. The bathroom door's internal side has a brown and tan marble doorknob with a metal or brass skeleton plate cover. This side of the door also has an eleven inch by 20-inch, white wooden frame under glass, picture of the state of Florida depicted in a greenish blue color, with silver words saying, "Have found paradise send more vodka." This picture has a white background. The interior side of the bathroom door has areas where the paint is removed down to a brown painted area. I cannot see any wooding grains. This may be brown paint instead of wood or it could be a brown primer. The next or second layer of paint out from the surface of the door is a greenish blue paint, the third layer of paint is a light yellow, and the fourth layer of paint is white. The interior bathroom door matches part of the exterior door side, except for the doorknob and the skeleton key plate cover which has a decorative design embossed into the metal or brass doorknob. The skeleton key cover plate which have the same design on both sides of the bathroom door, only differ in that the skeleton key cover plate on the interior side is not painted. The interior side of the bathroom door's knob is not painted. The interior side of the bathroom door has a clothes hanger mounted into the door located between the first and second sunken door panels, from the top. The interior side of the bathroom door's white wooden trim appears to be modern, 4-inch-wide wood, with a 4-inch piece of shoe molding near the floor. The interior side of the bathroom door when closed, is on the bathrooms west wall.

The bathrooms entrance is on the bath room's west wall and there is a wooden shelf on the west wall. This wooden shelf has three layers of different colored of paint. The layer of paint closest to the wood is brown, the second layer is yellow and the third layer is green. The bathrooms west wall has two mounted towel racks and a 18" x 28" painting of a river and trees.

The bathroom's south wall has a white trashcan, white stand-alone sink, above the sink is an oval mirror, and above the mirror is a mounted wall light. On the bathrooms southeast corner is a bathtub and shower with plumbing handles and fixtures that look like they could be from the 1940's or 1950's. The bathtub and shower have a shower curtain.

The bathrooms east wall has a 14" x 18" jalousie window with modern white wooden trim. Also, on the east wall is a white toilet with a towel rack mounted on the wall above the toilet.

On the bathrooms north wall there is an area that is boarded up. This area is the same size as the bathroom door, this use to be the bathroom's closet from 1942 to 1996. After 1996 when Doris Sweet Shop moved into the Kitchen and Dining Room at the Hays House there was a need for a Lady's and Men's room. So, a small Lady's and Men's room was built on to the back porch and made available to the patrons of Doris Sweet Shop. The Small Men's room was created in the space where the Bathroom's closet had been up until 1996. The Lady's room took away part of the back-porch space, just the right side of the rear door and between were the bathroom's closet use to be. The Bathroom's north wall at this boarded-up area is covered with the horizontal tongue and groove type boards. The bathrooms north wall also has a 20" x 26" piece of metal with a painting of a cat's face, with a fish body playing a guitar, and with three butterflies flying around the guitar. There are two decorative white shelves mounted on the north wall of the bathroom. On the top shelf is a painting of a lady with dark brown hair and a bird on shoulder. This painting has a light blue background. There are also five silver metal butterflies mounted on the bathroom's north wall. There are only one silver metal butterflies mounted on the bathroom's east wall.

The bottom half of all of the bathrooms walls are covered with white 4" x 4" square tiles. The top half of all the bathrooms walls are covered with white horizontal tongue and groove 2 1/2-inch boards. The bathroom's ceiling is about 9 foot tall. The ceiling is covered with green tongue and groove ceiling boards that are approximately 2 1/2 inches wide. These boards are running in a north to south direction. The bathrooms floor is covered with a stone looking type multi-colored, tan, brown, silver, and gray, 12" x 12" square titles.

The north wall of the Den Room has the entrance, with an original white wooden door with five sunken panels, the original brass doorknob and matching skeleton key base plate. The threshold boards between the First Floor Back Stairway Room and the Den Room has a 6-inch-wide board closer towards the First Floor Back Stairway Room and a two and three-quarter inch threshold board closer to the Den Room side. There are three modern paintings of various sizes mounted on the room's North wall. There is also an Oster baking stove, on top of a green wooden counter along the room's North wall. This counter has one drawer and one open shelf. Also mounted on the room's North wall is a large 12" x 20" messenger board with a pink and green butterfly at the top. There are an additional two silver metal butterflies on the room north wall. In the rooms northeast corner there is a green wooden stool and a white plastic trash can.

On this room's east wall is a wooden counter top with cabinets above and below the waist level counter top, a sink for washing dishes, and a white magic chef microwave oven. Also, along the room's East wall is a white Dissani refrigerator and freezer, a coffee maker on top of the counter and a 4-foot-tall chest of drawers. The room's East wall has three modern paintings of various sizes and four silver metal butterflies. The entrance to the bathroom is on the room's East wall.

The room's South wall has two windows that appear to be original. Both windows are approximately 30" x 60". The internal white wooden window trim is modern. Each top and bottom window pane has two sections. The lower half glass of both Windows is opaque which allows light through, but you cannot see through. The lower half of both of the windows are obscured by a window netting. The left side of the window has a white Frigidaire air conditioner. Along the room's south wall is a full bed with a modern six-foot tall headboard. There is a green wooden bench with an orange cushion on top, at the foot of the bed. The bed has a decorative white bedspread with six different pillows that differ in size and color. Also, on the room's south wall is a white wooden table with a pink lamp. This lamp has a pink and white lamp shade.

On the rooms west wall is a wooden six-foot tall coat hanger stand and a door leading into Pat & Kathleen's Room. This interior door is an original white wooden door with five sunken panels that are approximately 9 inches in height and 20 inches long. This door has a decorative brass or metal doorknob with the matching skeleton key cover plate that is painted white. On this door there is mounted a painting of a fish. Also, on the room's west wall is a round white table with a green supporting stand. This table is about 27 inches in diameter.

The Den Room's ceiling has the original green tongue and groove ceiling boards that are approximately 2 1/2 inches wide and running in an east to west direction. The ceiling and floor trim are white and appear to be original. At the top of all four walls there is a strip of modern molding at about 9 inches below the original ceiling trim. This molding is painted white but the 9-inch area between the modern molding and the original trim, there is an area painted green. The ceiling has a white ceiling fan and light, located in the center of the room's ceiling. Also, there is a white smoke detector on the ceiling. This room has 2 1/2-inch tongue and groove hardwood heart pine flooring, that is running in an east to west direction. Directly in front of the rooms entrance, there is a 3-foot-wide area of tongue and groove heart pine flooring that looks to have been repaired. This area of tongue and groove hardwood floor is lighter in color then the rest of the room's tongue and groove hardwood floor. This 3-foot-wide area of tongue and groove heart pine flooring that has a different width and does not match up with the original tongue and groove hardwood, heart pine flooring. The threshold floorboard at the floor level of this room's entrance is pieced together, because the wood grains do not match, but both threshold board appear to be original. This could be a replacement threshold that was not the correct size. The threshold floorboard under the door on this room's West wall cannot be seen. This door is locked. The threshold floorboard on the room's East wall that leads to the bathroom entrance appears to be original.

The history of the Den Room, Hays House.

In 1942 the Den room was Patsy Hays' bedroom until she was 8 years old. The same year Patsy became eight years old, her sister Frances was born. The Den Room became France's room until she was eight years old. The patched area on the tongue & groove, heart pine, hard wood flooring once held the create for a floor furnace that was install in the early 1950's. After Pat passed away in 1978, Kathleen moved the TV from the TV Room to the Den. In 2016, when I first started my Paranormal Investigations within the Den room, I did not know at that time, that this room had been a bedroom and or what this room was used for. I thought maybe it had been Mary's room. It turned out that Mary's room, was in the same location within the Hays House, but above this room on the second floor. The Den room was part of the walkway that both Pat and Kathleen Hays used as they travel from their bedroom to the first-floor bathroom. After Frances turn eight years old, this room was used as a Den up until 1996.

Mel Meter based readings for the Den Room, Sunday, 22nd May 2016, Hays House.

5:11 PM The electrical outlet on the bathroom's North West wall. This outlet was not in use.

The electromagnetic frequency range was 0.7 mG to 1.4 mG.

The temperature range was 71.1°F to 71.9°F.

5:12 PM The South wall mounted light over the bathroom sink. This light is on.

The electromagnetic frequency range was 2.2 mG to 2.9 mG.

The temperature range was 74.4°F to 75.4°F.

5:13 PM The electrical outlet on the room's North wall. My laptop is plugged into this outlet.

The electromagnetic frequency range was 87.7 mG to 90.4 mG.

The temperature range was 71.2°F to 71.9°F.

5:14 PM The double switch light and ceiling fan on the room's North wall. The light is on and the ceiling fan is off.

The electromagnetic frequency range was 0.9 mG to 1.4 mG.

The temperature range was 71.4°F to 72.1°F.

5:15 PM The electrical outlets near the room's Northeast corner and on the room's North wall. The electrical outlet is not in use.

The electromagnetic frequency range was 0.0 mG to 0.0 mG.

The temperature range was 71.7°F to 72.4°F.

5:16 PM The white Magic Chef microwave oven sitting on the counter, located on the room's East wall. This microwave oven is not in use.

The electromagnetic frequency range was 0.3 mG to 0.6mG.

The temperature range was 71.4°F to 71.5°F.

5:17 PM The electrical outlet on the room's East wall. The microwave oven is plugged into the outlet.

The electromagnetic frequency range was 0.0 mG to 0.0 mG.

The temperature range was 70.5°F to 71.0°F.

5:18 PM The white Vissani refrigerator and freezer located on the room's East wall. The refrigerator and freezer are in use.

The electromagnetic frequency range was 0.0 mG to 0.1 mG.

The temperature range was 71.6°F to 72.2°F.

5:18 PM The double light switch on the room's East wall. Both light switches are in the on position.

The electromagnetic frequency range was 0.8 mG to 1.0 mG.

The temperature range was 70.7°F to 71.5°F.

5:19 PM The electrical outlet on the room's East wall. The white Frigidaire air conditioner is plugged into this outlet.

The electromagnetic frequency range was 5.0 mG to 5.4 mG.

The temperature range was 71.9°F to 72.2°F.

5:19 PM The white Frigidaire air conditioner window unit, in the left side window, located on the room's South wall. This air conditioner window unit is in use.

The electromagnetic frequency range was 26.2 mG to 37.8 mG.

The temperature range was 70.7°F to 71.6°F.

5:20 PM The electrical outlet on the room's West wall. The lamp is plugged into this outlet.

The electromagnetic frequency range was 0.1 mG to 0.3 mG.

The temperature range was 71.9°F to 72.3°F.

5:22 PM The pink lamp on the white nightstand, near the room's Southwest corner, and on the room's South wall. This pink lamp is in use.

The electromagnetic frequency range was 0.0 mG to 0.3 mG.

The temperature range was 71.4°F to 71.4°F.

5:22 PM The white ceiling fan and ceiling light. The ceiling fan is not on, but the ceiling light is on.

The electromagnetic frequency range was 0.0 mG to 0.0 mG.

The temperature range was 73.5°F to 74.6°F.

Paranormal Investigation, Session 1, Sunday, 22nd May 2016, Den Room, Hays House. The ceiling fan and the air conditioner are off.

I did not get any strong Paranormal emotions prior to the Paranormal Investigation. My knees were hurting so bad that I was not picking of any emotions that any Ghosts and or Spirits may have had.

6:01 PM Keith: "Hello, I am Keith Evans. If you would like to talk, you may use your energy to choose words from the Ovilus IV's data base. The Ovilus IV will not hurt you." (Hold the Ovilus IV up.)

6:01 PM Keith: "This is the Mel Meter. The Mel Meter measures temperature and electromagnetic frequencies. The Mel Meter will not harm you." (Hold it up.)

6:03 PM Keith: "The Ovilus IV has not given me any background words."

6:03 PM Keith: "I have observed the readings from the Mel Meter to be 0.4 mG and 75.6°F." (Picture)

6:03 PM Keith: "Hello Sunshine, how are you doing today."

6:04 PM Keith: "The Ovilus IV gave me the word while, which is spelled W-H-I-L-E. The Ovilus IV pronounced the word while at a normal conversational level and speed."

6:04 PM Keith: "I have observed the Mel Meter readings to be 0.5 mG and 76.1°F." (Picture)

6:06 PM Keith: "The Ovilus IV gave me the word out, which is spelled O-U-T. The Ovilus IV pronounced the word out at a louder than normal conversational level and faster than a normal conversational speed, like a command was given."

6:06 PM Keith: "I observed the Mel Meter readings to be 0.4 mG and 76.3°F." (Picture)

6:06 PM Keith: "I observed the Mel Meter readings to be 0.4 mG and 76.4°F." (Picture)

6:07 PM Keith: "The Ovilus IV has given me the word me, which is spelled M-E. The Ovilus IV pronounced the word me at a normal conversational level and speed."

6:07 PM Keith: "I observed the Mel Meter readings to be 0.8 mG and 76.4°F." (Picture)

6:11 PM Keith: "The Ovilus IV has given me four words; bridge, which is spelled B-R-I-D-G-E, watch, which is spelled W-A-T-C-H, and can you, which is spelled C-A-N Y-O-U. The Ovilus IV pronounced the words, bridge, watch, and you can at a normal conversational level and speed."

6:11 PM Keith: "I observed the Mel Meter readings to be 0.5 mG and 77.1°F." (Picture)

6:11 PM Keith: "I observed the Mel Meter readings to be 0.5 mG and 77.0°F." (Picture)

6:16 PM Keith: "At 6:03 PM I asked my last question."

6:17 PM Keith: "The Ovilus IV has given me the following words: while, out, me, bridge, watch, and can you."

6:18 PM Keith: "Okay, the Ovilus IV gave me the word out. Are you telling me to get out?"

6:19 PM Keith: "The Ovilus IV has given me six words fast and back-to-back stick, which is spelled S-T-I-C-K, period, which is spelled P-E-R-I-O-D, and Poem, which is spelled P-O-E-M. Unfortunately, I do not have any pictures of the first three words. Homicide, which is spelled H-O-M-I-C-I-D-E, present, which is spelled P-R-E-S-E-N-T, and magic, which is spelled M-A-G-I-C. I have pictures of the last three words. All six words were pronounced by the Ovilus IV at a normal conversational level but at a very fast speed."

6:19 PM Keith: "I observed the Mel Meter readings to be 0.4 mG and 77.2°F." (Picture)

6:25 PM Keith: "Stick, period, and poem, Sunshine, do these three words have anything to do with the Edgar Allan Poe poem that I read to you about a year ago?"

6:27 PM Keith: "The words homicide, present, and magic, I do not feel that these words are in response to any of the questions that I have asked during this session."

6:29 PM Keith: "Kathleen and Pat, are you here today?"

6:30 PM Keith: "Kathleen and Pat, I just want to tell you that you have a beautiful house."

6:32 PM Keith: "Mr. Buck, are you here today?"

6:33 PM Keith: "Mr. Buck, thank you for building such a beautiful house."

6:34 PM Keith: "The Ovilus IV gave me the word copper, which spelled C-O-P-P-E-R. The word copper was pronounced by the Ovilus IV at a normal conversation level, but at a fast speed."

6:34 PM Keith: "I observed the Mel Meter readings to be 0.6 mG and 78.2°F." (Picture)

6:36 PM Keith: "That was a motorcycle outside."

6:37 PM Keith: "What does copper have to do with me?"

6:38 PM Keith: "Sunshine, described yourself to me."

6:39 PM Keith: "Sunshine, thank you for helping me with my knees yesterday. My knees feel better today."

6:40 PM Keith: "Sunshine, is this the room that you passed away in back in 1956?"

6:41 PM Keith: "Sunshine, which room in this house was yours when you were living here?"

6:42 PM Keith: "The Ovilus IV has given me two words; rent, which is spelled R-E-N-T, and ravine, which is spelled R-A-V-I-N-E. Rent and ravine were both pronounced by the Ovilus IV at a normal conversational level but at a very fast speed."

6:42 PM Keith: "I observed the Mel Meter readings to be 0.4 mG and 78.0°F." (Picture)

6:45 PM Keith: "Sunshine, did you pay rent when you lived here at the Hays House?"

6:46 PM Keith: "I observed the Mel Meter readings to be 0.4 mG and 77.7°F." (Picture)

6:47 PM Keith: "It appears that the Ovilus IV may have frozen up, with two white dots in the upper left-hand side of its display."

6:49 PM Keith: "Thank you for talking to me. Have a good evening."

6:49 PM Keith: "I observed the Mel Meter readings to be 0.5 mG and 77.9°F." (Picture)

6:50 PM Keith: "This Session 1 ended on Sunday, 22nd May 2016."

Mel Meter base readings for the Den Room, Monday, 23rd of May 2016, Hays House. The ceiling fan is off and the air conditioner is on.

4:07 PM The top of the white round table on the west wall.

The electromagnetic frequency range was 0.5 mG to 0.5 mG.

The temperature range was 72.3°F to 72.3°F.

4:08 PM The electrical outlet on the bathroom's west wall. This electrical outlet is not in use.

The electromagnetic frequency range was 0.2 mG to 0.7 mG.

The temperature range was 73.4°F to 73.8°F.

4:09 PM The south wall mounted light over the bathroom sink. This light is in the on position.

The electromagnetic frequency range was 0.0 mG to 0.0 mG.

The temperature range was 77.6°F to 78.0°F.

4:10 PM The electrical outlet on the room's north wall. My laptop is plugged into this electrical outlet.

The electromagnetic frequency range 65.0 mG to 66.9 mG.

The temperature range was 73.3°F to 73.6°F.

4:10 PM The double light switch on the room's north wall. The light switch was in the on position. The ceiling fan switch was in the off position.

The electromagnetic frequency range was 0.3 mG to 0.9 mG.

The temperature range was 73.5 °F to 73.7 °F.

4:11 PM The electrical outlet near the room's north east corner. This electrical outlet is located on the room's north wall. This outlet is not in use.

The electromagnetic frequency range was 0.1 mG to 0.1 mG.

The temperature range was 74.1°F to 78.8°F.

4:12 PM The white Magic Chef microwave oven on the countertop. The microwave is located on the room's east wall.

The electromagnetic frequency range was 0.2 mG to 0.3 mG.

The temperature range was 74.6°F to 74.7°F.

4:13 PM The electrical outlet on the room's east wall. The microwave is plugged into this outlet.

The electromagnetic frequency range was 0.0 mG to 0.3 mG.

The temperature range was 73.2°F to 73.7°F.

4:14 PM The white Vissani refrigerator and freezer on the room's east wall. The freezer and refrigerator are in use.

The electromagnetic frequency range was 0.0 mG to 0.2 mG.

The temperature range was 74.4°F to 74.8°F.

4:15 PM The double light switch on the room's east wall. Both switches are in the on position.

The electromagnetic frequency range was 0.0 mG to 0.1 mG.

The temperature range was 74.4°F to 75.4°F.

4:16 PM The electrical outlet on the room's east wall. The Frigidaire air conditioner is plugged into this electrical outlet.

The electromagnetic frequency range was 7.6 mG to 7.8 mG.

The temperature range was 75.6°F to 76.4°F.

4:16 PM The white Frigidaire air conditioner window unit, in the left side window, on the room's south wall. This air conditioner is in use.

The electromagnetic frequency range was 3.2 mG to 3.6 mG.

The temperature range was 77.6°F to 78.5°F.

4:17 PM The pink lamp on the white nightstand, near the room's southwest corner. This pink lamp is located on the room's south wall. This lamp is in use.

The electromagnetic frequency range was 0.1 mG to 0.3 mG.

The temperature range was 75.3°F to 75.4°F.

4:18 PM The electrical outlet on the room's west wall. The lamp is plugged in to this electrical outlet.

The electromagnetic frequency range was 0.0 mG to 0.1 mG.

The temperature range was 75.1°F to 75.4°F.

4:19 PM The white ceiling fan and ceiling light. The ceiling fan is not on, but the ceiling light is on.

The electromagnetic frequency range was 0.0 mG to 0.0 mG.

The temperature range was 75.1°F to 76.3°F.

The Paranormal Investigation, Session 2, Den Room, Hays House, Monday, 23 May 2016. The ceiling fan is off and the air conditioner is on.

6:01 PM Keith: "Hello, I am Keith Evans. If you would like to talk, you may use your energy to choose words from the Ovilus IV's data base. The Ovilus IV will not hurt you. This is the Ovilus IV. (Hold it up.) Today I only want to talk to spirits that lived at the Hays House between the years of 1942 through 1996."

6:01 PM Keith: "This is the Mel Meter. The Mel Meter measures temperature and electromagnetic frequencies. The Mel Meter will not harm you." (Hold it up.)

6:03 PM Keith: "The Ovilus IV has not given me any background words."

6:03 PM Keith: "I observed the Mel Meter readings to be 0.9 mG and 72.8°F." (Picture)

6:03 PM Keith: "Sunshine, are you here today?"

6:03 PM Keith: "Sunshine, are you shy?"

6:04 PM Keith: "The Ovilus IV gave me the word stirred, which is spelled S-T-I-R-R-E-D. The Ovilus IV pronounced the word stirred at a normal conversational level and speed."

6:05 PM Keith: "I observed the Mel Meter readings to be 1.1 mG and 72.9°F." (Picture)

6:06 PM Keith: "The Ovilus IV has given me the word finish, which is spelled F-I-N-I-S-H. The Ovilus IV has pronounced the word finish in a normal conversational level and speed."

6:06 PM Keith: "I observed the Mel Meter readings to be 1.1 mG and 73.2°F." (Picture)

6:10 PM Keith: "Sunshine, are you finished being shy?"

6:11 PM Keith: "Sunshine, what are you stirring?"

6:12 PM Keith: "Sunshine, do you have any questions that you would like to ask?"

6:13 PM Keith: "Are you upset with me?"

6:14 PM Keith: "What is my name?"

6:15 PM Keith: "I have observed the Mel Meter readings to be 1.0 mG and 73.4°F." (Picture)

6:16 PM Keith: "Kathleen Hays, would like to ask me a question?"

6:17 PM Keith: "Today, I took pictures of where your daughter Frances placed her hand print, name, and the date, 20th March 1953, into the soft cement back in 1953, located on the back-porch step."

6:18 PM Keith: "Today, I also took pictures of where both of your daughters, Frances and Patsy Hays, wrote their names into the soft cement on the porch steps located on the north side of the house."

6:22 PM Keith: "Can your spirit see my laptop?"

6:23 PM Keith: "I have a picture of Frances' right hand print and it is dated 20th March 1953."

6:24 PM Keith: "Kathleen, Pat, and Sunshine, you are all welcome to look at the pictures I have of Frances' right hand print."

6:26 PM Keith: "Who said the word stirred which is spelled S-T-I-R-R-E-D?"

6:27 PM Keith: "I observed the Mel Meter readings to be 1.0 mG and 73.1°F." (Picture)

6:29 PM Keith: "Here's another picture of the steps on the North Side of the house, where Patsy Ann Hays placed her name, Patsy Ann, into the soft cement."

6:29 PM Keith: "Everyone is welcomed to look at the pictures."

6:32 PM Keith: "Here is another picture of the steps on the north side of the Hays House where Frances Hays placed her name into the soft cement."

6:33 PM Keith: "Did anyone like those pictures?"

6:35 PM Keith: "I observed the Mel Meter readings to be 1.1 mG and 72.6°F."

6:36 PM Keith: "The Ovilus IV has given me the word abort, which is spelled A-B-O-R-T. The word abort was pronounced by the Ovilus IV in a normal conversational level and speed."

6:36 PM Keith: "I have observed the Mel Meter readings to be 1.0 mG and 73.3°F." (Picture)

6:38 PM Keith: "What do you want to abort?"

6:39 PM Keith: "Do you no longer want to look at the pictures?"

6:41 PM Keith: "Who would like to talk to me tonight?"

6:42 PM Keith: "Pat, when is Dove season?"

6:43 PM Keith: "Pat, what did you hunt besides Doves?"

6:44 PM Keith: "That was a car alarm going off directly south from my location."

6:45 PM Keith: "Pat, would you like to ask me any questions?"

6:46 PM Keith: "Kathleen, would you like to ask me any questions?"

6:47 PM Keith: "I have a question? Was the bathroom added to this room on the southeast corner of the Hays House in 1953?"

6:49 PM Keith: "Does anyone know what year the bath tub was made that is in the bathroom near the southeast corner of the Hays House?"

6:51 PM Keith: "Sunshine, what do you think of me?"

6:52 PM Keith: "I like the brass doorknobs and the skeleton key covers that are throughout the Hays House."

6:53 PM Keith: "Thank you for talking to me. Have a good evening."

6:54 PM Keith: "I observed the Mel Meter readings to be 0.5 mG and 73.5°F." (Picture)

6:54 PM Keith: "This Session 2 ended on Monday, 23rd May 2016."

Mel Meter base readings Den Room, Tuesday, 24th May 2016, Hays House.

4:14 PM The top of the white round table located along the room's west wall.

The electromagnetic frequency range was 0.4 mG to 0.5 mG.

The temperature range was 72.3°F to 72.4°F.

4:15 PM The electrical outlet on the bathroom's west wall. This electrical outlet is not in use.

The electromagnetic frequency range was 0.4 mG to 0.4 mG.

The temperature range was 72.0°F to 73.0°F.

4:15 PM The bathroom's south wall mounted light, over the sink. This light is in the on position.

The electromagnetic frequency range was 0.4 mG to 0.5 mG.

The temperature range was 76.3°F to 77.6°F.

4:16 PM The electrical outlet on the room's north wall. My laptop is plugged into this electrical outlet.

The electromagnetic frequency range was 76.7 mG to 77.4 mG.

The temperature range was 73.0°F to 73.2°F.

4:16 PM The double light switch on the room's north wall. Both light switches are in the off position.

The electromagnetic frequency range was 0.7 mG to 0.8 mG.

The temperature range was 73.5°F to 74.0°F.

4:16 PM The electrical outlet near the room's northeast corner and on the room's north wall. This electrical outlet is not in use.

The electromagnetic frequency range was 0.0 mG to 0.0 mG.

The temperature range was 73.7°F to 74.2°F.

4:17 PM The Magic Chef microwave oven on the countertop, located on the room's north wall. The microwave oven is plugged into this electrical outlet.

The electromagnetic frequency range was 0.2 mG to 0.3 mG.

The temperature range was 74.2°F to 74.4°F.

4:17 PM The electrical outlet on the room's east wall. The microwave oven is plugged into this electrical outlet.

The electromagnetic frequency range was 0.0 mG to 0.1 mG.

The temperature range was 72.8°F to 73.7°F.

4:18 PM The white Vissani refrigerator and freezer on the room's east wall. This refrigerator and freezer is in use.

The electromagnetic frequency range was 0.0 mG to 0.2 mG.

The temperature range was 73.5°F to 73.9°F.

4:18 PM The double light switch on the room's east wall. Both switches are in the on position.

The electromagnetic frequency range was 0.4 mG to 0.9 mG.

The temperature range was 72.6°F to 73.3°F.

4:19 PM The electrical outlet on the room's east wall. The Frigidaire air conditioner is plugged into this outlet.

The electromagnetic frequency range was 25.7 mG to 26.0 mG.

The temperature range was 72.3°F to 72.8°F.

4:19 PM The white Frigidaire air conditioner window unit, in the left side window, on the room's south wall. This air conditioner is in use.

The electromagnetic frequency range was 25.6 mG to 26.0 mG.

The temperature range was 73.7°F to 74.3°F.

4:20 PM The pink lamp on the white nightstand, in the room's southwest corner, located along the room's south wall. This pink lamp is in use.

The electromagnetic frequency range was 0.3 mG to 0.6 mG.

The temperature range was 72.8°F to 73.3°F.

4:21 PM The electrical outlet on the room's west wall. The pink lamp is plugged into this electrical outlet.

The electromagnetic frequency range was 0.0 mG to 0.1 mG.

The temperature range was 74.0°F to 74.3°F.

4:21 PM The white ceiling fan is in the off position. The ceiling light is in the on position.

The electromagnetic frequency range was 0.0 mG to 0.0 mG.

The temperature range was 75.3°F to 76.8°F.

The Paranormal Investigation, Session 3, Den Room, Tuesday, 24 May 2016, Hays House. The ceiling fan is off and the air conditioner is on.

4:52 PM Keith: "Hello, I am Keith Evans. Today I only want to talk to spirits who lived at the Hays House between 1942 in 1956. You may use your energy to choose words from the Ovilus IV's data base. This is the Ovilus IV and it will not hurt you." (Hold it up.)

4:53 PM Keith: "This is the Mel meter. The Mel Meter measures temperature and electromagnetic frequencies. The Mel Meter will not harm you." (Hold it up.)

4:53 PM Keith: "The Ovilus IV has given me two background words; pound which is spelled P-O-U-N-D, and Buddha which is spelled B-U-D-D-H-A. Pound and Buddha were pronounced by the Ovilus IV at a normal conversational level and speed."

4:53 PM Keith: "I have observed the Mel Meter readings to be 1.1 mG and 73.6°F."

4:55 PM Keith: "The Ovilus IV gave me the word manifest which is spelled M-A-N-I-F-E-S-T. The Ovilus IV has pronounced the word manifest at a normal conversational level and speed."

4:56 PM Keith: "I have observed the Mel Meter readings to be 1.3 mG and 73.9°F."

4:58 PM Keith: "What do you mean by saying the words pound, Buddha, and manifest?"

5 PM Keith: "The Ovilus IV gave me the word movie which is spelled M-O-V-I-E. The Ovilus IV pronounced the word movie in a normal conversational level and speed."

5 PM Keith: "I have observed the Mel Meter readings to be 1.0 mG and 74.0°F."

5:01 PM Keith: "The Ovilus IV gave me the word tool which is spelled T-O-O-L. The Ovilus IV pronounced the word tool in a normal conversational level and speed."

5:01 PM Keith: "I have observed the Mel Meter readings to be 1.1 mG and 74.7°F."

5:04 PM Keith: "Are you watching a movie?"

5:05 PM Keith: "I do not have cable TV, so I'm not watching anything."

5:06 PM Keith: "When you said the word tool. Which tool are you talking about? The Mel Meter, Ovilus IV, cell phone, digital camera, and or laptop."

5:08 PM Keith: "Hello Sunshine, Pat, and Kathleen."

5:09 PM Keith: "Sunshine, do you have a question for me?"

5:11 PM Keith: "Pat, do you have any questions for me?"

5:12 PM Keith: "The Ovilus IV gave me the word Norman which is spelled N-O-R-M-A-N. Norman was pronounced by the Ovilus IV at a normal conversational level but faster than the normal conversational speed. It sounded like an African-American woman's voice happy to see Norman. The voice was high pitch, with a lot of happy emotion. I have the Ovilus IV set for male voices. There was a choice between either male or female voices. Even though I've chosen male voices, sometimes female voices still come through."

5:12 PM Keith: "I have observed the Mel Meter readings to be 1.1 mG and 74.5°F."

5:13 PM Keith: "Kathleen, do you have any questions for me?"

5:17 PM Keith: "I have observed the Mel Meter readings to be 1.2 mG and 74.3°F."

5:18 PM Keith: "Hello, have you mistaken me for Norman? My name is Keith."

5:20 PM Keith: "Pat, when was the bathroom added on to this room?"

5:21 PM Keith: "Pat, was the bathroom already added onto this room, when you purchased this house in 1942?"

5:22 PM Keith: "Kathleen, when was the bathroom added onto this room?"

5:23 PM Keith: "Kathleen, was the bathroom already added to this room, when you purchased this house in 1942?"

5:24 PM Keith: "Sunshine, what is on your mind?"

5:26 PM Keith: "Sunshine, a penny for your thoughts."

5:27 PM Keith: "Pat, do you know why the floor near the entrance to this room had to be repaired."

5:28 PM Keith: "Kathleen, do you know why the floor near the entrance to this room had to be repaired."

5:30 PM Keith: "Sunshine, do you know why the floor near the entrance to this room had to be repaired."

5:32 PM Keith: "I have the feeling that the Ovilus IV may have frozen up. There are two dots on the left-hand side of the top of its display."

5:32 PM Keith: "The Ovilus IV gave me the word yell which is spelled Y-E-L-L. The Ovilus IV has pronounced the word yell at a louder than a normal conversational level and faster than a normal conversational speed."

5:32 PM Keith: "I have observed the Mel Meter readings to be 1.0 mG and 74.8°F.

5:35 PM Keith: "I have observed the Mel Meter readings to be 0.9 mG and 74.5°F.

5:36 PM Keith: "The Ovilus IV still appears to be frozen up, with two dots in the upper left-hand side display."

5:37 PM Keith: "The Ovilus IV will not go back to the home position. I have attempted several times to touch the home icon at the lower left-hand side of the Ovilus IV's screen."

5:38 PM Keith: "I have turned the Ovilus IV off without going to the home position."

5:40 PM Keith: "The batteries in the Ovilus IV our dead and I am out of AAA batteries."

5:41 PM Keith: "Thank you for talking to me. Have a good evening."

5:41 PM Keith: "I have observed the Mel Meter readings to be 0.9 mG and 73.9°F."

5:41 PM Keith: "This session 3 ended on Tuesday, 24th May 2016."

Unexplained events in the Den Room, Monday, 3rd July 2017, Hays House.

I had spent the month of July at the Hays House in what is today called the Petit Jardin room. At 1 PM on 3rd July 2017, I was lying in bed, I had not fallen asleep yet. The cat, Jill had been playing out in the hall making a lot of noise with the rug and tapping her, Paul's at my door. I decided to look to see if she wanted to come in. When I opened the door. The rug was all wrinkled up and she looked at me and walked inside the room. I straighten up the rug so no one would trip. I laid back down on the East side of the bed. I had the five or six pillows stacked on the side of the bed towards the West wall. Jill jumped up on the bed from the west side and attempted to find a place to lay down on top of the pillows. I assisted her by rearranging the pillows so she had a flat area to lay down. Jill laid down and was facing me and looking at me. I assume that she might've been play-ing in the hallway with a ghost cat or ghost dog. And perhaps that the ghost cat or dog had followed Jill into my room. I was looking at Jill and facing the rooms West wall. When I heard and felt something sit down at the West side foot of the bed. It sounded and felt like an adult female had sat down on my bed. I was looking at Jill, who did not seem to be worried about what had just happened. It was almost as if she was looking at me to see how I would react. To the best of my knowledge, I had no reaction. A few minutes later. While I still was looking at Jill, I heard a sound like a dog shaking with a collar and a dog tag on. I have heard this type of sound before when a dog would shake themselves after they had come in from outside after be-ing wet. I was still looking at Jill when this sound took place. Jill had not moved and I had not moved. There was one dog in the house and there was no living dog in my room. The sound of a dog shaking with a collar and a metal license on that collar sounded like it was coming from the West side foot of the bed. The same location where I heard and felt a female adult sitting down. I was very happy that some para-normal activity was happening without me even doing a paranormal investigation. I felt like the ghosts or spirits which could have been a human, and or a dog, and or a cat had such a good relationship with Jill that they were willing to come in with her and make themselves known. It was almost as if Jill was helping me by introducing me to one or two ghosts and or spirits. I did not hear and or feel anything unexplained for the remainder of the night. I said good night to Jill and Sunshine and then I went to sleep.

Analysis of the Paranormal Investigation, Session 1, Sunday, 22nd May 2016, Den Room. The date of analysis was Tuesday, 25th April 2017.

The first three words given to me by the Ovilus IV during Session 1 were while, out, and me. I do not feel that the words while and me are responding to any questions that I have asked. I do feel that the word out was a spirit telling me to get out. And I base this on the fact that the Ovilus IV pronounced the word out loud and fast. I feel in was the intelligent spirit of Jeff Buck, who passed away in the Hays House. I not sure which room Jeff Buck passed away in. I was given me an order to get out now. I find that until you build a relationship with the ghosts and spirits they don't want to be bothered with you at all. You have to find something in common with the ghosts and spirits that dwell in the places you are writing about. That is why it's very important to know the history of the people that lived there in the pass, what type of work they did, what their hobbies were, and what their likes and dislikes were during their life time. The word out may have been spoken by an intelligent spirit, Kathleen Hays who spend many years of her using this Den room as a TV Room. As you can see the Ovilus IV did not give me the word get. I do not believe that the ghosts and or spirits realize that not every word they attempt to display on the Ovilus IV, by using their energy, is actually success-fully displayed. So many times, when Ghosts and Spirits are trying to speak to me, I'm getting bits and pieces of a fragmented sentence coming through on the Ovilus IV. Until Ghosts and Spirits have used the Ovilus IV enough times to learn that I'm not getting the total mes-sage that they're trying to have me understand. There will be a certain degree of disconnect in the communications between me and the spirits. The analysis of all paranormal investigations is very subjec-tive. One has to be able to take bits and pieces of sentences and try to make meaningful conclusions from those few words.

The fourth through seventh words given to me by the Ovilus IV during this paranormal investigation were bridge, watch, can, and you. It appears to me that someone is asking me if I can watch the bridge. Watching the bridge may be a naval and or a term used by someone navigating a ship or a boat. These words seem to be from an intelligent spirit that may be communicating with me concerning a boat or ship. On the second hand this could be Kathline Hays, Sunshine Gibson, and Annie Gibson Hays Palmer inviting me to watch them play the card game bridge.

The eighth through 14th words given to me during this paranormal investigation were stick, period, poem, homicide, present, and magic. I believe that these words come from Sunshine Gibson and she is referring to a poem that I read to her over a year ago. The poem was written by Edgar Allan Poe and is titled the Raven. The words stick and period maybe referring to a style in which a poem is written. The words poem, homicide, present, and magic, are talking about the poem the Raven. I feel that Sunshine is trying to give her opinion about the poem the Raven, by saying that it is a dark poem about a homicide and magic. Sunshine's use of the word stick and present may be her way of saying that Edgar Allan Poe has a certain way of sticking it or presenting it to cause fear. Sunshine is definitely zeroing in on the way Edgar Allan Poe is presenting his words and his thoughts within the poem the Raven.

The 15th through 17th words given to me by the Ovilus IV during this paranormal investigation were copper, rent, and ravine. I do not believe that any of these words are answering any of the questions that I have asked so far during this Session 1. The word ravine may be the closest choice that Sunshine could find within the data base of the Ovilus IV for the word Raven. Sunshine may have been trying to choose the word Raven. Raven is the name of the Edgar Allen Poe poem that I read to Sunshine over a year ago. I feel that there is a connection there. I have conducted over two years' worth of Paranormal Investigations concerning the Hays, Gibson, and Buck families at other locations.

I obtained 12 different Mel Meter readings between 6:04 PM to 6:49 PM. The electromagnetic frequency range was between 0.4 mG to 0.8 mG. The electromagnetic frequency range during this paranormal investigation indicates that a spirit was near the Mel Meter nearly the entire 50-minute paranormal investigation. This is an indication that one or more Ghosts and or Spirits had an intense interest in what was going on during this Session.

Ovilus IV words: Bridge, Watch Can You.

Analysis of the Paranormal Investigation, Session 2, Monday, 23rd May 2016, Den Room. The date of this analysis was Wednesday, 26th April 2017.

The first word given to me by the Ovilus IV during this Paranormal Investigation was stirred. There were no background words at the beginning of this Paranormal Investigation Session 2. The words stirred was given to me by the Ovilus IV at 6:04 PM, just three minutes after the Paramount Investigation started. The last question that I asked, prior to the Ovilus IV giving me the word stirred, was, "Sunshine are you shy?" I feel that this stirred Sunshine up. That was Sunshine's way of saying that I aggravated her and annoyed her, when I asked if Sunshine was shy.

The second word given to me by the Ovilus IV during this Paranormal Investigation was finish, at 6:06 PM. I feel that this is the intelligent spirit of Sunshine stating that she is finished talking to me today.

From 6:16 PM to 6:33 PM I talked about several pictures that I had taken on the locations where Patsy and Frances Hays as children had left their names and their palm prints in the soft cement on the back-porch step's and the steps on the north side of the Hays House. At 6:36 PM Ovilus IV gave me the word abort. I feel that this is an intelligent response from the spirit of Sunshine and she is saying, I am tired of looking at the pictures, move on. I feel that ghosts and spirits still retain their human emotions and will respond to events in an emotional way. If a ghost or a spirit is having a bad day and you do something to upset them or annoy them, then they will be short and unresponsive to anything that you want to do during that paranormal investigation.

I have compared the first session in the Den Room to the second session and discovered that eight separate readings of the electro-magnetic frequency range are higher during Session 2. This range for the 1st Session was between 0.5 mG to 1.1 mG. This indicates that a spirit was near the Mel Meter nearly the entire 54 minutes Paranormal Investigation. This is an indication that Sunshine and or maybe other spirits or ghosts have an intense interest in what I was doing during the Paranormal Investigation. They had decided that they were not going to verbally communicate and did not using their energy to manipulate the Ovilus IV's database. I have often wondered if ghosts and or spirits are restricted to staying inside of the structure that they are able to visit after they pass away. It appears that during this Session 2 Paranormal Investigation that the ghosts and spirits were not all that impressed with the pictures of Patsy and Frances' names and hand-prints. This may denote that the spirits and ghosts within the Hays House are able to travel outside and see the steps where Patsy and

Frances' placed their names and handprints, into the soft cement in 1953. If the ghosts or spirits were restricted to just staying inside the Hays House, I think they would have paid a lot more attention to the pictures that were taken on the outside of the Hays House. The ghosts and or spirits that were present during the Session 2 Paranormal Investigation, seem to say that they could see these pictures anytime they wanted to.

Analysis of the Paranormal Investigation, Session 3, Tuesday, 24th May 2016, Den Room. The date this analysis was Wednesday, 26 April 2017.

The first two background words given by the Ovilus IV during this Paranormal Investigation, were found and Buddha. I do not feel that these two words have a connection with me and or any questions that I have asked in the past.

The third through fifth words given to me by the Ovilus IV during this Paranormal Investigation Session 3 were manifests, movie, and tool. I do not feel that any of these words have a connection with me and or any of the questions I've asked so far during this Paranormal Investigation Session 3. It is only logical to think that some ghost and or spirit may be asking a question about a movie and or a question about a tool. Depending on when the ghosts and or spirits lived, they may consider my digital camera, Ovilus IV, Mel Meter, cell phone or laptop, to be a tool that I am using. I'm not sure which tool they may be asking about. Manifest as a verb means to display, show, or reveal. A ghost and or spirit may be suggesting that they will materialize, so that I may be able to see them. I did not see any unexplained individuals during my stay between the 21st May 2016 to the 24th May 2016. So, a ghost and or spirit did not materialize, and a connection between the word manifest and any action is just not there.

The sixth word given to me by the Ovilus IV during this Paranormal Investigation Session 3 was Norman. I have received this word Norman by the same sounding voice, a high-pitched female, possibly African-American, many times, at other locations in Apalachicola. This is a very welcoming voice, it sounds like a voice of the person who knows me well and is happy to see me again. I have no idea if the ghost and or spirit is talking to me or another ghost or spirit in the area. If this ghost or spirit is talking to me, I can only assume that they had mistaken me for Norman. I do not know Norman's last name. I do not know any Norman associated with the Buck, Hays, and or Gibson family's.

I have compared the second session in the Den Room to the third session and I have noticed that from the nine separate readings of the electromagnetic field, that the range is higher between 0.9 mG to 1.3 mG. I have noticed over the three-day period, that each day the electromagnetic frequency range increased in value. This increase in the electromagnetic frequency range that I have observed is an indication that the spirits or ghosts were applying more electromagnetic energy which is equivalent to an increase in their intensity of interest concerning the Paranormal Investigations. I cannot tell if more ghosts were monitoring me, from a closer distance to the Mel Meter or if just one or a few ghosts were monitoring me, near the Mel Meter, but were using more energy while they were observing.

Digital pictures of the Den room and it's bathroom, Saturday, 21st May 2016, Hays House.

I obtained four pictures of the room's South wall.

I obtained one picture of the room's West wall.

I obtained three pictures of the room's East wall.

I obtained one picture of the room's Northeast corner.

I obtained three pictures of the room's North wall.

I obtained one picture of the room's ceiling.

I obtained five close up pictures of the pictures, and or paintings within the room.

I obtained one close up picture of the chest of drawers which are located on the room's East wall.

I obtained two pictures of the room's hardwood flooring.

I obtained two pictures of the threshold board at the bathroom door.

I obtained two pictures of the exterior side of the bathroom door's trim.

I obtained two pictures of the patched area on the room's hardwood claiming groove floor in front of the interior side of the room's door.

I obtained one picture of the interior side of the room's entrance door.

I obtained two pictures of the threshold board at the entrance door.

I obtained two pictures of the entrance door's interior side doorknob and skeleton key baseplate.

I obtained two close up pictures of the room's horizontal wallboards.

I obtained one close up picture of the room's South wall window netting.

I obtained three pictures of the room's wall and ceiling trim.

I obtained two close up pictures of the room's kitchen cabinets, located on the room's East wall.

I obtained one picture of the bathroom's floor.

I obtained two pictures of the bathroom's North wall.

I obtained one picture of the bathroom's door, interior side.

I obtained one picture of the bathroom's door exterior side.

I obtained two pictures of the bathroom's door, exterior side doorknob and skeleton key baseplate.

I obtained two pictures of the bathroom's door, interior side doorknob and skeleton key baseplate.

I obtained two pictures of the bathroom's door, interior side.

I obtained one close up picture of the bathroom's North wall's decorations.

I obtained one close up picture of the bathroom's white toilet.

I obtained one close up picture of the window, located on the bathroom's East wall.

I obtained two pictures of the bathroom's sink and mirror.

I obtained one picture of the bathroom's West wall.

I obtained two pictures of the bathroom's ceiling trim.

I obtained three pictures of the bathroom's bathtub.

I obtained two pictures of the bathroom's bathtub's spigots and handles for the hot water, cold water, and shower.

Please see the author's website at www.keithoevans.com to view each of the above digital pictures.

CHAPTER **3**

Second Floor Bath Room, Hays House, Ghosts are People too.

A brief description on what used to be the 2nd Floor Bathroom and what is today divided into the Second Floor Bathroom and the Second Floor North Side Kitchen.

Starting with the second-floor bathroom. The South wall of the second-floor bathroom is new and was built in sometime after 1996. Along this wall is a modern zinc and above the sink is a mirror. On the bathroom's South wall is the entrance door. This entrance door is white and has five sunken panels. It appears to be one of the original doors that was taken from another area in the house to be placed at this new wall after 1996.

Along the bathrooms West wall is a washer and dryer.

The bathrooms North wall has a, modern white toilet. There is a signal window on the room's North wall that is covered on the internal side with stained-glass window. The stained-glass image looks like a saint emblem.

The bathrooms East wall shows the outline of the wood-burning stove's brick fire place chimney that was in the kitchen's up until the early 1950's. Also, on the bathrooms East wall is a modern bathtub with shower curtain.

The Second Floor North Side Kitchen Room is approximately 10 feet along the north and south walls. The Second Floor North Side

40

Kitchen's east and west walls are approximately 5 feet wide. The Second Floor North Side Kitchen's South wall is the original wall prior to 1996, to what was the south wall of the second-floor bathroom. In 2017 the room's South wall doorway had no door. The white electric stove and oven are on the room's South East corner.

On the Second Floor North Side Kitchen's West wall is no door at the doorway, that before 1996 led to the Second Floor Bathroom's closet. Today, 2017, this doorway leads to a small area, approximately 3-foot-wide by 5 feet long and has a white refrigerator and freezer along its South wall and wooden shelves along its North wall. The West wall has a door that leads into what used to be Annie's Room. This doorway was put in sometime after 1996 and has a five-sunken panel door, that appears to be original.

The Second Floor North Side Kitchen's North wall has the entrance to the bathroom. Also, along the room's North wall is a modern double-sided stainless-steel sink, which was placed here when the Second Floor North Side Kitchen was built sometime after 1996.

Along the room South East corner is a white electrical stove and oven. There is a utility table on this room's Southwest corner.

A description of the 2nd Floor Bathroom from two 1996 pictures.

To the left side of the window on the Second Floor Bathroom's North wall is a pedestal type stand approximately 3-foot-tall with one small drawer. Attached to the back and top of the stand is a 12 inch by 18-inch mirror. The interior side of the bathroom's window has a stain glass window insert covering each of the four window panes. Each individual windowpane has a yellow saints symbol in the center that is outlined in black. The overall stain glass window is outlined with light green rectangles. At the bottom and top of the window are black or dark green diamonds. On each of the top of the diamonds in the bottom row and on each of the bottom diamonds in the top row there is a connecting black vertical line. There is a white background behind the two rows of diamonds and their vertical black lines. The second-floor bathroom's white horizontal tongue and groove wallboards and ceiling trim are original and painted white. To the right of the second-floor bathroom's window is the top of the white toilet which has a green potted plant sitting on the top of the toilets tank. Mounted on the north wall above the toilet is a vertical row of three, 12" x 18" frame pictures or paintings. Each of the pictures or paintings portray a harbor, a bay, and a marsh land scene.

The history of the Second Floor Bathroom, Hays House.

In 1942 when the Hays family moved into the Hays House the toilet was along the room's north wall and resting on a marble slab. It is believed that this marble slab was moved to the Second Floor Southside Bathroom, which was installed sometime after 1996. Today, in 2017, the modern white toilet in the Second Floor Southside Bathroom rest on a piece of marble slab. This appears to be the same size as the marble slab that the toilet prior to 1996, in the Second Floor Northside Bathroom rested on.

Back in the 1950s there was a small gas heater which was used to heat the Second Floor Bathroom. This gas heater was located between the toilet and the white sink, located along the room's East Wall.

In 1942 there was a white sink in the center of the 2nd Floor North Side Bathroom's east wall. This sink was taken out. A modern sink was located on the room's new south wall sometime after 1996.

In 1942 when the Hays family moved into the Hays House, there was a white clawfoot bathtub, located along the room's East wall and close to the room's South East corner. The white clawfoot bathtub remained in the Hays House until approximately 2012.

The lime green porcelain toilet paper holder that was still in the Hays House in 2017 was the original lime green porcelain toilet paper holder that was in the house when the Hays family moved in to the house in 1942.

Mel Meter base readings for the Second Floor North Side Kitchen Room, Hays House, Tuesday, 14th, March 2017.

The light switch on the left side and the cover plate on the right side, located on the room's South wall. The light switch on the left side is in the on position.

Electromagnetic frequency range 0.3 mG to 0.4 mG.

Temperature range 73.7°F to 74.6°F.

The white-hot point stove and oven, located on the room's East wall. The stove and oven are not in use.

Electromagnetic frequency range 0.0 mG to 0.4 mG.

Temperature range 74.6°F to 74.6°F.

The electrical outlet located on the room's East wall. The food lamp warmer is plugged into this electrical outlet.

Electromagnetic frequency range 0.0 mG to 0.0 mG.

Temperature range 74.4°F to 74.5°F.

The white Americana fridge and freezer located on the room's South wall. This white Americana fridge and freezer is in use.

Electromagnetic frequency range 0.0 mG to 0.1 mG.

Temperature range 72.9°F to 73.3°F.

The white tabletop located along the room's South wall.

Electromagnetic frequency range 0.0 mG to 0.2 mG.

Temperature range 72.0°F to 72.3°F.

The Mel Meter base readings for the Second Floor Bathroom, Hays House, Tuesday, 14 March 2017.

The electrical outlet on the room's West wall. The lamp is plugged into this electrical outlet.

Electromagnetic frequency range 0.0 mG to 0.1 mG.

Temperature range 72.2°F to 73.7°F.

The lamp sitting on top of the washer located along the room's West wall. This lamp is on.

Electromagnetic frequency range 0.0 mG to 0.1 mG.

Temperature range 74.2°F to 74.6°F.

The white Whirlpool washer located along the room's West wall. This washer is not in use.

Electromagnetic frequency range 0.0 mG to 0.3 mG.

Temperature range 73.5°F to 73.5°F.

The white whirlpool dryer located along the room's West wall. This dryer is not in use.

Electromagnetic frequency 0.0 mG to 0.0 mG.

Temperature range 72.5°F to 73.2°F.

The Paranormal Investigation, Session 1, 2nd Floor Bath Room, Hays House, Tuesday, 14th March 2017.

3 PM Keith: "Hello, I am Keith Evans. If you would like to talk, you may use your energy to choose words from the Ovilus IV's database. The Ovilus IV will not hurt you. This is the Ovilus IV." (Hold it up.)

3:01 PM Keith: "This is the Mel Meter. The Mel Meter measures temperature and electromagnetic frequencies. The Mel Meter will not harm you." (Hold it up.)

3:02 PM Keith: "The Ovilus IV has given me the following background words; have which is spelled H-A-V-E, and Lynn which is spelled L-Y-N-N. Have and Lynn were pronounced by the Ovilus IV at a normal conversational level and speed."

3:02 PM Keith: "I have observed the Mel Meter readings to be 0.0 mG and 68.7°F."

3:02 PM Keith: "I have observed the Mel Meter readings to be 0.0 mG and 68.6°F."

3:03 PM Keith: "The Ovilus IV has given me the word Rodger which is spelled R-O-D-G-E-R. The Ovilus IV pronounced the name Roger in a British accent, at a normal conversational level and speed."

3:03 PM Keith: "I have observed the Mel Meter readings to be 0.0 mG and 68.7°F."

3:06 PM Keith: "Is your name Lynn?"

3:07 PM Keith: "Lynn, what is your last name?"

3:08 PM Keith: "How are you doing today Roger?"

3:10 PM Keith: "The Ovilus IV has given me the word sub which is spelled S-U-B. I only heard an "S" sound. The word sub was pronounced by the Ovilus IV at a lower than normal conversational level. Almost like a whisper, but at a faster than normal conversational speed."

3:10 PM Keith: "I have observed the Mel Meter readings to be 0.0 mG and 69.5°F."

3:13 PM Keith: "What are you trying to tell me about a sub?"

3:14 PM Keith: "Is there an active enemy sub in the waters near Apalachicola, Florida?"

3:15 PM Keith: "Lynn are you still here?"

3:16 PM Keith: "Lynn are you related to any of the family's that use to live here?"

3:17 PM Keith: "The Ovilus IV is frozen, with two white dots in the upper left-hand corner of its display. I will place new batteries into the Ovilus IV."

3:20 PM Keith: "The Ovilus IV has given me two background words; break which is spelled B-R-E-A-K, and happy which is spelled H-A-P-P-Y. The words break and happy were pronounced by the Ovilus IV at a normal conversational level and speed."

3:20 PM Keith: "I have observed the Mel Meter readings to be 0.0 mG and 69.4°F."

3:21 PM Keith: "The Ovilus IV has given me the word ledge which is spelled L-E-D-G-E. The Ovilus IV has pronounce the word ledge at a normal conversational level and speed."

3:22 PM Keith: "I have observed the Mel Meter readings to be 0.0 mG and 69.9°F."

3:24 PM Keith: "So your happy to have a break out on the ledge?"

3:25 PM Keith: "Are you happy that it is spring break?"

3:26 PM Keith: "Roger and Lynn is your last name, Buck, Hays, or Gibson?"

3:28 PM Keith: "Roger and Lynn, can you tell me what you remember about the Hays House?"

3:29 PM Keith: "Kathleen, was this your sewing room when you lived here? I know that there was not a bathroom and kitchen in this room, when you lived here."

3:31 PM Keith: "Kathleen Hays, do you like what has been done to the house so far?"

3:34 PM Keith: "Kathleen, what was this room used for, if it was not used for sewing room?"

3:35 PM Keith: "Lynn do you know Roger?"

3:36 PM Keith: "I have observed the Mel Meter readings to be 0.7 mG and 70.3°F."

3:36 PM Keith: "I have observed the Mel Meter readings to be 0.8 mG and 70.5°F."

3:37 PM Keith: "I have observed the Mel Meter readings to be 0.7 mG and 70.6°F."

3:38 PM Keith: "I have observed the Mel Meter readings to be 0.7 mG and 70.8°F."

3:40 PM Keith: "I have observed the Mel Meter readings to be 0.7 mG and 70.9°F."

3:40 PM Keith: "I have observed the Mel Meter readings to be 0.6 mG and 70.9°F."

3:40 PM Keith: "I have observed the Mel Meter readings to be 0.7 mG and 71.2°F."

3:41 PM Keith: "I have observed the Mel Meter readings to be 0.7 mG and 70.7°F."

3:41 PM Keith: "I have observed the Mel Meter readings to be 0.6 mG and 70.9°F."

3:41 PM Keith: "I have observed the Mel Meter readings to be 0.7 mG and 70.9°F."

3:41 PM to 3:42 PM Keith: "I walked on the stairway going from the second to the third floor."

3:43 PM Keith: "I have observed the Mel Meter readings to be 0.7 mG and 70.9°F."

3:43 PM Keith: "I have observed the Mel Meter readings to be 0.7 mG and 70.9°F."

3:45 PM Keith: "I have observed the Mel Meter readings to be 0.7 mG and 71.0°F."

3:45 PM Keith: "I have observed the Mel Meter readings to be 0.7 mG and 71.2°F."

3:45 PM Keith: "Miss Kitty, Jill, stop making bread." (Jill craws are making sounds on the door trim.)

3:47 PM Keith: "I have observed the Mel Meter readings to be 0.7 mG and 71.2°F."

3:48 PM Keith: "The Ovilus IV has given me two words; finish which is spelled F-I-N-I-S-H, and student which is spelled S-T-U-D-E-N-T. The words finish and student were pronounced by the Ovilus IV at a normal conversational level and speed."

3:48 PM Keith: "I have observed the Mel Meter readings to be 0.7 mG and 71.2°F."

3:49 PM Keith: "I have observed the Mel Meter readings to be 0.7 mG and 71.5°F."

3:52 PM Keith: "Thank you for talking to me. Have a good day."

3:52 PM Keith: "I have observed the Mel Meter readings to be 0.7 mG and 71.4°F."

3:53 PM Keith: "A lady walked into frame and said hello."

3:54 PM Keith: "I have observed the Mel Meter readings to be 0.7 mG and 71.3°F."

3:54 PM Keith: "This Session 1 ended on Tuesday, 14th, March 2017."

The Paranormal Investigation, Session 2, 2nd Floor Bath Room, Tuesday, 14th March 2017.

4 PM Keith: "Hello, my name is Keith Evans. If you would like to talk, you may use your energy to choose words from the Ovilus IV's database. This is the Ovilus IV. The Ovilus IV will not hurt you." (Hold it up.)

4:01 PM Keith: "This is the Mel Meter. The Mel Meter may measure temperature and electromagnetic frequency. The Mel Meter will not harm you." (Hold it up.)

4:01 PM Keith: "The Ovilus IV has given me two background words; button which is spelled B-U-T-T-O-N, and read which is spelled R-E-A-D. The Ovilus IV has pronounced the words button and read in an angry man's voice, at a lower than conversational level and at a faster speed than normal conversational speed."

4:01 PM Keith: "I have observed the Mel Meter readings to be 0.0 mG and 71.0°F."

4:03 PM Keith: "Are you asking me to stop reading?"

4:04 PM Keith: "What do you mean by saying the words button and read."

4:05 PM Keith: "Kathleen, are you telling me that you use to use this room to sew buttons on and to read?"

4:05 PM Keith: "I have observed the Mel Meter readings to be 0.0 mG and 71.5°F."

4:06 PM Keith: "The Ovilus IV has given me two words; real which is spelled R-E-A-L, and the word and which is spelled A-N-D. The Ovilus IV has pronounced the words real, and the word and at a normal conversational level and speed."

4:06 PM Keith: "The Ovilus IV has given me the word drunk which is spelled D-R-U-N-K. The Ovilus IV has pronounce the word drunk at a normal conversational level and speed."

4:06 PM Keith: "I have observed the Mel Meter readings to be 0.0 mG and 71.3°F."

4:11 PM Keith: "I'm not drunk, are you drunk?"

4:12 PM Keith: "I do not know that ghosts could drink alcohol?"

4:13 PM Keith: "I obtained thermal images of camcorder one, which is located by the sink and camcorder two, which is located by the stove."

4:16 PM Keith: "Kathleen, what would you like to tell me?"

4:19 PM Keith: "The Ovilus IV has given me three words fast and back to back, but at a normal conversational level. These words were West which is spelled W-E-S-T, nor which is spelled N-O-R, and gasp which is spelled G-A-S-P."

4:19 PM Keith: "I have observed the Mel Meter readings to be 0.0 mG and 71.6°F."

4:23 PM Keith: "What do you mean by saying the words West, nor, and gasp."

4:24 PM Keith: "Is this Sunshine talking?"

4:25 PM Keith: "How are you doing Sunshine?"

4:26 PM Keith: "May I call you Sunshine, or do you prefer Miss Gibson?"

4:27 PM Keith: "Is West a first name or a last name?"

4:28 PM Keith: "Was it West or Roger that showed me how the back-stair steps used to go perpendicular to how the steps are today?"

4:29 PM Keith: "I appreciate your help on how the construction of the house used to be."

4:30 PM Keith: "What year did you use to live in the Hays House?"

4:31 PM Keith: "Which room in this house was your favorite room?"

4:32 PM Keith: "Was this room, a bedroom, when you lived here?"

4:33 PM Keith: "Kathleen, do you miss living in this house?"

3:34 PM Keith: "Kathleen, how many guardian angels are connected with this house?"

4:36 PM Keith: "All right, now all I am getting is silence."

4:37 PM Keith: "Are you all given me the cold shoulder?"

4:38 PM Keith: "Yes, it has been a long day for me to."

4:39 PM Keith: "Kathleen, what did you like to knit?"

4:40 PM Keith: "Kathleen, do you preferred that I call you Mrs. Hays?"

4:41 PM Keith: "Pat Hays, are you here today?"

4:41 PM Keith: "The Ovilus IV has given me the word deal which is spelled D-E-A-L. The Ovilus IV has pronounce the word deal at a normal conversational level and speed."

4:41 PM Keith: "I have observed the Mel Meter readings to be 0.9 mG and 71.2°F."

4:41 PM Keith: "I have observed the Mel Meter readings to be 0.8 mG and 71.2°F."

4:42 PM Keith: "Pat are you causing the electromagnetic frequency reading to be 0.8 mG?"

4:42 PM Keith: "I have observed the Mel Meter readings to be 0.8 mG and 71.5°F."

4:43 PM Keith: "The Ovilus IV has given me two words; idol which is spelled I-D-O-L, British which is spelled B-R-I-T-I-S-H, Fay which is spelled F-A-Y, beer which is spelled B-E-E-R, and Tesla which is spelled T-E-S-L-A. These five words were spoken louder than normal

51

conversational level and faster than normal conversational level. Since these words are spoken fast and back to back, I was unable to obtain a picture of the first two words. I believe that I heard the first two words to be idol and British. I was able to obtain a picture of the third, fourth, and fifth words."

4:43 PM Keith: "I have observed the Mel Meter readings to be 0.7 mG and 72.1°F."

4:43 PM Keith: "I have observed the Mel Meter readings to be 0.8 mG and 71.5°F."

4:44 PM Keith: "I have observed the Mel Meter readings to be 0.9 mG and 72.3°F."

4:45 PM Keith: "The Ovilus IV has given me the word Akasha which is spelled A-K-A-S-H-A. The word Akasha was pronounced by the Ovilus IV in a louder than normal conversational level and a faster than normal conversational speed."

4:45 PM Keith: "I have observed the Mel Meter readings to be 0.7 mG and 71.9°F."

4:50 PM Keith: "I have observed the Mel Meter readings to be 0.7 mG and 71.5°F."

4:51 PM Keith: "Okay Pat, you said that this was a deal to use both the Ovilus IV and the Mel Meter?"

4:53 PM Keith: "So Pat, you are familiar with any of these words; idol, beer, British, Tesla, and Akasha?"

4:55 PM Keith: "I have observed the Mel Meter readings to be 0.6 mG and 71.5°F."

4:55 PM Keith: "I have obtained three thermal images. The first thermal image is of the camcorder one, which is on top of the counter, beside the sink, located on the thermal image at center left. This image is located on the Northside Kitchen Room's North wall. The second, thermal image is of the camcorder two which is on top of the white stove and oven, located along the Northside Kitchen Room's East wall. The third thermal image is a pen sitting on top of the white table, on top of my notebook, and located along the tables Northside and along the Kitchen Room's South wall. On the thermal image the yellow pen is located in the center of the image."

4:55 PM Keith: "This Session 2 ended on Tuesday, 14th, March 2017."

Analysis of the Paranormal Investigation Session 1, 2nd Floor Bath Room, Tuesday, 14th March 2017. The data was analyzed on Sunday, 14th May 2017.

The first two background words that the Ovilus IV gave me during session 1 were have and Lynn. I have not asked any questions yet during this session 1. I do not know any Lynn connected with the Buck, Gibson, and Hays families. It is my belief that the ghosts and spirits speak in full sentences, but that the Ovilus IV is only picking up a few words from that sentence. If I am missing words from a sentence. It is only my guess as to what the sentence could be. One guess would be the following sentence. Have you talked to Lynn? A second guess could be, have you seen Lynn. The possible sentences that one could make from the words have and Lynn are limitless.

The third word given to me by the Ovilus IV during this session 1 was Roger. The Ovilus IV pronounced the word Roger with a British accent at a normal conversational level and speed. I had not asked any questions yet, between the first word that was given to me by the Ovilus IV at 3:02 PM and the second word was given to me by the Ovilus IV at 3:03 PM. So, I guess Roger was in response to the words have and Lynn. If we use the guess question from the above paragraph. Have you talked to Lynn? Then Roger would be a yes response. Roger may also be the name of a spirit and or Roger may be the person that the spirit is asking for.

The fourth word given to me by the Ovilus IV during this session 1 was sub. The word sub was pronounced by the Ovilus IV at a lower level than normal conversational level and at a faster than normal conversational speed. I only heard a whisper of a "S" sound. At 3:08 PM I had asked a question. How are you doing today Roger? I received the word sub at 3:10 PM. There may or may not be any connection between the last two words. Roger and sub may be considered to be military type words. Roger may just be a man's name. Sub could be a name of a sandwich. I cannot say with any degree of accuracy that the last two words are answering any of my questions that I've asked so far during this session number one.

At 3:17 PM the Ovilus IV froze up on me with two white dots in the upper left-hand corner of the display. Usually when the batteries keep going dead in the any of the equipment, it's due to a lot of the paranormal activity. I placed new batteries into the Ovilus IV and obtained two background words at 3:20 PM. The fifth and sixth words given to me by the Ovilus IV during this session were break and happy. I don't see where the words break and or happy are answering any of the questions that I have asked so far during this session. This may be an intelligent response from a spirit just stating that they are happy to have a break from the Ovilus IV. While I'm changing batteries, this may give the spirit's time to figure out a new way to choose words or a new system to use their energy to choose words from the Ovilus IV. I can only imagine that it may be difficult for some spirits to figure out how to use the Ovilus IV.

At 3:21 PM the Ovilus IV gave me the seventh word during this session 1, ledge. At 3:15 PM during this session 1, I asked Lynn if she was still here? This may be a possible intelligent response from the spirit name Lynn stating that she is on the ledge. I'm not sure what ledge Lynn maybe referring to. If I was just pure energy and did not take up much space. I guess she could fit on the window ledge, on the porch ledge, and on the bookshelf ledge.

At 3:35 PM, I asked Lynn if she knew Roger? At that point in session 1, I had not received any type of electromagnetic reading from the Mel Meter. After I asked that question the electromagnetic reading for the Mel Meter range was between 0.6 mG to 0.8 mG up until this session ended at 3:54 PM. The increase electromagnetic readings may indicate a connection between Lynn and Roger.

At 3:48 PM, the Ovilus IV gave me the eighth and ninth words from this session 1, which were finish and students. I know that Sunshine Gibson was an elementary school teacher for a while, so this could be her saying that she is finished with the students. The words finish and students are not answering any of the questions that I have presented during this session 1.

Analysis of the Paranormal Investigations, Session 2, 2nd Floor Bath Room, Tuesday, 14th March 2017. The data was analyzed on Thursday, 18th May 2017.

The first and second background words given to me by the Ovilus IV today were button and read. Background words are given by the Ovilus IV, within 60 seconds after starting the Ovilus IV and are a reading of the energy in the environment. So far during this session 2, I have not asked any questions. These two words button and read are not in response to any questions that I have asked. Kathleen may have used this room to sew buttons on, and to read. Another way of looking at these two words button and read could be that the word button has a nice slang term used in the early 1960's for shut up. So, some spirit or ghost maybe telling someone, maybe me, to shut up and read.

At 4:06 PM, the Ovilus IV gave me the third through fifth words during this session 2, and those words were real, and, and drunk. I do not feel that any of these words are in response to any of the questions that I have asked during this session number two.

4:13 PM I obtained one, thermal image of camcorder one to the left side of the kitchen sink, located along the room's North wall, a thermal image of camcorder to on top of the white stove located on the room's East wall, and I obtained thermal image of my pen, warmed by my hand, and laying on top of the white table top, located on this room's South wall. Scanning the room from top to bottom, left to right, and from wall to wall, I don't see anything thermally unexplained and or Paranormal about this room.

At 4:19 PM the Ovilus IV has given me three more words fast and back to back. The sixth through eighth words given to me during this session 2 were; West, nor, gasp. I do not feel that the words West, nor, and gasp, are in response to any of the questions I've asked during this session 2. A ghost may be unhappy with my use of describing the rooms by using West, North, East, and South terms.

At 4:43 PM the Ovilus IV gave me five more words pronounced by the Ovilus IV at a louder than normal conversational level and at a faster than normal conversational speed. The ninth through 13th words during this session number two were; idol, British, Fay, beer, and Tesla. I do not know of anyone with the first name of Fay who has any type of relationship with the Hays House. These words might be the intellectual spirit of Sunshine just given me a hard time by giving me groups of unconnected words simply because she doesn't want to help me with the history. Then again, I might be wrong, it could be group of spirits that are randomly talking to each other, in the environment and my Ovilus IV is just picking up their conversations.

Between 4:41 PM and 4:45 PM the electromagnetic frequency range on the Mel Meter were from 0.7 mG to 0.9 mG. This is an indication of high levels of paranormal activity for this period of time.

At 4:45 PM, the Ovilus IV gave me 14th word during this session number two. That word was akasha. I do not feel that this word is responding to any of the questions I've asked during this session. Akasha is a word that has many meanings. The word akasha is used by Western religion and philosophy as a large library or records of endless knowledge and history that only a few people can tap into via with supernatural means. In India the word akasha is used by philosopher's, who state that it is in regards to material and nonmaterial entities in a common medium.

Digital Pictures of the Second Floor Bathroom, Hays House, Tuesday, 14th March 2017.

One picture of the room's Northeast corner ceiling trim.

One picture of the room's Northeast corner floor area.

One picture of the room's North wall window.

One picture of the room's Northwest corner ceiling trim.

One picture of the room's Northwest corner, left side of the picture, right side part of the window.

One picture of the room's ceiling tongue and groove boards.

Two pictures of the brass window handles, right side window, located on the room's North wall.

Two pictures of the room's East wall pipe openings.

Two pictures of the room's South wall entrance door.

Two pictures of the room's tongue and groove hardwood floor.

One picture of the room's horizontal tongue and groove wallboards.

Two pictures of the kitchen side, bathroom door, black brass doorknob.

Please see the author's website at www.keithoevans.com to view each digital picture.

Digital pictures of the Second Floor North Side Kitchen, Tuesday, 14th, March 2017, Hays House.

Two pictures of the wall with the double door way.

One picture of the Northwest corner of the ceiling, to include trim.

Three pictures of the East wall.

Two pictures of the South wall.

Two pictures of the threshold floorboard between the two small rooms.

One picture of the door between the North side kitchen room and the I love you more room.

One picture of the Southwest corner of the ceiling trim.

One picture of the ceiling's tongue and groove boards.

One picture of the five-panel sunken door between the north kitchen and the north bathroom.

Two pictures of the hardwood floor.

Four pictures of the threshold board between the kitchen and the bathroom.

One picture of the threshold board between the two small rooms and the North side kitchen room.

Two pictures of the kitchen side of the bathroom North side entrance door.

Please see the author's website at www.keithoevans.com to view each digital picture.

The Thermal Images of the Second Floor Bathroom, Hays House, Tuesday, 14 March 2017.

One thermal image of the lamp on top of the washer, right side of the picture, on the room's West wall.

One thermal image of the warm just stopped dryer, bottom left corner of the picture, located along the room's North wall.

One thermal image of the room's East wall with the bathtub on the left, and the shower curtain on the right.

One thermal image of the room's South wall with the Mirror top, sink bottom, and the entrance door on the right side of the picture.

One thermal image with the ceiling vent on the picture's center to the bottom left corner.

One thermal image of the cover plate for previous stove, heat pipe, and or ductwork located in the center of the picture.

One thermal image of the room's floor in front of the bathtub.

One thermal image of the room's floor, in front of the bathtub, with the image of the shower curtain at the top of the picture.

Please see the author's website at www.keithoevans.com to view each thermal image.

Thermal Images of the Second Floor North Side Kitchen Room, Hays House, Tuesday, 14 March 2017.

One thermal image of the West wall in the double door ways.

One thermal image of the North wall to include bath room door, left side.

One thermal image of the East wall stove at the bottom right side.

One thermal image South wall door leading to the second-floor back stair room.

One thermal image of the room's ceiling with the ceiling light, bottom left corner.

One thermal image of the table located along the room's South wall.

One thermal image of the floor near the table located on the room's South.

Please see the author's website at www.keithoevans.com to view each thermal image.

CHAPTER 4

The First Floor Kitchen Room, Hays House, Ghosts are People too.

The description of the First Floor Kitchen Room, Monday, 13 March 2017.

The room's South wall has an original white wooden door that is 34 inches wide and 82 inches in height and has five sunken panels. This door has an original brass doorknob and matching skeleton key plate cover. This door is located near the room's South East corner. The threshold board between the 1st Floor Kitchen Room and the 1st Floor Back Stairway Room is 7 1/2 inches wide. There is a stainless-steel table located along the room's South wall. There is one modern wooden shelf located across the room's South wall.

On the room's West wall is an original white wooden door that is 34 inches wide and 82 inches in height and has five sunken panels. This door also has an original brass doorknob and matching skeleton key plate. This door is located near the room's Southwest corner. Next, along the room's West wall are the modern wooden cabinets that are mounted on the wall and also standing on the floor. The countertop is from the 1980s, which is located to the left and right sides of the white stove and stainless steel Nikme Heritagg hood and fan.

The room's North wall has an original double window with six glass panes on the top and the bottom sections. Each of the six panes dimensions are 7 1/2 inches by 12 inches. Each window has a bottom section with brass window grips. These window grips are what one would hold onto when opening and closing these windows. Within the right-side window, there is a white air conditioner window unit. Along the room's North wall are the wooden cabinets mounted on the wall and standing on the floor. There countertop is modern process wood, with delamination on top, from the 1980s. Also, on the countertop is a stainless-steel sink, and sitting on the floor between the cabinets is a white dishwasher. In the room's Northeast corner there is a refrigerator.

On the room's East wall is an approximately a 6-foot-tall natural wooden cabinet mounted on the wall and standing on the floor. This cabinet is located near the Northeast corner of the room. On the room's East wall is an original doorway opening that is 32 inches wide and 80 inches in height. This doorway once opened between the kitchen and the area that was once the back porch. This door way appears to have the original threshold that is 6 inches wide and painted gray. On top of the original threshold is another threshold board that is 3 1/2 inch wide and is painted gray. This doorway leads to what was at one time the back porch. Now, this original door way opening, which is missing a door, leads to the two small rooms that occupy part the space where the back porch used to be. On the room's East wall and located near the room's South East corner is an original window that is approximately 27 inches wide and 52 inches in height, with two glass panes in the top and bottom sections. The bottom section has the two original brass handholds.

The description of the First Floor Kitchen Room from two pictures taken in 1996.

This is a picture of the Northwest corner of the First Floor Kitchen showing the kitchen cabinets, the white stove, oven, silver hood and fan, and microwave oven, all on the room's West wall. On the kitchen's North wall is the kitchen cabinets, the black dishwasher, the double side stainless steel kitchen sink, and the double window with the white security bars. On the North wall and in front of each window is a green potted plant which is hanging from the ceiling. In the top center of the photo is the kitchen light which has a pink, orange, and green lamp cover all hanging from the kitchen ceiling.

In the bottom center of the photo is a wooden round table with three matching wooden chairs. The West, North, and east walls are covered with decorative wallpaper that have red and pink roses with a yellow background.

The photo of the First Floor Kitchen's East wall shows the wallpaper, the exterior kitchen door, the wooden covered clock that is mounted on the East wall between the exterior door and the window. The window on the room's East wall has the white security bars, and approximately 12″ x 18″ wooden frame stained glass with two yellow flowers with green leaves. The bottom half of the window on the First Floor Kitchen's East wall, had white wooden louvered shutters. There are three items sitting on top of a small stand or table situated in front of the First Floor Kitchen's East window. The three items are a 2 1/2-inch diameter white candle on a candleholder, a glass cup sitting on a glass saucer, and the top of a green plant. To the far right of the photo it shows the Southeast corner of the First Floor Kitchen. Mounted on the First Floor Kitchen's South wall there is a small yellow frying pan with a black handle. Part of the white wooden original trim from the doorway that leads from the First Floor Kitchen to the First Floor Back Stairway room can be seen within this photo. The exterior kitchen door is seen in part within the photo, and only the black side bolt lock can be seen on the far-right side of this door.

The history of the First Floor Kitchen Room, Hays House.

In 1996, the kitchen walls were all covered with drywall and painted an off-white. In 1996 there was still a red brick chimney in the Northeast corner of the kitchen. Back in the 1950's there was a coal and or wood burning stove that had a black pipe that led to the red brick chimney. From 1942 up until 1978 the First Floor Kitchen Room had metal kitchen cabinets. In 1978 the kitchen cabinets were replaced with modern wooden kitchen cabinets, that remain in the kitchen as of 2017. Today on the kitchen's West wall there is a General Electric stove and oven that was installed in 1978. At one time, Kathleen had the kitchen walls covered with decorative wallpaper. Some of this decorative wallpaper had red and pink roses with a yellow background and could still be seen on the wall above the kitchen sink, and on the walls behind the kitchen cabinets when these cabinets were taken down during renovations of the kitchen in 2017. In 1996, the exterior original off-white door with five sunken panels, was still on the kitchen's East wall and led to the back porch.

Mel Meter base readings of the First Floor Kitchen Room, Monday, 13 March 2017.

The two separate electrical outlets on the room's south wall. These two electrical outlets are not in use.

The electromagnetic frequency range was 0.0 mG to 0.0 mG.

The temperature range was 61.3°F to 62.0°F.

The gray electrical fuse box in the room's South West corner. The electrical fuse box is in use.

The two separate electrical outlets on the room's south wall. These two electrical outlets are not in use.

The electromagnetic frequency range was 0.7 mG to 1.2 mG.

The temperature range was 61.3°F to 62.0°F.

The electric meter on the room's West wall. This electrical meter is in use.

The electromagnetic frequency range was to 21.3 mG to 47.4 mG.

The temperature range was 62.3°F to 62.6°F.

The light switch on the room's West wall. This light switch is in the on position.

The electromagnetic frequency range was 0.0 mG to 0.1 mG.

The temperature range was 62.1°F to 62.4°F.

The double electrical outlet on the room's West wall. This double electrical outlet is not in use.

The electromagnetic frequency range was 0.0 mG to 0.0 mG.

The temperature range was 62.0°F to 62.3°F.

The electrical outlet on the room's West wall. This electrical outlet is not in use.

The electromagnetic frequency range was 0.2 mG to 0.2 mG.

The temperature range was 62.2°F to 62.4°F.

The white General Electric stove and oven on the room's West wall. The stove and oven are not in use.

The electromagnetic frequency was 0.0 mG to 0.2 mG.

The temperature range was 62.1°F to 62.2°F.

The electrical outlet on the room's West wall. This electrical outlet is not in use.

The electromagnetic frequency range was 3.0 mG to 3.6 mG.

The temperature range was 62.2°F to 63.1°F.

The double electrical outlet on the room's West wall. This double electrical outlet is in use, the small vacuum is plugged in and charging in this electrical outlet.

The electromagnetic frequency range was 164.8 mG to 19 5.7 mG.

The temperature range was 63.5°F to 63.8°F.

The white Comfort Aire air conditioner window unit on the room's North wall and within the right side of the double window. This air conditioner was not in use.

The electromagnetic frequency range was 0.0 mG to 0.0 mG.

The temperature range was 62.0°F to 63.4°F.

The electrical outlet on the room's North wall. The window air conditioner unit is plugged into this outlet.

The electromagnetic frequency range was 0.0 mG to 0.0 mG.

The temperature range was 61.0°F to 61.2°F.

The white Whirlpool refrigerator located in the room's north east corner. This refrigerator is not in use.

The electromagnetic frequency range was 0.0 mG to 0.0 mG.

The temperature range was 61.5°F to 61.8°F.

The white plate covering an electrical box, on the right side of the door way that leads into the two-small rooms located on the room's East wall.

The electromagnetic frequency range was 0.0 mG to 0.0 mG.

The temperature range was 61.7°F to 62.1°F.

The double electrical outlet on the room's East wall. This double electrical outlet is not in use.

The electromagnetic frequency range was 0.0 mG to 0.0 mG.

The temperature range was 62.3°F to 62.9°F.

The electrical outlet on the room's South wall. This electrical outlet is not in use.

The electromagnetic frequency range was 0.0 mG to 0.0 mG.

The temperature range was 62.4°F to 62.6°F.

The light switch on the room's South wall. This light switch was in the off position.

The electromagnetic frequency range was 0.0 mG to 0.1 mG.

The temperature range was 62.4°F to 62.7°F.

The white Vissani refrigerator position in the middle of the room. This refrigerator is not in use.

The electromagnetic frequency range was 0.0 mG to 0.0 mG.

The temperature range was 62.1°F to 62.9°F.

The white dishwasher on the room's north wall. This dishwasher is not in use.

The electromagnetic frequency range was 0.0 mG to 0.0 mG.

The temperature range was 62.0°F to 62.0°F.

Paranormal Investigation Session 1, 1st Floor Kitchen Room, Wednesday, 15 March 2017.

It was very cold outside in Florida for month of March. It was cold in the Kitchen and my hands were cold. I was planning to complete this Paranormal Session as soon as possible. I felt like at least the Spirit of Kathleen was in the room before I started the Paranormal Investigation. I was feeling that she had no use for a man that worked as a Paranormal Investigator. I was thinking to myself, "I hope I can win Kathleen Hays over," otherwise this is going to be a boring book. I had this feeling that Kathleen was telling me that I was in her territory now.

2:41 PM Keith: "Hello, I am Keith Evans. If you would like to talk, you may use your energy to choose words from the Ovilus IV's database. This is the Ovilus IV. The Ovilus IV will not hurt you." (Hold it up.)

2:42 PM Keith: "This is the Mel Meter. The Mel Meter measures temperature and electromagnetic frequencies. The Mel Meter will not harm you." (Hold it up.)

2:43 PM Keith: "The Ovilus IV has not given me any background words."

2:44 PM Keith: "I have observed the Mel Meter readings to be 0.0 mG and 52.2°F."

2:45 PM Keith: "That is unusual to not get any background words. The batteries are fully charged. Since I'm seeing the lights moving on the Ovilus IV's display, I know that the Ovilus IV is working fine."

2:45 PM Keith: "The Ovilus IV has given me the word remember which is spelled R-E-M-E-M-B-E-R. The Ovilus IV has pronounced the word remember in a normal conversational level and speed."

2:45 PM Keith: "I have observed the Mel Meter readings to be 0.0 mG and 53.0°F."

2:48 PM Keith: "What is it that you want to remember."

2:49 PM Keith: "Hello Kathleen and Pat."

2:50 PM Keith: "Do you remember all of the Christmas and Thanksgiving meals that you cooked here in this kitchen from the 1940's to the 1990's."

2:51 PM Keith: "The Ovilus IV has given me the word bright which is spelled B-R-I-G-H-T. The Ovilus IV has pronounced the word bright in a normal conversational level and speed."

2:51 PM Keith: "I have observed the Mel Meter readings to be 0.0 mG and 53.0°F."

2:51 PM Keith: "Did you mean to choose the word right instead of the word bright?"

2:54 PM Keith: "What were the Thanksgiving and Christmas meals like here at the Hays House?"

2:55 PM Keith: "What was your favorite meal for Thanksgiving and Christmas Pat and or Kathleen?"

2:58 PM Keith: "I am obtaining four thermal images of dark blue areas on the ceiling located on the South West and South East sides of the ceiling."

2:59 PM Keith: "The Ovilus IV has given me the word diction which is spelled D-I-C-T-I-O-N. The Ovilus IV has pronounced the word diction at a normal conversational level and speed."

3 PM Keith: "I have observed the Mel Meter readings to be 0.0 mG and 52.7°F."

3:02 PM Keith: "Hello Sunshine, that sounds like you. Are you correcting my speech?"

3:03 PM Keith: "Sunshine, do you remember cooking Thanksgiving and Christmas dinners in this kitchen during the 1940's and the 1950's?"

3:05 PM Keith: "Sunshine, what do you like to cook?"

3:06 PM Keith: "Sunshine, does the cat got your tongue?"

3:07 PM Keith: "I can hear loud talking outside on the north side porch."

3:08 PM Keith: "All right, I need someone to talk to me. I'm not a mind reader. I may look like one, but I'm not a mind reader."

3:09 PM Keith: "Pat, what did this kitchen look like back in the 1940's, when you first purchase the Hays House?"

3:10 PM Keith: "The batteries are dead and the Ovilus IV has frozen up, with three dots located in the upper left-hand corner of the Ovilus IV display. I will change the batteries."

3:14 PM Keith: "The Ovilus IV has given me three back ground words: someone which is spelled S-O-M-E-O-N-E, crowd which is spelled C-R-O-W-D, language which is spelled L-A-N-G-U-A-G-E. The Ovilus IV has pronounced the words someone, crowd, and language at a normal conversational level and speed."

3:14 PM Keith: "I have observed the Mel Meter readings to be 0.0 mG and 52.9°F."

3:15 PM Keith: "The Ovilus IV has given me the word ran which is spelled R-A-N. The Ovilus IV has pronounced the word ran with an angry voice, at a very loud level, but at a normal conversational speed."

3:18 PM Keith: "I have observed the Mel Meter readings to be 0.0 mG and 53.1°F."

3:20 PM Keith: "Sunshine, are you saying that my language is crowded?"

3:21 PM Keith: "Sunshine, could you be a little more specific about that statement?"

3:22 PM Keith: "Sunshine, did you teach English?"

3:23 PM Keith: "Pat said you called my speech Pig Latin!"

3:24 PM Keith: "Who is running? Who needs to run?" (I laughed.)

3:25 PM Keith: "It must be about 40°F in here?"

3:29 PM Keith: "I obtained two thermal images of dark blue areas on the southeast corner of the room's ceiling."

3:30 PM Keith: "I obtained two thermal images of dark blue areas on the northwest corner of the room's ceiling and kitchen cabinet area."

3:34 PM Keith: "The Ovilus IV is making a dial tone, sound, noise, and or chirping sound."

3:36 PM Keith: "The number one camcorders batteries are dead. I have moved the number two camcorder over to the number one camcorder's position. I want the Ovilus IV to be closer to the number two camcorder so that the tone sounds will be recorded by the number two camcorder."

3:38 PM Keith: "I can hear loud talking in the hallway."

3:40 PM Keith: "The Ovilus IV is still making the tone and chirping sounds."

3:41 PM Keith: "I have observed the Mel Meter readings to be 0.0 mG and 53.0°F."

3:41 PM Keith: "Thank you for talking to me. Have a good day."

3:41 PM Keith: "This session 1 has ended on Wednesday, 15 March 2017."

The Paranormal Investigation, Session 2, 1st Floor Kitchen Room, Thursday, 16th March 2017.

10:31 AM Keith: "Hello, I am Keith Evans. If you would like to talk, you may use your energy to choose words from the Ovilus IV's database. This is the Ovilus IV. The Ovilus IV will not harm you." (Hold it up.)

10:32 AM Keith: "This is the Mel Meter. The Mel Meter measures temperature and electromagnetic frequencies. The Mel Meter will not harm you." (Hold it up.)

10:32 AM Keith: "The Ovilus IV has given me three background words: right which is spelled R-I-G-H-T, beast which is spelled B-E-A-S-T, and sentence which is spelled S-E-N-T-E-N-C-E. The Ovilus IV has pronounced the words right, beast, and sentence in a faster than normal conversational speed and at a normal conversational level."

10:32 AM Keith: "I have observed the Mel Meter readings to be 0.0 mG and 49.9°F."

10:33 AM Keith: "The Ovilus IV has given me four words fast and back to back, the first word sounded like design which is spelled D-E-S-I-G-N. I have a picture of the second, third, and fourth words: sacrifice which is spelled S-A-C-R-I-F-I-C-E, judge which is spelled J-U-D-G-E, and head which is spelled H-E-A-D. The Ovilus IV has pronounced the words design, sacrifice, judge, and head in a faster

70

than normal conversational speed and at a normal conversational level."

10:33 AM Keith: "I have observed the Mel Meter readings to be 0.0 mG and 50.0°F."

10:35 AM Keith: "There are people in the hallway talking and walking."

10:36 AM Keith: "The Ovilus IV has given me three words fast and back to back: students which is spelled S-T-U-D-E-N-T-S, once which is spelled O-N-C-E, and alone which is spelled A-L-O-N-E. The Ovilus IV has pronounced the words students, once, and alone, in a faster than normal conversational speed and at a normal conversational level."

10:36 AM Keith: "I have observed the Mel Meter readings to be 0.0 mG and 50.3°F."

10:39 AM Keith: "Is that my car alarm. I think the ghost's likes to play with my car alarm." (I used my remote control to turn my car alarm off. The car alarm that I heard stopped at the same moment that I pressed the stop button. I did not have a visual of my car.)

10:40 AM Keith: "Well the horn stopped right as I turned off my car alarm by using the remote control. So, it was my cars alarm going off."

10:43 AM Keith: "I have observed the Mel Meter readings to be 0.0 mG and 50.2°F."

10:43 AM Keith: "I have not been showing the words that I had been receiving on the Ovilus IV to the camcorder to my right side, because the words were coming so fast."

10:44 AM Keith: "My camera is continuously going in and out of focus."

10:46 AM Keith: "Pat, when you were alive, most cars did not have car alarms, airbags, and other types of safety features that cars have today. In the 1970's only, some cars had safety belts. I guess you are interested in my car's safety equipment? Are you?"

10:53 AM Keith: "Right, beast, sentence."

10:53 AM Keith: "The Ovilus IV has given me the word rapture which is spelled R-A-P-T-U-R-E. The Ovilus IV has pronounced the word rapture in a lower than normal conversational level and a slower than normal conversational speed."

10:53 AM Keith: "I have observed the Mel Meter readings to be 0.1 mG and 50.4°F."

10:56 AM Keith: "Right, beast, and sentence, are you saying that I am not using the correct grammar, full sentences, and that this makes me a beast?"

10:58 AM Keith: "Someone is walking in the hallway."

10:59 AM Keith: "Someone is walking above me on the second floor."

11 AM Keith: "Sunshine, why don't you tutor me on how to use better grammar and how to use complete sentences when I speak?"

11:01 AM Keith: "So Sunshine, will you help me with that?"

11:02 AM Keith: "I obtained two thermal images of a dark blue area on the wall above the cabinets in this room's northwest corner."

11:02 AM Keith: "This is the FLIR Thermal Imager. I can see the temperature as it reads the location shown were the crosshairs are placed. The thermal imager shows an image of the heat in a colored code."

11:03 AM Keith: "For example cold colors are black, blue, and dark purple."

11:04 AM Keith: "When an object is 60°F it will appear to be purplish red."

11:05 AM Keith: "When an object is 70°F it will appear to be orange, at 80°F or above the object will appear to be yellow."

11:10 AM Keith: "The Ovilus IV has given me the word Halo which is spelled H-A-L-O. It sounded to me as if the Ovilus IV had said the word hit. This word was spoken at a faster than normal conversation speed and at a very loud level as compared to normal conversational levels."

11:10 AM Keith: "I have observed the Mel Meter readings to be 0.0 mG and 49.8°F."

11:11 AM Keith: "The Ovilus IV has given me the word shop which is spelled S-H-O-P. The Ovilus IV has pronounced the word shop at a normal conversational level but at a faster than normal conversational speed. The only thing I heard was a "S" sound. My hearing is not very good."

11:12 AM Keith: "My digital camera keeps going in and out of focus. Annie is that you? Okay, I know that you are here."

11:12 AM Keith: "I have observed the Mel Meter readings to be 0.0 mG and 50.2°F."

11:14 AM Keith: "How are you doing today Annie?"

11:18 AM Keith: "Annie, do you like to shop?"

11:20 AM Keith: "It was nice talking to you Pat, Kathleen, Sunshine, and Annie."

11:20 AM Keith: "I have observed the Mel Meter readings to be 0.0 mG and 49.9°F."

11:21 AM Keith: "Thank you for talking to me. Have a good day."

11:21 AM Keith: "This session 2 has ended on Thursday, 16th March 2017."

The analysis of the Paranormal Investigation, Session 1, 1st Floor Kitchen Room, Wednesday, 15th March 2017.

At 2:43 PM I noticed that there were no background words given by the Ovilus IV within the first minute after turning the Ovilus IV on. Just reminder the background words are the words given by the Ovilus IV, just from analyzing the energy within the environment upon the first 60 seconds after turning the Ovilus IV on. Not obtaining background words is rare and I've noticed that when there are no background words the session is usually very active.

At 2:45 PM the Ovilus IV gave me the first word during this session 1. The first word was remember. I had not asked a question yet. I feel that this is an intelligent spirit stating that I am going to ask them to remember things that had happened in the past. This is true, within the majority of my questions, I am asking spirits and ghosts about what they remember concerning the past.

AT 2:51 PM I received the second word given to me during this session by the Ovilus IV was bright. The word bright is not connected in any way with answering any of the questions I've asked so for during this session 1. I was concerned that maybe a ghost or spirit was attempting to choose the word right and by mistake chose the word bright. It is only logical to me that a ghost or spirit might say the word right in response to me asking them if they remember having a good holiday at the Christmas and Thanksgiving. It is a long shot assumption but possibly Sunshine is referring to me not being too bright for being a Paranormal Investigator. I do not feel that throughout their lifetimes that Sunshine, Kathleen, Annie, and Pat, valued anyone who would complete Paranormal Investigations. All Ghosts and Spirits retained the same values after their death's that they held while they were alive.

At 2:58 PM I evaluated the southwest corner and the southeast corner of the ceiling. I obtained four thermal images of dark blue areas. I am unable to identify what is causing the dark blue areas on the First Floor Kitchen's ceiling. There are no air conditioning ducts nearby that could cause the dark blue areas.

At 2:59 PM the Ovilus IV gave me the third word from this session, diction. I feel that this is an intelligent response from Sunshine Gibson, who is correcting me on my diction. I have noticed throughout my Paranormal Investigations the word diction is stated by the Ovilus IV more often than other words. I know that Sunshine Gibson was a school teacher for a while before she went full-time into the hotel business. I know that Sunshine Gibson is not happy with my choice of words and the way I construct sentences.

At 3:10 PM I noticed that the batteries in the Ovilus IV were dead and causing the Ovilus IV to freeze up. I coined the phrase, "frozen up", to denote the fact that the dots that constantly move on the upper left side of the Ovilus IV's display, stop moving when the Ovilus IV's four AAA batteries are dead. When the ghosts or spirits are draining all of the energy from my batteries on the Paranormal Investigating equipment, that is usually an indication of a very active paranormal session.

At 3:14 PM I received the fourth through sixth words given to me by the Ovilus IV during this session were someone, crowd, and language. There is an intelligent spirit pleading with a large crowd of ghosts or spirits to use their language to speak to me. I had heard loud talking coming from the north side porch. In addition to the first interpretation of what these three words I had heard, at 3:07 PM may mean. I had heard loud talking coming from the north side porch. This intelligent spirit may just be acknowledging that they know someone in the crowd that was talking loudly. The analysis of a Paranormal Investigation can be very subjective.

At 3:15 PM I received the seventh word given to me by the Ovilus IV during this session was ran. This word was spoken loud and angrily but at a normal conversational speed. It was not an order telling me to run, but it was past tense of run, ran. Seems to me like a spirit was upset about having to run. This could be an intelligent spirit talking to another spirit, but I do not feel they are responding to me or any of the questions I've asked so for during this session.

At 3:22 PM and 3:23 PM I am teasing Sunshine about being a teacher who teaches Pig Latin and I'm blaming it on Pat. I guess I'm doing this to get under Sunshine skin. At 3:34 PM I noticed that the Ovilus IV is making a dial tone sound, noise, and more chirping sound. It would be nice to receive words on the Ovilus IV that were answering my questions, but instead I am just getting a dial tone noise.

At 3:29 PM I obtained thermal images from the southeast corner of the room's ceiling. I obtained two thermal images with dark blue areas, that are unexplained. I cannot determine any source for this cold air. I know this cold air is not coming from the air conditioner ducts. This dark blue area may be the ghosts and or spirits of Pat, Kathleen, Sunshine, and or Annie.

At 3:30 PM I obtained thermal images from the northwest corner of the room's ceiling. I obtained two thermal images with dark blue areas, that are unexplained. I cannot determine any source for this cold air. I know this cold air is not coming from any air conditioner ducts. This dark blue area may be the ghosts and or spirits of Pat, Kathleen, Sunshine, and or Annie.

3:36 PM I noticed that the number one camcorder's batteries were dead. I quickly moved the number two camcorder over to the position where the number one camcorder had been recording, so I could obtain a close-up view and recording of the Ovilus IV. I wanted to capture the videotape and the sound that the Ovilus IV was making. I feel that the strange noise that the Ovilus IV was making and the camcorder 1's batteries going dead, was a direct result of me teasing Sunshine at 3:22 PM and 3:23 PM during this session.

The analysis of the Paranormal Investigation, Session 2, 1st Floor Kitchen Room, Thursday, 16th March 2017.

At 10:32 PM I received the first three words given to me by the Ovilus IV during Session 2, were background words; right, beast, and sentence. The words right, beast, and sentence were spoken at a normal conversation level but at a faster than normal conversational speed. I feel that these background words were from Sunshine. I feel that she was waiting to urgently let me know that I must improve on my sentence structure and to use proper grammar. I feel that Sunshine was saying that if I write incorrectly, people will consider me to be a beast.

At 10:33 PM I received the fourth through seventh words given to me by the Ovilus IV were given to me very fast and back to back. The first word sounded like design, but I do not have a picture of this word. I do have a picture of the second through fourth words; sacrifice, judge, and head. These four words were pronounced by the Ovilus IV at a normal conversational level but at a faster than normal conversational speed. The Ovilus IV only stores the last three words on its display. In a situation where four or more words are given fast and back to back by the Ovilus IV, it is next to impossible to obtain a digital picture of the first word. I feel that this is an intelligent respond from Sunshine Gibson. Sunshine is telling me that I need to design a book, sacrifice to learn how to write well, to make the judgement on how and what to write about, and to use my head or good judgement.

At 10:36 PM I received the eighth through tenth words given to me by the Ovilus IV were given to me very fast and back to back. These three words were pronounced by the Ovilus IV at a normal conversational level, but at a faster than normal conversational speed. The words were students, once, and alone. I feel that this was an intellectual respond from Sunshine and that she was telling me that I would be a student once and I must do this on my own and alone.

At 10:39 AM I noticed my car alarm started going off. I know it was my car alarm going off because the alarm stopped when I pressed the alarm stop button on my car's remote control. I feel that Pat Hays was the spirit that caused my car alarm to go off. I think that Pat is interested in the new car protection technology.

At 10:44 AM I noticed that my digital camera was continuously going in and out of focus. I feel that this is Annie.

At 10:53 AM the eleventh word rapture was given to me by the Ovilus IV during this Session 2. This word rapture was pronounced by the Ovilus IV at a lower than normal conversational level and a slower than normal conversational level. I do not believe that this word rapture was in response to any of the questions that I have asked during this Session 2.

At 10:53 AM I observed the Mel Meter reading for the electromagnetic frequency to be 0.1 mG. This is the only time during this Session 2 that I received any reading for the electromagnetic frequency. It is rare but sometimes when the spirits or ghosts manipulates the Ovilus IV, they also manipulate the Mel Meter readings.

At 11:02 AM I obtained two thermal images of dark blue areas on the wall and above the cabinets near the first floor Kitchen Room's north west corner. I feel that this could be the ghost and or spirit of Pat, Kathleen, Sunshine, and or Annie.

At 11:10 AM the Ovilus IV gave me the twentieth word Halo, during this Session 2. Only heard the word hit. The word Halo was pronounced by the Ovilus IV at a louder than normal conversation level and at a faster speed than normal conversational speed. I do not believe that the word Halo is in response to any of the questions I've asked so for during this Session 2.

At 11:11 AM the Ovilus IV gave me the 13th word, shop during this Session 2. The word shop was pronounced by the Ovilus IV at a normal conversational level but spoken at a faster than normal conversational speed. All I heard from the Ovilus IV was a "S" sound. In the past Sunshine has spoken at a normal conversational level but faster than normal conversational speed. So, I would have to say that this is probably a trademark of Sunshine Gibson. This is the intelligent response from Sunshine telling me that she wants to go shopping and that she does not want to help me with the history concerning the book.

At 11:12 AM I noticed that my digital camera going in and out of focus. I said Annie is that you. Okay, I know you're here. I have always thought that when my digital camera goes in and out of focus that it is Annie Gibson because when I was at a relative's house and taking pictures of Annie's most favorite possession, a music box, at that point in time my camera went in and out of focus. So, that gave me

Annie's name to connect this action of my digital camera going in and out of focus.

Digital pictures of the First Floor Kitchen Room, Hays House, Monday, 13 March 2017.

Two pictures of the Southwest corner interior door, located on the first-floor kitchen rooms West wall, that leads from the First Floor Kitchen Room to the dining room.

One picture of the First Floor Kitchen Room's West wall to include the oven and the stove.

Two pictures of the Northwest corner of the First Floor Kitchen Room, to include the oven, the stove, and the dishwasher.

One picture of the First Floor Kitchen Room's North wall to include the double window with the window unit air condition unit.

Two pictures of the black on door knob, to the door between the kitchen and the dining room, located on the first-floor kitchen room's North wall.

Two pictures of the exterior door with the five sunken panels, on the door between the kitchen and the dining room, located on the First Floor Kitchen Room's North wall.

One picture of the Northeast corner of the First Floor Kitchen Room. This picture is very blurry.

One picture of the First Floor Kitchen Room's North wall, to include the white dishwasher, sink, and the white air conditioner window unit.

Two pictures of the drywall ceiling and ceiling light.

One picture of the First Floor Kitchen Room's tongue and groove hardwood floor.

One close up picture of the Nickmee Heritage hood fan that is located on the room's West wall.

One close up picture of the two-brass window holds, on the left side window, of the double windows located on the First Floor Kitchen Room's North wall.

Two close up pictures of one brass window hold, located on the left side of the window located on the First Floor Kitchen Room's North wall.

One picture of the six-panel window, located on the left side window, on the first level kitchen room's North wall.

Two pictures of the First Floor Kitchen Room's East wall, left side, the open door with no door, leading to the two small rooms built on top of what used to be the original back porch to the Hays house.

One picture of the First Floor Kitchen Room's South East corner, left two panel windows, exterior five panel door that leads to the back-stair room.

Two pictures of the First Floor Kitchen Room's South wall. The white refrigerator and freezer are not in use.

One picture of the two fluorescent lights on the ceiling the First Floor Kitchen Room.

Two pictures of the wooden threshold between the back-kitchen door that is leaving towards the two small rooms that were built on the original back porch.

Two pictures of the floor molding on the First Floor Kitchen Room's East wall.

10 pictures of the white door trim, and door leading from the kitchen to the two small rooms built on the original back porch area.

Two pictures of the brass window grips or holds located on the First Floor Kitchen Room's East wall.

Three pictures of the window located on the First Floor Kitchen Room's East wall.

One picture of the black doorknob located on the door leading to the back stairs room, located on the First Floor Kitchen Room's South wall.

Two pictures of the five sunken panels white door leading to the back stairs room, located on the First Floor Kitchen Room's South wall.

Two pictures of the threshold between the First Floor Kitchen Room and the First Floor Back Stairway Room.

Three pictures of the flower paper behind the sink on the First Floor Kitchen Room's North wall.

Please visit my website at www.keithoevans.com to view each digital picture.

Thermal Images of the First Floor Kitchen Room Hays House, Monday, 13th March 2017.

One picture South West corner of the First Floor Kitchen Room.

One picture of the white oven and stove, located at the center of the room's West wall.

One picture of the warm, yellow, small vacuum cleaner, that was charging, and was located on the room's northwest corner.

One picture of the room's North wall double window.

One picture of the far-left side part of the window that is located on the room's North East corner.

One picture of the open doorway that leads to the two small rooms built over what used to be the original back porch and located on the room's East wall.

One picture of the room's southwest corner.

One picture of the ceiling area.

One picture of the ceiling area and the ceiling florescent light.

One picture which could be of the floor or the ceiling area.

One close up picture of the white oven and stove located on the room's West wall.

One picture of the white oven and stove's far left side, and the warm area of the small vacuum that is charging at the electrical outlet, on this picture's top right, located on the room's West wall.

One picture of the open oven door viewed as orange, at the top center of the picture, and located on the room's West wall.

Please visit my website at www.keithoevans.com to view each thermal image.

CHAPTER 5

The Dining Room, Hays House, Ghosts are People too.

The description of the Dining Room, Hays House, Monday, 13th March 2017.

On the Dining Room's West wall are one door and two door ways. The first doorway opening is near the room's Southwest corner. This door-way opening leads to the TV Room and is approximately 34 inches wide and six-foot and 8 inches in height. The second door is located on the room's West wall and is near the room's Northwest corner and leads outside to the wraparound porch. This door is approximately 36 inches wide and six-foot 10 inches in height. This door appears to be original. The top half of this door has a large glass window that is approximately 30 inches wide and 36 inches long. The bottom half of this white wooden door has two decorative sunken panels. The door in the room's Northwest corner, also has a decorative original brass doorknob and a decorative original skeleton key cover plate. The majority of the room's West wall has a beautiful original natural wooden Tiger Striped yellow oak fireplace mantle with a right and left side natural wooden Tiger Striped yellow oak column that hold up the first shelf on the mantle. There is a second shelf held up by a left and right side natural wooden Tiger Striped yellow oak decorative columns. On the wall space that spans between the area under the columns holding up second shelf is the original mirror. This mirror is approximately 35 inches long and 17 inches wide. The fireplace wood burning area is surrounded by a mixture of original olive green, light green, and white, colored tiles. These rectangular shaped tiles are approximately 1 9/16 of an inch wide and 6 1/8 inches long. There is a black fireplace insert within the fireplace which is original. The dimensions of the fireplace insert are approximately 26 1/4 inches wide and 31 5/8 inches in length.

The west wall, Dining Room.

On the Dining Room's North wall there are two original white wooden windows with a top and bottom half. Each window has an overall dimension approximately 36 inches wide and 18 inches in length. The top and bottom half each has two rectangular glass panes.

On the Dining Room's East wall, there is one original white wooden window, located near the room's North East corner. This windows dimensions are approximately 18 inches wide and 4 feet and 18 inches in length. This window has a top and bottom half with one pane of glass within each half. In the room's South East corner there is an original white wooden interior door with five decorative sunken panels. This door's dimensions are approximately 34.5 inches wide and 6'8" in height. This door has the original brass doorknob and the original matching skeleton key cover plate. This door in the room's South East corner leads to the First Floor Kitchen. The threshold board between the Dining Room and the First Floor Kitchen is approximately 3 1/8 inches wide.

On the Dining Room's South wall and near the room's Southwest corner, there is a double door. Each door has 10 individual glass panes that are approximately 8 1/4-inch-wide and 13 inches long. The overall dimensions of the double doors are approximately 48 inches wide and 6 feet 9.5 inches in height. The right-side door's, dimensions from standing within the Dining Room, are approximately 23 1/4-inch-wide and 6'9" in height. The left side door's dimensions, from standing within the Dining Room, are approximately 23 inches wide and six-foot 9 inches in height. This door leads to the First Floor Front Stairway Room. This door may be original.

The Dining Room has 2 1/2-inch-wide tongue and groove heart pine hardwood floors. The hardwood floors are running in an East to West direction. The hardwood floor has three openings for heat ducks. Two ducks are located near the room's North wall and one heat duck is located near the room's South East corner. The Dining Room also has a white decorative wooden trim on all four walls, located between the top of each wall and the ceiling. The ceiling has 2 1/2-inch tongue and groove boards that are running from an East to West direction.

Each wall in this room has a white wainscoting which is a decorative wooden wall covering from the floor to approximately 4 feet and 8.5 inches in height, with a 5-inch shelf on the top border. The top portion of all walls in this room are covered with the 3-inch-wide white horizontal tongue and groove wallboards.

So, much of the original dining room still remains here in 2017. The original house I feel gives the connection that allows the Ghosts and Spirits an avenue between haven and the places and things that they loved during their lives. This is why it is so important to save the Victorian Homes and Victorian structures and restore these structures to their original states. Once these Victorian structures are gone the connection between the Ghosts and Spirits are loosed forever.

The description of the Dining Room, Hays House, from pictures taken in 1996.

On top of the 5-inch ledge going around the top of the Wainscoting on each wall within the dining room, were various small and large China type plates and saucers. There is a small plate or saucer resting on the short five-inch piece of the top ledge of the wainscoting that is located between the double doors on the dining room's South wall and the door that leads from the Dining Room into the TV room on the Dining Room's West wall. The door on the Dining Room's west wall opens into the Dining Room and stops against the left side of the fireplace. On the Dining Room's West wall was the white fireplace mantle with the different shades of blue tiles surrounding the fireplace opening. Within the fireplace opening is a gas heater insert. On the top shelf over the fireplace mantle was three glass pitchers. On the bottom shelf over the fireplace mantle were two glass pitchers on each side of a porcelain clock. Sitting on the different shades of blue tiles, on the floor in front of the fireplace was a golden fireplace hearth. To the left side of the fireplace is a golden coal bucket. Against the West wall is a dark wooden China cabinet that is approximately 4-foot-tall, 4-foot-wide, and 12 inches deep. The China cabinet has glass doors and is full of clear glasses. On the room's West wall and near the room's Northwest corner is an original white exterior door that leads to the North side of the wraparound porch. The top of this door has a window and the bottom half of the door has two sunken panels. Near the room's Northwest corner is a 4-foot-tall, four leg, dark wooden teapot holder with a teapot on top.

In the center of the dining room is an 8-foot-long dark wooden dining room table with its two, 1 foot long, wooden inserts. The table has six matching wooden chairs around its perimeter. The table is decorated with two antique bowls that are sitting on top of their pedestals on each side of an antique candleholder with four white candles and white and pink flowers on top of the candles. Above this table is what I call a grand chandelier with clear crystals and 10 or 12 small candle looking electrical lightbulbs hanging from the center of the Dining Room ceiling. The Dining Room's floor had a light gray or off-white rug covering most of the hardwood flooring.

Along the North wall are two wooden chairs with a textile covered seats on each side of a dark wooden cabinet with three drawers and a silver punch bowl on top, surrounded by four punch bowl cups. The North wall has two windows, and both are covered with a silver, and or off-white drapery.

There is one narrow window on the room's East wall, that is covered with a silver and off-white drapery. In the room's North East corner, there is a live green potted plant sitting on a dark wooden pedestal. A long the Dining Room's East wall is a dark wooden piece of furniture with several drawers and cabinets doors. This piece of furniture appears to be an antique. On top of this piece of furniture are a silver candleholder and a silver set of serving containers on a silver tray. To the right of this piece of furniture is a dark wooden pedestal with a pinkish gray marble top. On top of this pedestal is a bust of a woman who is wearing a white and light orange bonnet.

The Dining Room's South wall has an approximately a 6-foot-tall, and 5-foot-wide China cabinet. The top half of this China cabinet has three shelves with glass doors. Each shelf contains clear glassware, such as plates and glasses. The bottom half of this China cabinet has three layers of drawers. On the top of the China cabinet are two decorative pitchers on each side of a large decorative serving plate that has two handles. To the right of the China cabinet is a dark wooden pedestal that has a pinkish gray marble top. On top of this pedestal is an antique vase. To the top right side of the antique vase and on the Dining Room's south wall is the light switch.

The History of the Dining Room from approximately 1942 to 1996, Hays House.

From 1942 to 1996 Mrs. Kathleen Hays decorated the dining room's narrow 5-inch shelf located at the top of the Wainscoting that surrounds each wall in the dining room, with decorative plates. Pictures taken in 1996 and 1959 have shown that all of the 5-inch shelves within the dining room had several decorative and very colorful plates. I'm going to talk about a few of the plates that the Mrs. Kathleen Hays had on her 5-inch shelf in the dining room. The first plate is a golden trim plate with roses around the perimeter of the plate and two off-shoot vines, with one in the center, depend on how you orientate the plate, one on the left side of the plate. Written on the back of this plate are the words P. S. Bavaria Hand-painted. The Bavaria china was made in Bavaria Germany. This fine china was made form white clay called Kaolin. Kaolin is fired at extremely high temperatures for a long time. This results in a very glossy, slightly translucent, and very hard porcelain. This porcelain makes a ping sound upon being struck. Bavaria Germany was known for having high quality clay quarries. Next are the second and third plate and small tray plate with two handles and golden trim around the edges. Both items were hand-painted and have small blue flowers around the perimeter and a large Daisy, depending on how you have the dish orientated, shaped like a rainbow near the center of the plate. The words on the back of the plate read, Berisch Studios Ginorin, Italy. The fourth and fifth pieces of China that were located on the room's narrow 5-inch shelf are a plate and a small tray plate with two golden handles, each having golden edges. Each plate is decorated and or hand-painted with three yellow roses on the diameter. The words on the back of the plates are Berisch Studios Ginorin, Italy. The sixth and seventh plate and small tray plate, located on the top of the wainscoting and are each having golden trim with the small tray having to golden handles. Each item is hand-painted with four light orange roses on the diameter. The artist for both pieces was A. Dimi. The words on the back of the plate are Berisch Studios Ginorin Italy.

From 1942 until approximately the mid-1950s the dining room was heated by a coal and wood-burning stove located in the kitchen. The fireplace, located on the dining room's West wall, had the same decorative iron crate over the front of the fire place in 1996 as was there in 2017. The fireplace wood burning area was surrounded by a mixture of original olive green, light green, and white, colored tiles. These rectangular shaped tiles are approximately 1 9/16 of an inch wide and 6 1/8 inches long. Some of these tiles are gone now. Patsy Hays remembers playing with the loose and removeable titles when she with a little girl.

Sometime between 1987 and the early 1990's Mrs. Kathleen Hays had central heat placed in all rooms on the first floor. The central heat for the first floor was transferred through ducks that ran under the first floor within the crawlspace. You can still see two duct openings on the floor near the room's North wall. It appears that one duck has been covered over with a piece of metal. This duck is located near the room's South East corner in front of the door that goes between the dining room and the kitchen.

From 1942 to 1996 Mrs. Kathleen Hays had a large dining room table, in the center of the dining room. This table had two 24-inch table inserts to lengthen the table.

When the Hays family purchased and moved into the Hays House in 1942, Mrs. Kathleen Hays pledged to paint all of the natural dark wood within the house white. She made this pledge because she wanted to brighten up the house. Many people within the town told her that it would not be a good ideal to place white paint over such a beautiful, buy very dark natural wooden grain. Mrs. Kathleen Hays had already made up her mind and the fireplace mantle with its beautiful yellow oak Tiger stripe wood was painted white shortly after 1942. It wasn't until after 1996, when a new owner decided to spend the time and the money to remove the white paint and allow the natural wood and its beauty to be seen by all.

Keeping with Mrs. Kathleen Hays' promised to brighten up the dining room, she also had the Wainscoting, the walls, and the ceiling painted white. It is believed that the Wainscoting had never been painted until Mrs. Kathleen Hays had it painted white. So, up until 1942 the Wainscoting revealed the original wooden grain. It is believed that the horizontal tongue and groove walls above the Wainscoting and the tongue and groove ceiling may have already been painted with some unknown color prior to 1942.

Between 1960 and 1961 Mrs. Kathleen Hays had beige Cornish curtains made by a local business in Apalachicola. The top of these curtains had plywood behind the curtain to give it support. These curtains were hung in the dining room sometime between 1960 and 1961 and stayed there until the house was sold by Mrs. Kathleen Hays in 1996.

Kathleen Hays had a large beautiful crystal chandelier hanging from the ceiling and in the center the Dining Room from 1942 until 1996.

From 1942 to 1996 Mrs. Kathleen Hays prepared meals for her family and they ate in the dining room. Mrs. Kathleen Hays may have used three of her decorative bowls if needed, for daily use. The first one of these decorative bowls is the 8 inches in diameter scallop shaped bowl with the hand-painted rose in the middle and four roses around the perimeter. The writing on the back of the bowl states M. Z. Austria. The markings M. Z. stands for Moritz Zdekauer. Moritz Zdekauer purchase the porcelain factory in 1884 and he owned this factory until 1909. During the period that Moritz Zdekauer owned the porcelain factory in Altrohlau Austria all the porcelain manufactured there was marked M. Z. Austria. Altrohlau Austria is today known as Stara Role and it is located in the Czech Republic. The second of the hand-painted decorative 8-inch bowls has golden trim around the perimeter and flowers along the water in the center of the interior side of the bowl. Documented on the back of this bowl are the letters and word R. S. Prussia which was use prior to 1917. R. S.

stand for Reinhold Schlegelmilch, who started his porcelain factory in Suhl Germany in 1869. The third of the decorative 8-inch bowls has a wide golden edge around the perimeter of the bowl and four red and two pink roses hand-painted on the interior side of the bowl. There are no manufacturing name or markings on the backside of this bowl.

From 1942 to 1996 Mrs. Kathleen Hays prepared Thanksgiving Day meal for her family at the Hays House and they ate in the dining room. In 1953 Mrs. Kathleen Hays saw the plates with a turkey in the middle. On the back of the King Tom plates are the words an American tradition, hand decorated under glaze genuine ironstone. She had to have these plates. So, she purchased the King Tom plates size 11 3/8 inches and the King Tom large serving plate size 18 inches. This started a tradition in the Hays family where the King Tom plates and large serving plate were used at the Hays House for every Thanksgiving Day meal from 1953 until 1996. I was told that the family continues to use the King Tom plates and large serving plate for their Thanksgiving dinner up to the present date, which is 2017. The menu that Mrs. Kathleen Hays prepared for Thanksgiving dinner from 1942 to 1996 was as follows:

baked turkey
cornbread dressing
oyster dressing
cranberry relish
sweet potato casserole baked inside of a hollowed-out half of an orange peel, with marshmallows on top from 1942 to 1965
sweet potato casserole from 1966 to 1996
fresh green beans
corn casserole
homemade yeast rolls
pecan pie with vanilla ice cream
unsweetened iced tea

Between 1942 and 1978 the Hays family had their Thanksgiving Day meal between 12 noon and 1 PM. Mr. Pat Hays preferred to eat his Thanksgiving meal at this time. From 1978 to 1996 the Hays family had their Thanksgiving dinner at 5 PM.

From 1942 to 1968 the Dining Room had Christmas decorations on top of the fire place mantle. In the center of the fire place mantle was an electrical five candles that were surrounded by home handed decorations. Such as branches and leaves that were hand painted silver or gold and inserted into a soft piece of foam within a vase. These colorful leaves and branches had store bought Christmas balls hanging from them.

From 1942 to 1996 Mrs. Kathleen Hays prepared the Christmas Day meal for her family at the Hays House and they ate in the dining room. The Hays family used the King Tom plates and large serving plate with the picture of the turkey in the middle of the plate for their Christmas day meal. This started a tradition in the Hays family where the King Tom plates and large serving plate were used at the Hays House for their Christmas meal from 1953 until 1996. I was told that the family continues to use the King Tom plates and large serving plate for their Christmas Day meal up to the present date, which is 2017. For the Christmas Day meal Mrs. Kathleen Hays used a large and a small stainless-steel Christmas tree molds to hold her green congealed salad. There are no manufacturing name or markings on either stainless steel mold. The menu that Mrs. Kathleen Hays prepared for Christmas Day dinner from 1942 to 1996 was as follows:

baked turkey
baked ham
cornbread dressing
oyster dressing
sweet potato casserole
cream corn
white acre peas
asparagus casserole
green congealed salad in Christmas tree molds
cranberry relish
homemade yeast rolls
lane cake is a yellowcake flavored with bourbon and topped with a cooked white icing
unsweetened iced tea

Between 1942 and 1978 the Hays family had their Christmas Day meal between 12 noon and 1 PM. Mr. Pat Hays preferred to eat his Christmas Day meals at this time. From 1978 to 1996 the Hays family had their Christmas day dinner at 5 PM.

The double doors that lead from the Dining Room to the 1st Floor Front Stairway Room are the same doors that were there in 1996. The Dining Room double doors and the double doors that use to be there at the wall in the 1st Floor Front Stairway Room, that was taken down sometime after 2015, were matching double doors. These double doors where installed by Pat and Kathleen Hays shortly after they purchased the Hays House in 1942. It is not clear if there were any doors, located on the Dining Room's South wall leading to the 1st Floor Front Stairway Room prior to 1942. The Exterior door, located on the Dining Room's west wall and leading from the Dining Room to the North Side of the wrap-around Front Porch is the same door that was there in 1996. It is believed that the exterior door on the room west wall is an original door and was there in 1942.

Mel Meter Base Readings, The Dining Room, Hays House, Monday, 13th March 2017.

The white ceiling fan and light. Both were in the on position.

The electromagnetic frequency range was 0.0 mG to 0.0 mG.

The temperature range was 63.4°F to 63.7°F.

The cast iron gas heater fireplace insert. This gas heater fireplace insert is in use.

The electromagnetic frequency range was 0.0 mG to 0.0 mG.

The temperature range was 64.5°F to 65.7°F.

The double light switch and one covered plate, to the left of the hallway entrance, located on the room's South wall. Both light switches are in the on position.

The electromagnetic frequency range was 0.4 mG to 2.4 mG.

The temperature range was 63.4°F to 63.6°F.

The Paranormal Investigation, Session 1, The Dining Room, Hays House, Thursday, 16th, March 2017.

2:07 PM Keith: "Hello, I am Keith Evans. If you would like to talk, you may use your energy to choose words from the Ovilus IV's database. This is the Ovilus IV. The Ovilus IV will not hurt you." (Hold it up.)

2:08 PM Keith: "This is the Mel Meter. The Mel Meter measures temperature and electromagnetic frequencies. The Mel Meter will not harm you." (Hold it up.)

2:08 PM Keith: "The Ovilus IV has given me three background words; weapon which is spelled W-E-A-P-O-N, process which is spelled P-R-O-C-E-S-S, and wonder which is spelled W-O-N-D-E-R. The Ovilus IV has pronounce the words weapon, process, and wonder in a normal conversational level and speed."

2:08 PM Keith: "I have observed the Mel Meter readings to be 0.0 mG and 66.3°F."

2:10 PM Keith: "The Ovilus IV has given me the word momma which is spelled M-O-M-M-A. The Ovilus IV has pronounced the word momma in a louder than normal conversational level and in a faster than normal conversational speed. This voice sounded disparate."

2:10 PM Keith: "I have observed the Mel Meter readings to be 0.0 mG and 66.4°F."

2:11 PM Keith: "I have observed the Mel Meter readings to be 0.0 mG and 67.4°F."

2:14 PM Keith: "No, the Ovilus IV and Mel Meter are not weapons. You do not need to process, think, and or worry about the, Ovilus IV and the Mel Meter because they are not weapons and will not harm you."

2:16 PM Keith: "Who is calling for their momma?"

2:17 PM Keith: "The Ovilus IV is frozen up and will not respond to my touch to return it to the home position. I am going to turn the Ovilus IV off and change the batteries."

2:19 PM Keith: "The Ovilus IV has given me three background words; distance which is spelled D-I-S-T-A-N-C-E, completed which is spelled C-O-M-P-L-E-T-E-D, and wonder which is spelled W-O-N-D-E-R. The Ovilus IV has pronounced the words; distance, completed, and wonder in a normal conversational level and speed."

2:19 PM Keith: "I have observed the Mel Meter readings to be 0.0 mG and 67.9°F."

2:21 PM Keith: "The Ovilus IV has given me the word porch which is spelled P-O-R-C-H and breaker which is spelled B-R-E-A-K-E-R. The Ovilus IV has pronounced the word porch and breaker in a normal conversational level and speed."

2:21 PM Keith: "I have observed the Mel Meter readings to be 0.0 mG and 70.3°F."

2:21 PM Keith: "The Ovilus IV has given me the word preacher which is spelled P-R-E-A-C-H-E-R. The Ovilus IV has pronounced the word preacher at a normal conversational level and speed."

2:22 PM Keith: "I have observed the Mel Meter readings to be 0.0 mG and 68.4°F."

2:26 PM Keith: "Distance, complete, wonder, porch, breaker, and preacher, what do these words mean?"

2:27 PM Keith: "The Ovilus IV has given me the word bank which is spelled B-A-N-K. The Ovilus IV has pronounced the word bank at a normal conversational level and speed."

2:27 PM Keith: "I have observed the Mel Meter readings to be 0.0 mG and 70.5°F."

2:30 PM Keith: "Yes, I went to the bank today to get rolls of Jefferson Nickels, so I can look for Error coins."

2:32 PM Keith: "I heard talking out in the hallway."

2:35 PM Keith: "Pat, did you work in a bank?"

2:36 PM Keith: "The Ovilus IV has given me the word bell which is spelled B-E-L-L. The Ovilus for has pronounced the word bell in a lower than normal conversational level and in a faster than normal conversational speed."

2:36 PM Keith: "I have observed the Mel Meter readings to be 0.0 mG and 71.6°F."

2:37 PM Keith: "I have heard talking in the hallway."

2:39 PM Keith: "What does Bell have to do with the bank, Pat?"

2:39 PM Keith: "I hear talking in the first-floor kitchen room."

2:40 PM Keith: "The Ovilus IV has given me two words; hop which is spelled H-O-P, and divided which is spelled D-I-V-I-D-E-D. The Ovilus IV has pronounced the words hop and divided at a lower than normal conversational level and at a faster than normal conversational speed. I could not understand what the Ovilus IV had said."

2:40 PM Keith: "I have observed the Mel Meter readings to be 0.0 mG and 71.6°F."

2:41 PM Keith: "I have observed the Mel Meter readings to be 0.0 mG and 71.8°F."

2:44 PM Keith: "Hop and divide, are words that are telling me what?"

2:45 PM Keith: "I do not understand what you're trying to tell me."

2:46 PM Keith: "I am going to check the camcorders. Camcorder one is working fine. Camcorder 2 is over, on top of the fireplace mantle and it has turned itself off. I have turned camcorder 2 on and it is working fine."

2:49 PM Keith: "Pat, did you work as an accountant for one of the local banks?"

2:50 PM Keith: "The Ovilus IV is frozen up again. I will change the batteries. The Ovilus IV will not go back to the home position. I have turned the Ovilus IV off."

2:52 PM Keith: "The Ovilus IV has given me two background words; red which is spelled R-E-D, and key which is spelled K-E-Y. The Ovilus IV has pronounce the words red and key at a normal conversational level and speed."

2:52 PM Keith: "I have observed the Mel Meter readings to be 0.0 mG and 72.9°F."

2:52 PM Keith: "I have observed the Mel Meter readings to be 0.0 mG and 73.6°F."

2:53 PM Keith: "I have observed the Mel Meter readings to be 0.0 mG and 73.9°F."

2:54 PM Keith: "The Ovilus IV has given me the word press which is spelled P-R-E-S-S. The Ovilus IV has pronounced the word press at a normal conversational level and speed."

2:55 PM Keith: "I have obtained two thermal images of the dark blue area, located on the room's South wall near the double light switches. I have obtained two thermal images of the dark blue area, located on the room's South East corner wall."

2:55 PM Keith: "Yes, your easy all right."

2:55 PM Keith: "This session 1 ended on Thursday, 16 March 2017."

The Paranormal Investigation, Session 2, The Dining Room, Hays House, Thursday, 16th, March 2017.

4:07 PM Keith: "Hello, I am Keith Evans. You may use or energy to choose words from the Ovilus IV's database. This is the Ovilus IV and it will not hurt you." (Hold it up.)

4:07 PM Keith: "This is the Mel Meter. The Mel Meter measures temperature and electromagnetic frequencies. The Mel Meter will not harm you." (Hold it up.)

4:08 PM Keith: "The Ovilus IV has given me two background words; mass which is spelled M-A-S-S, and let which is spelled L-E-T. The words mass and let were pronounced by the Ovilus IV at a normal conversational level and speed."

4:08 PM Keith: "I have observed the Mel Meter readings to be 0.0 mG and 77.9°F."

4:09 PM Keith: "The Ovilus IV has given me the word cupcake which is spelled C-U-P-C-A-K-E. It sounded to me like the Ovilus IV had said hey cupcake or eat cupcake. I heard the sounds of hey or eat to be at a lower level than normal conversational level and slower than normal conversational speed. There is no evidence recorded by the Ovilus IV of the word hey and or eat. The Ovilus IV pronounced the word cupcake at a normal conversational level and speed."

4:09 PM Keith: "I have observed the Mel Meter readings to be 0.0 mG and 78.4°F."

4:10 PM Keith: "The Ovilus IV has given me the word 40 which is spelled F-O-R-T-Y. The word 40 was spoken at a normal conversational level and speed."

4:11 PM Keith: "I have observed the Mel Meter readings to be 0.0 mG 77.9°F."

4:15 PM Keith: "The words mass, let, cupcake, and 40, what do these words mean?"

4:16 PM Keith: "Sunshine, is that you just spouting off a lot of words without any certain theme and or meaning?"

4:17 PM Keith: "Who has good memories about eating meals in this dining room?"

4:18 PM Keith: "Did anyone enjoy Christmas dinner in this dining room?"

4:20 PM Keith: "I have observed that camcorder number two, which is in the close-up position, was not functioning at all, so I moved camcorder 2 to the Southwest corner of the yellow room. At that location I can plug in camcorder 2 directly into the electrical outlet. I then moved camcorder one to the close-up position which is besides the table where I am documenting the transcript."

4:24 PM Keith: "Did anyone enjoy Thanksgiving dinner in this room?"

4:25 PM Keith: "Mary did you enjoy Thanksgiving dinner and or Christmas dinner in this dining room?"

4:26 PM Keith: "Does anyone from the Buck family have any good memories of eating in this dining room?"

4:27 PM Keith: "Does anyone from the Gibson, and Hays families have any good memories of eating in this dining room?"

4:28 PM Keith: "Are you all given me the cold shoulder today?"

4:29 PM Keith: "Sunshine, cat got your tongue?"

4:30 PM Keith: "Pat, can you make another car alarm go off?"

4:31 PM Keith: "Did you enjoy eating cupcakes in this dining room?"

4:32 PM Keith: "What flavor was the cupcake and what flavor was the icing on your cupcake?"

4:33 PM Keith: "Did you bake your own cupcakes?"

4:34 PM Keith: "What else did you bake besides cupcakes?"

4:35 PM Keith: "Pat, were you a good cook?"

4:35 PM Keith: "I heard someone coming in the front door."

4:36 PM Keith: "I heard someone in the front room, walking."

4:37 PM Keith: "Pat, was that you who made the car alarm go off?"

4:38 PM Keith: "Sunshine, was that Pat that made the car alarm go off, yes or no?"

4:39 PM Keith: "Is there anyone present that enjoyed meals in this dining room, when they were alive?"

4:40 PM Keith: "Who ate turkey in this dining room?"

4:41 PM Keith: "Kathleen, did you eat turkey in this dining room, when you were alive?"

4:42 PM Keith: "Kathleen, did you enjoy Thanksgiving meals in this dining room during the 1940's through the 1990's?"

4:43 PM Keith: "Kathleen, did you enjoy Christmas meals in this dining room during that time period between the 1940's to the 1990's?"

4:44 PM Keith: "Are you all afraid to talk to me?"

4:45 PM Keith: "Kathleen, what do you want to talk about?"

4:46 PM Keith: "Kathleen, what do you want to tell me?"

4:47 PM Keith: "Kathleen, how did you have this dining room area decorated?"

4:48 PM Keith: "The camcorders are working fine."

4:54 PM Keith: "Would anyone like to talk?"

4:55 PM Keith: "I have observed the Mel Meter readings to be 0.0 mG and 74.6°F."

4:56 PM Keith: "Thank you for talking to me. Have a good day."

4:57 PM Keith: "I have obtained two thermal images of dark blue areas on the South wall near the double light switch. I have obtained two thermal images of dark blue areas on the room's South East corner wall."

4:57 PM Keith: "This session 2 ended on Thursday, 16 March 2017."

The analysis of the Paranormal Investigation, Session 1, The Dining Room, Hays House, Thursday, 16th, March 2017. Date of analysis is Saturday, 20 May 2017.

At 2:08 PM I obtained the first three background words from the Ovilus IV during this session 1 and they were; weapon, process, and wonder. I feel that an intelligent spirit was thinking out loud, that I may have a weapon. The spirit must've felt vulnerable to the different types of equipment that I have and that they could be used to cause harm. To process is to decided and to wonder if their conclusion with correct.

At 2:10 PM I obtained the fourth word from the Ovilus IV during this session 1 and it was the word Momma. I guess a spirit is really frighten, because they are screaming for their mother. The Ovilus IV pronounce the word Momma at a louder than normal conversational level and at a faster than normal conversational speed. This voice sounded desperate. This could be a child spirit.

At 2:16 PM I had asked a question who was calling for their mother? At 2:17 PM the Ovilus IV is frozen up and will not respond to my touch to return it to the home position. It seems like when the spirits are unhappy with me. They just shut my machine down by draining the batteries in the Ovilus IV. I don't think that was a child spirit frighten of me and calling for its mother. I think it was just a ghost being sarcastic. Ghosts and spirits only have their wit two mess with you. As you can see I'm not getting very much information on the history of the Hays House and or any History about the three major families that lived here.

At 2:19 PM the Ovilus IV gave me the fifth through seventh words during this session number one; distance, complete, and wonder. I feel this is an intelligent spirit, is probably Sunshine and she is wondering how long it is going to take me to complete this book. Today during this session one at 2:08 PM, I obtained a group of three words from the Ovilus IV, with the last word of that group of three words being the word wonder. This is the second time today that I have got a group of three words with the third word being the word wonder. This type of trait of ending a group of words with the word wonder would have to mean that the Spirit that stated this at 2:19 PM, is the same Spirit that made this statement at 2:08 PM. If one says I wonder, that is no more than a question, like a what if. Some Ghost and or Spirit is asking me something and I am just not getting the question.

At 2:21 PM I obtained the eighth word during this session number one from the Ovilus IV, porch. Maybe this spirit is saying that they are out on the porch.

At 2:21 PM within the same minute, but a different response, I obtained the ninth word during this session number one from the Ovilus IV, breaker. I do not feel that this word breaker is responding to any of the questions that I've asked so far during this session number one.

At 2:22 PM I obtained the 10th word during this session number one from the Ovilus IV, preacher. I do not feel that this word preacher is responding to any of the questions that I have asked so for during this session number one.

At 2:27 PM I obtained the 11th word during this session number one from the Ovilus IV, bank. I had taken this to be an intelligent spirit telling me that they had observed me earlier today going to the bank, where I obtain a roll of Jefferson Nickels, which I looked through to try to find error coins. In addition to me, going to the bank today. Pat Hays was on the Board of Directors at the Apalachicola State Bank.

So maybe this could have been Pat Hays communicating with me about his past employment.

At 2:36 PM I obtained the 12th word during this session number one from the Ovilus IV, Bell. The word Bell was pronounced by the Ovilus IV in a very lower than normal conversational level and at a faster than normal conversational speed. I do not feel that the word Bell is responding to any of the questions that I have asked so far during this session number one.

At 2:40 PM I obtained the 13th and 14th words during this session number one from the Ovilus IV, hop and divided. The words hop and divided were pronounced by the Ovilus IV and a very lower than normal conversational level and at a faster than normal conversational speed. The words hop and divided were spoken by the Ovilus IV in a low level and so fast that I could not hear what the Ovilus IV had said. That tells me that the last three words given to me by the Ovilus IV were spoken by the same ghost or spirit because each of those words were spoken at a very low level and at a very fast speed. I do not feel that the words hop and divide are in response to any of the questions that I have asked so far during this session number one.

At 2:46 PM I noticed that camcorder two located on top of the fireplace mantle, had turned itself off. I turned camcorder two back on. I didn't turned camcorder number two off and camcorder two definitely has power on its battery.

At 2:50 PM the Ovilus IV is frozen again. The batteries are dead, so I am going to change the batteries and place four brand new AAA batteries into the Ovilus IV. Something is draining the energy from these batteries and is not me.

At 2:52 PM I obtained the 15th and 16th words during this session number one from the Ovilus IV, red and key. The last question that I asked this session number one was at 2:49 PM, Pat, did you work as an accountant for one of the local banks? What does the words red and key have to do with Pat, working as an accountant for local bank? Was Pat saying that I'm in the red? Was Pat saying that is a key question? I do not know. I feel that the words red and key are not in response to any of the questions that I have asked during this session number one.

At 2:54 PM I obtained the 17th words during this session number one from the Ovilus IV, press. I do not feel that the word press is in response to any of the questions that I have asked during this session number one.

At 2:55 PM. I obtained two thermal images of dark blue areas, located on the room's South wall near the double light switches. I obtained two thermal images of dark blue areas, located on the room's South East corner wall area. All of the dark blue areas in the thermal images are unexplained. These two dark blue areas could be one or more Ghosts and or Spirits grouped together.

The analysis of the Paranormal Investigation, Session 2, The Dining Room, Hays House, Thursday, 16th, March 2017. Date of analysis is Saturday, 20 May 2017.

At 4:08 PM the Ovilus IV gave me the first and second background words for session number two, mass and let. I have not asked any questions yet during this session number two. Maybe a Ghost is telling me that I need to let some mass go and lose some weight.

4:09 PM, the Ovilus IV gave me the third word for session number two, cupcake. The Ovilus IV did not pick this up, but prior to the Ovilus IV pronouncing the word cupcake, I thought I heard either hey or eat cupcake. Now this could have been a disembodied voice and not the Ovilus IV saying the word hey or eat, but even with my bad hearing, it sounded like somebody said hey cupcake or eat cupcake. The hey or eat was pronounced at a normal conversational level, but at a slower than normal conversational speed. The word cupcake was pronounced by the Ovilus IV at a normal conversational level and speed. The difference in the speed of the words hey or eat, and cupcake would denote two different spirits and or two different delivery methods, one via Ovilus IV and the other by disembodied voice. This could be a Ghost and or Spirit egging me on to eat more cupcakes and not to lose weight.

At 4:10 PM the Ovilus IV gave me the fourth word for session 2, the word 40. I have not had time to ask any questions during this session number two. Your guess is as good as mine as to what 40 stands for.

4:20 PM I observed that camcorder 2, my close-up camera's batteries were dead. I moved camcorder number two over to the Southwest corner of the Dining Room so I could plug camcorder 2 into the electrical outlet. I moved camcorder number one to the close-up position, besides the tabletop.

4:57 PM I obtained two thermal images of a dark blue area on this room's South wall near the double light switch. I obtained two thermal images of a dark blue area on this room's South East corner wall area. I cannot explain why there are any dark blue areas in any of the four thermal images that I obtained in the Dining Room. During today's session number two, I obtained five words from the Ovilus IV within the first four minutes of the session number two, however after that, I did not receive any more words from the Ovilus IV. There is no rhyme or reason as to if or when a room will be filled with a lot of paranormal activity.

Digital Pictures, The Dining Room, Hays House, Monday, 13th March 2017.

Seven pictures of the fireplace.

Five pictures of the cast iron gas fireplace insert heater.

Two pictures of the cast iron gas heaters on and off switch.

Tw the history of the dining room pictures of the green and white fireplace tile.

13 pictures of the tiger stripe decorative fireplace mantle wood.

Six pictures of the West wall.

One picture of the North wall.

Three pictures of the East wall.

Two pictures of the South wall.

Two pictures of the doorknob on the interior door side, which leads to the old kitchen.

Two pictures of the doorknob, exterior door, interior side of the door.

Four pictures of the heart pine hardwood floor.

Four pictures of the old dining room's decorative trim and shelving.

One picture of the horizontal tongue and groove wallboards.

One unknown picture.

Three pictures of the interior door, leading from the old dining room to the front hallway room.

Please see the author's website at www.keithoevans.com to view each of these digital pictures.

Digital Pictures, The Dining Room, Hays House, Wednesday, 7th June 2017.

Eight pictures of the greenish blue fireplace mantle tile on the room's West wall.

Two pictures of the room's tongue and groove heart pine floor.

Four pictures of the room's horizontal wallboards.

Please see the author's website at www.keithoevans.com to view each of these digital pictures.

Digital Pictures, The Dining Room, Hays House, Thursday, 8th June 2017.

Four pictures of the room's Northwest corner.

Eight pictures of the room's West wall.

Four pictures of the room's Southwest corner.

Four pictures of the room's South East corner.

Two pictures of the Kitty named Jill.

Two pictures of the double door on the room's South wall, in the room's South West corner.

Two pictures of the room's Southwest corner.

Two pictures of the room's top wall and ceiling area located in the room's Northwest corner.

Two pictures of the room's lower North wall and floor area.

Two pictures of the red metal patched floor near the room's South East corner.

Two pictures of the white original wooden door, located on the room's North East corner.

Two pictures of the left side window, on the room's North wall.

Two pictures of the door leading to the porch in the room's Northwest corner.

Two pictures of the room's South wall.

Two pictures of the double door glass panes, located on the room's South wall.

Two close-up pictures of the doorknob on the right side double door, located on the room's South wall.

Please see the author's website at www.keithoevans.com to view each of these digital pictures.

Thermal Images, The Dining Room, Hays House, Monday, 13th March 2017.

One image of the rooms Southwest corner.

One image of the center of the rooms West wall, the cast iron gas heater on images bottom center.

One image of the room's Northwest corner, interior door on the image's left side center, part of the window on the image's right side.

One image of the room's North wall, two Windows.

One image of the rooms Northeast corner, to Windows.

One image of the rooms East wall.

One image of the room's South East corner, top right side of the ceiling fan and lights.

One image of the room's South wall.

One image of the rooms Southwest corner, gas heater fireplace insert at the bottom right of the image.

One image of the ceiling fan and lights.

Two images of a close-up of the double light switch and cover plate to the left of the entrance leading from the old dining room to the front hallway, located on the dining room's South wall.

Please see the author's website at www.keithoevans.com to view each of these thermal images.

CHAPTER 6

TV Room, Hays House, Ghosts are People too.

Description of the TV Room, Hays House, Friday, 10th March 2017 and Thursday, 8th June 2017.

On the room's West wall there are two Windows, with a top and bottom half. Each half has two glass panes. The dimensions of the left side window are approximately 34 1/4 inches wide and 5'9" in height. The dimensions of the right side, window are approximately 34 inches wide and 5'9" in height.

The room's North wall has one window that is approximately 34 1/2 inches wide and 5'9" in height.

The room's East wall has the original decorative Tiger striped wooden fireplace mantle with a left column and a right column. The decorative wooden wreath on the front and center of the fireplace mantle, just above the vertical fireplace tile, is partially damaged and partially missing most of the top reef. Up until 1996, the fireplace mantle was covered with light yellow paint. The fireplace's original tile is colored, light blue, pink, and white. The fireplace tile's dimensions are approximately one 9/16-inch-wide and 6 1/16 inch in length. The fireplace's original mantle mirror's dimensions are approximately 17 1/2 inches wide and 36 inches in length. The antique iron decorative fireplace cover located on the room's East wall, is approximately 27 ½ inchers wide and 33 inches in height. This iron cover was there when Pat and Kathleen purchased the Hay House in 1942. There is a door way opening with no door, located in the room's South East corner and on the room's East wall. This doorway appears to have modern white wooden trim. The threshold board between the TV Room and the Dining Room is three and three-quarter inches wide and maybe original.

The East wall TV Room.

The South wall's opening is narrowed by an original, 4 feet in height decorative natural wooden wall with a right and left natural wooden column. After 1996, the light-yellow paint was removed from the 4-foot-high decorative natural wooden wall and its right and left side natural wooden column.

The room's ceiling has 2 1/2-inch-wide original white tongue and groove ceiling boards that are running from an East to West direction. The room's original white horizontal wall boards are approximately 3 1/4 inches wide. The room's original heart pine hardwood flooring is approximately two 9/16 inches wide. This hardwood floor is running in an East to West direction. The TV room's original tongue and groove heart pine hardwood floor was last stripped sometime after 1996.

A description of the TV Room from pictures taken in 1996.

This description of the TV Room is from eight pictures taken by Frances Hays Toulon in 1996 before her Mother, Kathleen Hays soled the Hays House. The west wall has two windows that are covered with silver or off white decorative drapery. Along the west wall is a 36-inch-tall, three leg, dark wooden table with one center post that is supporting an approximately thirty inches in diameter circular dark wooden table top. On this table top are the following items: a golden framed mirror, a golden lamp standing three feet tall, with a white and clear glass globe, one candy dish, and a decorative multi-colored glass pitcher. All of the items on top of this round table top appears to be antiques. Also, along the west wall is a green and pink multi-colored antique cough.

On the Northwest corner of the TV room, there is a natural wooden china cabinet with porcelain figurines on its shelves. On the North wall, there is one window that is covered with silver or off-white decorative drapery. Near the room's Northwest corner is an antique chair with decorative wooden trim and matching gold colored seat and back rest. A long the room's North wall is an antique wooden small stand with four legs and two shelves. On this small stand's top shelf there is a decorative antique golden colored lamp with a white glow cover. This lamp is decorated with hanging clear crystals that are 4 to 5 inches long. Other items on this shelf are one framed picture, and one candy bowl. On this small stand's bottom shelf is one candy dish. The lamp is plugged in to the electrical outlet just below the window on the room's North wall. On the floor below this window on the room's North wall is a heating and air conditioner vent. The TV Room's Northeast corner had a framed portrait of Patsy Hays hanging on the room's North wall. There are golden colored candleholders mounted on the wall on each side of Patsy's portrait. Each candleholder has a white candle. Along the North wall is a black or dark wooden antique chair and a small black or dark wooden antique stand with flowers on top.

Mounted on the room's East wall is a framed picture of flowers and a waiter pull that Kathleen knitted. Along the room's East wall is a 36 inches tall narrow table that is black or dark natural wood. The table has two items with white marble bases and golden candle holders that are decorated with 3 to 4-inch clear crystals, and a porcelain rectangular shaped container with a matching led. In front of the fireplace gas insert is a decorative golden fireplace hearth and to the left-hand side of the fireplace is a golden coal container with a golden handle. On the fireplace's lowest shelf are two antique golden pitchers and between these two pitchers is a multicolored porcelain clock. This clock shows the time to be 3:30 PM. The top shelf on this fireplace mantle there are two glass pitchers. In the room's South East corner and on the room's East wall is an open doorway with a white original door with five sunken panels. In this Northeast corner, in front of the doorway is an antique wooden chair with decorative wooden arms and legs and a brown textile seat and brown textile back rest which has a multi-colored flower design.

In the room's South East corner and along the room's South wall was an antique dark wooden stand with flowers on top. Mounted on the room's South wall is a framed picture of three or four individuals. Against the room's South wall and near the room's South East corner is a 4-foot-tall narrow stand with six shelves. Each shelf contains several porcelain figurines and small framed pictures. On the South wall near the South East corner is one half of the white flexible curtain like wall that can be drawn across the opening on the room's South wall. On this room's Southwest corner is a decorative antique chair with four wooden legs and, two wooden arms with a yellow textile covered seat and back rest. Mounted on the room's right side's South wall is a framed wedding picture of Patsy and or Frances.

The majority of the TV Room's floor is covered with a light grey or silver colored rug. Family members have told me that Kathleen liked only off-white colored rugs. The TV Room's original horizontal tough and grooved boards are painted white. The Fire Place Mantle was painted white.

The history of the TV Room, Hays House.

In 1942, shortly after Pat and Kathleen moved into the Hays House, Kathleen had the natural dark wood of the fire place mantle, walls, and ceiling in the TV Room painted an off white. The TV Room did not have its first TV until sometime in the early 1950's.

The fireplace mantle titles that were there in 2017 are the same title that were there from 1942 to 1996. This fireplace mantle had no loose titles in 1996. The gas heater fireplace insert was purchased by Kathleen in 1958 and maybe a reproduction of the Ray Glo original from the 1920's. In 2017 the outer shell of the Ray Glo gas heater fireplace insert is the same as in 1958, but the interior part to the gas heater fireplace insert has been replaced sometime after 1996. Up until 1996 there was a decorative golden colored fire place harp in front of the fireplace in the TV Room.

There was a TV in the TV Room's north east corner at least until Pat Hays passed away in 1978. From 1942 until 1996 there was a white Baby Grand Penna in the TV Room's north west corner.

Kathleen Hays had a large beautiful crystal chandelier hanging from the ceiling and in the center of the TV Room from 1942 until 1996.

From 1942 to 1968 the TV Room had Christmas decorations on top of the fire place mantle. In the center of the fire place mantle's lowest shelf was an electrical five candles that were surrounded by home handed decorations. These decorations included branches and leaves that were hand painted silver or gold and inserted into a soft piece of foam within a vase. These colorful leaves and branches had store bought blue Christmas balls hanging from them. From 1942 until 1950 the Christmas tree was placed in the north-west corner of the TV Room. From 1942 until 1969 Pat Hays would go out to the woods and cut down a ten-foot-tall Christmas tree. This Christmas tree would be decorated with store bought Christmas balls of different colors.

TV Room, Mel Meter Base Readings, Hays House, Friday, 10th March 2017.

The worn area on the hardwood floor located in the room's Northwest corner.

The electromagnetic frequency range was 0.0 mG to 0.0 mG.

The temperature range was 72.3°F to 72.8°F.

The green lamp on top of the wooden furniture, located along the room's West wall.

The electromagnetic frequency range was 0.0 mG to 0.0 mG.

The temperature range was 72.5°F to 72.7°F.

The area between the two lamps located along the room's West wall.

The electromagnetic frequency range was 0.0 mG to 0.0 mG.

The temperature range was 72.8°F to 72.8°F.

The electrical outlet located on the room's North wall. This electrical outlet is not in use.

The electromagnetic frequency range was 0.0 mG to 0.0 mG.

The temperature range was 72.8°F to 73.0°F.

The electrical outlet located on the room's North wall. This electrical outlet is in use.

The electromagnetic frequency range was 0.0 mG to 0.0 mG.

The temperature range was 73.2°F to 73.2°F.

The electrical outlet located on this room's East wall. This electrical outlet is not in use.

The electromagnetic frequency range was 0.0 mG to 0.0 mG.

The temperature range was 73.0°F to 73.0°F.

The white cable running vertically along the left side of the fireplace, located on the room's East wall.

The electromagnetic frequency range was 0.0 mG to 0.0 mG.

The temperature range was 73.4°F to 73.8°F.

The gas burning insert heater, with polit light on, located on the room's East wall.

The electromagnetic frequency range was 0.0 mG to 0.0 mG.

The temperature range was 75.6°F to 75.8°F.

The double light switch on the room's South wall. Both switches are in the on position.

The electromagnetic frequency range was 0.0 mG to 0.0 mG.

The temperature range was 73.8°F to 74.0°F.

The electrical outlet, located on the room's South East corner, and the room's South wall. This electrical outlet is not in use.

The electromagnetic frequency range was 0.0 mG to 0.0 mG.

The temperature range was 72.9°F to 73.9°F.

The electrical outlet, located on this room's South West corner and on this room's South wall. This electrical outlet is not in use.

The electromagnetic frequency range was 0.0 mG to 0.0 mG.

The temperature range was 73.2°F to 73.4°F.

Paranormal Investigation, Session 1, TV Room, Hays House, Friday, 17 March 2017.

10:30 AM Keith: "Hello, I am Keith Evans. If you would like to talk, you may use your energy to choose words from the Ovilus IV's database. This is the Ovilus IV. The Ovilus IV will not hurt you." (Hold it up.)

10:30 AM Keith: "This is the Mel Meter. The Mel Meter measures temperature and electromagnetic frequencies. The Mel Meter will not harm you." (Hold it up.)

10:31 AM Keith: "The Ovilus IV has given me two background words; began which is spelled B-E-G-A-N, and Bunny which is spelled B-U-N-N-Y. The Ovilus IV has pronounced both words at a normal conversational level and speed."

10:31 AM Keith: "I have observed the Mel Meter readings to be 0.0 mG and 60.0°F."

10:32 AM Keith: "The Ovilus IV has given me the word waters which is spelled W-A-T-E-R-S. The Ovilus IV has pronounced the word waters at a normal conversational level and speed."

10:32 AM Keith: "I have observed the Mel Meter readings to be 0.0 mG and 60.4°F."

10:33 AM Keith: "The Ovilus IV has given me the word aim which is spelled A-I-M. The Ovilus IV has pronounced the word aim in a normal conversational level and speed."

10:33 AM Keith: "I have observed the Mel Meter readings to be 0.0 mG and 60.2°F."

10:33 AM Keith: "I have observed the Mel Meter readings to be 0.0 mG and 60.5°F."

10:37 AM Keith: "Is your last name Waters?"

10:38 AM Keith: "What are you aiming at?"

10:39 AM Keith: "Pat, are you hunting?"

10:40 AM Keith: "Is there anyone from the Buck family here today?"

10:40 AM Keith: "The kitty, Jill, is in the video frame right now."

10:41 AM Keith: "I hear two people entering the front door and talking."

10:42 AM Keith: "Pat, are you going hunting for doves?"

10:42 AM Keith: "The Ovilus IV has given me the word bank which is spelled B-A-N-K. The word bank was pronounced by the Ovilus IV at a normal conversational level and speed."

10:42 AM Keith: "I have observed the Mel Meter readings to be 0.0 mG and 61.1°F."

10:45 AM Keith: "Are you working at the bank today?"

10:45 AM Keith: "I hear another person walking by and going out the front door."

10:46 AM Keith: "Pat, were you on the board of directors of the Apalachicola State Bank?"

10:47 AM Keith: "What do you do as a member of the Board of Directors of the Apalachicola State Bank?"

10:48 AM Keith: "Pat, what do you want to tell me about the bank?"

10:49 AM Keith: "I go to the bank to get rolls of Nickels to look for error coins."

10:50 AM Keith: "Pat, were you a coin collector?"

10:52 AM Keith: "Pat, what do you want to talk about?"

10:53 AM Keith: "How was this room furnished when you lived here? What did this room look like?"

10:54 AM Keith: "Who said the word bank?"

10:55 AM Keith: "The Ovilus IV has given me two words; rich which is spelled R-I-C-H, and actually which is spelled A-C-T-U-A-L-L-Y. The Ovilus IV has pronounce the words rich and actually at a normal conversational level and speed."

10:55 AM Keith: "I have observed the Mel Meter readings to be 0.0 mG and 61.9°F."

10:55 AM Keith: "Are you actually Rich?"

10:58 AM Keith: "Why are you telling me that you are rich?"

10:59 AM Keith: "Pat, are you telling me that you are rich?"

11 AM Keith: "Are you asking if I am rich?"

11:01 AM Keith: "I have observed the Mel Meter readings to be 0.0 mG and 62.6°F."

11:01 AM Keith: "I heard a person walking in the hallway."

11:02 AM Keith: "I can hear furniture being moved across the second floor."

11:03 AM Keith: "Okay Pat, tell me about the bank?"

11:03 AM Keith: "I can hear furniture being moved across the second floor."

11:04 AM Keith: "Pat, what is your favorite coin?"

11:04 AM Keith: "The Ovilus IV is frozen up. It will not go to the home position."

11:05 AM Keith: "I will turn the Ovilus IV off and change the batteries."

11:08 AM Keith: "I hear a vacuum cleaner on the second floor."

11:09 AM Keith: "I am going to leave the Camcorder frame to obtain four new AAA batteries."

11:10 AM Keith: "I am back with the new batteries."

11:12 AM Keith: "The Ovilus IV has given me two background words; best which is spelled B-E-S-T, and case which is spelled C-A-S-E. The Ovilus IV has pronounced the words best and case at a normal conversational level and speed."

11:12 AM Keith: "I have observed the Mel Meter readings to be 0.0 mG and 63.6°F."

11:16 AM Keith: "The Ovilus IV has given me four words; pending which is spelled P-E-N-D-I-N-G, nor which is spelled N-O-R, up which is spelled U-P, and Gail which is spelled G-A-I-L. These four words were pronounced by the Ovilus IV at a faster than normal conversational speed and back to back, but at a normal conversational level. I did not obtain a picture of the first word. The first word sounded like pending. I did not get to see the first word on the Ovilus IV's display. I was able to obtain a picture of the words; nor, up, and Gail."

11:16 AM Keith: "I have observed the Mel Meter readings to be 0.0 mG and 63.4°F."

11:16 AM Keith: "I hear a vacuum cleaner, running on the second floor."

11:19 AM Keith: "This is not the way to conduct a Paranormal Investigation."

11:19 AM Keith: "Thank you for talking to me. Have a good day."

11:19 AM to 11:25 AM Keith: "I obtained thermal images of the front room. I obtain two thermal images of a yellow square centered on the left side of image on the room's Northeast corner. I obtained five thermal images of a dark blue area near the ceiling fan and ceiling light."

11:25 AM Keith: "This Session 1 ended on Friday, 17th, March 2017."

Paranormal Investigation, Session 2, TV Room, Hays House, Friday, 17 March 2017.

1:27 PM Keith: "Hello, I am Keith Evans. If you would like to talk, you may use your energy to choose words from the Ovilus IV's data base. This is the Ovilus IV. The Ovilus IV will not hurt you." (Hold it up.)

1:28 PM Keith: "This is the Mel Meter. The Mel Meter measures temperature and electromagnetic frequencies. The Mel Meter will not harm you." (Hold it up.)

1:29 PM Keith: "The Ovilus IV has given me two background words; hunted which is spelled H-U-N-T-E-D, and stirred which is spelled S-T-I-R-R-E-D. The Ovilus IV has pronounced the words hunted and stirred at a normal conversational level and speed."

1:29 PM Keith: "I have observed the Mel Meter readings to be 0.0 mG and 69.9°F."

1:30 PM Keith: "What are you hunting?"

1:31 PM Keith: "Pat, are you hunting doves?"

1:32 PM Keith: "Kathleen, how did you have this room furnished when you lived here?"

1:33 PM Keith: "Did this room have a gas burning fireplace insert in the 1940's?"

1:34 PM to 1:37 PM Keith: "I obtained two thermal images of this room's right side of the North wall."

1:38 PM Keith: "The Ovilus IV has given me the word dinner which is spelled D-I-N-N-E-R. The Ovilus IV has pronounce the word dinner at a normal conversational level and speed."

1:38 PM Keith: "I have observed the Mel Meter readings to be 0.0 mG and 69.9°F."

1:38 PM Keith: "I have observed the Mel Meter readings to be 0.0 mG and 69.9°F."

1:40 PM Keith: "The Ovilus IV has given me the word linger which is spelled L-I-N-G-E-R. The Ovilus IV has pronounce the word linger at a normal conversational level and speed."

1:40 PM Keith: "The Ovilus IV has given me the word purified which is spelled P-U-R-I-F-I-E-D. The Ovilus IV has pronounce the word purified at a normal conversational level and speed."

1:40 PM Keith: "I have observed the Mel Meter readings to be 0.0 mG and 69.9°F."

1:44 PM Keith: "What do you mean by saying linger and dinner?"

1:45 PM Keith: "Do you feel that I am lingering in one spot to long?"

1:48 PM Keith: "Do you feel that I need to be purified?"

11:49 PM Keith: "Maybe it's you that needs to be purified?"

1:50 PM Keith: "What do you think about that?"

1:51 PM Keith: "Kathleen, was there a lot of furniture in this room, when you lived here?"

1:52 PM Keith: "What type of furniture was in this room in the 1940's?"

1:53 PM Keith: "What type of furniture was in this room in the 1950's?"

1:54 PM Keith: "What type of furniture was in this room in the 1960's?"

1:55 PM Keith: "Throw a dog a bone, say something?"

1:56 PM Keith: "I hear someone walking down the hall and going out the front door."

1:57 PM Keith: "Pat, what did you hunt besides doves?"

1:58 PM Keith: "Pat, what type of weapon did you use to hunt doves?"

1:59 PM Keith: "Pat, are you happy with the way the Hays House is today?"

2 PM Keith: "Pat, did you enjoy working at the bank?"

2:01 PM Keith: "Is there anyone from the Gibson family here today?"

2:02 PM Keith: "Sunshine, are you and or Annie here today?"

2:03 PM Keith: "Sunshine, if you're here knock on the floor?"

2:04 PM Keith: "Annie, if you are here knock on the room's North wall?"

2:05 PM Keith: "I did not hear any knocking sounds."

2:06 PM Keith: "Is there any one here from the Buck family today?"

2:07 PM Keith: "Sunshine, cat got your tongue?"

2:08 PM Keith: "The Ovilus IV has given me the word being which is spelled B-E-I-N-G. The Ovilus IV has pronounced the word being at a louder than normal conversational level and at a faster speed than a normal conversational speed. The word being was stated like it was despicable."

2:08 PM Keith: "I have observed the Mel Meter readings to be 0.0 mG and 69.9°F."

2:11 PM Keith: "The Ovilus IV has given me two words; Pinkie which is spelled P-I-N-K-I-E, and thank which is spelled T-H-A-N-K. The Ovilus IV has pronounce the words pinkie and thank at a normal conversational level and speed."

2:11 PM Keith: "I have observed the Mel Meter readings to be 0.0 mG and 69.9°F."

2:12 PM Keith: "I have observed the Mel meter readings to be 0.0 mG and 69.9°F."

2:14 PM Keith: "You're welcome Pinkie."

2:15 PM Keith: "What are you thanking me for?"

2:16 PM Keith: "Pinkie, are you a cat?"

2:18 PM Keith: "I have observed the Mel Meter readings to be 0.0 mG and 69.9°F."

2:18 PM Keith: "Thank you for talking to me. Have a good day."

2:18 PM Keith: "This Session 2 has ended on Friday, 17th, March 2017."

The analysis of the Paranormal Investigation, Session 1, TV Room, Hays House, Friday, 17 March 2017. Date of analysis was Sunday, 21st May 2017.

At 10:31 AM the Ovilus IV gave me the first two background words for Session 1, began, and bunny. I had not asked any questions during this session 1. Bunny could be a name. I am not aware of any person by the name bunny connected with the Hays House. Could this be Jeff Buck saying he began the Buck family's last name. The ghost or spirit of Jeff Buck may have misspelled his chosen last name of Buck, by spelling Bunny. We all make spelling mistakes. Remember Ghost are people too!

At 10:32 AM the Ovilus IV gave me the third word from Session 1, waters. I had not asked any questions during this session 1. Waters could be a last name. I am not aware of any person by the name waters, that is connected with the Hays House.

At 10:33 AM the Ovilus IV gave me the fourth word from Session 1, aim. I had not asked any questions during this session 1. The word aim is associated with aiming a weapon for hunting. This may be the spirit of Pat Hays talking about hunting. It could be that he is talking in a full sentence, but the Ovilus IV is only picking up one word of that sentence.

At 10:40 AM the kitty, Jill, is now in the video frame. I guess Jill wants to be a Kitty Paranormal Investigator.

At 10:42 AM I asked Pat if he was hunting for dove? At 2:42 AM, the Ovilus IV gave me the fifth word during this session 1, Bank. To me, that is an intelligent spirit of Pat Hays, responding right away that now he's not out hunting, he's working at the bank.

At 10:55 AM the Ovilus IV gave me the sixth and seventh words during session number one, rich and actually. Rich could be a first name or it could mean that you have plenty of money. I do not know anyone by the name of Rich that is associated with the Hays House. At 10:54 AM, I have asked the question who said the word bank? So maybe Rich is actually the one who said the word bank.

At 11:04 AM I noticed that the Ovilus IV is frozen up again and will not return to the home position. I manually turn off the Ovilus IV and change the batteries. At 11:12 AM, the Ovilus IV has given me the eighth and, ninth background words during this session 1, best and case. It seems to me that an intelligent spirit is talking about a best case which maybe referring to how the room was furnished in the pass. Then again, best case could be referring to best case a wine, best case scenario, and or the best case this Attorney I ever had. The analysis of a paranormal investigation is very subjective.

At 11:16 AM the Ovilus IV gave me the 10th through 13th words during this session number one, pending, nor, up, and Gail. I do not believe that the words pending, nor, and up, are in response to any of the questions that I have asked so far during this session number one. Gail is a ladies first name. I do not know anyone by the name of Gail that is associated with the Hays House. On the other hand, this could be a ghost or spirit warning me of pending northern or nor Gail or wind event coming up in the near future.

There was a lot of known human activity going on in the Hays House this morning, besides me and my paranormal investigating during this Session number one. I feel that a lot of human activity can be disruptive to the spirits that are attempting to communicate. You might get more activity, but it may not be the same spirit that you had before or, with the same attention span, responding to the same question that you asked. I feel that Ghosts and Spirits can be easily distracted by other activities that are going on inside of the house. At times it is difficult to be the only one in a house. I find that I have more credibility if I do my Paranormal Investigating during the day. I actually like to sleep at night.

The analysis of the Paranormal Investigation, Session 2, TV Room, Hays House, Friday, 17 March 2017. Date of analysis was Monday, 22nd May 2017.

At 1:29 PM the Ovilus IV gave me the first two background words for session 2, hunted and stirred. I had not asked any questions during this session 2. I can only imagine that this may be the spirit of Pat talking about hunting and maybe how the dogs would stir the doves from the underbrush, so the hunters could shoot them.

At 1:38 PM the Ovilus IV gave me the third word from session 2, dinner. My questions have been directed towards Pat, and Kathleen Hays. So, it is possible that one of their spirits has responded by saying that they ate dinner in the front room. I would imagine if there was a TV in the front room, that I would eat dinner in the front room while watching TV.

At 1:40 PM the Ovilus IV gave me the fourth and fifth words from session 2, linger and purified. I do not feel that the words linger and purified are in response to any of the questions I have asked so far during this session number two. Could be an intelligent spirit stating that I linger in one spot during my paranormal investigations.

At 2:07 PM I had asked Sunshine the following question, cat have your tongue? At 2:08 PM the Ovilus IV gave me the sixth word during this session number two, being. The Ovilus IV pronounced the word being at a louder than normal conversational level and at a faster than normal conversational speed. The word being was said like someone was angry and was serious about what they were saying. I feel that this is the spirit of Sunshine Gibson. When Sunshine ignores me, I will say something that will aggravate her, like cat got your tongue. Sometimes she ignores me or she's just not in the area where she can hear what I'm saying, but at other times she will respond back with something demeaning. Today, I think she said that I am not human being. The Ovilus IV only picked up the last word being. For those of you that want to linger in the negative, no she's not proclaiming me to be a demon. Sunshine is just comparing me to a dog or maybe pond scum.

At 2:11 PM the Ovilus IV gave me the seventh and eighth words during this session number two, Pinkie, and thank. I feel that Pinkie is a spirit of a cat. I have communicated with Pinkie at other investigations in Apalachicola. The last time that I communicated with Pinkie was about two years ago and I had asked pinkie if he or she wanted a snack. I gave the snack to a living cat and I guess pinkie receive some enjoyment from that, otherwise Pinkie would not be thanking me now. Other than that occasion, I don't really know why pinkie would be thanking me. Pinkie didn't give me any indication during this session number two as to why I was being thanked.

Digital Pictures, TV Room, Hays House, Friday, 10th March 2017.

Four pictures of the room's North wall.

Five pictures of the room's South wall.

Two pictures of the room's West wall.

Two pictures of the vent in the floor near the room's North wall.

Two pictures of the room's South East corner, upper wall trim and ceiling trim.

Two pictures of the room's horizontal wallboards.

Eight pictures of the fireplace mantle on the room's East wall.

Five close-up pictures of the fireplace mantle's gas heater insert, located on the room's East wall.

Eleven close-up pictures of the fireplace mantle's columns, located on the room's East wall.

Eight close-up pictures of the fireplace mantle's light blue, red, and, white, tile.

Six pictures of the room's heart pine hardwood floor.

Please go to the author's website at www.keithoevans.com to view each digital picture.

Digital Pictures, TV Room, Hays House, Thursday, 8th June 2017.

Two pictures of the room's white horizontal warm wallboard.

Four pictures of the room's heart pine hardwood floor.

Eight pictures of the room's fireplace mantle's tile, located on the room's East wall.

Two close-up pictures of the Ray Glo on and off knob for the gas heater fireplace insert.

Two close-up pictures of the fireplace mantle's decorative wooden wreath, located on the room's East wall.

Please go to the author's website at www.keithoevans.com to view each digital picture.

Thermal Images, TV Room, Hays House, Friday, 10 March 2017.

One thermal image of the room's West wall, between the windows.

One thermal image of the room's West wall, Southwest corner.

One thermal image of the room's West wall, Northwest corner.

One thermal image of the worn spot, on the hardwood floor, located on the room's Northwest corner.

One thermal image of the center window, on the room's North wall.

One thermal image of the room's North East corner.

One thermal image of the gas heater fireplace insert located on the room's East wall. The pilot light is on.

One thermal image of the room's South East corner and the door opening in to the dining room.

One thermal image of the left side of the room's South wall.

One thermal image of the center of the decorative opening within the room's South wall.

One thermal image of the right side of the room's South wall.

One thermal image of the worn spot in the hardwood floor. Located on this room's Northwest corner.

Please go to the author's website at www.keithoevans.com to view each thermal image.

CHAPTER 7

The Pat & Kathleen Room, Hays House, Ghosts are People too.

The description of Pat & Kathleen's Room, Hays House, Wednesday, 2nd November 2016.

The room's North wall has the entrance which does not have a door. There are two threshold boards between Pat & Kathleen's Room and the First Floor Front Stairway Room. The first threshold board which is closer to the First Floor Front Stairway Room and is 6 inches wide. The second threshold board that is closer to Pat & Kathleen's Room and is two and three-quarter inches wide. The trim around this doorway appears to be original white and wooden.

Near the room's north east corner and on the room's East wall is an original white wooden door with five sunken panels. This door has the original brass and or metal decorative doorknob with the matching original decorative skeleton key baseplate. This door is secured and I do not have a key, but there is an original threshold board that is approximately 3 and three-quarter inches wide. This doorway appears to have the original white wooden trim. A long the room's East wall there are two mounted flood lights on tripods.

The room's South wall has two windows with the original windows that have two panes of glass in the upper and lower sections. Each window is approximately 34 inches wide and 68 inches in height. The window trim in part appears to be original. The window trim along the left and right sides and the piece of trim across the top of the window appears to be modern wood painted white.

The room's West wall has the original fireplace and original wooden decorative fireplace mantle with a left and right, upper and lower column. Up until 1996, this fireplace mantle was covered with a light-yellow paint. At one time the fireplace had a decorated marble type tile, that is no longer there. The fireplace also has an antique look-ing gas heater insert that was placed in the Hays House's fireplace sometime after 1996. There is a round burnt area about 4 inches in diameter on the floor in front of the fireplace. This burnt area involves the trim that surrounded the area that once had tiles. Two of the tongue and groove 2 1/2-inch-wide heart pine hardwood floor boards are burnt also. In addition to the fireplace, the room's West wall has an opening that leads to the Living Room. It is said that up until 1996, the area now known as an opening to the next room, had a door which led to a closet off from Pat & Kathleen's Room. After 1996, the wall was removed from the back of the closet, allowing this to be a walkway between what is now known as Pat & Kathleen's Room to the Living Room. There is no door at the opening to what use to be the closest prior to 1996. The wooden trim around this doorway ap-pears to be original white and wooden. The original threshold board that is situated where the back wall to the closet that was between Pat & Kathleen's Room and the Living Room is three and three-quarter inches wide. After 1996, there was a six and three-quarter inch wide threshold board placed at this newly made doorway opening, at what used to be the back wall of the closet. This threshold board, appears to be as old as similar looking threshold board's in other areas of the Hays House, and may have come from one of the other doorways within the house.

The history of the Pat & Kathleen Room, Hays House.

In 1942 when Pat and Kathleen Hays first moved into the Hayes house, they had the large decorative bedroom suit that Pat's mother Annie gave Pat and Kathleen as a wedding gift. Pat and Kathleen used the large decorative bed and the chest of drawers until sometime before 1978, when Pat and Kathleen Hays had purchased a modern king size bed. At that time, they moved the bed and chest of drawers from their bedroom to the second floor and into Sunshine's bedroom. Sunshine had passed away in 1956. Sunshine's bedroom suit was moved into the room that Patsy had used prior to her marriage and 1958.

As a child, Patsy used to play with the loose tile's that were around the fireplace on the West wall of her parents' bedroom. Today there are no tiles left on the floor in front of this fireplace. The surviving relatives are not sure if Pat and Kathleen's room ever had a gas insert within the fireplace. A bat once flew down the Chimney into Pat and Kathleen's Room so that would show that there was no fireplace insert that at that time. The burnt area within the fireplace's wooden trim around where the tile use to be and the burnt area within three hardwood floor boards, was there when Patsy was a child.

Edward Ryan Hays, (Pat) was involved with the community. Pat went with the Chapman High School Parents and Teachers Association to the first regional meeting of the Florida Congress of Parents and Teachers held in Panama City on Wednesday, 27th of October 1937.

In 1937 Edward Ryan Hays was a member and or a visitor of the Delta Deck Card Club. The Delta Deck Card Club met weekly on Wednesday evenings. Pat Hays attended the Delta Deck Card Club meeting on Wednesday the third day of November 1937.

On Tuesday afternoon ninth of November 1937, E. R. Hays, better known as Pat, was a visitor while Kathleen played cards with the Comus Bridge Club.

Kathleen Hays was a good card player and was a member of the Comus Bridge Club during the 1930s. The Comus Bridge Club met every Tuesday afternoon. On Tuesday, 26 October 1937 Kathleen Hays better known at the time as Mrs. E. R. Hays won the grand slam during the afternoon of playing bridge. Pat, better known at the time as E. R. Hays was present that afternoon as a visitor.

On the Tuesday afternoon 2nd November 1937, Mrs. E. R. Hays, better known as Kathleen attended the Comus Bridge Club that was meeting at the home of Mrs. Porter. During the afternoon of cards playing, Kathleen had the second highest score.

Pat and Kathleen had close family bonds. During the weekend of Saturday, 30th of October 1937 and Sunday, 1st November 1937 Mr. and Mrs. F. W. Reames of Aucilla, FL were the weekend guests of their son-in-law and daughter, Mr. and Mrs. E. R. Hays.

The description of the Pat & Kathleen Room from three photos taken at the Hays House in 1996.

In a photo from 1996 of Pat and Kathleen's room, starting with the West wall and going from left to right, there is an antique dark brown chest of drawers with a mirror on top. On top of this chest of drawers are several porcelain items such as a plate, a teapot, and a porcelain figurine of a lady. There is a white wicker chair in front of the chest of drawers. In the center of the photo is the white wooden fireplace mantle with two shelves, each shelf is supported by a wooden column on each side. The fireplace mantle is original. Between the top shelf's bottom side and the bottom shelf, there is an original mirror. On the fireplace mantle's top shelf is a porcelain vase. On the fireplace mantle's bottom shelf are two porcelain figurines of a lady on each side of a picture. In front of the fireplace mantle is a small wooden desk with pictures on top. There is an antique wooden chair with an orange textile seat in front of the desk. To the right side of the fireplace mantle is the room's closet door. This door has an original white wooden door with five sunken panels and an original door knob that is not painted. The original skeleton key plate is painted white. There is a narrow view of the full body mirror that was mounted on the exterior of the closet door. In front of the closet door is a modern chair with wooden arms and a pink textile seat and back rest.

This is a photo taken in 1996 of the Northwest corner, and the North wall of Pat and Kathleen's Room. Starting from left to right on this photo and on the West wall is the closet door with the full-length mirror mounted on the front of the door. In front of the closet is a modern chair with wooden arms, wooden legs, a pink textile seat and back rest. Along the room's North wall is a narrow 1 foot tall and

3-foot-long table with some white and blue luggage sitting on top of this table. To the right of the narrow table is an antique wooden chest of drawers with a mirror attached to the top. On top of this piece of furniture are the following items: an antique multicolored glass lamp, a small framed picture, and a white alarm clock. Mounted on the room's North wall are six golden framed pictures of family members. To the far right of the photo is the white original wooden door way trim. This doorway leads from Pat and Kathleen's Room into the First Floor Front Stairway Room.

The next picture in Pat and Kathleen's Room, that was taken in 1996, is at the Southeast corner of the room starting from the left side of the photo. One can see a narrow strip of the original white wooden trim on the room's East wall. This is a door way that led from Pat and Kathleen's Room into the Den Room. To the right of the doorway is a dark wooden antique nightstand. On top of this nightstand was a small radio alarm clock. Above the nightstand and mounted on the East wall are two off-white thermostats. Between the nightstand and the South wall is a king-size bed with five pillows and a bedspread all covered with a matching white textured material. Mounted on the East wall are four golden framed pictures of family members. At the foot of the bed is a Brown footstool. Mounted on the room's South wall are two golden framed pictures of family members. There is a window, near the Southeast corner of the room with blue and white curtains. The room's floor is mostly covered with a light blue rug. All of the walls in Pat and Kathleen's Room are covered with the original white tongue and groove horizontal boards.

Some back-ground history concerning Pat & Kathleen.

Edward Ryan Hays, Pat, was born in on the 18 July 1907 and passed away in 1978 at the age of 71 on a Wednesday morning at Tallahassee Memorial Regional Medical Center. Pat was buried at the Magnolia Cemetery in Apalachicola, Florida. Pat was a member of the Apalachicola United Methodist Church. Pat was a Board of Director for the Apalachicola State Bank. Edward Ryan Hays, Pat, went to high school at Randolph Macon Academy in Bedford, Virginia. On the 10th October 1941, Pat Hays purchased a Franklin County game license number 1504 to fish and hunt migratory birds. Pat's hunting license described him as a 34-year-old white male with black hair, brown eyes, height 6'3", weighed 150 pounds and occupation as a hotel keeper. Pat also obtained a deer hunting license number 241904 for the years 1956 in 1957. This Deer hunting license states Pat's date of birth as 18 July 1907 and described him as a white male, black hair, brown eyes, 6 foot and 3 inches height, weight 150 pounds. The date that this deer hunting license was issued was the 11th day of October 1956 and his occupation was listed as an accountant. This license shows that the deer hunting season was the ninth through 26 November 1956 and turkey hunting season was 9th November 1956 through to the 15 January 1957. The next hunting licenses number 34323 with the name E. R. Hays, and the address 48 Avenue D, Apalachicola, Franklin County, Florida and shows a date of birth as being 18 July 1907, white male, brown hair, brown eyes, 6 foot and 3 inches in height, 170 pounds weight and the date that this hunting license was issued was 30 September 1971. Edward Ryan Hays is the son of Miss Annie Louise Gibson Hays and Mr. Alfred Gordon Hays of Bamberg, South Carolina. Pat's Maternal Grandfather is William Henry Gibson and Pat's Maternal Grandmother is Ella Byrd, Gibson. Pat was a smoker.

Kathleen Reams Hays was born on the second day of March 1910 in Greenville, Florida. Kathleen Reams Hays passed away at age 97 on a Thursday, 20th December 2007 in Tallahassee, Florida. Kathleen was interned at the Magnolia Cemetery in Apalachicola, Florida. Kathleen's parents were Maggie and Frances Reams. Kathleen was a member of the United Methodist Church in Apalachicola, Florida, a member of the Philaco Club, a member of the Apalachicola Historical Society and the Historic Apalachicola Organization. Kathleen Reams had taught at Chapman high school for three years before she married Pat Hays.

Mr. and Mrs. Edward Ryan Hays were married at the United Methodist Church in Apalachicola and they had their wedding reception at the Gibson hotel on a Saturday afternoon. At least 100 guests were there to meet the newlywed couple in the lobby and the dining room of the Gibson hotel. It is said that the lobby of the Gibson hotel was decorated with ferns and clusters of pink flowers. The hostesses of this wedding reception were Mrs. William Henry Gibson, Mrs. Counsil Bryan Palmer of Tallahassee and Miss Mary Ella Gibson. The grandmother, mother and aunt, respectively of the groom. Other family members, and friends that attended this wedding reception just to name a few were Mrs. Alice Rose Gibson, and Mrs. Gwendolyn Gibson, who are cousins of the groom and Miss. Carrie Lee Sutton.

In 1942 when Pat and Kathleen Hays first moved into the Hayes house, they had the large decorative bedroom suit that Pat's mother Annie gave Pat and Kathleen as a wedding gift. Pat and Kathleen used the large decorative bed and the chest of drawers until sometime before 1978, when Pat and Kathleen Hays had purchased a modern king size bed. At that time, they moved the bed and chest of drawers from their bedroom to the second floor and into Sunshine's bedroom. Sunshine had passed away in 1956. Sunshine's bedroom suit was moved into the room that Patsy had used prior to her marriage and 1958.

As a child, Patsy used to play with the loose tile's that were around the fireplace on the West wall of her parents' bedroom. Today there are no tiles left on the floor in front of this fireplace. The surviving relatives are not sure if Pat and Kathleen's room ever had a gas insert within the fireplace. A bat once flew down the Chimney into Pat and Kathleen's Room so that would show that there was no fireplace insert at that time. The burnt area within the fireplace's wooden trim around where the tile use to be and the burnt area within three hardwood floor boards, was there when Patsy was a child.

Edward Ryan Hays, (Pat) was involved with the community. Pat went with the Chapman High School Parents and Teachers Association to the first regional meeting of the Florida Congress of Parents and Teachers held in Panama City on Wednesday, 27th of October 1937.

In 1937 Edward Ryan Hays was a member and or a visitor of the Delta Deck Card Club. The Delta Deck Card Club met weekly on Wednesday evenings. Pat Hays attended the Delta Deck Card Club meeting on Wednesday the third day of November 1937.

On Tuesday afternoon ninth of November 1937, E. R. Hays, better known as Pat, was a visitor while Kathleen played cards with the Comus Bridge Club.

Kathleen Hays was a good card player and was a member of the Comus Bridge Club during the 1930s. The Comus Bridge Club met every Tuesday afternoon. On Tuesday, 26 October 1937 Kathleen Hays better known at the time as Mrs. E. R. Hays won the grand slam during the afternoon of playing bridge. Pat, better known at the time as E. R. Hays was present that afternoon as a visitor.

On the Tuesday afternoon 2nd November 1937, Mrs. E. R. Hays, better known as Kathleen attended the Comus Bridge Club that was meeting at the home of Mrs. Porter. During the afternoon of cards playing, Kathleen had the second highest score.

Pat and Kathleen had close family bonds. During the weekend of Saturday, 30th of October 1937 and Sunday, 1st November 1937 Mr. and Mrs. F. W. Reams of Aucilla, FL were the weekend guests of their son-in-law and daughter, Mr. and Mrs. E. R. Hays.

The Comus Bridge Club met at the home of Mrs. Annie R. Marks and was hosted by Mrs. Edward M. Crawford on Wednesday, 8th June 1938. Mrs. E. R. Hays won high score and Mr. E. R. Hays was in attendance.

The Comus Bridge Club met at the home of Mrs. Harry Cumming on Tuesday, 14th June 1938. Jay A. Shuler hosted three tables of Bridge. Mr. and Mrs. E. R. Hays were in attendance.

The Comus Bridge Club met at the home of Mrs. Hal Hoffman on Wednesday, 6th July 1938. Mrs. E. R. Hays won high game and Mr. E. R. Hays was in attendance.

On Monday, 19th November 1938, Pat Hays drove his new born daughter Patsy Ann and his wife Kathleen home from the Archbold Hospital in Thomasville, Georgia.

Mr. and Mrs. C. Bryan Palmer of Tallahassee, Florida would always spend the Christmas and New Year Holidays with Mr. and Mrs. Edward Ryan Hays at the Hays House on 48 Avenue D Apalachicola, Florida.

Mr. and Mrs. F. W. Reams of Aucilla, Florida always spend the Christmas and New Year Holidays with Mr. and Mrs. Edward Ryan Hays at the Hays House on 48 Avenue D Apalachicola, Florida.

The Comus Bridge Club met at the home of Mrs. Annie R. Marks on Tuesday afternoon, 26th September 1939. This was the first meeting of the fall season. The hostess was Mrs. Edward M. Crawford. Mrs. E. R. Hays won high score and Mr. E. R. Hays was in attendance.

The Comus Bridge Club met at the home of Dr. and Mrs. G. E. Weems on Tuesday afternoon, 28th November 1939. Miss Marjorie Weems was the hostess for three tables of Bridge. Mr. and Mrs. E. R. Hays were in attendance.

Mr. and Mrs. C. Bryan Palmer of Tallahassee, Florida would always spend the Thanksgiving Holidays with Mr. and Mrs. Edward Ryan Hays at the Hays House on 48 Avenue D Apalachicola, Florida.

Mr. and Mrs. F. W. Reams of Aucilla, Florida always spend the Thanksgiving Holidays with Mr. and Mrs. Edward Ryan Hays at the Hays House on 48 Avenue D Apalachicola, Florida.

The Comus Bridge Club met on Wednesday, 3rd January 1940. Mrs. Edward Ryan Hays won the second highest score. Mr. E. R. Hays was in attendance.

In 1940 Mr. and Mrs. Edward Ryan Hays and daughter Patsy spend the Christmas and New Year Holidays with Mr. and Mrs. C. Bryan Palmer of Tallahassee, Florida. Mr. and Mrs. C. Bryan Palmer are the Grandmother, Annie Gibson Hays Palmer and Step-Grandfather C. Bryan Palmer, to Patsy Hays and Frances Hays.

On Thursday, 27th November 1941, Mr. and Mrs. Edward Ryan Hays, (Pat and Kathleen), attended the monthly meeting of the Philaco Club at the Community House.

Mrs. E. R. Hays was the President of the Philaco Club in 1941. Under Kathleen's leadership the Philaco Club presented the play, "Cool Knights", at the High School auditorium on Tuesday evening at 8 PM on the 2nd December 1941.

The Tuesday Afternoon Bridge Club met at the home of Mrs. J. B. Spear on Tuesday, 16th December 1941. Mr. and Mrs. E. R. Hays were in attendance.

Mrs. E. R. Hays was involved when the Philaco Club had a Defense Benefit Bridge Party in early January 1942, to obtain funds to purchase a Defense Bond for the Philaco Club.

On Monday afternoon, 5th April 1943, during the April Business Meeting of the WSCS, (Women's Society of Christian Services of the Methodist Church), Mrs. E. R. Hays, Vice-President, led the meeting in the absence of the President, Mrs. Chas Brass. The WSCS assisted with various active such as cleaning the Church, fund raising Spaghetti Dinners, taking food to the sick Church Members.

In 1968 Pat and Kathleen Hays, James and Patsy Hays Philyaw, and Frances Hays were all members of the First United Methodist Church located on 75 Fifth Street Apalachicola, Florida.

On the 25th May 1969 the First United Methodist Church, (1839-1969), celebrated their 130th Anniversary at the Church on 75 Fifth Street Apalachicola, Florida. Mr. and Mrs. E. R. Hays and family where in attendance.

In 1996 Kathleen Hays was awarded her fifty years pin honoring her years of service with the Philaco Club.

Mel Meter Base Readings, the Pat & Kathleen Room, Hays House, Wednesday, 2nd November 2016.

11:30 AM The yellow standalone lights, located in the middle of the room. The yellow stand-alone lights are not in use.

The electromagnetic frequency range was 0.0 mG to 0.0 mG.

The temperature range was 79.4°F to 80.0°F.

11:30 AM The right side, white window unit air conditioner, located on the room's South wall. This window unit air conditioner was in use.

The electromagnetic frequency range was 0.0 mG to 0.5 mG.

The temperature range was 75.2°F to 77.9°F.

11:31 AM The electrical outlet on the right side of the rooms West wall. This electrical outlet was not in use.

The electromagnetic frequency range was 0.0 mG to 0.0 mG.

The temperature range was 77.6°F to 77.9°F.

11:31 AM The lime green stand-alone lights, located in the middle of the room. The lime green stand-alone lights are not in use.

The electromagnetic frequency range was 0.0 mG to 0.0 mG.

The temperature range was 78.6°F to 78.9°F.

11:32 AM The double electrical outlet on the left side of the room's West wall. This double electrical outlet was in use.

The electromagnetic frequency range was 0.0 mG to 0.0 mG.

The temperature range was 78.8°F to 78.8°F.

11:32 AM The white ceiling fan and lights. The ceiling fan and lights are in use.

The electromagnetic frequency range was 0.0 mG to 0.0 mG.

The temperature range was 79.4°F to 79.9°F.

Paranormal Investigation, Session 1, the Pat & Kathleen Room, Hays House, Tuesday, 28th, March 2017.

10:48 AM Keith: "Hello, I am Keith Evans. If you would like to talk, you may use your energy to choose words from the Ovilus IV's database. This is the Ovilus IV. The Ovilus IV will not hurt you." (Hold it up.)

10:49 AM Keith: "This is the Mel Meter. The Mel Meter measures temperature and electromagnetic frequencies. The Mel Meter will not harm you." (Hold it up.)

10:48 AM Keith: "The Ovilus IV has given me two background words; equate which is spelled E-Q-U-A-T-E, and Lark which is spelled L-A-R-K. The Ovilus IV has pronounced the words equate and Lark at a normal conversational level and speed."

10:48 AM Keith: "I have observed the Mel Meter readings to be 0.0 mG and 74.5°F."

10:54 AM Keith: "I have spoken to the two guests that are here at the Hays House."

10:54 PM Keith: "The Ovilus IV has given me the letter "U". The Ovilus IV pronounced the letter "U" at a normal conversational level and speed. The letter "U" was stated like it was pointing and speaking to me."

10:55 PM Keith: "I have observed the Mel Meter readings to be 0.0 mG and 74.9°F."

10:57 AM Keith: "Yes, I am Keith Evans. What do you have to tell me today?"

10:58 AM Keith: "Pat, were you involved with the obtaining of resin from the pine trees?"

10:59 AM Keith: "Pat, which pine trees had the most resin?"

11 AM Keith: "Pat, which pine trees were better the short needle pine trees, or the long needle pine trees?"

11:01 AM Keith: "Pat, what was the name of the bank that you work with?"

11:02 AM Keith: "Pat, how many Guardian Angels live-in the Hays House?"

11:03 AM Keith: "Pat, cat got your tongue?"

11:04 AM Keith: "Pat, do you have any questions for me today?"

11:05 AM Keith: "Pat, is Lark a bird that you use to hunt?"

11:11 AM Keith: "The Ovilus IV has given me the word sense which is spelled S-E-N-S-E. The Ovilus IV has pronounced the word sense at a normal conversational level and speed."

11:11 AM Keith: "I have observed the Mel Meter readings to be 0.0 mG and 75.0°F."

11:13 AM Keith: "Yes, I do sense someone in the room's North East corner, and someone near the fireplace."

11:14 AM Keith: "I am sensing someone near the North East corner of the room and at the fireplace because I'm getting colder than usual readings on my thermal images. There is no cold source that I should be detecting from the two walls that make up the Northeast corner of the room. There is no cold source coming from the iron fireplace cover insert which is located on this room's West wall." (I moved the camcorder number two to the Northeast corner. I used camcorder one to obtain a close-up footage of the fireplace. I have obtained two thermal images of the Northeast corner of this room and four thermal images of the fireplace which is located on this room's West wall.)

11:19 AM Keith: "This is camcorder number two, which is, located behind me."

11:20 AM Keith: "Who are you people that are standing at the Northeast corner of the room and the fireplace?"

11:21 AM Keith: "Are you someone from the Buck family?"

11:22 AM Keith: "Are you someone from the Gibson family?"

11:22 AM Keith: "The Ovilus IV gave me the word climbed which is spelled C-L-I-M-B-E-D. The Ovilus IV has pronounced the word climbed at a normal conversational level and speed."

11:23 AM Keith: "I have observed the Mel Meter readings to be 0.0 mG and 75.4°F."

11:26 AM Keith: "How is the word climbed, which is past tense, going to help me discover who is standing at the Northeast corner of this room and in front of the fireplace?"

11:28 AM Keith: "Does anyone from the Buck family want to tell me anything about this house?"

11:29 AM Keith: "What was this room used for when the Buck family lived here?"

11:30 AM Keith: "What was this room used for when the Hays family lived here?"

11:31 AM Keith: "I can hear the sound of a large tractor and trailer that is parked outside on fourth Street."

11:32 AM Keith: "Sunshine, are you here today?"

1133 Keith: "Sunshine, if you are here today, give me the word Sunshine on the Ovilus IV."

11:35 AM Keith: "Sunshine, what do you want to talk about?"

11:36 AM Keith: "The Ovilus IV gave me the word equal which is spelled E-Q-U-A-L. The Ovilus for has pronounced the word equal in a lower than normal conversational level and in a slower than normal conversational level."

11:36 AM Keith: "I have observed the Mel Meter readings to be 0.0 mG and 75.5°F."

11:37 AM Keith: "So Sunshine, are you saying that we are equal?"

11:39 AM Keith: "So Sunshine, how are we equal? Were we equal in age? Are we equal in weight? Are we equal in knowledge?"

11:41 AM Keith: "Some of your responses are very vague."

11:42 AM Keith: "Thank you for talking to me. Have a good day."

11:43 AM Keith: "I have observed the Mel Meter readings to be 0.0 mG and 75.5°F."

11:43 AM Keith: "This session number one ended on Tuesday, 28th, March 2017."

Paranormal Investigation, Session 2, the Pat & Kathleen Room, Hays House, Tuesday, 28th, March 2017.

12:24 PM Keith: "Hello, I am Keith Evans. If you would like to talk, you may use your energy to choose words from the Ovilus IV words database. This is the Ovilus IV. The Ovilus IV will not hurt you." (Hold it up.)

12:25 PM Keith: "This is the Mel Meter. The Mel Meter measures temperature and electromagnetic frequencies. The Mel Meter will not harm you." (Hold it up.)

12:25 PM Keith: "The Ovilus IV has given me two background words; own which is spelled O-W-N, and these which is spelled T-H-E-S-E. The Ovilus IV has pronounced the words; own and these at a normal conversational level and speed."

12:25 PM Keith: "I have observed the Mel Meter readings to be 0.0 mG and 75.4°F."

12:27 PM Keith: "You own these? What do you own?"

12:28 PM Keith: "I thought I heard the doorbell ring." (I looked, but no one had entered the house.)

12:29 PM Keith: "The Ovilus IV has given me the word sister which is spelled S-I-S-T-E-R. The Ovilus IV has pronounced the word sister at a normal conversational level and speed."

12:29 PM Keith: "I have observed the Mel Meter readings to be 0.0 mG and 75.7°F."

12:31 PM Keith: "Who is your Sister?"

12:32 PM Keith: "What is her name?"

12:33 PM Keith: "The Ovilus IV has given me the word stood which is spelled S-T-O-O-D. The Ovilus IV has pronounced the word stood at a normal conversational level and speed."

12:33 PM Keith: "I have observed the Mel Meter readings to be 0.0 mG and 75.9°F."

12:33 PM Keith: "Sunshine, and Annie are sisters?"

12:34 PM Keith: "The Ovilus IV has given me the word mop which is spelled M-O-P. The Ovilus IV has pronounced the word mop at a normal conversational level and speed."

12:34 PM Keith: "I have observed the Mel Meter readings to be 0.0 mG and 75.8°F."

12:37 PM Keith: "Did your sister mop the floor?"

12:38 PM Keith: "Did you mop the floor?"

12:39 PM Keith: "What is your name?"

12:42 PM Keith: "Mary did you mop the floor?"

12:43 PM Keith: "Sunshine, did you mop the floor?"

12:44 PM Keith: "Pat, did you mop the floor?"

12:45 PM Keith: "Kathleen, did you mop the floor?"

12:46 PM Keith: "Pat, did you like the Turpentine business better than the Hotel business?"

12:47 PM Keith: "James Fulton Buck, did you like the Turpentine business better than the Hotel business?"

12:49 PM Keith: "Lamb Gillam Buck, did you like the Turpentine business better than the Hotel business?"

12:50 PM Keith: "Terryss McBride Buck, did you like this house?"

12:51 PM Keith: "Terryss McBride Buck, what was your favorite thing about this house?"

12:52 PM Keith: "Does anyone from the Buck family have any questions for me?"

12:53 PM Keith: "Sunshine, how was this room furnished when you were alive?"

12:54 PM Keith: "The Ovilus IV has given me the words; begin which is spelled B-E-G-I-N and alone which is spelled A-L-O-N-E. The Ovilus IV has pronounce the words begin and alone at a normal conversational level and speed."

12:54 PM Keith: "I have observed the Mel Meter readings to be 0.0 mG and 76.4°F."

12:55 PM Keith: "The Ovilus IV has given me the word world which is spelled W-O-R-L-D. The Ovilus for has pronounced the word world at a normal conversational level and speed."

12:55 PM Keith: "I have observed the Mel Meter readings to be 0.0 mG and 76.4°F."

12:59 PM Keith: "Begin, alone, world, what is that supposed to be telling me?"

1 PM Keith: "What does begin, alone, world, have to do with mopping and or sister?"

1:01 PM Keith: "How many sisters do you have?"

1:02 PM Keith: "Do you have a brother?"

1:03 PM Keith: "Do you remember this room, when it had a wood-burning fireplace?"

1:05 PM Keith: "It does not look like the original tile is left near the fireplace?"

1:06 PM Keith: "Sunshine, when was this fireplace converted over to gas heat?"

1:07 PM Keith: "Sunshine, what year was this fireplace converted over to gas heat?"

1:08 PM Keith: "This fireplace mantle has the nice wooden tiger strip design."

1:09 PM Keith: "Sunshine, what was kept up on this fireplace mantle while you were alive?"

1:10 PM Keith: "Pat, is that the original mirror that was placed into that Fire Place Mantle?"

1:11 PM Keith: "If you do not know Pat. It is alright to say that you do not know."

1:12 PM Keith: "Would you like me to stop asking questions now?"

1:13 PM Keith: "I have obtained two thermal images of a dark purple area in the room's South East corner. I have obtained two thermal images of a pink area near the fire place insert plate. I have obtained two thermal images; first image has a pink area and the second image has a blue area in the room's North East corner."

1:13 PM Keith: "Thank you for talking to me. Have a good day."

1:13 PM Keith: "I have observed the Mel Meter readings to be 0.1 mG and 76.6°F."

1:14 PM Keith: "This Session 2 ended on Tuesday, 28th March 2017."

The analysis of the Paranormal Investigation, Session 1, the Pat & Kathleen Room, Hays House, Tuesday, 28th, March 2017. The date of analysis was Tuesday, 23rd May 2017.

At 10:48 AM the Ovilus IV gave me the first and second background words for session 1, equate and lark. I have not asked any questions yet during this session 1. I can only imagine that Pat may have brought up the word lark. Lark could be the name of a bird that he may have hunted at one time."

At 10:54 AM the Ovilus IV gave me the third letter for this session 1, "U". I have not asked any questions yet during this session 1. The Ovilus IV has pronounced the letter "U" like it was a command. I think this was some intelligent spirit pointing at me and saying you! It does not feel that the spirit is happy with me conducting a Paranormal Investigation.

At 11:11 AM the Ovilus IV gave me the fourth word for this session 1, sense. I do not feel that the words sense is in response to any of the questions I've asked so far during this session 1. This could be an intelligent spirit asking me to sense an answer. Up until Monday the 22nd of May 2017, I had forgotten the details of the Tuesday, 28 March 2017, Paranormal Investigation in Pat & Kathleen's Room. I still can't say why at 11:13 AM during this first session, that I was able to sense someone in the rooms Northeast corner and sense more than one person near the fireplace. I know I wrote it down in my transcript. I just don't remember the details. It was like a Ghost and or Spirit was forecasting that I was going to be sensing something soon, then the Ovilus IV gave me the word sense. On the second hand maybe, an intelligent spirit or ghost was surprised that I was able to sense them, thus saying you sense us!

At 11:14 AM I was using the FLIR thermal imager to obtain two thermal images of the Northeast corner of the room and four thermal images of the fireplace. I cannot explain why I was getting a dark blue line near the north east corner of the room and a pink color near the fireplace insert. There is no reason why there should be a dark blue line, which is a very cold area near the room's north east corner. There were no heat sorts to cause the Thermal Images to show a pink image, near the fireplace insert. I have thought maybe that the Northeast corner could have a sewage drain pipe within the wall. If someone on the second floor was running cold water that might give me a dark blue thermal image. There is no drainage pipe coming from the second floor to the first floor in the room's north east corner. As for the fireplace, I have seen what the polit light at the fireplace gas heater inserts looks like and this did not look the same. The polit light covers a small area and is bright yellow in color as seen by the thermal imager. The entire front of the fireplace gas insert was a pink color which is too cold to be a polit light and too warm to be a ghost or spirit. On the other hand, there may be some ghosts and or spirits that can use their electromagnetic energy to create heat.

Between 11:20 AM to 11:22 PM I had asked three questions to find out who the people were that were standing by the fireplace. At 11:22 AM the Ovilus IV gave me the fifth word during this session 1, climbed. I cannot see how the word climbed could be an intellectual response to any of my questions that I asked. I felt and saw three females on my thermal imager standing to the left of the fire place in real time. I felt like they could see me and were afraid of me. I thought it could be Kathleen Hays, Sunshine Gibson, and Annie Gibson Hays Palmer. After I reviewed the thermal images I noticed only two separate cold areas to the left of the fire place. This was one of the most unusual Paranormal Investigation that I have ever had. I had no member of this Paranormal Investigation until I set down to type the analysis on Tuesday, 23rd May 2017. After reading my hand-written transcript, reviewing the digital pictures, and reviewing the thermal images, I thought to myself woo that was an outstanding Paranormal Investigation with some intimate contact with at least four Ghosts and or Spirits. It is sad that I did not have that short-term memory of this event, to build on that day's contact with Pat Hays at the north east corner and Kathleen Hays, Sunshine Gibson, and Annie Gibson Hays Palmer to the left side of the Fire Place Mantle. I was startled by suddenly being surrounded by cold dark blue images on my FLIR thermal imager. I was disappointed that the Ghosts and or Spirits felt threaten by my presents. It was like they were seeing me as a Ghost and or Spirit and they were alive reacting to something very strange that was happening to them.

At 11:36 AM, the Ovilus IV gave me the word equal. The Ovilus IV pronounced the word equal at a lower than normal conversational level and at a slower than normal conversational speed. I sense that this is the spirit of Sunshine and she is saying softly and slowly, I am getting even with you. Somehow her equal means I'm getting even with you and she is doing this by giving open ended words on the Ovilus IV, that are so far from answering any of the questions that I've asked so for this Session number one. On the other hand, this could be a Ghost and or Spirit telling me that their world is equal to my world.

This has been one of the most unusual Paranormal Investigations that I have the ever been on. It is unexplained as to the pink and dark blue colors on the thermal images that I obtain during this Paranormal Investigation. It is unacceptable that I had very little memory of this Paranormal Investigation between 28th March 2017 to 23rd May 2017, until I started reading the transcript that I had written during that Session number one. I only remember feeling extra emotionally drained after Session One. I was not sure if I was going to do Session Two on that same day, but I started Session Two less than an hour after I had finished Session One.

The analysis of the Paranormal Investigation, Session 2, the Pat & Kathleen Room, Hays House, Tuesday, 28th, March 2017. The date of analysis was Tuesday, 23rd May 2017.

At 12:25 PM the Ovilus IV gave me the first and second background words for session 2, own and these. I have not asked any questions yet during this session 2. I do not believe that the words own and these are in response to any of the questions that I have asked during the previous session 1. This could be the Spirit of Jeff Buck or Pat and Kathleen Hays telling me that they own these premise's.

12:28 PM I thought I heard the doorbell ring. For some reason I got up to look to see who was at the door. There was no one at the door to ring the door bell and no one in the house other than me.

At 12:29 PM, the Ovilus IV gave me the third word for this session 2, sister. The last two questions that I had asked at 12:27 PM, was do you own these? What do you own? The last three words that the Ovilus IV has given me were; own, these, and sister. Maybe there is an intelligent spirit is trying to tell me that their sister owns these. I can only conclude that an intelligent spirit is saying that their sister owns the Hays House.

At 12:33 PM the Ovilus IV gave me the fourth word for this session 2, stood. I do not believe that the word stood is in response to any of the questions I've asked so far during this number two, session. A spirit maybe telling me that they understood what I was saying.

At 12:34 PM the Ovilus IV gave me the fifth word for this session number two, mop. I do not believe that the word mop is in response to any of the questions I've asked so far during this number two session.

At 12:54 PM the Ovilus IV gave the sixth and seventh words for this session number two, begin and alone. I believe that this is an intelligent response from Sunshine. Sunshine is telling me to begin my research to find out how this room was furnished and for me to do it alone and without her help.

At 12:55 PM the Ovilus IV gave me the eighth word for this session number two, world. I do not feel that the word world is in response to any of the questions that I have asked so far during this number two session. A spirit is telling me once I finish the book, I will be on top of the world.

At 1:13 PM I have obtained two thermal images of a dark purple area in the room's South East corner. I cannot explain why there are dark purple areas in the South East corner of Pat & Kathleen's Room. I have obtained two thermal images of a pink area near the fire place insert plate. I cannot explain why there are pink areas near the fireplace insert plate. I have seen the fireplace insert plates when they are hot and also when only the pilot light is on and these pictures do not look anything like that. I have obtained two thermal images of the room's north east corner. The first image has a pink area and the second image has a blue area. I cannot explain why the first image is pink and a couple of seconds later the second image is blue. Both images were taken pointing in the same direction, at the room's Northeast corner, and at a very close interval of time. There seemed to have been a very fast manipulation of the temperature, thus the color changes within the thermal images right while I am aiming at the room's North east corner. I have ruled out that there was a malfunction with the FLIR Thermal Imager. It does appear that the spirits here have mastered a certain ability to control and manipulation a quick temperature change within the environment of Pat & Kathleen's Room.

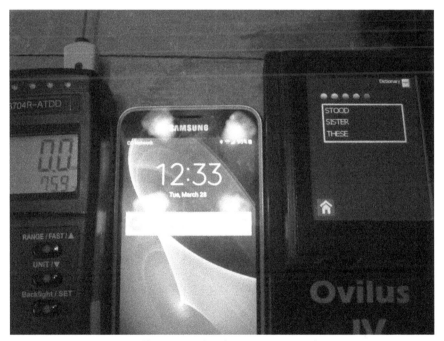

Ovilus IV words: These, Sister, Stood.

Digital Pictures, the Pat & Kathleen Room, Wednesday, 2nd November 2016.

One picture of the room's North wall.

One picture of the room's East wall.

Two pictures of the room's heart pine tongue and groove hardwood floor.

One picture of the room's West wall and Northwest corner.

One picture of the room's ceiling lights and fan.

One picture of the ceiling and wall on the room's South East corner.

Two pictures of the room's wall and ceiling trim.

One close up picture of the room's door that leads to the Petit Jardin room.

Two pictures of the room's horizontal wall boards.

Two close-up pictures of the room's horizontal wall boards.

One picture of the fireplace mirror and columns, located on the room's West wall.

One picture of the fireplace and lower columns, located on the room's West wall.

Two close-up pictures of the Tiger stripe natural would fireplace mantle on the room's West wall.

Four close-up pictures of the left column of the fireplace mantle on the room's West wall.

Two pictures of the room's Northwest corner.

Please see the author's website at www.keithoevans.com to view each digital picture.

Thermal images, the Pat & Kathleen Room, Wednesday, 2nd November 2016.

One thermal image of the door located on the room's North wall.

One thermal image of the interior door and the standalone lights within the room's Northwest corner.

One thermal image of the interior door, while close, left side of the door, located on the room's East wall.

One thermal image of the two Windows with the bottom left of the image showing the second standalone light and the top right of the image being the ceiling fan and light, located on the room's South wall.

One thermal image of the fireplace with the top left side of the image showing the ceiling fan and light, located on the room's West wall.

One thermal image of the ceiling fan and light.

Please see the author's website at www.keithoevans.com to view each thermal image.

CHAPTER 8

Living Room, Hays House, Ghosts are People too.

The description of the Living Room, Hays House, Friday, 11 November 2016.

On the room's East wall near the room's Northeast corner is a door way opening that leads to Pat & Kathleen's Room. This doorway was created after 1996 by removing the wall in the back of the closet that could be entered from Pat & Kathleen's Room. The white wooden trim surrounding this door way opening does not appear to be original because the door-way trim is not the same as the trim around the built in the wall shelves on the room's East wall located near the room's South East corner. All of the interior doors between rooms on the first floor are located near the interior wall bordering the central hallway, down the middle of the Hays House. With this in mind it would follow the pattern that this door opening was original. It may just be that over the years the door trim may have been updated and replaced. It may have been impossible to find matching wooden trim to place around this door. In the middle of the Living Room's East wall is an original fireplace with a decorative natural Tiger striped wooden fireplace mantle with columns on the right and left sides. The fireplace mantle has a mirror that is 17 1/2 inches wide and 36 inches in length. The fireplace mantle has an iron gas heater insert that is 27 1/2 inches wide and 32 and three-quarter inches in length. The fireplace mantle has olive green, brown, and white, tile, that is 1 1/2 inches wide and 6 1/16 inches long. On the room's East wall near the room's South East corner are seven white wooden shelves that are built into the wall. The shelves may be original, because the trim around the shelves match the trim around the rest of the room's windows and the floor's baseboard. This may have originally been a doorway leading to Pat and Kathleen's Room. This room may have originally had two doorway openings on each side of the fireplace along the room's East wall. The bottom two bookshelves are 12 inches in height. The second from the bottom bookshelf is approximately 12 1/4 inches in height. The bottom bookshelf is 12 1/2 inches deep. The second from the bottom bookshelf is 11 3/16 inches deep. The other five shelves vary from 9 inches in height to approximately nine 5/16th inches in height. The other five shelves vary from approximately 11 inches deep to 12 1/4 inches deep.

The Fire Place Mantle, East wall, Living 'Room.

Fire Place Gas Heater Insert, East wall, Living Room.

On the room's South wall are four windows. As I am facing the room's South wall, the narrow window to the far-left side of the room has a window with the following dimensions; 25 three-quarter inches wide and 68 and three-quarter inches in height. The narrow window to the far-right side of the room's South wall is approximate 25 1/4 inches wide and 69 1/4 inches in height. The two windows in the middle of the room's South wall both are approximately 34 1/4 inches wide and 68 1/4 inches in height. In front of the windows along the room's South wall is a white couch and in front of the white couch is a blue wicker coffee table.

On the room's West wall there are two windows, the left side window while facing the room's West wall is approximately 34 1/8 inches wide and 68 three-quarter inches in height. The right-side window while facing the room's West wall is approximately 34 1/4 inches wide and 68 1/2 inches in height. Along the room's West wall is a natural wooden double-sided desk. There is a Buck Deer head mounted on the room's West wall between the two windows.

All four walls within the Living Room have white horizontal wall-boards that are approximately 3 1/4 inches wide. The floors within the Living Room is covered with heart pine hardwood that is approximately two 9/16th inches wide. The ceiling within the Living Room has the 2 1/2-inch-wide tongue and groove ceiling boards.

On the Living Room's North wall is an opening to the First Floor Front Stairway Room. This opening has been reduced by what I believe to be a later added decorative natural short wall approximately 4 foot tall. This fencing extends out from both sides of the opening ending with a column on both sides, that extends up to the ceiling.

The North wall, Living Room.

The history of the Living Room, Hays House.

From 1942 to 1968 the Living Room had Christmas decorations on top of the fire place mantle. In the center of the fire place mantle was an electrical light with five candles that were surrounded by home handed decorations. These decorations included branches and leaves that were hand painted silver or gold and inserted into a soft piece of foam within a vase. These colorful leaves and branches had store bought blue Christmas balls hanging from them. From 1951 until 1968 the Christmas tree was placed in the south-west corner of the Living Room. Pat would go out to the woods and cut down a ten-foot-tall Christmas tree. From 1969 to 1977 Pat and Kathleen had an artificial Christmas tree that they placed in the south-west corner of the Living Room. From 1978 until 1996, which was Kathleen's last Christmas in the Hays House, the artificial Christmas tree was placed in the Living Room's south-west corner, in front of the Bay windows.

Kathleen Hays had a large beautiful crystal chandelier hanging from the center of the ceiling in the Living Room from 1942 until 1996.

In 1942 there was an oil or coal burning stove that sat out from the fireplace and vented through the fireplace. This stove was used to heated the Living Room. In 2017 the circular shaped black area on the hardwood floor in front of and to the right side of the fireplace, was caused from where the cold bucket has set there for years.

Nat Toulon and Frances Hays Toulon were married in the Living Room in 1968.

Sometime after 1996 a door way size opening was created at the rear wall of the closet in Pat and Kathleen's Room and on Living Room's east wall and near the room's north-east corner.

The description of the Living Room from ten pictures taken in 1996, Hays House.

I will be using 10 pictures of the living room to describe the room. I will be starting at the room's South wall and working around the room in a clockwise direction. The South wall has four windows called Bay Windows, and they are all covered with an off-white drapery. Each window has two glass panes in the upper and lower section. The window trim is painted white and appears to be original. There is a green potted plant on the far-left side of this room's South wall. A long the

South wall are two matching, antique chairs with dark wooden arms and legs. These chairs have an off white textured, textile covered seat and back rest. Between the two chairs on the room's South wall is a dark wooden antique table with a white round marble top. On top of this table, and from left to right are the following items; a pink china dish on a golden pedestal, a black ashtray or a back-glass coaster, and a multi-colored porcelain lamp with an octagon shape the white lamp shade. To the far-right side of the room is a golden metal stand, with four legs and a white marble top. Sitting on top of this stand is a large multi-colored, but mostly blue porcelain vase. On the floor, there is a central heat and air vent near the center of the room's South wall.

On the living room's West wall there are two original windows with two glass panes in the top and bottom section of the window. Each window has the white original wooden trim. These windows are covered with an off-white drapery. To the left side of the left window and mounted on the wall is a decorative plate. Between these two windows and mounted on the wall, is a wooden frame under glass, wedding photo of Frances Hays Toulon. From left to right along the room's West wall is a dark wooden antique round table with a golden crystal covered tree stand with five white candles like electrical light bulbs. On top of round table are two small porcelain items, one looks like a square box and the other item may be a porcelain candy dish. A long the far-right side of the room's West wall is a dark wooden round antique table that matches the above-described table on the left side of the West wall. On top of this round antique table is a matching golden tree shape crystal line lamp that matches the lamp on the top of the table on the left side of the room's West wall. On top of this round antique table are a moon shaped porcelain candy dish and a china cup and saucer. Between the two antique tables is a white textile covered antique couch with dark wooden legs and trim. In front of the couch is an oval shaped wooden coffee table with a white marble top. On top of the coffee table is a blue and white porcelain type items.

Near the room's Northwest corner is an antique chair with dark wooden arms, legs and a white textile covered seat. On the right side of the room's North wall is the room's light switch which is mounted on the wall and also mounted on the wall is a golden shelf with an olive porcelain vase on top. At the center of the room's North wall is a large open area that leads to the First Floor Front Stairway Room. On each side of this large opening is a white wooden column that sits on top of a 4-foot-tall part of the wall that extends out from the wall that extends from the floor to the ceiling. On the right side of the North wall is an antique chair with wooden legs, a white textile covered seat and back rest.

Starting from the left side and mounted on the living room's East wall is a golden framed painting of Frances Hays in her white wedding dress. To the left side of the fireplace mantle is a multi-colored waiter pull that Kathleen Hays knitted. Along the room's East wall is an antique dark wooden desk with two matching golden candleholders. Each candleholder has five white 8-inch candles. To the left side of the fireplace mantle is an antique chair with dark wooden arms, legs, and trim. This antique chair also has a yellow textile covered seat and back rest. In the center of the room's East wall is the fireplace with the original white decorative fireplace mantle that has a wooden column on each side. These columns hold the fireplace mantle's top shelf in place. On this top shelf are two matching porcelain vases with red flowers. Between the top and the bottom shelves and mounted on the wooden fireplace mantle is an 18" x 36" original mirror. On the fireplace mantle's bottom shelf are three porcelain baby dolls. Around the fireplace are decorative greenish blue tiles. In front of the fireplace gas heater insert is a decorative golden fireplace hearth. To the right side of the fireplace and built into the wall are seven book shelves. There are books on the bottom shelf and the other shelves are decorated with small pictures and different types of porcelain and glass items. The shelves that are built into the wall starting at the floor level and reach up to about 7 feet in height. To the right side of the fireplace is an antique chair with dark wooden arms, legs, and trim with a yellow textile covered seat and back rest.

All of the walls in the living room have the original horizontal wooden wall boards that are painted white. The majority of the living room's floor is covered with an off-white rug. In the middle of the room's ceiling is a grand chandelier with clear crystal's and several white candles like holders with electrical light bulbs. The ceiling has the original heart pine tongue and groove boards that are painted white.

Mel Meter Base Readings for the Living Room, Hays House, Friday, 11th November 2016.

2 PM The lamp on top of the wooden desks along the rooms West wall.

The electromagnetic frequency range was 0.0 mG to 0.0 mG.

The temperature range was 68.1°F to 68.5°F.

2:01 PM the electrical outlet, on the room's West wall. The lamp, my laptop, and the FLIR charger are all plugged in to this electrical outlet.

The electromagnetic frequency range was 0.0 mG to 0.0 mG.

The temperature range was 68.3°F to 68.3°F.

2:02 PM the double light switch to the right of the entrance on the room's North wall. This light switches in the off position.

The electromagnetic frequency range was 0.0 mG to 0.0 mG.

The temperature range was 68.4°F to 68.8°F.

2:03 PM the LG black flat screen TV 21" x 35", located on the room's North wall. The LG black flat screen TV is not in use.

The electromagnetic frequency range was 0.0 mG to 0.0 mG.

The temperature range was 68.2°F to 68.3°F.

2:04 PM the black spot on the floor, to the far-right side and in front of the fireplace.

The electromagnetic frequency range was 0.0 mG to 0.0 mG and.

The temperature range was 67.4°F to 67.6°F.

2:05 PM the decorative, top of the right-side wooding post of the fireplace mantle, located on the room's East wall.

The electromagnetic scene range was 0.0 mG to 0.0 mG.

The temperature range was 67.2°F to 67.4°F.

2:06 PM the white bookshelf on the right side of the room's East wall.

The electromagnetic frequency range was 0.0 mG to 0.0 mG.

The temperature range was 68.3°F to 68.4°F.

2:07 PM the right side wooden Tiger stripe fireplace mantle post located on the room's East wall.

The electromagnetic frequency range was 0.0 mG to 0.0 mG.

The temperature range was 68.3°F to 69.0°F.

2:08 PM the white Perfect Aire air conditioner window unit, mounted on the second window from the left, on the room's South wall.

The electromagnetic frequency range was 0.0 mG to 0.0 mG.

The temperature range was 68.5°F to 69.0°F.

2:09 PM the black Brother combination sound system on the stand, located along the room's South wall.

The electromagnetic frequency range was 0.0 mG to 0.0 mG.

The temperature range was 68.5°F to 68.8°F.

2:10 PM the double electrical outlet on the room's South wall. The air conditioner, Brothers Sound Center, and the lamp are all plugged into this electrical outlet.

The electromagnetic frequency range was 0.0 mG to 0.0 mG.

The temperature range was 68.5°F to 68.6°F.

2:11 PM the electrical outlet on the room's North wall. The TV and the VCR are plugged into this electrical outlet.

The electromagnetic frequency range was 0.0 mG to 0.0 mG.

The temperature range was 67.3°F to 68.1°F.

Paranormal Investigation, Session 1, Living Room, Hays House, Tuesday, 28th, March 2017.

3:31 PM Keith: "Hello, I am Keith Evans. If you would like to talk, you may use your energy to choose words from the Ovilus IV's data base. This is the Ovilus IV. The Ovilus IV will not hurt you." (Hold it up.)

3:32 PM Keith: "This is the Mel Meter. The Mel Meter measures temperature and electromagnetic frequencies. The Mel Meter will not harm you." (Hold it up.)

3:32 PM Keith: "The Ovilus IV has given me two background words; right which is spelled R-I-G-H-T, and early which is spelled E-A-R-L-Y. The Ovilus IV has pronounced the words right, and early at a normal conversational level and speed."

3:32 PM Keith: "I have observed the Mel Meter readings to be 0.0 mG and 80.1°F."

3:33 PM Keith: "The Ovilus IV has given me the word castle which is spelled C-A-S-T-L-E. The Ovilus IV has pronounced the word castle at a normal conversational level and speed."

3:33 PM Keith: "I have observed the Mel Meter readings to be 0.0 mG and 80.2°F."

3:34 PM Keith: "The Ovilus IV has given me the word heat which is spelled H-E-A-T. The Ovilus IV has pronounced the word heat at a normal conversational level and speed."

3:34 PM Keith: "I have observed the Mel Meter readings to be 0.0 mG and 80.2°F."

3:39 PM Keith: "I guess it is early to be a hot castle?"

3:40 PM Keith: "Do you consider the Hays House to be your castle?"

3:41 PM Keith: "It is hotter on the second and third floors."

3:42 PM Keith: "What floor are you on?"

3:42 PM Keith: "The Ovilus IV has given me the word thank which is spelled T-H-A-N-K. The Ovilus IV has pronounced the word thank in a normal conversational level and speed."

3:42 PM Keith: "I have observed the Mel Meter readings to be 0.0 mG and 80.7°F."

3:44 PM Keith: "What are you thanking me for?"

3:45 PM Keith: "I still do not know what floor you were on."

3:46 PM Keith: "I'm talking to a guest in the Living Room." (The Living Room is a common area for all of the bed-and-breakfast personnel that are staying at the Hays House.)

3:46 PM Keith: "I have stopped session 1, Tuesday, 28th, March 2017."

Continued Paranormal Investigation, Session 1, Living Room, Hays House, Wednesday, 29th, March 2017.

11:33 AM Keith: "The batteries in the digital camera are dead."

11:34 AM Keith: "Okay, I'm going to replace the batteries in the digital camera with two AA batteries."

11:35 AM Keith: "I have observed the Mel Meter readings to be 0.0 mG and 75.3°F."

11:35 AM Keith: "The Ovilus IV has given me one background word, drank which is spelled D-R-A-N-K. The Ovilus IV has pronounced the word drank in a normal conversational level and speed."

11:35 AM Keith: "I have observed the Mel Meter readings to be 0.0 mG and 75.0°F."

11:36 AM Keith: "Yes, I am drinking sweet tea." (I place my glasses of sweet tea in front of the camcorder.)

11:39 AM Keith: "I hear the housekeeper causing sounds of glasses touching together. I hear the housekeeper walking in the hallway."

11:40 AM Keith: "I hear the housekeeper walking up the stairs to the second floor."

11:40 AM Keith: "Do you like non-sweet tea?"

11:42 AM Keith: "The Ovilus IV will not go to the home position, upon pressing the home icon so, the batteries are dead. I will have to place four brand-new AAA batteries into the Ovilus IV."

11:44 AM Keith: "The Kitty, Miss Jill is my part-time helper with the Paranormal Investigating."

11:45 AM Keith: "I do not mind if Jill is on the video footage. She is a very loveable Kitty."

11:46 AM Keith: "The Ovilus IV has given me three background words; sometime which is spelled S-O-M-E-T-I-M-E, ground which is spelled G-R-O-U-N-D, and compare which is spelled C-O-M-P-A-R-E. The Ovilus IV has pronounced words sometime, ground, and compare, at a normal conversational level and speed."

11:46 AM Keith: "I have observed the Mel Meter readings to be 0.0 mG and 75.5°F."

11:46 AM Keith: "I have observed the Mel Meter readings to be 0.0 mG and 75.9°F."

11:47 AM Keith: "I heard a truck going past the Hays House."

11:48 AM Keith: "I hear the housekeeper making rattling sounds in the hallway."

11:49 AM Housekeeper: "You have some company."

11:50 AM Keith: "Yes, she, (Jill), likes to help."

11:50 AM Housekeeper: "What are you doing Jill? What are you doing Jill?" (Said the housekeeper in a whisper type voice.)

11:51 AM Keith: "I can hear the housekeeper mopping the hallway floor."

11:53 AM Keith: "The Ovilus IV has given me the word field which is spelled F-I-E-L-D. The Ovilus IV has pronounced the word field at a normal conversational level and speed."

11:53 AM Keith: "I have observed the Mel Meter readings to be 0.0 mG and 75.3°F.

11:55 AM Keith: "Are you comparing the ground to a field?"

11:56 AM Keith: "Are you measuring the pH in the ground soil?

11:57 AM Keith: "Are you looking at the type of land that would grow good trees for turpentine?"

12 noon Keith: "The Ovilus IV has given me the word lift which is spelled L-I-F-T. The Ovilus IV has pronounced the word lift at a normal conversational level and speed."

12 noon Keith: "I have observed the Mel Meter readings to be 0.0 mG and 79.1°F."

12:01 PM Keith: "I could lift Jill out of the way, but I will leave her be."

12:02 PM Keith: "The Ovilus IV has given me the word milk which is spelled M-I-L-K. The Ovilus IV has pronounced the word milk at a normal conversational level and speed."

12:02 PM Keith: "I have observed the Mel Meter readings to be 0.0 mG and 76.9°F."

12:04 PM Keith: "I could give Jill some milk. I bet Jill would love that."

12:05 PM Keith: "I can hear the housekeeper walking upstairs."

12:07 PM Keith: "How do you feel about me doing the Paranormal Investigations?"

12:08 PM Keith: "I know that you are observing what is going on in this room because you have made comments about me drinking the non-sweet tea, you have commented on Jill being in the way of the video camera, and you have stated that Jill may like some Milk."

12:10 PM Keith: "What are your concerns when it comes to comparing ground and Field dirt?"

12:11 PM Keith: "Miss Jill, can you sit over here for me please."

12:12 PM Keith: "Miss Jill, you're just holding up the video camera. Yes, I need my notes to write on."

12:13 PM Keith: "I can hear the housekeeper walking down the stairs."

12:14 PM Keith: "Pat, what is the best type of soil to grow the long-needled Pine trees?"

12:15 PM Keith: "Who said the words; sometime, ground, compare, and field?"

12:16 PM Keith: "I have obtained two thermal images of the dark blue area near the room's North East corner, and lower down towards the floor. I have obtained two thermal images of the pink areas on the deer's head that is mounted on the room's West wall. I have obtained one thermal image of my cold non-sweet tea that is sitting on the blue wicker coffee table, in front of the couch, located along the room's South wall."

12:17 PM Keith: "My name is Keith. What is your name?"

12:18 PM Keith: "Okay, what do you want to talk about?"

12:19 PM Keith: "I can hear the housekeeper walking down the Front Stairway."

12:20 PM to 12:22 PM Keith: "I was talking to the housekeeper concerning my website and contact information. Jill was loving the camcorder number two, and almost pushed the camcorder number two off of the tabletop."

12:24 PM Keith: "Sunshine, are you here today?"

12:25 PM Keith: "Pat, what time of the year, did you hunt doves?"

12:26 PM Keith: "So, your advice is to compare the ground dirt of the field, that I wish to purchase?"

12:28 PM Keith: "If I buy a house here in town and want to have a small vegetable garden, I could just put down topsoil in the location that I want to have my small garden."

12:30 PM Keith: "Pat, did you ever have a vegetable garden here at the Hays House?"

12:31 PM Keith: "Sunshine, did you ever have a vegetable garden here at the Hays House?"

12:32 PM Keith: "Mary, did you ever have a vegetable garden here at the Hays House?"

12:32 PM Keith: "That's thud sound was Jill the cat, as she jumped from the desk down to the floor."

12:33 PM Keith: "Kathleen, did you ever have a vegetable garden here at the Hays House?"

12:34 PM Keith: "Thank you for talking to me. Have a good day."

12:34 PM Keith: "I have observed the Mel Meter readings to be 0.0 mG and 75.9°F."

12:35 PM Keith: "The Ovilus IV has given me the word cloud which is spelled C-L-O-U-D. The Ovilus IV has pronounced the word cloud at a normal conversational level but at a slower than normal conversational speed."

12:35 PM Keith: "I have observed the Mel Meter readings to be 0.0 mG and 77.0°F."

12:35 PM Keith: "This Session 1 ended on Wednesday, 29th, March 2017."

Paranormal Investigation, Session 2, Living Room, Hays House, Wednesday, 29th, March 2017.

2:04 PM Keith: "Hello, I am Keith Evans. If you would like to talk to me, please use your energy to choose words from the Ovilus IV's database. This is the Ovilus IV. The Ovilus IV will not hurt you." (Hold it up.)

2:05 PM Keith: "This is the Mel Meter. The Mel Meter measures temperature and electromagnetic frequencies. The Mel Meter will not harm you." (Hold it up.)

2:05 PM Keith: "The Ovilus IV has given me two background words; clockwise which is spelled C-L-O-C-K-W-I-S-E, and happy which is spelled H-A-P-P-Y. The Ovilus IV has pronounced the words clockwise and happy at a louder than normal conversational level and at a faster than normal conversational speed."

2:05 PM Keith: "I have observed the Mel Meter readings to be 0.0 mG and 78.7°F."

2:06 PM Keith: "I observed a shadow from a slow-moving pickup truck going eastbound on fourth Street."

2:08 PM Keith: "Clockwise, and happy, it sounds like Sunshine is saying that I'm going in too much detail. Sunshine wants to know if that makes me happy? Yes, it makes me happy."

2:09 PM Keith: "The words that the Ovilus for gave me at 2:05 PM were of a higher pitch female voice with more energy."

2:10 PM Keith: "What I mean by more energy, is more emotion as to how the words were spoken."

2:11 PM Keith: "The Ovilus IV gave me the word soil which is spelled S-O-I-L. The Ovilus IV has pronounced the word soil at a normal conversational level but at a slower conversational speed with a deep male's voice."

2:11 PM Keith: "I have observed the Mel Meters readings to be 0.0 mG and 78.2°F."

2:13 PM Keith: "Okay, what about the soil."

2:15 PM Keith: "The Ovilus IV gave me two words portal which is spelled P-O-R-T-A-L, and Chris which is spelled C-H-R-I-S. The Ovilus IV has pronounced the words portal and Chris in a deep male voice, at a normal conversational level and speed."

2:15 PM Keith: "I have observed the Mel Meter readings to be 0.0 mG and 78.4°F."

2:17 PM Keith: "Chris, what can you tell me about the portal?"

2:18 PM Keith: "Is the portal the way spirits travel from heaven to the Hays House?"

2:18 PM Keith: "The Ovilus IV gave me the word stood which is spelled S-T-O-O-D. The Ovilus IV has pronounced the word stood with a male's voice, at a normal conversational level and speed."

2:18 PM Keith: "I have observed the Mel Meter readings to be 0.0 mG and 78.2°F."

2:21 PM Keith: "You did not answer my question about how one travels within the portal with a yes or no. Who is traveling within the portal? Did Chris travel with the portal? Who is Chris?"

2:23 PM Keith: "Am I talking to Chris?"

2:24 PM Keith: "Chris, did you ever live in the Hays house?"

2:24 PM Keith: "Both camcorder one and two are working fine."

2:25 PM Keith: "That was me tapping on my notebook with my finger."

2:26 PM Keith: "Chris, are you related to the Buck family?"

2:27 PM Keith: "Chris, are you related to the Gibson, and or Hays family?"

2:28 PM Keith: "If you understood my question, is the portal the way spirits travel from heaven to the Hays house? How come you cannot answer that question with a yes or no answer?"

2:30 PM Keith: "Are my questions, just to deep or what?"

2:31 PM Keith: "The Ovilus IV has given me the word pastor which is spelled P-A-S-T-O-R. The Ovilus IV has pronounce the word pastor with a higher pitch male's voice spoken at a normal conversational level and speed."

2:31 PM Keith: "I have observed the Mel Meter readings to be 0.0 mG and 78.9°F."

2:33 PM Keith: "If you're the pastor you should be able to speak the truth. I am all ears, go ahead."

2:34 PM Keith: "Pastor, is the portal the way the spirits travel from heaven to the Hays House."

2:35 PM Keith: "So Pastor, you do not know?"

2:36 PM Keith: "Pastor, what is your name?"

2:37 PM Keith: "My name is Keith. What is your name?"

2:38 PM Keith: "Sunshine, tell me some details about this room? How was this room decorated in the 1940s?"

2:39 PM Keith: "Sunshine, what type of furniture was in this room in the 1940s."

2:40 PM to 2:42 PM Keith: "I have obtained thermal images with the FLIR Thermal Imager. I obtained two thermal images of a dark blue area on the room's lower Northeast corner. I obtained four thermal images of the mounted deer head on the room's West wall. I obtained one thermal image of my cold unsweetened tea on the coffee table in front of the couch, located along the room's South wall."

242 PM Keith: "That was my sunglasses rattling in my pocket as I sat down."

2:46 PM Keith: "Sunshine, did you use all of your energy when you said the words clockwise and happy?"

2:47 PM Keith: "It appears that the Ovilus IV is frozen up again."

2:48 PM Keith: "The Ovilus IV will not go back to the home position. I have tapped the home icon several times. The four AAA batteries are new, I just place them into the Ovilus IV today. They cannot be dead already. I guess this is a good time to stop."

2:51 PM Keith: "I have observed the Mel Meter readings to be 0.0 mG and 78.7°F."

2:52 PM Keith: "Thank you for talking to me. Have a nice day."

2:52 PM Keith: "This Session two ended on Wednesday, 29th, March 2017."

The analysis of the Paranormal Investigation, Session 1, Living Room, Hays House, Tuesday, 28th, March 2017. The date of analysis was Sunday, 28th May 2017.

At 3:32 PM the Ovilus IV gave me the first two background words for session 1; right and early. I have not asked any questions yet during this session 1. I believe that this background energy are spirits talking amongst themselves.

At 3:33 PM the Ovilus IV gave me the third word for this session 1, castle. I have not asked any questions yet during this session number one. I do feel that spirits are free to talk amongst themselves constantly and consistently. Ghost and spirits do not need a Paranormal Investigator around to be communicating with each other.

At 3:34 PM the Ovilus IV gave me the fourth word for this session 1, heat. I have not asked any questions yet during this session number one. It seems like this is a very active area for spirits to be communicating amongst themselves. It could be that there is an old well nearby that still brings water close to the surface. This well and its water will allow more activity between spirits and ghosts. The old maps show the well, located somewhere on the far North East side of the Gibson in property. The Hays House is very close to the river water to the north and the bay water to the Southeast.

Let's take a look at all four words that have been given so far this session number one, right, early, castle, and heat. I could assume that a ghost or spirit is making a statement that I'm there right early arriving at the castle. The castle would be the Hays House and it is hot because the air conditioning is off on the first floor and it is warm outside. So, this may be an intelligent spirit communicating with me even though I haven't asked any questions yet.

At 3:42 PM the Ovilus IV gave me the fifth word for this session number one, thank. I do not believe that the word thank is responding to any of the questions that I've asked so far during this session number one.

At 3:46 PM a guest walked into the Living Room. The Living Room is a common area for all guest to use, who are renting rooms here at the Hays House. I promptly ended my Paranormal Investigating for the day. I feel that my paranormal investigating is an activity that obtains the best results if it's just me and the ghosts.

The analysis of the continued Paranormal Investigation, Session 1, Living Room, Hays House, Wednesday, 29th, March 2017. The date of analysis was Sunday, 28th May 2017.

11:33 AM already. The batteries are dead in the digital camera. It seems like the spirits are getting energy from wherever they can.

11:35 AM the Ovilus IV gave me the sixth background word for this session number one, drank. I can't help but think that drank and thank at least rhyme and are the last two words that I received on the Ovilus IV over the last two days. This could be the intelligent spirit of Sunshine showing me that she knows how to use words that rhyme. Sunshine refuses to talk about the history of her family or the Hays House. She may be trying to fill the space with poetry. Or maybe she wants me to read more of the Edgar Allen Poe poem the Raven. I had read parts of the Edgar Allan Poe poem the Raven to Sunshine at another location in Apalachicola about a year and 1/2 ago. I do not feel that the word drank is responding to any of the questions that I had asked yesterday during the first part of session 1. I have not asked any questions today during the second part of session 1. I have brought with me from lunch a glass of non-sweet tea and it could be that the ghost or spirit is given a play-by-play detail of the fact that I am drinking non-sweet tea. This would be an intelligent response. Drank is past tense and I still had more non-sweet tea to drink at 11:35 AM.

At 11:39 AM and 11:40 AM I tagged my transcript with the sounds of hearing, the housekeeper in the hallway, with the sounds of glasses touching together and housekeeper walking up and down the stairs. I find that any other activity in the house may distract the spirits and ghosts from effectively communicating with the Paranormal Investigator.

At 11:42 AM the Ovilus IV has frozen up again. The Ovilus IV will not go back to its home position. Upon pressing the home icon. Looks like the spirits have draining the energy from the batteries of the Ovilus IV. This gets expensive when you're change in batteries all the time. The Ovilus IV requires four brand-new AAA batteries to function properly.

At 11:44 AM during this session number one. The kitty, Miss Jill has joined me as my part-time helper for this Paranormal Investigation. Miss Jill was also on the video footage.

At 11:46 AM the Ovilus IV gave me the seventh through ninth words for this session number one; sometime, ground, and compare. I do not feel that the words sometime, ground, and compare are in response to any of the questions that I have asked so for during session number one.

At 11:47 AM, a loud truck drove by.

At 11:48 AM I hear sounds from the housekeeper rattling things in the hallway on the first floor.

At 11:49 AM the Housekeeper has walked into the Living Room and starts talking to me and to Jill.

At 11:53 AM the Ovilus IV gave me the 10th word for this session number one, field. I do not believe that the word field is in response to any of the questions that I have asked so far during this session number one.

At 12 noon the Ovilus IV gave me the 11th word for this session number one, lift. I do not believe that the word lift is in response to any of the questions I have asked so for during this session number one.

12:01 PM the Ovilus IV gave me the 12th word for this session number one, milk. I do not believe that the word milk is in response to any of the questions that I have asked so far during this session number one. Even though the spirit is not responding to any of my questions, they may be saying that Jill the cat would like some milk. This could be an intelligent spirit responding to what the spirit sees in the environment.

At 12:05 PM. I can hear the housekeeper walking upstairs.

At 12:11 PM and 12:12 PM Miss Jill is sitting on my transcript and blocking me from taking notes. Miss Jill is laying up against the camcorder thus blocking any footage that may be taken of the Living Room.

At 12:13 PM I can hear the housekeeper walking down the steps.

At 12:16 PM I obtained two thermal images of a dark blue area that was low, towards the floor and near the room's Northeast corner. I cannot find a reason for this area to be dark blue which indicate that it's much colder than the rest of the room. I obtained two thermal images of the warm areas near the mounted Deer's head on the room's West wall. I do not know why the Deer's head would indicate an almost life-like temperature in certain places. I obtained one picture of my cold non-sweet tea which is sitting on the blue Wickard coffee table that is in front of the couch, located along the room's South wall.

At 12:19 PM I heard the housekeeper walking down the stairs.

12:20 PM to 12:22 PM I was talking to the housekeeper concerning my website and my contact information. Jill the cat was loving the camcorder number two and almost pushed the camcorder number two off of the desk.

At 12:32 PM the thugs sound was Jill the cat jumping down from the desk.

At 12:35 PM the Ovilus IV gave me the 13th word for this session number one, cloud. I do not see any connection between the word cloud and any of the questions that I have asked so far during this session number one. The disconnect between the questions that I asked and the words the Ovilus IV gave me, may be due to all the interruptions starting with sounds in the background, other people talking to me in the house, and maybe even the cat moving the camcorder number two around, maybe there was enough distractions to keep the spirits from intellectually communicating.

The analysis of the Paranormal Investigation, Session 2, Living Room, Hays House, Wednesday, 29th, March 2017. The date of analysis was Sunday, 28th May 2017.

At 2:05 PM the Ovilus IV gave me the first two background words for this session number two; clockwise and happy. The Ovilus IV pronounced the words clockwise and happy at a louder than normal conversational level and at a faster than normal conversational speed. The words clockwise and happy sounded like a high-pitched female's voice with a lot of emotional energy. This sounds like an intelligent response from Sunshine, who is very excited to point out that I am (Keith) all too happy to go into a great deal of detail. The use of the word clockwise was used by me in the past to describe the rooms of other places in Apalachicola where I have conducted paranormal investigations and have spoken to the spirit of Sunshine or Mary Ella Gibson.

At 2:11 PM the Ovilus IV gave me the third word for this session number two, soil. The Ovilus IV pronounced the word soil with a deep male voice, at a normal conversational level, but at a slower than normal conversational speed. I do not think that the word soil was in response to any of the questions that I have asked so far during this session number two. The word soil could be in response to several of the questions that I asked at the end of the session number one. I have asked questions about having a vegetable garden at the Hays House. Soil might be one word out of the whole sentence that a spirit has spoken. The Ovilus IV only has the ability the pickup certain words from a possible sentence spoken by spirits or ghosts as they use their energy to choose words from the Ovilus IV.

At 2:15 PM the Ovilus IV gave me the fourth and fifth words for this session 2; portal and Chris. The words portal and Chris were pronounced by the Ovilus IV with a deep male's voice, at a normal conversational level and speed. I find that the word portal may be the intelligent spirit of Chris, who is talking about a method of traveling from heaven to the Hays House for spirits and ghosts. A portal is a way and means for spirits to travel from heaven to the Hays House. Today it is popular for portal to be used in a negative light as a way for negative individuals to travel from someplace to a location on earth. I believe that a portal is a method of travel that we do not understand and that human beings are not permitted to use. A portal may only be used by individuals who have passed away and are in heaven and have a deep emotional connection with a house, a place, and or a person, and these spirits or ghosts can use a portal to travel from heaven to that person or place on earth where that spirit or ghost have a deep emotional connection. I do not know of any Chris who has a connection with, lived and or worked at the Hays House. That does not mean that there is not a Chris who has a connection with the Hays House. It just means that I have not discovered a Chris who has a connection with the Hays House.

At 2:18 PM the Ovilus IV gave me the sixth word for this session number two, stood. The Ovilus IV pronounced the words good with a male's voice, at a normal conversational level and speed. At 2:18 PM I had just asked the question, is the portal the way spirits travel from heaven to the Hays House? Within a couple of seconds, I received the words stood. I feel that some intelligent spirit was trying to say the word understood. Maybe when I said, is the portal the way spirits travel from heaven to the Hays House, the spirit understood me to be making a statement and not asking a question. At that point it would make sense for the spirit to say I understand you, without the spirit making any judgments statement on agreeing or disagreeing with what I said.

At 2:31 PM the Ovilus IV gave me the seventh word for this session number two, Pastor. The Ovilus IV pronounced the word pastor with a higher pitch male's voice spoken at a normal conversational level and speed. I do not feel that the word pastor is responding to any of the questions that I have asked so for during this session number two.

From 2:40 PM to 2:42 PM I obtained thermal images. I obtained two thermal images of dark blue areas near the room's lower northeast corner. I obtained four thermal images of the mounted deer head on the room's West wall. I obtained one thermal image of my cold non-sweet tea on top of the blue wicker table, in front of the couch, and along the room's South wall.

At 2:47 PM the Ovilus IV had frozen up again. I was surprised that the batteries were so drained because they were not that old. I had just placed the four AAA batteries into the Ovilus IV that day. I did not believe that these batteries had been use that much to be dead. I feel that in a very active paranormal location, the spirits and ghosts use the power and or energy from the battery sources to give themselves energy.

Unexplained Events in the Living Room, Thursday, 15th June 2017, Hays House.

2:35 PM Keith: "I heard a tapping sound coming from the front right side of my laptop's keyboard. I said that I can hear a strange light tapping sound. I also said I know you're here. This light tapping sound lesson for about four minutes. It sounded like an electrical type sound and it was definitely coming from the right front side of my laptop. I have never heard that type of sound coming from any part of my laptop.

Every time I do a Paranormal Investigation at the Hays House. I always use one side of the double wooden desks, located along the Living Room's West wall, to download and save my video footage, EDI data, digital pictures, and, thermal images onto my laptop. Each day that I complete a Paranormal Investigation at the Hays house, I spend as much time at this desk as I do completing Paranormal Investigating. The ghosts and spirits have noticed this and are using it as an occasion to attempt to communicate with me. I would like to think electronic tapping sound was an attempt to re-create music. Even though it didn't sound like any song that I'm familiar with. It seemed to be the continuous pattern of electronic tapping sounds. The ghosts and spirits at the Hays House now are using my laptop computer to try to communicate. If you were a ghost, and or a spirit and were just pure energy, what would you do to occupy your time while Earth bound?

Digital Pictures, Living Room, Friday, 11th November 2016.

Three pictures of the room's North wall.

Two pictures of the room's Northeast corner.

Three pictures of the fireplace on the room's East wall.

Two pictures of the room's Northeast corner.

Two pictures of the fireplace tile on the room's East wall.

Six pictures of the fireplace gas heater insert on the room's East wall.

Eight close-up pictures of the fireplace decorative wood and columns.

Two pictures of the room's hardwood floor.

Two pictures of the black stain on the hardwood floor in front of and to the right side of the fireplace.

Two pictures of the room's East wall.

Two pictures of the room's South wall.

Two pictures of the room's ceiling fan.

Two pictures of the room's South wall.

Two pictures of the rooms West wall.

Two pictures of the room's Southwest corner.

Two pictures of the room's Northwest corner.

Four pictures of the room's ceiling.

Two pictures of the window on the room's South wall.

Four close-up pictures of the window handles.

Please see the author's website at www.keithoevans.com to view each digital picture.

Digital Pictures, Living Room, Friday, 10th March 2017.

Seven pictures of the fireplace on the room's East wall.

Two pictures of the fireplace tile on the room's East wall.

Six pictures of the fireplace gas heater insert on the room's East wall.

Please see the author's website at www.keithoevans.com to view each digital picture.

Digital Pictures, Living Room, Thursday, 8th June 2017.

Two pictures of the room's white horizontal wallboards.

Five pictures of the olive green, brown, and white fireplace mantle tiles, located on the room's East wall.

Two pictures of the room's heart pine hardwood floor.

Please see the author's website at www.keithoevans.com to view each digital picture.

Digital Pictures, Living Room, Wednesday, 14th June 2017.

16 pictures of the built in the East wall bookshelves.

Please see the author's website at www.keithoevans.com to view each digital picture.

Thermal Images, Living Room, Friday, 11th November 2016.

One image of the room's North wall.

One image of the room's Northeast corner.

One image of the fireplace on the room's East wall.

One image of the South side of the room's East wall.

One image of the East side of the room's South wall.

One image of the room's South West corner.

One image of the South side of the room's West wall.

One image of the North side of the room's West wall.

One image of the room's Northwest corner.

One image of the ceiling fan.

Please see the author's website at www.keithoevans.com to view each thermal image.

CHAPTER 9

First Floor Back Stairway Room, Hays House, Ghosts are People too.

The description of the First Floor Back Stairway Room, Hays House, Thursday, 17th, November 2016.

The Back Stairway is located in the Northwest corner of the room. This stairway is narrow and has some hand railing to hold on to as one advances up or down these stairs. The steps start down from the second floor going from a Southern to the northern direction along the room's West wall. Then the steps wind around at a 90° angle with no landing. The steps continued down from a Western to an Eastern direction, located along the room's North wall. Then the steps end on the first floor, at the left side of the door that leads to the first-floor kitchen. The steps and railing are both painted black. Along the North wall is a storage area with two shelves situated under the back-stairway steps. This open closet and or storage area under the back stairway is 29 inches wide by 55 inches in height. There is a natural wooden chair sitting in front of this storage area. Next to the chair and along the interior North wall that is created by the back stairway, there is a dark blue chest of drawers. The original five panel white wooden door that measures 34 inches wide and 82 inches in height, leads into the first-floor kitchen and is on the room's North wall and close to the rooms Northeast corner. This door has the original brass doorknob and the skeleton key plate cover.

The room's East wall has a window that is 34 inches wide and 69 inches tall. The two top and bottom windows sections have two window panes each. Along the room's East wall is a tan wicker basket, and a white wooden bookshelf with a lamp on top. The base of this lamp is pink and the lamp's, shade has diamond-shaped pink designs with a white background. Mounted on the East wall between the window and the rear door is a modern red fire extinguisher. On the room's East wall and towards the room's South East corner is the rear entrance to the Hays House. This rear door is approximately 36 inches wide by 80 inches in height. This is a modern wooden door with nine glass panels, on the top half. Each of the nine glass panels measures 8 inches wide and 11 inches in height. The rear entrance also has a modern wooden screen door. The width of the threshold board between the Back-Stairway Room and the rear entrance cannot be determined because of the new thresholds that have been place on top of the original wooden threshold board.

The room's South wall has a white wooden cabinet with shelves. The South wall has the entrance to the Den Room. The door to this entrance is original, white, wooden with five sunken panels and is 34 inches wide and 82 inches in height. This door has the original brass doorknob and skeleton key plate cover. Mounted on the South wall is a painting of a sunflower with a pink background.

The room's West wall has the original white wooden door that is 34 inches wide and 82 inches in height, with five sunken panels. The threshold board between the First-Floor Back Stairway room and the First-floor Front Stairway room is 3 5/8 inches wide. This doorway leads to the First-floor Front Stairway room. This opening was designed to have two separate doors within the same opening. The door jamb is double wide and designed to have a door to open towards the West side and another door to open, towards the east side. This door has the original brass doorknob and skeleton key plate cover.

The history of the First Floor Back Stairway Room, Hays House.

From 1942 to 1996 the safe that the Gibson Hotel used up and until 1942, was placed in the South-west corner of the First Floor Back-Stairway Room. I was told that the door between the First Floor Front Stairway Room and the First Floor Back Stairway Room swung open into the First Floor Back Stairway Room. This door could not open all the way because of were the 48-inch-wide safe was setting. That is the reason why Kathleen never used the door between the First Floor Front Stairway Room and the First Floor Back Stairway Room.

In 1996 there was a large round table in the center of the First Floor Back Stairway Room. This table was pushed at times near to the safe and the door on the room's west wall. Between 1978 to 1996 Kathleen would eat her meals on this table. Between 1978 and 1996, Kathleen and her family did not use the exit door located on this room's east wall. They would use the exit door in the kitchen to exit the Hays House to the back porch.

Mel Meter Base Readings, First Floor, Back Stairway Room, Hays House, Thursday, 17 November 2016.

The interior side of the door leading to the hallway on the room's West wall.

The electromagnetic frequency was range 0.1 mG to 0.7 mG.

The temperature range was 69.7°F to 70.8°F.

The electrical outlet on the room's South wall. This electrical outlet is not in use.

The electromagnetic frequency range was 2.5 mG to 3.4 mG.

The temperature range was 70.2°F to 72.0°F.

The light switch on the room's North wall. This light switch in the off position.

The electromagnetic frequency range was 0.0 mG to 0.0 mG.

The temperature range was 70 .5°F to 71.5°F.

The lamp on the white Wooden bookshelf located on the room's East wall. This lamp is not in use.

The electromagnetic frequency range was 0.0 mG to 0.0 mG.

The temperature range was 71.0°F to 71.5°F.

The extension cord on the floor, located on the room's North East corner. This extension cord is in use.

The electromagnetic frequency range was 0.0 mG to 0.0 mG.

The temperature range was 70.4°F to 70.8°F.

The Rhnai thermostat on the room's East wall. This thermostat is in use.

The electromagnetic frequency range was 0.0 mG to 0.0 mG.

The temperature range was 73.1°F to 74.2°F.

The light switch to the left side of the back door, located on the room's East wall. This light switch is in the on position.

The electromagnetic frequency range was 0.0 mG to 0.0 mG.

The temperature range was 71.4°F to 72.2°F.

Paranormal Investigation, Session 1, First Floor Back Stairway Room, Hays House, Friday, 7th April 2017.

I feel like this room may be more important then I may know at this time. It seems like a small room like this may only be used as a hallway to get to the rear door, the Den room, First Floor Stairway Room, back stairway, and kitchen. At the time I am starting this paranormal investigation, session 1. I do not know the history on how this room was furnished and or how it was used by the families that had lived here prior to the present owner. Since the present family has the home up for sale, is very important that I obtained all of my paranormal investigations sessions one and two in each room before the Hays House is sold.

12:50 PM Keith: "Hello, I am Keith Evans. If you would like to talk, you may use your energy to choose words from the Ovilus IV's database. The, Ovilus IV will not hurt you. This is the Ovilus IV." (Hold it up.)

12:51 PM Keith: "This is the Mel Meter. The Mel Meter measures temperature and electromagnetic frequencies. The Mel Meter will not harm you." (Hold it up.)

12:51 PM Keith: "The Ovilus for has given me three background words: force which is spelled F-O-R-C-E, embark which is spelled E-M-B-A-R-K, and Captain which is spelled C-A-P-T-A-I-N. The words force and embark were pronounced by the Ovilus IV at a normal conversational level and speed. The word captain was pronounced by the Ovilus IV at a louder than normal conversational level and at a faster than normal conversational speed."

12:52 PM Keith: "I have observed the Mel Meter readings to be 0.0 mG and 65.2°F."

12:54 PM Keith: "The Ovilus IV has given me the word idle which is spelled I-D-L-E. The word idle was pronounced by the Ovilus IV at a normal conversational level and speed."

12:54 PM Keith: "I have observed the Mel Meter readings to be 0.0 mG and 64.8°F."

12:56 PM Keith: "My nickname was Captain when I went to UCF. Did you know me when I went to UCF?"

12:58 PM Keith: "Can you elaborate on the word force and embark?"

12:59 PM Keith: "What is the name of the person that said the word idle?

1 PM Keith: "What is the name of the person that showed me where the back stairway used to come out towards where I am setting, in the middle of the room?"

1:02 PM Keith: "The Ovilus IV gave me the word British which is spelled B-R-I-T-I-S-H. The word British was pronounced by the Ovilus IV at a normal conversational level and speed."

1:02 PM Keith: "I have observed the Mel Meter readings to be 0.0 mG and 65.7°F."

1:04 PM Keith: "Are you British?"

1:05 PM Keith: "What is your name?"

1:06 PM Keith: "My name is Keith Evans."

1:07 PM Keith: "I am going to scan the room with my thermal imager."

1:07 PM to 1:09 PM Keith: "I obtained the following thermal images in the First Floor Back Stairway Room. I obtained two pictures of the cleaning cloth draped over the bucket on the table near the back stairways along the room's North wall. The thermal imager's laser was aimed at the cloth draped over the bucket. I obtained temperatures between the range of 55.2°F to 55.9°F. I obtained two pictures of the back stairway while I was standing near the back door. While obtaining the last two pictures, the laser pointer was aimed at the North wall, near the first floor back-stair way. I did not see anything unusual and or Paranormal while I was taking these thermal images."

1:10 PM Keith: "I observed the Mel Meter readings to be 0.0 mG and 65.4°F."

1:11 PM Keith: "Pat are you here today?"

1:12 PM Keith: "Kathleen, what type of furniture did you have in this little room here? What I call the First Floor Back Stairway Room."

1:13 PM Keith: "Kathleen, when you lived here was the ceiling light right there were the two little holes are in the ceiling?" (I am pointing to the ceiling.)

1:14 PM Keith: "The Ovilus IV gave me the word Chloride which is spelled C-H-L-O-R-I-D-E. The Ovilus IV pronounced the word chloride at a normal level and speed, but the voice was gargled."

1:15 PM Keith: "I have observed the Mel Meter readings to be 0.0 mG and 65.2°F."

1:16 PM Keith: "The Ovilus IV gave me the words logical which is spelled L-O-G-I-C-A-L, and deal which is spelled D-E-A-L. The Ovilus IV pronounce the words logical and deal at a normal conversational level and speed."

1:16 PM Keith: "I have observed the Mel Meter readings to be 0.0 mG and 65.7°F."

1:16 PM Keith: "Someone is hammering next door."

1:20 PM Keith: "Is your voice gargled because you were exposed to a chemical agent?"

1:21 PM Keith: "It sounded like someone dragging something across the ground."

1:22 PM Keith: "There is that dragging sound again."

1:23 PM Keith: "That was the people next door talking."

1:24 PM Keith: "What is the logical deal? I said hello to two guests."

1:25 PM Keith: "Sunshine, are you here today?"

1:26 PM Keith: "Sunshine, please grade my English."

1:27 PM Keith: "It looks like the Ovilus IV is frozen up again. So, I am going to manually turn off the Ovilus IV for a couple of minutes."

1:28 PM to 1:29 PM Keith: "I can hear the next-door neighbors talking."

1:29 PM Keith: "I am turning the Ovilus IV back on. Because I do not believe that the batteries are dead."

1:30 PM Keith: "The Ovilus IV gave me to background words Brad which is spelled B-R-A-D, and explain which is spelled E-X-P-L-A-I-N. The Ovilus IV has pronounced the words Brad and explain at a normal conversational level and speed."

1:30 PM Keith: "I have observed the Mel Meter readings to be 0.0 mG and 65.9°F."

1:31 PM Keith: "The Ovilus IV gave me the word, rent which is spelled R-E-N-T. The Ovilus IV pronounced the word, rent, at a normal conversational level and speed."

1:31 PM Keith: "I have observed the Mel Meter readings to be 0.0 mG and 65.6°F"

1:33 PM Keith: "I hear people talking upstairs and one person walking down the front stair way. One person has exited out through the front door."

1:34 PM Keith: "That is my stomach growling constantly."

1:38 PM Keith: "The front door opened due to the wind, so I had to close front door."

1:39 PM Keith: "That is my stomach growling again."

1:40 PM to 1:41 PM Keith: "That is my stomach constantly growling."

1:42 PM Keith: "That is people talking next door."

1:43 PM Keith: "How can you do a paranormal investigation under these circumstances."

1:44 PM Keith: "Thank you for talking to me. Have a nice day."

1:44 PM Keith: "This session 1 ended on Friday, 7th, April 2017."

Paranormal Investigation, Session 2, First Floor, Back Stairway Room, Hays House, Friday, 7th April 2017.

2:52 PM Keith: "Hello, I am Keith Evans. This is the Ovilus IV. You may use your energy to choose words from the Ovilus IV. The Ovilus IV will not hurt you." (Hold it up.)

2:53 PM Keith: "This is the Mel Meter. The Mel Meter measures temperature and electromagnetic frequencies. The Mel Meter will not harm you." (Hold it up.)

254 Keith: "The Ovilus IV has given me for background words fast and back to back. I could not understand what the first word was and I do not have any picture of the first and second words. I have a picture of the third and fourth words. The word index which is spelled I-N-D-E-X, dig which is spelled D-I-G, and New Moon which is spelled N-E-W M-O-O-N. The last four words were pronounced by the Ovilus IV at a normal conversational level, but at a faster than normal conversational speed."

2:54 PM Keith: "I have observed the Mel Meter readings to be 0.0 mG and 65.7°F."

2:56 PM Keith: "The Ovilus IV gave me the word cupcake which is spelled C-U-P-C-A-K-E. The Ovilus IV pronounced the word cupcake at a normal conversational level and speed."

2:57 PM Keith: "I have observed the Mel Meter readings to be 0.0 mG and 66.1°F."

2:58 PM Keith: "The Ovilus IV gave me the word hammer which is spelled H-A-M-M-E-R. The Ovilus IV pronounced the word hammer so fast that all I heard was a "S" sound."

2:58 PM Keith: "I have observed the Mel Meter readings to be 0.0 mG and 66.3°F."

3:02 PM Keith: "The words index, dig, new moon, cupcake, and hammer, it sounds like you want to put me to work?"

3:03 PM Keith: "During session 1, I got the words Brad and explained. Brad what you mean by explain?"

3:04 PM Keith: "Amy's husband, Andrew came home and walked into the frame where I was taping with my two camcorders to say hello and shake my hand."

3:04 PM Keith: "I waved to Jill the cat who is in the First Floor Front Stairway Room looking at me."

3:10 PM Keith: "I have observed the Mel Meter readings to be 0.0 mG and 67.2°F."

3:10 PM Keith: "Due to the house being so busy and the First Floor Back Stairway Room is a common area hallway which is readily used. I am going to discontinue session 2 for today and resume session 2 tomorrow."

Continued Paranormal Investigation, Session 2, First Floor Back Stairway Room, Hays House, Saturday, 8th April 2017.

1:59 PM Keith: "The Ovilus IV has given me two background words; become which is spelled B-E-C-A-M-E, and dollar which is spelled D-O-L-L-A-R. The Ovilus IV has pronounced the words become and dollar at a normal conversational level and speed."

1:59 PM Keith: "I have observed the Mel Meter readings to be 0.0 mG and 66.0°F."

2 PM Keith: "The Ovilus IV has given me the word bottom which is spelled B-O-T-T-O-M. The word bottom was pronounced by the Ovilus IV in a normal conversational level and speed."

2:01 PM Keith: "I have observed the Mel Meter readings to be 0.0 mG and 66.7°F."

2:02 PM Keith: "The Ovilus IV has given me the word year which is spelled Y-E-A-R. The word year was pronounced by the Ovilus IV at a normal conversational level and speed."

2:02 PM Keith: "I have observed the Mel Meter readings to be 0.0 mG and 66.5°F."

2:07 PM Keith: "Became, dollar, bottom, year, Pat, what do you mean by that."

2:08 PM Keith: "Pat, in 1926 the housing market fell and the bank had problems with people giving the property back to the bank's."

2:10 PM Keith: "The Ovilus for gave me two words angry which is spelled A-N-G-E-R-Y, and Witch which is spelled W-I-T-C-H. The Ovilus IV pronounced the words angry so fast that I cannot understand what had been said. The Ovilus IV pronounced the word angry lower than a normal conversational level and faster than normal conversational speed."

2:10 PM Keith: "I have observed the Mel Meter readings to be 0.0 mG and 66.6°F."

2:10 PM Keith: "I have observed the Mel Meter readings to be 0.0 mG and 66.9°F."

2:15 PM Keith: "That is the dog barking upstairs. Poochie dog it's okay. It is me downstairs doing the Paranormal Investigations."

2:16 PM Keith: "Pat, I can understand that you were angry about the housing collapse in 1926 and the Great Depression in 1930."

2:17 PM Keith: "That is the next-door neighbor talking to my right."

2:19 PM Keith: "Who said the word Witch?"

2:20 PM Keith: "Are you a witch?"

2:21 PM Keith: "I'm not a Witch, but I am a Paranormal Investigator."

2:22 PM Keith: "Pat, what can you tell me about the housing collapse here in Florida in the 1920s?"

2:23 PM Keith: "Pat, what can you tell me about the Great Depression?"

2:24 PM Keith: "The Ovilus IV is frozen up again with two dots on its upper left-hand side of its display. The Ovilus IV will not go back to the home position. I am going to turn the Ovilus IV off for two minutes and turn it back on. Yesterday, the Ovilus IV was working fine without having to add new batteries."

2:25 PM Keith: "I am going to complete a thermal scan of the First-floor Back Stairway Room."

To 2:26 PM to 2:28 PM Keith: "I obtained the following thermal images; two images of the North wall behind the back stairway, two images of the table with no cleaning cloth, and eight images of my mirror image against the interior kitchen door. Concerning the eight pictures of my mirror image against the interior kitchen door, four images were taken far back, two images were taken close up, and two images were taken close up, with my legs wide apart."

2:30 PM Keith: "I see an image of a person that is pink. This images temperature is between 62.0°F to 63.0°F."

2:32 PM Keith: "The person and pink image that I am looking at is a mirror image of me coming off of the interior first floor kitchen door. I cannot explain this."

2:33 PM Keith: "Yesterday, while I was using the FLIR TG-165, I did not obtain any mirror image of myself on the interior kitchen door."

3:37 PM Keith: "I did not have time to turn the Ovilus IV back on during this session 2."

2:38 PM Keith: "Thank you for talking to me. Have a good day."

2:38 PM Keith: "I have observed the Mel Meter readings to be 0.0 mG and 66.2°F."

2:38 PM Keith: "This continued session 2 ended on Saturday, 8th, April 2017."

The analysis of the Paranormal Investigation, Session 1, First Floor Back Stairs Room, Hays House, Friday, 7th April 2017. The date analyzed was Sunday, 18th June 2017.

At 12:51 PM the Ovilus IV gave me the first three words of Session 1. These words are background words and they are force, embark, and Captain. The Ovilus IV pronounced these three words, at a loud level and a fast speed. It was almost like someone was given a military order while training for combat or possibly in combat. The background words are coming from the Ovilus IV's ability to measure the background energy in the environment. I had not asked any questions yet during this Session 1, so these three background words are not in response to any questions that I have asked. When I worked for parking services at UCF my nickname was Captain, but I do not feel that there's any connection here.

At 12:54 PM the Ovilus IV gave me the fourth word of this Session 1, idle. I have not asked any questions yet during this Session 1, so this word, idle, is not in response to any questions that I have asked.

At 1:02 PM the Ovilus IV gave me the fifth word of this Session 1, British. The word British may be responding to the question I asked at 12:58 PM, can you elaborate on the word force and embark? This may have been a ghost or spirit of a British soldier speaking when the Ovilus IV was reading the energy in the environment and picking up the background words force, embark, and Captain.

At 1:14 PM the Ovilus IV gave me the sixth word of this Session 1, chloride. The word chloride was spoken with a gargled or unclear sound. I do not feel that the word chloride is in response to any of the questions I have asked so far during this session number one. The ghosts or spirits voice might be gargled or unclear due to the exposure to chlorine gas. I know that during World War I soldiers in Europe were exposed to chloride gas.

At 1:16 PM the Ovilus IV gave me the seventh and eighth words of this Session 1, logical, and deal. Logical could be responding to the question, not I asked, at 1:13 PM, Kathleen, when you lived here was the ceiling light right there were the two little holes are in the ceiling? Kathleen may be responding with, that is logical. A yes or no would be a more direct answer. I do not feel that the word deal is in response to any of the questions that I have asked so far during this Session 1.

At 1:27 PM I noticed that the Ovilus IV was frozen up. When there is a lot of paranormal activity. It seems like the ghosts, and or spirits like to drain the batteries within the Ovilus IV. The ghost or spirits will interfere with the batteries, and somehow stop the Ovilus IV from being able to properly function. So sometimes just turning the Ovilus IV off and turn it back on will break the hold that the ghost or spirit has on the Ovilus IV and then the energy from the batteries will be allowed to properly allow the Ovilus IV to function. After turning the obelisk for back on. It gave me the following background words.

At 1:30 PM the Ovilus IV gave me the ninth and 10th words of this session one, Brad and explain. I do not know anyone with the first name Brad that is connected with the Hays house and or had ever lived at the Hayes house. That doesn't mean that there was not a Brad who was somehow associated with the Hays house, it just means that I don't know of one yet. I do not feel that the word explain is in response to any of the questions that I have asked so far during this Session 1.

At 1:31 PM the Ovilus IV gave me the 11th word of this Session 1, rent. I do not feel that the word rent is in response to any of the questions that I have asked so far during this Session 1.

There were a lot of interruptions and noise during this Session 1. Session 1 was conducted in a common area, which is used as a hallway, and which I call the First Floor Back Stairway Room. It is likely that the ghosts and spirits are distracted by the activities going on in the other rooms of the Hays House. I feel that noise, and other distractions within the Hays House may contribute to ghosts and spirits not responding to the questions that I have asked during this Session 1.

The analysis of the Paranormal Investigation, Session 2, First Floor, Back Stairway Room, Hays House, Friday, 7th April 2017. The date analyzed was Monday, 19th June 2017.

At 2:54 PM the Ovilus IV gave me the first four words of the Session 2. The four words are given fast and back to back. I cannot understand what the first word was and I was unable to get a picture of the first word. The second, third and fourth words. I did obtain pictures and those background words were index, dig, and New Moon. The Ovilus IV pronounced the words index, dig, and New Moon at a normal conversational level but at a much faster speed than normal conversational speed. I had not asked any questions yet during Session 2. So, the words that I have received via the Ovilus IV cannot be answering any of the questions that I have asked.

At 2:56 PM the Ovilus IV gave me the fifth word of this Session 2, cupcake. I had not asked any questions yet during Session 2. Therefore, the words that I have received via the Ovilus IV cannot be answering any questions that I have asked.

At 2:58 PM the Ovilus IV gave me the sixth word of this Session 2, hammer. The Ovilus IV pronounced the word hammer so fast and low that all I heard was an "S" sound. I had not asked any questions yet during Session 2. Therefore, the words that I have received via the Ovilus IV cannot be answering any of the questions that I have asked.

Due to the amount of individual traffic in the hallway, I decided to discontinue Session 2 until Saturday, 8th, April 2017.

Continuing the analysis of the Paranormal Investigation, Session 2, First Floor, Back Stairs Room, Hays House, Saturday, 8th April 2017. The date analyzed was Monday, 19th June 2017.

At 1:59 PM the Ovilus IV gave me the seventh and eighth background words of this Session 2, become and dollar. I have not asked any questions yet during session 2. Therefore, the words that I have received via the Ovilus IV cannot be answering any of the questions that I have asked. I feel that this is the intelligent spirit of Jeff Buck, and he is telling me that he became a dollar. A slang word for dollar is a buck. Sometime before 1900, Jeff Belin changed his last name to Buck, after having an estate dispute with his family. It is also believed that Jeff buck passed away at the Hays House in 1922. On the eighth day of April 2017, while I was conducting the session 2 paranormal investigation. I did not yet know that Jeff buck had earlier changed his last name, so these words did not have any meaning to any of the questions that I had been asking throughout my earlier paranormal sessions. It just goes to show that the better history one has on the family and the people that lived in the house where you're doing the paranormal research, the words you receive will have a higher probability of having some meaning.

At 2 PM the Ovilus IV gave me the ninth word of this Session 2, bottom. I have not asked any questions yet during Session 2. Therefore, the word that I have received via the Ovilus IV cannot be answering any of the questions that I have asked.

At 2:02 PM the Ovilus IV gave me the 10th word of this Session 2, year. I have not asked any questions yet during Session 2. Therefore, the word that I have received via the Ovilus IV cannot be answering any of the questions that I have asked. If I were to connect the words bottom of the year, I could draw the conclusion that a ghost and or spirit is referring to the month of December as the bottom of the year.

At 2:10 PM the Ovilus IV gave me the 11th and 12th words of this Session 2, angry and witch. At 2:08 PM I asked Pat the question in 1926 the housing market fell and the banks have problems with people giving the mortgaged property back. I feel that the word angry is an intelligent response from Pat Hays as he shows his feelings towards the 1926 housing market fall. I do not feel that the word, witch is in response to any of the questions I've asked so for during this Session 2. The words, angry, and witch, may be Jeff Buck who is angry and is blaming a witch for his family having to give the Hays House back to the Apalachicola State Bank shorting after his death in August 28th 1922.

At 2:24 PM the Ovilus IV had frozen up again, with two white dots displayed on its upper left-hand corner. The Ovilus IV will not return to the home position. I do not believe that the batteries had been totally drained. I felt that somehow the ghosts and or spirits were just interfering with the flow of energy which causes the Ovilus IV to freeze up and not function properly. So, I have decided to turn the Ovilus IV off manually for two minutes and then I will turn it. I feel that the Ghosts and or Spirits are trying so hard to communicate with me that they are inadvertently drawing the energy from the four AAA batteries within the Ovilus IV.

At 2:26 PM to 2:28 PM I scanned the room with my thermal imager. I obtained eight images of my mirror image reflected on to the interior kitchen door. I cannot explain why my mirror image was reflected on to this interior door that leads to the first-floor kitchen. While I completed a thermal scan of this same room one day prior, I did not see any reflected thermal image of myself on the interior kitchen door. This door does not seem to have any type of high glossy white paint. I proved to myself that it was a reflective image by moving up close to the door. As I move closer to the door, my image became larger. As I spread my legs far apart the image on the interior kitchen door did the same. So, it was definitely my image being reflected on to the interior kitchen door. The pink image that I saw on the interior kitchen door was showing a temperature between 62.0°F and 63.0°F.

At 2:38 PM, Session 2 ended and I had not had time to turn the Ovilus IV back on.

After this session 2, I felt physically drained more so then usual. I always feel somewhat emotional and physically drain after all of my Paranormal Investigations. This time was different, I was getting good Paranormal evidence and should have continued on once I noticed that I had not turned the Ovilus IV back on. I was just to physically drained and I wanted to lay down and sleep. I did not have time to sleep, so instead I did what I always do after an hour long Paranormal Investigation. I spend another hour saving my evidence and labeling each folder. I transfer the footage from the two video camcorders into two separate folders and labeled each within my computer. I saved the digital and thermal pictures into two separate folders and labeled each within my computer. Sometimes I regret not spending more time on this Paranormal Investigation. As the older people would say back in the 1960's, tomorrow is another day.

Digital Pictures, First Floor Back Stairway Room, Hays House, Thursday, 17th, November 2016.

Two pictures of the room's West wall.

Two pictures of the room's Northeast corner.

Eight pictures of the room's North wall.

Six pictures of the room's ceiling.

Four pictures of the door on the room's West wall.

Two pictures of the room's Southwest corner.

Six pictures of the doorknob on the door located on the room's West wall.

Six pictures of the room's floorboard trim.

Four pictures of the room's horizontal wallboards.

Two pictures of the room's Northeast corner.

Four pictures of the room's North wall.

Four pictures of the door on the room's North wall.

Eight pictures of the back stairway.

Four pictures of the horizontal wallboards, located on the room's North wall.

Two pictures of the room's Southwest corner.

Two pictures of the ceiling trim, located at the room's Southwest corner.

Eight pictures of the doorknob on the room's North wall.

Six pictures of the threshold board from the door on the room's North wall.

Four pictures of the floor trim near the door on the room's North wall.

Two pictures of the room's East wall.

Five pictures of the room's ceiling.

Two pictures of the room's East wall.

Four pictures of the room's South East corner.

Four pictures of the room's Southwest corner.

Four pictures of the room's South wall.

10 pictures of the room's back stair way.

Two pictures of the room's South wall.

Two pictures of the room's North wall.

Two pictures of the rooms hardwood floor.

Two pictures of the threshold board, for the rear door.

Six pictures of the floor trim near the rear door.

Two pictures of the threshold floorboard between the first-floor back stairway room and the first-floor front stairway room.

15 pictures of the door, and wall board trim between the first-floor back stairway room and the first-floor front stairway room.

Please see the author's website at www.keithoevans.com to view each digital picture.

Thermal Images of the First Floor Back Stairway Room, Hays House, Thursday, 17th November 2016.

One image with orange area at the top left interior center of the room's West wall.

One image of dark blue two legs, body, and a head, right bottom of the image, room's Northwest corner.

One image of the back-stair way view, room's North West corner.

One image of the room's North wall.

One image of an orange and yellow light, located on the center right side of the image on the room's ceiling.

One image of the right side of the window room's North East corner.

One image of the left side of the window and the right side of the door on the room's East wall.

One image of the left side of the door on the room's South East corner.

One image of the bottom and center of the door on the room's South wall.

One image of the room's Southwest corner.

Two images of the back-stair way in the room's Northwest corner.

Two close up images of the third step in the room's North West corner.

Two images of the back-stair way in the room's Northwest corner.

Three close up images of the spatula and the room's Northwest corner.

Two close up images of the fifth step in the room's North West corner.

Please see the author's website at www.keithoevans.com to view each thermal image.

CHAPTER 10

Sunshine Room, Hays House, Ghosts are People too.

Description of the Sunshine Room, Hays House, Wednesday, 2nd November 2016.

Along the room's North wall is a brown wooding home entertainment center. The room's North wall also has the original white wooden door with five sunken panels. The room's North wall has various size paintings, mounted on the wall.

Brass or Metal Door Knob & Skeleton Key Base Plate, North wall, The Sunshine Room.

The room's East wall has a small closet near the Northeast corner of the room. The room's East wall has a fireplace mantle with a black iron cover over the fireplace. This black iron cover is embossed with an image of a lady climbing a tree. There is a door way opening that leads to Frances Room which is located on the room's East wall near the room's South East corner. There is a bed along the room's East wall.

The Fire Place Mantle, East wall, The Sunshine Room.

The room's South wall has four windows. All the windows have a top and a bottom section with each section having two glass panels. These four windows appear to be original, and most of these windows have the original brass handgrips on the left and right sides at the bottom of the lower half sections. Along the room's South wall there are two blue cloth covered chairs and an antique chest of drawers with a mirror mounted on the wall.

The room's West wall has two original windows. All of these windows have a top and bottom section with two glass panes in each section.

Each window has the brass handgrips located at the bottom of the lower section. Along the room's West wall is a wooden table and a stand-a-lone lamp. There are various size paintings, mounted on the West wall.

A description of the Sunshine Room from four pictures taken in 1996.

I will be observing four pictures taken in sunshine's room. In 1996 to describe this room starting with the room's South wall and continuing around in a clockwise direction. The South wall has four Windows that are covered with white curtains. Along the room's South wall is an antique dark wooden chest of drawers with a large mirror that stands approximately 9 feet tall and has decorative designs and a large scallop shell carved into the top center of the trim around the mirror. On top of this piece of furniture are the following items a hairbrush, a handheld mirror, and for white porcelain items. In front of the chest of drawers is an antique wooden stool with a golden textile covered seat. There are antique wooden chairs on each side of the chest of drawers.

Along the room's West wall starting from left to right, is an antique stand-a-lone oval shaped full left wooden mirror. Next to the left side of the bed is an antique wooden night stand. On top of this nightstand is a golden lamp with a white glass covered shade, four candy dishes, one looks to be white porcelain, one candy dish is red and two of the candy dishes are clear glass. Next to the nightstand is an antique bed with a Tiger striped wooden head and footboard. This bed is covered with a white bedspread and has five pillows, to the pillows are under the bedspread, two pillows are golden, and the center top pillow is a multicolored. The headboard stands about 9-foot-tall and has a large scallop shell carved at the very top center of the headboard. In the middle and center of the headboard is a bust of a carving of a bust of a human. The head of the bed covers most of the two Windows on the room's West wall. Part of the right window can be seen in this one photo and the window is covered with white curtains. To the right side of the bed is a small antique wooden three-legged stand with an approximately 12 inch round white marble top.

On the room's North wall and near the Northwest corner of the room is another matching piece of furniture, an antique dark wooden armoire with two doors on each side. Both doors are covered with a full-length mirror. In the center of the armoire is a vertical row of five narrow drawers. At the top half of this narrow area between the two doors is a narrow door covered with a mirror. This piece of furniture, stands at least 9-foot-tall with decorative wooden trim covering its front to include a large scallop shell at the top center of the armoire. As I am observing a photo which is showing me the South East corner of this room and moving from left to right on the room's East wall. There is a fireplace with its original white wooden fireplace mantle. The opening around the fireplace is covered with white and light blue tiles. On the fireplace mantle's shelf is one golden lamp decorated with clear crystals and this lamp has a clear or white glass lamp shade. To the right of the fireplace and at about 3 feet in height is an electrical outlet. To the right side of the fireplace is a light colored wooden antique matching deaths and chair, both with a heart-shaped mirror. So, one could look in the mirror that is mounted onto the desk and see the back of their head from the mirror that is mounted on the back of the chair. On top of the desks are three white porcelain items.

This room has a golden assembly system of lights hanging down from the center of the ceiling with four light bulbs that are covered with white glass lamp shades. Each wall in this room has the original tongue and groove horizontal wallboards that are painted light blue. The wall and the ceiling trim boards are original and painted either a light blue or white. The room's ceiling is covered with the original tongue and groove boards that are painted white and are running in an East to West direction.

Some back-ground history about Sunshine's Room and Mary Ella Gibson (Sunshine).

Sunshine Gibson had a nice decorative light colored wooden bedroom set that Frances, Sunshine's nice, still has as of 2017. I was told that the head board of Sunshine's bed was against the room's west wall. This head board had covered parts of the lower half of the two west wall windows.

On the east wall is the original wooden fire place and the black iron fireplace cover with the embossed image of a lady climbing a tree. This black iron insert cover was there in 1942.

Miss Mary Ella Gibson, (Sunshine), was a member of the Tuesday afternoon bridge club. Sunshine enjoyed playing bridge every Tuesday from the 1920s, up until the 1950s. On many occasions she would host the Tuesday bridge club meeting at the location where she was living.

Miss Mary Ella Gibson, (Sunshine), frequently visited her sister Mrs. C. Bryan Palmer, (Annie) for the weekend at her home in Tallahassee, Florida.

Miss Mary Ella Gibson, (Sunshine), may have been a member of the Philaco club. On Thursday afternoon November 4, 1937 at the Philaco club meeting at the community house. With Mrs. Byron D. Morris, Pres. and Mrs. Mildred Davis, Vice President, Miss Mary Ella Gibson read the poem, "Waukeenah's Save". An ice cours was served at the social hour. J. P. Coombs, Jerome Sheip, L. D. Walters, and Clyde Brown were present.

On Tuesday, 2nd November 1937, Miss Mary Ella Gibson was the hostess for the Tuesday Afternoon Bridge Club.

On Tuesday, 16th November 1937, the Tuesday Afternoon Bridge Club meet at the home of Mrs. John Marshall Jr. Miss Mary Ella Gibson was in attendance.

Miss. Mary Ella Gibson, (Sunshine), accompanied her brother-in-law and sister, Mr. and Mrs. C Bryant Palmer of Tallahassee to New Orleans for the weekend and returned to Apalachicola on Monday, 8th November 1937.

Reverin F. E. Steinmeyer and Mrs. Steinmeyer of Madison, Florida, were the guests of Miss Mary Ella Gibson during the District Conference of the Methodist Church held during the first week of December 1937.

Miss Mary Ella Gibson, (Sunshine), was a member of the woman's auxiliary for the Methodist Church. On Monday afternoon 6th December 1937, in the churches auditorium following the business meeting, the annual election of officers was held and Miss Mary Ella Gibson was elected to serve as treasurer for 1937 to 1938.

On Tuesday, at three o'clock, 7th December 1937, the Tuesday Afternoon Bridge Club meet at the home of Mrs. L. D. Walton. Miss Mary Ella Gibson was in attendance.

On Monday, 13th December 1937, Miss Mary Ella Gibson return home from a weekend visit with relatives in Tarpon Springs and St. Petersburg, Florida.

On Monday, at three o'clock, 27th December 1938, the Woman's Missionary Society of the Methodist Church had their monthly business meeting. Miss Mary Ella Gibson who is a member of Mary Fowler's Circle, was in attendance.

On Tuesday, 4th December 1938, Miss Mary Ella Gibson was the hostess for the Tuesday Afternoon Bridge Club. Mrs. E. R. Hays joined the club for tea.

On Monday afternoon, 6th June 1938, the Methodist Auxiliary met at the Church. The President Mrs. A. B. Ham and twenty-five members were in attendance to include Miss Mary Ella Gibson.

On Tuesday, 7th June 1938, the Tuesday Afternoon Bridge Club meet at the home of Mrs. J. H. Cook. Miss Mary Ella Gibson was in attendance.

On Friday, 10th June 1938, Miss Gwendolyn Gibson of Jacksonville, Florida graduated from Robert E. Lee High School. Her Aunt Mary Ella Gibson was present.

On the second weekend in December 1938, Miss Mary Ella Gibson went to Jacksonville, Florida to visit Mrs. Harry Gibson, Miss Alice Rose, Gwendolyn Gibson, and Harry Gibson Jr.

On Wednesday, 28th December 1938, Author Gibson of Tarpon Springs arrived in Apalachicola, Florida to visit Miss Mary Ella Gibson.

During the 1938 Christmas Holidays Mrs. Jason Sykes and daughter Louis of Tarpon Springs, Florida, Miss Alice Rose, Gwendolyn Gibson and Harry Gibson of Jacksonville, Florida, were the guests of Miss Mary Ella Gibson.

On Sunday, 19th February 1939, Miss Mary Ella Gibson returned to her home in Apalachicola, Florida, from her trip to Atlanta Georgia, and Tarpon Springs, Florida.

On Tuesday, 17th October 1939, the Tuesday Afternoon Bridge Club meet at the home of Mr. J. P. Coombs for the first time since early Summer. Mrs. Elizabeth Porter Coombs was the hostess. Miss Mary Ella Gibson was in attendance.

Arthur B. Gibson and granddaughters Miss Louise Sykes and Mary Ann Ziegler of Tarpon Springs Florida and Mr. and Mrs. C. Bryan Palmer of Tallahassee, Florida, arrived on Wednesday, 22nd November 1939 to spend the Thanks Giving Holidays with Mr. and Mrs. Edward Hays and Miss Mary Ella Gibson.

During the last week of November 1939, the members of the Philaco Club assisted with a Banquet. The following members of the Philaco Club assisted with this Banquet: Mrs. Elizabeth Coombs, Mrs. Percy Coombs, Miss Mary Ella Gibson, and Mrs. S. E. Montgomery.

On New Year's Day, Monday, 1st January 1940, Mr. and Mrs. Frank Ziegler and their little daughter Mary Ann, Mrs. James N. Sykes, and Louise Sykes of Tarpon Springs, Florida and Mr. and Mrs. C. Bryan Palmer of Tallahassee, Florida, were the guests of Miss Mary Ella Gibson, and Mr. and Mrs. Edward Ryan Hays.

During the first week of January 1940 Miss Peba Byrd of Columbus, Georgia visited Miss Mary Ella Gibson.

On Monday, 8th January 1940 at 3:30 PM the Woman's Missionary Society of the Methodist Auxiliary met at the Methodist Church. Miss

Mary Ella Gibson who is a member of Mary Fowler's Circle, was in attendance.

On Tuesday, 25th November 1941, the Tuesday Afternoon Bridge Club meet at the home of Mrs. John Marshall Jr. Miss Mary Ella Gibson and Miss Elizabeth Coombs were in attendance.

On Wednesday, 26th November 1941, Mary Ella Gibson and Little Miss Patsy Ann Hays left for a trip to Tallahassee, Florida, where they joined Mr. and Mrs. Bryan Palmer, and they all travel to Tarpon Springs, Florida to spend the Thanksgiving Holiday with Mr. and Mrs. Arthur Gibson.

On Tuesday, 16th December 1941, the Tuesday Afternoon Bridge Club meet at the home of Mrs. J. B. Spear. Miss Mary Ella Gibson, Miss Elizabeth Coombs, Mr. and Mrs. Edward Ryan Hays were in attendance.

The Mel Meter base readings, the Sunshine Room, Wednesday, 2nd November 2016, Hays House

10:15 AM The light switch on the room's north wall, by the room's entrance. The light switches are in the off position.

The electromagnetic frequency range was 0.0 mG to 0.0 mG.

The temperature range was 72.1°F to 72.6°F.

10:15 AM The mounted left side East wall light. This light is off.

The electromagnetic frequency range was 0.0 mG to 0.0 mG.

The temperature range was 71.9°F to 72.1°F.

10:16 AM The mounted right side East wall light, on the right side of the bed. This light is off.

The electromagnetic frequency range was 0.0 mG to 0.0 mG.

The temperature range was 70.9°F to 71.3°F.

10:16 AM The lamp along the room's East wall, on the left side of the bed. This lamp is off.

The electromagnetic frequency was 0.0 mG to 0.1 mG.

The temperature range was 72.7°F to 72.9°F.

10:17 AM The electrical outlet on the room's East wall. This electrical outlet is not in use.

The electromagnetic frequency was 0.0 mG to 0.0 mG.

The temperature range was 71.1°F to 71.9°F.

10:17 AM The lamp along the room's East wall, on the right side of the bed. This lamp is not in use.

The electromagnetic frequency range was 0.0 mG to 0.0 mG.

The temperature range was 72.1°F to 72.6°F.

10:18 AM The electrical outlet on the room's South wall. This electrical outlet is not in use.

The electromagnetic frequency range was 18.5 mG to 39.9 mG.

The temperature range was 72.1°F to 72.9°F.

10:18 AM The ceiling fan. This fan is not on.

The electromagnetic frequency range was 0.0 mG to 0.0 mG.

The temperature range was 72.9°F to 73.1°F.

Paranormal Investigation, Session 1, the Sunshine Room, Saturday, 15 April 2017

11:35 AM Keith: "Hello, I am Keith Evans. You may use your energy to choose words from the Ovilus IV's database. This is the Ovilus IV. The Ovilus IV will not hurt you." (Hold it up.)

11:36 AM Keith: "This is the Mel Meter. The Mel Meter measures temperature and electromagnetic frequencies. The Mel Meter will not hurt you." (Hold it up.)

11:37 AM Keith: "The Ovilus IV has given me two background words: agent which is spelled A-G-E-N-T, and orb which is spelled O-R-B. Agent and orb were both pronounced by the Ovilus IV at a normal conversational level and speed."

11:37 AM Keith: "I have observed the Mel Meter readings to be 0.0 mG and 67.9°F."

11:38 AM Keith: "Sunshine, what do you mean by saying the words agent and orb?"

11:40 AM Keith: "Sunshine, will you talk to me today. I know this was your room when you were alive."

11:41 AM Keith: "The Ovilus IV has given me the word mini which is spelled M-I-N-I. Mini was pronounced by the Ovilus IV at a normal conversational level and speed."

11:41 AM Keith: "I have observed the Mel Meter readings to be 0.0 mG and 69.2°F."

11:43 AM Keith: "I have observed the Mel Meter readings to be 0.0 mG and 69.9°F."

1:43 AM Keith: "The Mel Meter has been readings the electromagnetic frequency for a period of time to be back and forth between 0.0 mG and 0.1 mG. When I tried to take a picture of the electromagnetic frequency on the Mel Meters display, the reading for the electromagnetic frequency would return to 0.0 mG."

11:44 AM Keith: "It is okay Sunshine, if you want to be close to the Mel Meter. The Ovilus IV is the piece of equipment that you will use your energy to talk with me."

11:45 AM Keith: "I have observed the Mel Meter readings to be 0.1 mG and 70.7°F."

11:48 AM Keith: "I have observed the Mel Meter readings to be 0.1 mG and 70.5°F."

11:49 AM Keith: "Sunshine, I am moving the equipment so that the video camera can see the information that the Ovilus IV has given me."

11:49 AM Keith: "The Ovilus IV has given me the word walk which is spelled W-A-L-K. Walk was pronounced by the Ovilus IV at a normal conversational level and speed."

11:50 AM Keith: "I have observed the Mel Meter readings to be 0.1 mG and 70.5°F."

11:50 AM Keith: "I have observed the Mel Meter readings to be 0.0 mG and 70.4°F."

11:50 AM Keith: "The Ovilus IV has given me the word surface which is spelled S-U-R-F-A-C-E. The Ovilus IV has pronounce the word surface with a deep man's voice, at a very low level and slow speed."

11:50 AM Keith: "I have observed the Mel Meter readings to be 0.0 mG and 70.4°F."

11:55 AM Keith: "Mini, walk, surface, what are you trying to tell me Sunshine, and or whoever is trying to talk to me?"

11:56 AM Keith: "Surface, are you asking me a question about why I was taking a picture of the light blue-and-white tile surface around the fireplace and the fireplace cover plate?"

11:58 AM Keith: "I took pictures of the tile and the fireplace cover plate, so that I could write about these items in the book. I hope to include some of these pictures in the book called the Hays House."

12 noon Keith: "Sunshine, when you were alive, how was this fireplace being used?"

12:01 PM Keith: "The Ovilus IV appears to be frozen up."

12:02 PM Keith: "The Ovilus IV will not return to the home position. I am going to replace the four AAA batteries."

12:05 PM Keith: "My camera keeps going in and out of focus. Annie Gibson is that you?"

12:05 PM Keith: "The Ovilus IV did not give me any background words upon turning it on."

12:05 PM Keith: "I have observed the Mel Meter readings to be 0.1 mG and 70.5°F."

12:07 PM Keith: "The Ovilus IV has given me the word answer which is spelled A-N-S-W-E-R. The Ovilus IV has pronounced the word answer in a normal conversational level and speed."

12:07 PM Keith: "I have observed the Mel Meter readings to be 0.1 mG and 71.0°F."

12:07 PM Keith: "Yes I would like an answer."

12:09 PM Keith: "The Ovilus IV has given me the words stay which is spelled S-T-A-Y. The Ovilus IV has pronounce the word stay at a normal conversational level and speed."

12:10 PM Keith: "I observed the Mel Meter readings to be 0.0 mG and 71.5°F."

12:13 PM Keith: "Sunshine, I would like to stay in Apalachicola, but I have to return to Panama City so I may receive the hyper barometric chamber treatments. These treatments will help my toes to heal and help the blood circulation to my feet to improve."

12:16 PM Keith: "Sunshine, I will be in Apalachicola every weekend."

12:17 PM Keith: "Sunshine, is it you or Annie that is increasing the electromagnetic frequency on my Mel Meter from 0.0 up to 0.1 mG?"

12:18 PM Keith: "Sunshine, can you cause the electromagnetic frequency on my Mel Meter to go up to 0.5 mG?"

12:19 PM Keith: "Annie, can you cause the electromagnetic frequency on my Mel Meter to go up to 0.5 mG?"

12:20 PM Keith: "Pat, can you cause the electromagnetic frequency on my Mel Meter to go up to 0.5 mG?"

12:21 PM Keith: "I have obtained nine thermal images in Sunshine's Room. I have obtained images of two purple cold spots on the ceiling near the north wall, and over the entrance door, from two different angles. Both cold areas seem to change in shape and color. The color change from light purple to dark purple. The central air condition for the second floor is on, but the air conditioner vent in this room was not close to these two cold spots. I have obtained two thermal images of this room's Northwest corner, to include walls and ceiling area."

1223 PM Keith: "Pat, a family member saw you in this room shortly after your death."

12:24 PM Keith: "I have observed the Mel Meter readings to be 0.0 mG and 70.2°F."

12:24 PM Keith: "Thank you for talking to me. Have a nice day."

12:24 PM Keith: "This Session 1 ended on Saturday, 15 April 2017."

Paranormal Investigation, Session 2, Sunshine's Room, Saturday, 15 April 2017

2:54 PM Keith: "Hello, I am Keith Evans. This is the Ovilus IV. You may use your energy to choose words from the Ovilus IV's database. The Ovilus IV will not hurt you." (Hold it up.)

2:55 PM Keith: "This is the Mel Meter. The Mel Meter measures temperature and electromagnetic frequencies. The Mel meter will not harm you." (Hold it up.)

2:56 PM Keith: "The Ovilus IV has given me no background words."

2:56 PM Keith: "My digital camera keeps going in and out of focus."

2:57 PM Keith: "I have observed the Mel Meter readings to be 0.0 mG and 72.3°F."

2:58 PM Keith: "The Ovilus IV has given me the word answer which is spelled A-N-S-W-E-R. The Ovilus IV has pronounce the word answer in a normal conversational level and speed."

2:59 PM Keith: "I have observed the Mel Meter readings to be 0.0 mG and 73.2°F."

2:59 PM Keith: "The Ovilus IV has given me the word starve which is spelled S-T-A-R-V-E. The word starve was pronounced by the Ovilus IV in a deep man's whisper type voice and a very slow speed."

3 PM Keith: "I have observed the Mel Meter readings to be 0.0 mG and 74.1°F."

3:03 PM Keith: "I have observed the Mel Meter readings to be 0.1 mG and 74.1°F."

3:04 PM Keith: "Sunshine, yes or no, are you here today."

3:05 PM Keith: "I have observed the Mel Meter readings to be 0.2 mG and 74.4°F."

3:05 PM Keith: "I have observed the Mel Meter readings to be 0.1 mG and 74.4°F."

3:05 PM Keith: "I have observed the Mel Meter readings to be 0.2 mG and 74.4°F."

3:05 PM Keith: "I have observed the Mel meter readings to be 0.2 mG and 74.4°F."

3:06 PM Keith: "Who used this room when the Buck family lived here?"

3:07 PM Keith: "Sunshine, I see that you like to play with my Mel Meter. I noticed that you like to increase the electromagnetic frequency readings from 0.1 mG to 0.2 mG."

3:09 PM Keith: "Sunshine, can you please make the electromagnetic frequency reading on my Mel Meter go up to 0.5 mG? Are you shy or something? As soon as I take the Mel Meter away from the camcorder the electromagnetic frequency reading on my Mel Meter's display increases to 6.3 milliguass for about one second."

3:12 PM Keith: "Pat, what would you like to talk about today?"

3:13 PM Keith: "Pat, shortly after your death when you appeared in this room, it was said that you were standing on the right side, at the foot of the bed. Was the head of the bed to my back, towards the west wall of this room? Were you standing near the south east corner of this room, near the right side of the fireplace?"

3:16 PM Keith: "Who wants to talk to me today? Tell me your name first?"

3:17 PM Keith: "I know that a spirit is very close to the Mel Meter because the electromagnetic frequency reading on the Mel Meter's display is showing me a reading between 0.1 mG up to 2.0 mG."

3:18 PM Keith: "The Ovilus IV has given me the word developed which is spelled D-E-V-E-L-O-P-E-D. The word development was pronounced by the Ovilus IV at a normal conversational level and speed."

3:18 PM Keith: "I have observed the Mel Meter readings to be 0.6 mG and 72.0°F."

3:18 PM Keith: "I have observed the Mel Meter readings to be 0.1 mG and 72.3°F."

3:22 PM Keith: "Developed, no the pictures from this digital camera do not have to be developed. I can just transfer the pictures electronically from the digital camera right into my laptop."

3:24 PM Keith: "Sunshine, did you own a camera?"

3:25 PM Keith: "Sunshine, did you like to take pictures?"

3:26 PM Keith: "All of the pictures that you took when you were alive, are now in the possession of Patsy and Frances."

3:27 PM Keith: "Mary are you here today?"

3:28 PM Keith: "Sunshine, what type of camera did you have?"

3:29 PM Keith: "I thought I heard something outside of the porch roof or window. There is nothing out there." (I moved to look at the outside the left side window on the room's west wall. I did not take any of the two camcorders with me.)

3:30 PM Keith: "What is the question, so I can give you an answer?"

3:31 PM Keith: "Starve, are you hungry?"

3:32 PM Keith: "I have observed the Mel Meter readings to be 0.1 mG and 74.1°F."

3:33 PM Keith: "Sunshine, put all of your energy towards choosing a word from the Ovilus IV's data base. I am holding the Ovilus IV in my right hand."

3:36 PM Keith: "The Ovilus IV has given me the word percent which is spelled P-E-R-C-E-N-T. Percent was pronounced by the Ovilus IV at a normal conversational level and speed."

3:36 PM Keith: "I have observed the Mel Meter readings to be 0.2 mG and 75.1°F."

3:37 PM Keith: "Percentage of what?"

3:39 PM Keith: "I am disappointed that you're not answering my questions."

3:41 PM Keith: "Sunshine, how was this room furnished when you were alive."

3:43 PM Keith: "Sunshine, when you lived here did you have the fire-place plate cover with a lady standing in the tree?"

3:45 PM Keith: "Thank you for talking to me. Have a nice day."

3:45 PM Keith: "I have observed the Mel Meter readings to be 0.0 mG and 72.4°F."

3:46 PM Keith: "I obtained two thermal images of two cold purple areas on the ceiling near the room's north wall and the room's entrance. I obtained two thermal images, from two different angles, of the air conditioner vent which has no cover. I obtained two thermal images of a cold purple areas and some hot red areas on the ceiling towards the room's South wall."

3:46 PM Keith: "This Session 2 ended on Saturday, 15 April 2017."

The Paranormal Investigation the Sunshine Room, Hay House, Sunday,16th April 2017.

12:15 PM Keith: "I have learned that the left side of the window located on the room's west wall, had the hair line crack for at least two years."

Analysis of the Paranormal Investigation, Session 1, Sunshine's Room, Saturday, 15 April 2017. The date of the analysis was Saturday, 6th May 2017.

The first three words that I received from the Ovilus IV during this Session 1 were agent, orb, and mini. I do not feel that any of these words are directed towards me and or that any of these words are in response to any of the questions that I've asked during this Session 1. The word mini may be a woman's name or a woman's nickname. I am not aware of any females within the Buck, Gibson, and or Hays family that had the name Mini.

At 11:43 AM during this Session 1, I noticed that the electromagnetic frequency on the Mel Meter continuously went from 0.0 mG to 0.1 mG. When I tried to take a picture of the higher of the two frequencies the reading would return to zero. I felt like the spirit was just playing with me and trying to keep me from getting the data that showed the manipulation of the electromagnetic frequency.

11:49 AM during this Session 1, I told Sunshine that I was moving the equipment so that the video camcorder would be able to obtain footage of the information I was obtaining. Immediately after saying that the Ovilus IV gave me the fourth word during this Session 1, walk. This was an intelligent response from a ghost or spirit who was giving me a play-by-play of what I was doing. As if to say I know you're walking.

The fifth word that the Ovilus IV gave me during this Session 1 was surface. I feel that this was the intelligent spirit of Sunshine, who had noticed earlier that I was taking pictures of the decorative, light blue and white, tile surface that surrounds the fireplace on the east wall.

12:05 PM during this Session 1, my camera started to go in and out of focus. This activity is usually the calling card of Annie Gibson.

The sixth word that the Ovilus IV has given me during this session 1, was answer. At 12:07 PM I said yes, I would like an answer.

The seventh words that the Ovilus IV gave me was stay. I feel that this was the intelligent spirit of Sunshine asking me to stay in Apalachicola and or stay at the Hays House.

When I was obtaining thermal images of Sunshine's Room, I detected two purple cold spots on the ceiling near the north wall directly over the entrance to the room. These two cold spots were not in any way related to the air conditioner vent. Even though the central air-conditioning was on for the second floor, the one air conditioning vent within the room, was on the south side of the room's ceiling. I cannot explain the origins of the two cold purple spots on the ceiling near the north wall directly over the room's entrance. Maybe this was Sunshine and Annie.

Analysis of the Paranormal Investigation, Session 2, the Sunshine Room, Saturday, 15 April 2017. The date of the analysis was Saturday, 6th May 2017.

There were no background words from the Ovilus IV, within one minute after turning the Ovilus IV on. Background words are just the Ovilus IV's reading the environmental energy that existed nearby.

At 2:57 PM, I noticed that my digital camera keeps going in and out of focus. I'm contributed this to Annie Gibson, since that seems to be her trademark way of let me know that she is present.

At 2:58 PM, the Ovilus IV gave me the first word for this Session 2, answer. As you can remember during Session 1 analysis, the 6th word given to me was answer and I had said yes, I would like an answer. During session 2, I did not respond to the word answer in any direct way. I guess you could say I ignored it to see what the possible response there could be.

2:59 PM, the Ovilus IV gave me the second word for session 2, starve. The Ovilus IV had pronounced the word starve in a deep whisper type voice and very slow. Seems to me that the spirit of Sunshine was not happy with my failure to respond similarly to the way I did in Session 1, when I said, yes, I would like an answer. This time I said nothing. I had stopped Sunshine from asking me to stay and I feel this made her angry and she told me to starve. It seems to me that Sunshine knows how much I like to eat, and how much I do not like to be hungry. So, for her to wish me or threatened me with starvation would be a severe punishment.

From 3:03 PM to 3:07 PM I noticed that the electromagnetic frequency readings on the Mel Meter's display where between 0.1 mG to 0.2 mG. At 3:07 PM I stated, Sunshine, I see you like to play with my Mel Meter. At 3:09 PM I asked Sunshine if she could increase the reading to larger than 0.5 mG. I attempted to obtain pictures of the increase in the electromagnetic frequency, but each time Sunshine return the frequency to zero almost like she was teasing me so she could make sure that I was not obtaining any evidence that she was present. At one-point Sunshine increased the electromagnetic frequency up to 6.3 mG for about a second. I was unable to get any pictures of this increase in the electromagnetic frequency.

At 3:17 PM I noticed that the Mel Meter readings for the electromagnetic frequency were going between 0.1 mG up to 2.0 mG. At 3:18 PM the Ovilus IV gave me the second word during this session 2, developed. I feel that this was a ghost or spirit asking me if I had to develop the pictures that I took with my digital camera. I explained to the ghosts or spirit that I did not have to develop any pictures from the digital camera. That I could just transfer the pictures electronically from the digital camera right into my laptop for storage.

At 3:28 PM I had just completed asking Sunshine several questions about her camera when she was alive, when I heard a sound at the left window on the room's west wall. It sounded like a plastic bag had move up against the outside of the window. I immediately got up from my chair and looked at the window and I looked outside the window. I could clearly see nothing that could have made that sound. I did notice that there was a crack in the window, but I'm pretty sure that crack had been there and later I did confirm that the crack in the window had been there for a couple of years. So, the sound that I heard was not the window cracking. I feel that when a spirit or ghost's electromagnetic energy travels between different materials, like air, glass of a window, and when back to air, human beings can hear the sound made by the frequencies changes made by that spirit or ghost's electromagnetic energy as it goes through different materials.

At 3:32 PM I noticed that the no meter readings for the electromagnetic frequency was 0.1 mG.

At 3:33 PM I asked Sunshine to use all of her energy to choose one word from the Ovilus IV's database. At 3:36 PM the Ovilus IV gave me the 3rd word from this Session 2, percent. I'm not sure what you are trying to tell me, by saying a word percentage.

I obtained two thermal images of two cold purple areas on the ceiling near the north wall and the room's entrance. These two cold purple areas are not caused by the air conditioner. I also obtained two thermal images from different angles to show that the cold air coming from the air conditioner vent was not connected to the two purple areas on the ceiling near the north wall over the room's entrance. I also obtained two thermal images of cold purple and hot red areas on the ceiling towards the south wall. The ceiling over the South half of the Sunshine Room is only covered by a low angled tin roof. So, this allows for heat to build up on part of this room's ceiling. The other half of the ceiling on the north side of the room is covered by part of the third-floor apartment.

Digital pictures the Sunshine Room, Wednesday, 2nd November 2016, Hays House.

Two pictures of the room's South East corner.

One close-up picture of the right-side window of the room's West wall.

One picture of the room's West wall.

Two pictures of the room's Southwest corner.

Three pictures of the room's South.

Two close-up pictures of the room's painted hardwood floor.

Three close-up pictures of the room's doorknob.

Two pictures of the room's exterior side of the entrance door.

One picture of the room's Northeast corner ceiling and trim.

Four pictures of the room's.

One picture of the room's North wall.

One picture of the room's Northwest corner.

One picture of the room's Northeast corner.

Two pictures of the room's entrance threshold board.

Two pictures of the room's entrance door trim.

Two pictures of the exterior of the room's entrance.

Please see the author's website at www.keithoevans.com to view each digital picture.

The Thermal Images, the Sunshine Room, Wednesday, 2nd, November 2016, Hays House.

One thermal image of the door on the room's North wall.

One thermal image of the bed on the room's East wall.

One thermal image of the left side, two windows on the room's South wall and South East corner.

One thermal image of the right side, two Windows on the room's South wall and South West corner.

One thermal image of the center, two Windows on the room's South wall.

One image of the two Windows on the room's West wall.

One image of the room's ceiling fan.

Please see the author's website at www.keithoevans.com to view each thermal image.

The Thermal Images, the Sunshine Room, 1215 PM, Sunday, 6th April 2017, Thermal Images.

Two thermal images of two cold areas on the ceiling near the rooms entrance near the room's North wall.

Two thermal images of the air conditioning opening that has no cover.

Two, thermal images of the ceiling on the room's South East side.

Please see the author's website at www.keithoevans.com to view each image.

CHAPTER 11

1st Floor Front Stairway Room, Hays House, Ghosts are People too.

Description of the 1st Floor Front Stairway Room, Thursday, 17th November 2016.

The room's West wall has the front entrance with the original natural wooden door. This door appears to be original and has two sunken wooden panels at the bottom and at the top half of the door is a modern glass window approximately 25.5 inches x 35 inches. On each side of the door, there are the original natural wooden decorative panels, with two bottom sunken wooden panels and at the top half of the panels has a glass window which is approximately 9.5 inches x 35 inches. The threshold board between the First Floor Front Stairway Room and the front entrance is approximately 4 1/8 inches wide, and the overall threshold area is 9 inches wide. Above the door to the front entrance and the right and left side panels is the original decorative panes of glass. The glass pane above the door is lead glass and has the dimensions of approximately 12 inches wide by 68 inches long. The interior of the front doorway area was refinished with a red mahogany type stain, that allows the natural grain to be seen.

The interior side of the Front Entrance, West Wall, 1st Floor Front Stairway Room.

The First Floor Front Stairway Room is the main hallway starting at the front entrance leading through to the First Floor Back Stairway Room. The First Floor Front Stairway Room also leads to two rooms on the left side of the house, the TV Room and the Dining Room. The right side of the First Floor Front Stairway Room leads to two rooms, the Living Room and Pat and Kathleen's Room. The First Floor Front Stairway Room leads to the front stairway which goes to the Second Floor Front Stairway Room.

There is a coat rack in the room's Northwest corner. The room's North wall has the decorative natural wooden open entrance leading to the TV Room. After 1996 the light-yellow paint that covered the decorative natural wood at the entrance to the TV Room was removed to reveal the natural wooden grain. There is no threshold board between the First Floor Front Stairway Room and the TV Room. There is a 36" x 47" painting on the room's North wall between the entrance leading to the TV Room and the entrance leading to the Dining Room. The entrance leading to the Dining Room has two doors that are wooden and painted white with 10 glass panes in each door. Each of these glass panes are approximately seven and three-quarter inches wide and 13 3/8 inches long. There is no threshold board between the First Floor Front Stairway Room and the Dining Room, where the double doors are located. At the Northeast corner of the room there is the front stairway. The crown of each front stairway post and stairway railing are natural wood and are much darker than the steps which are natural wood also. Sometime after 1996, the steps on the front stairway were stripped, but not the top railing, so the top railing is a darker color natural wood and the steps are a lighter color natural wood. The other areas of the front stairway are all painted white. Along the interior North wall that is created by the front stairway, there is a white wooden six leg table with a lamp on top. The first landing of the front stairway has a wooden table with a lamp on top. There is a door that leads to the closet which is under the stairway, that is created by the front stairway. The natural wooden threshold board between the First Floor Front Stairway Room and the closet under the stairway is approximately three and three-quarter inches wide.

The Hard Wood Floor, 1ˢᵗ Floor Front Stairway Room.

The Stairway, North East Corner, 1ˢᵗ Floor Front Stairway Room.

The room's East wall has the original white wooden door with five sunken panels. This door has the original decorative brass doorknob and a matching skeleton key plate. The East wall has two various sizes of paintings. The room's South East corner has a metal lawn chair.

The room's South wall has the entrance to Pat and Kathleen's Room. Between the entrance to Pat and Kathleen's Room and the entrance to the Living Room, and along the South wall is a natural wooden table. Above the table and mounted on the South wall is a decorative frame and mirror with the approximate dimensions of 38" x 58". There are various sizes, paintings, mounted on to the room's South wall. The South wall has the decorative natural wooden opening with a column of each side, that leads to the Living Room. Prior to 1996, this natural wooden opening was covered with light yellow paint. There is no threshold board between the First Floor Front Stairway Room and the Living Room.

This room has the original tongue and groove, approximately 2.5 inches wide, heart pine floors that are running in an East to West direction. All of the walls in the First Floor Front Stairway Room have the original horizontal wall boards which are approximately 3 inches wide. The room's ceiling has the original ceiling boards which are approximately 2.5 inches wide. There is no threshold board where a wall that once stood in the center of what is now the First Floor Front Stairway Room. One can see the opening of where the double doors use to be at this location where the wall once stood. This wall was there in 1996 when the floors within the First Floor Front Stairway Room were stripped. Stripping the hardwood floors took off about 1/16 of an inch to maybe 1/8 of an inch of wood from the top of the hard wood floor surface. When this wall stood over the hardwood floor it saved the area of the floor under the wall from being stripped. Upon the wall being taken down sometime after 2012, it revealed that to double doors have been located in the center of the wall. The total opening for the double doors that stood were this wall once was is 48 1/8 inches.

The history of the First Floor Front Stairway Room.

Shortly after 1942 the Hays family had a new wall built in the First Floor Front Stairway Room between TV Room and Dining Room on the room's north wall and between the Living Room and Pat and Kathleen's Room on the room's south wall. This wall was built to keep all of the heat during cold weather from going up to the second floor.

At Christmas time the family decorated the entry room table's bottom shelf and In front of the peer mirror with a Nativity Set that Included the Christ Child, Mary, Joseph, the Three Wise Men, and several animals. The peer mirror was used by ladies to check their petti coat and by everyone to check their shoes during the Victorian era. This entry room table sat along the First Floor Front Stairway Room's South wall and directly to the left of the entrance to the Living Room.

When Frances was in Elementary and High School she enjoyed decorating the 24 individual panes of glass to the two doors located at the wall that her parents built in the First Floor Front Stairway Room. Frances use the stencils of Christmas Trees, Snow Men, Reindeer, and many other Christmas related items, to hold up to each glass pane and spray artificial snow around each stencil to create a Christmas image.

The description of the First Floor Front Stairway Room from eleven pictures taken in 1996.

I will be observing 11 pictures taken in 1996. Of the first-floor front stairway room and describing this room, as depicted in those pictures. Starting with the room's West wall from left to right, there is a green potted plant on the floor in the room's Southwest corner. The West wall has the original front door, which is painted white. There was a round doorbell looking device near the top of the left side of the interior of the front door. This door's window and the two side windows have matching white curtains. This front door has two sunken panels and the original door knob and skeleton key baseplate. To the far right of the room's West wall are two light switches.

On the left side of the North wall and to the left side of the opening to the TV room, are two golden framed under glass pictures of Patsy

Hays and Frances Hays when they were young children. On the shelf to the left of the original column that was painted white is a porcelain or glass multi-colored, pitcher with a handle. In the room's Northwest corner is an antique, dark wooden table with a white marble top. On top of this table are the following items; an electrical lamp with a white marble base and a golden post that support a pink glass lamp shade, to porcelain candy dishes, and a candleholder with a marble base and a golden supporting stand with three, 8-inch, white candles. Hanging below each candle are some clear crystals. To the right of the antique white marble top table is a decorative antique wooden chair with a multi-colored textile covered seat. On the room's North wall and to the right of the opening to the TV room is a golden and silver colored glass, pitcher sitting on the shelf to the right of the original wooden column that was painted white. Mounted on the room's north wall is a golden frame under glass, picture of Patsy. A long the North wall is an antique dark wooden triangular stand with three legs and a dark green marble top. On this triangular stand is a white porcelain figurine. In the Northeast corner that was created by the wall that Kathleen and Pat added to the room after 1942, was an antique chair with wooden legs, arms and trim that has a tan textured textile covered seat, arms and back rest. On each side of this chair's back rest are wooden sculptures of an angel and or a winged human.

Mounted on the left side of this wall, that was added after 1942 and was the East wall to the front room, there was a porcelain figurine of a lady that is surrounded by an oval reef of flowers. There is a similar porcelain figurine of a lady with an oval reef mounted on the right side of the double doors on this wall that was added after 1942.

Mounted on the room's South wall is a golden frame tombstone shape mirror. On the shelf and to the left of the original wooden column is a multi-colored, pitcher with a handle. A long the room's South wall was an antique dark wooden entry way table with a rectangular white marbled tabletop. This entry way table has a mirror in the back of the lower section that extends down to the bottom shelf. On the bottom shelf is a pink porcelain candy dish. On the top of the white marble rectangular entryway table top are from left to right; an antique lamp with a white marble base, a golden post, clear crystals hanging from below the white glass lamp shade, a porcelain candlestick holder with three, 8-inch, white candles, and a light green porcelain apple with three bite marks. To the right side of the entryway table is an antique decorative dark wooden trim chair with a purple textile covered seat and back rest. On the room's South wall is an opening to the living room with the original wooden columns on each side that are painted white. To the right side of the white wooden column on the room's South wall and on the shelf is a multi-colored vase or teapot looking porcelain item. A long the right side of the room's South wall is a 3-foot-tall wooden antique, four level shelf type of furniture with a mirror on its back wall. The top shelf has a golden colored porcelain boat looking candy dish. The second shelf from the top has a golden vase, the third shelf from the top has a golden and white glass or porcelain pitcher. The fourth shelf from the top or bottom shelf, has two white porcelain figurines of a lady and a man. On the right side of the South wall is a golden framed, under glass picture of Frances Hays.

In 1996 the president day First Floor Front Stairway Room was divided into two rooms. I will describe the middle room that existed in 1996. Starting at the south side of the wall that was installed in 1942 and moving from the left side of the door way, located on the middle room's West wall is an antique dark wooden chair with a pink textile seat. The double door on the room's West wall opens towards the stairway.

On the room's North wall and near the middle room's northwest corner is the double door that leads to the dining room. To the right side of the stairway is an antique dark wooden pedestal with a large golden vase on top. The stairway goes along the middle room's North wall. As you are going up the steps from left to right there are three golden framed under glass, wedding pictures. I think these pictures are, Patsy's wedding pictures. The steps are covered with a grey carpet. There is white wainscoting on bottom half of the North and East wall's going along this stairway. The North wall created by the stairway has white wainscoting on its bottom half. There is an antique dark wooden three leg stand with the moon shape white marble top

231

that has a low slope tombstone white marble backing that extends up above the top of the moon shape table on top. On top of this moon shape table are from left to right, a black porcelain candy dish, a white porcelain candy dish, an electric lamp with a golden metal and white porcelain stand, that has a multi-colored design with a matching porcelain or glass lamp shade, and a decorative dish on a golden stand. This moon shaped stand has a shelf that is close to the floor. Sitting on this shelf is a dark glass candy dish. To the right of the moon shape stand is an original white door with two long and two short sunken panels that are vertically side by side. This is the only door in the house that has too long and too short sunken panels that are vertically side by side. This white door has the original matching brass or metal doorknob and skeleton key baseplate that are unpainted on the exterior side. The door trim appears to be original. This door leads to the closet that is under the stairway.

There is white wainscoting on the bottom of the middle room's East wall and on both sides of the door that leads into the First Floor Back Stairway Room. This door is covered by a large 6-foot-tall, decorative golden framed mirror. This mirror has an irregular shape 1-foot tall table in front of the mirror. This irregular shaped table has a white marble top with a white, gold, and blue porcelain dish on top. On each side of the mirror are golden frame under glass pictures of Patsy on the left side and Frances on the right side.

The middle room's South wall has white wainscoting on each side of the door that leads into Pat and Kathleen's room. This door is a white original five sunken panel door, with the original white wooden trim. Mounted on the room's South wall are four golden framed, under glass, pictures of family members. To the right side of the door to enter Pat and Kathleen's room is an antique dark wooden entry hall table with the following on top; from left to right, a white porcelain candy dish, a golden metal lamp stand, with a pink glass lamp shade, and next to the lamp was a Golden antique telephone. To the right side of this dark wooden entry hallway table is an antique dark wooden chair. Under this chair and mounted on the wall and at the level of the baseboard is an electrical outlet. Mounted on the South wall and near the middle room's Southwest corner is a decorative, dark wooden coat rack. Below the coat rack is an antique dark wooden stand with a square white marble top. On top of this antique dark wooden stand is a multi-colored porcelain dish.

The Mel Meter base readings for the 1st Floor Front Stairway Room, Thursday, 17th November 2016.

12 noon the triple light switch on the right side of the entrance on the room's West wall. One switch is in the on position and two switches are in the off position.

The electromagnetic frequency range was 4.5 mG to 5.0 mG.

The temperature range was 67.6°F to 67.9°F.

12:01 PM The electrical outlet on the room's North wall near the entrance to the TV Room. This electrical outlet is not in use.

The electromagnetic frequency range was 0.0 mG to 0.0 mG.

The temperature range was 67.0°F to 67.1°F.

12:02 PM The lamp on the green round three-leg wooden table sitting on the first landing on the Front Stairway. The lamp was on.

The electromagnetic frequency range was 0.0 mG to 0.0 mG.

The temperature range was 67.6°F to 68.3°F.

12:03 PM The lamp on the white oval six leg wooden table, near the stairway, located along the room's North wall. The lamp was on.

The electromagnetic frequency range was 0.0 mG to 0.0 mG.

The temperature range was 68.0°F to 68.3°F.

12:04 PM The electrical outlet near the stairway, located on the room's North wall. The outlet is in use. The lamp on the oval six leg wooden table is plugged into this electrical outlet.

The electromagnetic frequency range was 0.0 mG to 0.0 mG.

The temperature range was 67.2°F to 67.6°F.

12:05 PM The cable wire near the stairway, located along the room's North wall. This cable wire is not in use.

The electromagnetic frequency range was 0.0 mG to 0.0 mG.

The temperature range was 67.0°F to 67.0°F.

12:06 PM The electrical outlet near the entrance to Pat and Kathleen's Room, located on the room's South wall. This electrical outlet is not in use.

The electromagnetic frequency range was 0.0 mG to 0.0 mG.

The temperature range was 67.6°F to 67.9°F.

12:07 PM The electrical outlet near the Living Room entrance and located on the room's South wall. This electrical outlet is not in use.

The electromagnetic frequency range was 0.0 mG to 0.0 mG.

The temperature range was 67.9°F to 68.3°F.

Paranormal Investigation, Session 1, First Floor Front Stairway Room, Hays House, Sunday, 16th, April 2017.

10:30 AM Keith: "Hello, I am Keith Evans. You may use your energy to choose words from the Ovilus IV's database. The Ovilus IV will not hurt you." (Hold it up.)

10:31 AM Keith: "This is the Mel Meter. The Mel Meter measures temperature and electromagnetic frequencies. The Mel Meter will not harm you." (Hold it up.)

10:31 AM Keith: "The Ovilus IV has given me two background words; plains which is spelled P-L-A-I-N-S, and add which is spelled A-D-D. The Ovilus IV has pronounced the words plains and add at a normal conversational level and speed."

10:31 AM Keith: "I have observed the Mel Meter readings to be 0.0 mG and 74.9°F."

10:33 AM Keith: "Are you talking about the wide-open plains? What do you want to add?"

10:34 AM Keith: "I hear someone is walking up the back steps."

10:35 AM Keith: "The Ovilus IV has given me the word shirt which is spelled S-H-I-R-T. The Ovilus IV has pronounced the word shirt with a man's deep voice, but with a normal conversational level and speed."

10:35 AM Keith: "I have observed the Mel Meter readings to be 0.0 mG and 75.2°F."

10:36 AM Keith: "The Ovilus IV has given me the word fade which is spelled F-A-D-E. The Ovilus IV has pronounced the word fade at a normal conversational level and speed."

10:37 AM Keith: "I have observed the Mel Meter readings to be 0.0 mG and 75.7°F."

10:40 AM Keith: "The decorative beads on the table are making sounds as they rattle together."

10:42 AM Keith: "It sounds like someone is talking about me wearing a brand-new royal blue shirt instead of an old faded shirt."

10:44 AM Keith: "Sunshine, would that be you that said the word shirt and fade?"

10:45 AM Keith: "The Ovilus IV has given me the word recuse which is spelled R-E-C-U-S-E." The Ovilus IV has pronounced the word recuse at a normal conversational level and speed."

10:45 AM Keith: "I have observed the Mel Meter readings to be 0.0 mG and 75.2°F."

10:47 AM Keith: "Recuse means when a judge steps away from making decisions on the case because he has a conflict of interest."

10:49 AM Keith: "Who said the word recuse?"

10:50 AM Keith: "Are you an attorney that used to work at the Hays House?"

10:51 AM Keith: "Let us see what we have. Nothing out of the ordinary."

10:51 AM to 10:53 AM Keith: "I completed a thermal scan of the room. I obtained two images of the upper stairway, and two images of the lower stairway. I did not obtain any thermal images that were related to the paranormal and or that were unexplained."

10:53 AM Keith: "The Ovilus IV has given me the word bracelet which is spelled B-R-A-C-E-L-E-T. The Ovilus IV has pronounced the word bracelet at a normal conversational level and speed."

10:54 AM Keith: "I have observed the Mel Meter readings to be 0.0 mG and 75.4°F."

10:55 AM Keith: "Someone is walking down the front stairway."

10:56 AM Keith: "Yes, there is one other person in the house, besides me."

10:56 AM Keith: "I have observed the Mel Meter readings to be 0.0 mG and 75.9°F."

10:59 AM Keith: (My cell phone is ringing.) "Hey Dale, I'm in the middle of a paranormal investigation, I will call you back in 30 minutes. Sorry. Thank you. Goodbye."

11 AM Keith: "I hear church music playing from outside." (It is the Catholic Church bells ringing.)

11:01 AM Keith: "Someone is walking up the back stairway."

11:03 AM Keith: "Sunshine, are you talking about a bracelet that a relative has, that was once yours?"

11:04 AM Keith: "It looks like the Ovilus IV is frozen up again. The batteries are new. So, I am going to turn it off and back on again."

11:05 AM Keith: "I heard a ringing sound coming from the front stairway for several seconds."

11:07 AM Keith: "I have turned the Ovilus IV on."

11:07 AM Keith: "The Ovilus IV has given me the words; sat which is spelled S-A-T, add which is spelled A-D-D, and level which is spelled L-E-V-E-L. The Ovilus IV has pronounced the words sat, add, and level at a normal conversational level and speed."

11:07 AM Keith: "I have observed the Mel Meter readings to be 0.0 mG and 76.4°F."

11:08 AM Keith: "The Ovilus IV gave me the word industry which is spelled I-N-D-U-S-T-R-Y. The Ovilus IV has pronounced the word industry at a normal conversational level and speed."

11:09 AM Keith: "I have observed the Mel Meter readings to be 0.0 mG and 75.6°F."

11:09 AM Keith: "The pictures that I'm taking with my camera are blurry and out of focus."

11:13 AM Keith: "Pat, are you saying that as an accountant you use to sit and add your client's paperwork to make sure that everything was adding up right and level? Level as in balancing the financial records."

11:15 AM Keith: "Who said the word industry?"

11:16 AM Keith: "Mr. Coombs, was that you. I'm sorry, I just have not had time to get over to talk to you."

11:18 AM Keith: "Sunshine, and or Annie, can you tell me more about the bracelet."

11:18 AM Keith: "I can hear someone is walking down the back stairway."

11:20 AM Keith: "Yesterday, the Ovilus IV gave me the word percent. Was that you Pat, talking about the public accounting job?"

11:21 AM Keith: "I can hear someone walking up the back stairway."

11:22 AM Keith: "Thank you for talking to me. Have a good day."

11:22 AM Keith: "This session 1 ended on Sunday, 16th, April 2017."

Paranormal Investigation, Session 2, First Floor Front Stairway Room, Hays House, Sunday, 16th, April 2017.

2:50 PM Keith: "Hello, I am Keith Evans. You may use your energy to choose words from the Ovilus IV's data base. This is the Ovilus IV. The Ovilus IV will not hurt you." (Hold it up.)

2:50 PM Keith: "That is, Jill, walking in front of the camcorder one."

2:51 PM Keith: "This is the Mel meter. The Mel meter measures temperature and electromagnetic frequencies. The Mel meter will not harm you." (Hold it up.)

2:52 PM Keith: "The Ovilus IV has given me two background words; edged which is spelled E-D-G-E, and allow which is spelled A-L-L-O-W. The Ovilus IV has pronounced the words edge and allow at a normal conversational level and speed."

2:53 PM Keith: "I have observed the Mel Meter readings to be 0.0 mG and 78.4°F."

2:54 PM Keith: "The Ovilus IV has given me the word factories which is spelled F-A-C-T-O-R-I-E-S. The Ovilus IV has pronounced the word factories at a normal conversational level and speed."

2:54 PM Keith: "I have observed the Mel Meter readings to be 0.0 mG and 78.3°F."

2:54 PM Keith: "I have observed the Mel Meter readings to be 0.0 mG and 78.4°F."

2:58 PM Keith: "Edge, allow, factories, edge and allow maybe referring to me not allowing the cat to push items off the edge of the desk."

2:58 PM Keith: "The Ovilus IV gave me the word entered which is spelled E-N-T-E-R-E-D. The Ovilus IV has pronounced the word entered at a normal conversational level and speed."

2:58 PM Keith: "I have observed the Mel Meter readings to be 0.0 mG and 78.4°F."

3:03 PM Keith: "I hear music from outside and or church bells ringing."

3:03 PM Keith: "Factories may be referring to the fish and seafood canneries that have been and are here in Apalachicola, Florida."

3:05 PM Keith: "There are still fish and seafood canneries here in Apalachicola, Florida."

3:06 PM Keith: "What can you tell me about the fish and seafood canneries that used to be here in Apalachicola, Florida between 1907 to the 1970s?"

3:07 PM Keith: "Earlier the Ovilus IV gave me the word entered. Yes, I entered the Hays house around 2:30 PM."

3:08 PM Keith: "I have observed the Mel Meter readings to be 0.0 mG and 78.4°F."

3:09 PM Keith: "Jill, is that you? I heard some noise coming from the back of the house."

3:10 PM Keith: "I do not think it was Jill because she just walked down the front stairway, from the second floor."

3:11 PM Keith: "I am still hearing sound coming from the back of the house."

3:12 PM Keith: "I am going to walk around with camcorder two to check out the sounds coming from the rear of the house."

3:13 PM Keith: "The noises I'm hearing may be coming from the First Floor Back Stairway Room, The Den Room, the First Floor Kitchen Room, and the two room's off of the First Floor Kitchen Room."

3:14 PM Keith: "The noises I heard could have been Jill running up the Back Stairway before she appeared on camcorder two, walking down the Front Stairway."

3:18 PM Keith: "If you are a spirit making noise, please make the noise in this room."

3:19 PM Keith: "Who was watching me today and given me the feedback about what I am physically doing?"

3:20 PM Keith: "I need feedback about the history of the Hays House, the Buck, Gibson, and Hays families. That is what I really need."

3:22 PM Keith: "It is nice to know that you are an intelligent spirit or ghost. Your feedback shows me that you are intelligent."

3:23 PM Keith: "Do you not remember the history of your life?"

3:24 PM Keith: "I know my memory is not as good as it used to be."

3:25 PM Keith: "Yes or no, are ghost's, and or spirit's memory's not good?"

3:25 PM Keith: "That was a car horn blowing outside."

3:26 PM Keith: "The Ovilus IV has frozen up again. The Ovilus IV will not respond to me touching the home icon. So, I am going to turn it off."

3:28 PM Keith: "I have turned the Ovilus IV on."

3:29 PM Keith: "The Ovilus IV has given me the word falls which is spelled F-A-L-L-S. The Ovilus IV pronounced the word falls at a lower than normal conversational level and at a normal conversational speed. I could not understand what the Ovilus IV had said."

3:29 PM Keith: "I have observed the Mel Meter readings to be 0.0 mG and 78.7°F."

3:30 PM Keith: "That is a motorcycle going by."

2:32 PM Keith: "The word falls is very ambiguous. Are you talking about a water fall? Are you referring to someone is going to fall many times."?

3:34 PM Keith: "Is falls the name of a company that you use to work for in Apalachicola?"

3:35 PM to 3:38 PM Keith: "I am going to obtain thermal images of the room. I obtained two images of the lower part of the front stairway. I obtained two images of the upper part of the front stairway. I did not obtain any images that were related to the paranormal and or anything unexplained."

3:38 PM Keith: "Is falls a last name of a person?"

3:40 PM Keith: "I have moved the decorative chimes that was on the center of the table, because the chimes made sounds as I was writing."

3:42 PM Keith: "Thank you for talking to me. Have a good day."

3:42 PM Keith: "This session 2 ended on Sunday, 16th, April 2017."

The analysis of the Paranormal Investigation, Session 1, First Floor Front Stairway Room, Hays House, Sunday, 16th, April 2017. The date of the analysis was Friday, 23rd of June 2017.

At 10:31 AM the Ovilus IV gave me the first two background words of this session 1, plains and add. I have not asked any questions yet, so I do not believe that the words plains and add are responding to any questions that I have asked during my last paranormal investigation.

At 10:35 AM the Ovilus IV gave me the third word of this session 1, shirt. I do not feel that this word is in response to any questions that I have asked during this session 1. I believe that this is an intelligent spirit or ghost that is responding to the fact that I'm wearing a bright brand-new Royal blue shirt. Just recently I have switched out my old faded shirts for brand-new shirts.

At 10:36 AM, the, Ovilus IV gave me the fourth word of this session 1, fade. I do not believe that this word is in response to any questions that I have asked during this session 1. I believe that this is an intelligent spirit or ghost that is responding to the fact that I use to wear and that I had several faded shirts within my wardrobe. This spirit or ghost may be Miss Sunshine Gibson, who is letting me know that she is aware that I am wearing a brand-new shirt.

At 10:45 AM the Ovilus IV gave me the fifth word of this session 1, recuse. I do not believe that this word is in response to any questions that I have asked during this session 1. Recuse is a legal term and is used by a judge to dismiss him or herself from a case that he or she may have a conflict of interest with deciding the outcome.

At 10:53 AM the Ovilus IV gave me the sixth word of this session 1, bracelet. I do not believe that this word bracelet is in response to any of the questions that I have asked during this session 1. This may be an intelligent spirit or ghost, who is observing, and listening to the sounds of the beads that are rattling or chiming while they are coming in contact with each other, as I am writing on top of the table. This table is moving from side to side, as a result of me writing the transcript of this paranormal investigation session 1.

At 11:04 AM the Ovilus IV has frozen up again. I turned the Ovilus IV off. I do not believe that the Ovilus IV has drained the energy out of the four AAA batteries. I do believe that a ghost or spirit is somehow blocking the energy from leaving the batteries, thus this is causing the Ovilus IV to not function properly.

At 11:07 AM, I turned the Ovilus IV on. Now the Ovilus IV to function properly. The Ovilus IV gave me the seventh, eighth, and ninth words of this session 1, sat, add, and level. I do not believe that the words; sat, add, and level are in response to any of the questions that I have asked during this session 1. I do feel that this is the spirit or ghost of Pat, Edward Ryan Hays, stating that when he was a public accountant. He would sit down and add up the client's financial records and make sure that the records were all balanced and level.

At 11:08 AM the Ovilus IV gave me the 10th word of this session 1, industry. I do not feel that the word industry is in response to any of the questions I have asked during this session 1.

At 11:09 AM my digital camera was going in and out of focus. This is a trademark of Sunshine sister Annie Gibson Hays Palmer. Annie is letting me know that she is here. Annie is using her electromagnetic energy to interfere with the digital camera automatic focusing mechanism.

Ovilus IV words: Add, Shirt, Fade.

The analysis of the Paranormal Investigation, Session 2, First Floor Front Stairway Room, Hays House, Sunday, 16th, April 2017. The date of the analysis was Friday, 23rd of June 2017.

At 2:52 PM the Ovilus IV gave me the first two background words of session 2, edge and allow. I have not asked any questions yet. And I feel that edge and allow is just the Ovilus IV picking up the energy in the environment. Although, this could be an intelligent spirit and or ghost who has observed me in the pasted allowing Jill the cat to push items like the camcorder 1 and 2, my digital camera, the FLIR TG 165, the Ovilus IV, and the Mel Meter towards the edge of the desk. I have never allowed any of those items to fall to the floor.

At 2:54 PM the Ovilus IV gave me the third word of session 2, factories. I have not asked any questions yet during this session 2. I do not feel that the word factories are in response to any questions that I have asked during the first session.

At 2:58 PM the Ovilus IV gave me the fourth word of session 2, entered. I feel that this may be an intelligent spirit asking me what time I entered the Hays House. After lunch I came back into the Hays House at about 2:30 PM. The word entered is past tense, so the ghost and or spirit is talking about a past entry, not something that is taking place right now.

At 3:09 PM I heard some noise coming from the back of the house. I said, "Jill, is that you?" I have determined that wasn't Jill because she just walked down the front stairway. I'm still hearing sound coming from the back of the house with Jill within my site. So, I know it's not the cat, Jill. I pick up camcorder two and walked to the rear the house to determine what is making this sound. I checked the First Floor Back Stairway Room, the Den Room, the First Floor Kitchen Room, the two small rooms off from the kitchen, and I looked out onto the back porch and did not see any cause for the noise. There is no one in the Hays House except for me. These sounds coming from the back of the house will remain unexplained. I cannot say that the sounds I heard were cause by the paranormal. I just do not know what caused these sounds.

At 3:25 PM I heard a car horn blow outside. It seems like if a car horn blows outside. I am usually in the middle of a paranormal investigation. I do not remember ever hearing a car horn blow while I am at the Hays House when I'm not involved in a paranormal investigation.

At 3:26 PM the Ovilus IV had frozen up and will not function properly. The Ovilus IV will not respond to my pressing the home icon. I manually turn the Ovilus IV off. I do not believe that all the energy has been drained from the four AAA batteries. I feel that the ghosts and or spirits somehow are preventing the energy from the batteries from reaching the Ovilus IV. This causes the Ovilus IV to fail to function properly.

At 3:28 PM I turned the Ovilus IV on.

At 3:29 PM the Ovilus IV gave me the fifth word of session 2, falls. The Ovilus IV pronounced the word falls at a lower than normal conversational level and at a faster than normal conversational speed. I do not feel that the word falls is in response to any of the questions that I have asked so far during this session 2.

At 3:35 PM to 3:38 PM I did a thermal scan of the First Floor Front Stairway Room. I obtained two thermal images of the lower portion of the front stairway. I obtained two thermal images of the upper area of the front stairway. While I was scanning with the thermal imager, I did not see anything that could be considered unexplained and or paranormal.

At 3:40 PM I noted that session 2 was quieter because I have moved the decorative beads or chimes from the middle of the table to the floor along the South wall. While I was writing the transcript for session 2, the table was still moving but the decorative beads or chimes were not there to make those sounds.

Digital pictures of the 1st Floor Front Stairway Room, Thursday, 17th, November 2016.

Two pictures of the room's North wall.

Two pictures of the room's East wall.

Two pictures of the room's Northeast corner.

Two pictures of the room's South East corner.

Two pictures of the room's South wall.

10 pictures of the room's hardwood floor and wall where a wooden barrier was at one time.

Two pictures of the room's South wall.

Eight pictures of the room's wall and ceiling trim.

Two pictures of the room's lower 1st Floor Front Stairway.

Three pictures of the room's West wall.

Eight close-up pictures of the room's South wall.

Two pictures of the room's Northeast corner.

Two close-up pictures of the room's North wall.

Two pictures of the room's East wall.

Six pictures of the room's Northeast corner.

Two pictures of the room's 1st Floor Front Stairway steps.

Two close-up pictures of the room's North wall.

Four close-up pictures of the room's Northeast corner.

Two pictures of the room's North wall.

Six close-up pictures of the door knob.

Four pictures of the room's hardwood floor.

Two pictures of the room's original electrical outlet, located within the white wall floor trim.

Two close-up pictures of the room's white wall floor trim.

Two close-up pictures of the room's threshold board at the entrance door.

Two close-up pictures of the room's white horizontal wall boards.

Please see the author's website at www.keithoevans.com to view each digital picture.

Thermal images of the 1st Floor Front Stairway Room, Thursday, 17th November 2016.

One picture of the orange and red lamp on the round three leg wooden table, that is sitting on the 1st Floor Front Stairway's landing, on the room's Northeast corner.

One picture of the room's East wall, with the stairs to the left side.

One picture of the, left side of the room's South wall.

One picture of the two windows, in the Living Room, on the right side of the room's South wall.

One picture of the interior front entrance with the exit sign on the room's West wall.

One picture of the right side of the entrance wooden area on the room's West wall.

One close-up picture of the right side of the entrance wooden area on the room's West wall.

One picture of the row of the ceiling light and showing the room's North wall in the background.

One picture of the ceiling lights and the room's North wall.

One picture of the left side entrance leading to the TV Room on, the room's North wall.

One picture of the lamp on the 1st Floor Front Stairway's first landing, on the room's North wall.

One picture of the orange lamp on the 1st Floor Front Stairway's first landing, on the room's Northeast corner.

Please see the author's website at www.keithoevans.com to view each thermal image.

CHAPTER **12**

Back Porch, Hays House, Ghosts are People too.

The description of the Back Porch, 11th November 2016, Hays House.

The exterior West, North, and South walls of the back porch are all covered with modern vertical natural wooden boards. Starting from the left to right on the back porch's West wall and in the back porches South West corner is the small ladies room original door with green paint and five sunken panels. The store has the original brass or metal doorknob and skeleton key plate. Next part of the porches South wall has a white vent at about 3 feet from the floor. Continuing with the porches West wall is an exterior modern green painted door with nine glass panels, on the top half of the door and two vertical sunken plates on the lower half of the door. To the right of the exterior door is an original window with two glass panes in the upper and lower half's. The window trim is painted green and white and may be original. Covering this window on the exterior side are white security bars.

On the porch's East exterior wall is a Sonny Boy, Rinnai, hot water heater control system. A long the porches East wall is a modern white wooden bench. On this porch's East side are cemented steps that were built on 20 March 1953. We know this because Frances Hays left her hand print and documented the date that she left her hand print into the soft cement. There is a modern white wooden railing along the back-porch steps on the right side.

The back porches South wall has a green original men's room door with five sunken panels and the original brass or metal doorknob and skeleton key plate.

The ceiling of the back porch has modern white wood. There is a hanging light in the center of the back-porch's ceiling. The back porch has a modern wooden floor with 6-inch-wide boards that are running in an East to West direction.

History of the Back Porch, Hays House.

In 1908 when the Hays House was built, the Back Porch stretched all the way across the east side of the house.

It is believed that while the Buck family still own the Hays House, they built a second bathroom, which is located on the southeast side of the back porch. This bathroom was almost the same length as the Den Room. This bathroom extended the full width of the back porch. This bathroom also had a large closet for storage on the north side of the bathroom.

Sometime between the 1960's and the 1970's Kathleen Hays needed a place for her washer and dryer. Pat and Kathleen decided to build an outside shed for the washer and dryer on the far northeast side of the back porch. This little shed extended out to the right side of the exterior kitchen door and to the full width of the back porch.

Sometime after 1996, the door between the bathroom and the closet on the bathroom's North wall was closed in. The bathroom closet be-came a small men's room with a toilet and a sink. Connected to this bathroom and on the men's bathroom's North wall is a small ladies room. This small lady room is about half the width of the back porch. This ladies room has a toilet and a sink.

Sometime after 1996, there was a room built on the full width of the back porch between the washer and dryer room and the right-side exterior of the First Floor Back Stairway Room's window. This room closed off the kitchen from having an exterior exit. This left the Hays House with a very narrow back porch.

Mel Meter Base Readings of the Back Porch, Friday, 11th November 2016, Hays House.

10:40 AM Near the gas tank along the south side of the Hays House's exterior East wall.

The electromagnetic frequency range was 0.0 mG to 0.0 mG.

The temperature range was 75.1°F to 75.4°F.

10:41 AM The back-porch step's, near the Frances Hays documented 20th of March 1953 name and date.

The electromagnetic frequency range was 0.0 mG to 0.0 mG.

The temperature range was 72.6°F to 74.5°F.

10:42 AM The back-porch steps close to Frances Hays's hand print.

The electromagnetic frequency range was 0.0 mG to 0.0 mG.

The temperature range was 75.5°F to 76.4°F.

10:43 AM The Vent mounted on the Back Porches' exterior's South wall.

The electromagnetic frequency range was 0.0 mG to 0.0 mG.

The temperature range was 73.7°F to 73.7°F.

10:44 AM Near the white Sonny Boy device that is mounted on the Back Porches', exterior North wall.

The electromagnetic frequency range was 58.3 mG to 60.6 mG.

The temperature range was 74.0°F to 74.5°F.

10:45 AM The blue bench along the Back Porch's North wall.

The electromagnetic frequency range was 1.2 mG to 1.6 mG.

The temperature range was 73.4°F to 74.0°F.

10:46 AM The boxlike device named Rinnai water heater mounted on the Back Porches' exterior East wall.

The electromagnetic frequency range was 0.0 mG to 0.0 mG.

The temperature range was 74.3°F to 75.2°F.

10:47 AM The electrical outlet on the Back Porches', exterior North wall. This electrical outlet is not in use.

The electromagnetic frequency range was 9.0 mG to 9.4 mG.

The temperature range was 72.6°F to 72.8°F.

10:48 PM The accidental picture that I obtained near or on the Back Porch.

The electromagnetic frequency range was 0.3 mG to 1.3 mG.

The temperature range was 75.2°F to 75.9°F.

Paranormal Investigation, Session 1, Back Porch, Friday, 21st April 2017, Hays House.

Before I started my first paranormal investigation, session 1, I felt an increase in energy on the back porch. I thought that this might be caused by the Rinnai water heater on the back porch's exterior North wall. When I feel, increase energy. I feel agitated and uncomfortable. I still am not sure whether this was caused by the Rinnai water heater or had a paranormal origin.

11:48 PM Keith: "Hello, I am Keith Evans. You may use your energy to choose words from the Ovilus IV's data base. This is the Ovilus IV. The Ovilus IV will not hurt you."

11:49 PM Keith: "This is the Mel Meter. The Mel Meter measures temperature and electromagnetic frequencies. The Mel meter will not harm you."

11:50 PM Keith: "The Ovilus IV has given me two background words. Own, and add which are spelled O-W-N and A-D-D. The Ovilus IV pronounced the words own and add at a normal conversational level and speed."

1:50 PM Keith: "I have observed the Mel Meter readings to be 1.2 mG and 79.2°F."

1:51 PM Keith: "Own and mad. What are you mad? Correction, it was own and add."

1:52 PM Keith: "The Ovilus IV gave me the word molecules which is spelled M-O-L-E-C-U-L-E-S. The Ovilus IV has pronounced the word molecules at a normal conversational level and speed."

1:52 PM Keith: "I have observed the Mel meter readings to be 1.3 mG and 78.6°F."

1:53 PM Keith: "So, you know that I am a chemist."

1:55 PM Keith: "The Ovilus IV gave me the word animal which is spelled A-N-I-M-A-L. The Ovilus IV pronounced the word animal at a normal conversational level and speed."

1:55 PM Keith: "I have observed the Mel Meter readings to be 1.0 mG and 81.0°F."

1:56 PM Keith: "The Ovilus IV gave me the letter M. M was pronounced at a normal conversational level and speed."

1:56 PM Keith: "I have observed the Mel Meter readings to be 1.0 mG and 80.7°F."

1:58 PM Keith: "I have observed the Mel Meter readings to be 0.9 mG and 80.0°F."

1:58 PM Keith: "The electromagnetic frequency is going to be high here because of the Sonny Boy electrical equipment, that is close by. There is not much that I can do about that because the porch is small."

2:02 PM Keith: "Pat, Kathleen, and Sunshine, did you spend your time sitting on this back porch?"

2:03 PM Keith: "The Ovilus IV gave me the word eggs which is spelled E-G-G-S. The Ovilus IV pronounced the word eggs at a normal conversational level and speed."

2:03 PM Keith: "I have observed the Mel Meter readings to be 0.9 mG and 80.2°F."

2:04 PM Keith: "The Ovilus IV gave me the word slur which is spelled S-L-U-R. The Ovilus IV pronounced the word slur at a normal conversational level and speed."

2:04 PM Keith: "I have observed the Mel Meter readings to be 0.9 mG and 81.4°F."

2:08 PM Keith: "Who said the words egg and slur?"

2:09 PM Keith: "Are you throwing eggs at me because you feel that it was a slur for me to ask you if you sat out on your back porch?"

2:10 PM Keith: "I wonder if the Ovilus IV is just picking up energy between two ghosts that are talking amongst themselves?"

2:11 PM Keith: "Pat, what are your favorite memories about this back porch?"

2:12 PM Keith: "Kathleen, what are your favorite memories about this back porch?"

2:13 PM Keith: "The Ovilus IV has frozen up again. I am going to turn the Ovilus IV off and back on to see if that will help it to function properly."

2:14 PM Keith: "The Ovilus IV has given me three background words case which is spelled C-A-S-E, and quiet, which is spelled Q-U-I-E-T, and real which is spelled R-E-A-L. The words case, quiet, and real, were all pronounced by the Ovilus IV at a normal conversational level and speed."

2:14 PM Keith: "I have observed the Mel Meter readings to be 0.9 mG and 81.2°F."

2:14 PM Keith: "The Ovilus IV has given me the word wicked which is spelled W-I-C-K-E-D. The Ovilus IV has pronounced the word wicked at a normal conversational level and speed."

2:16 PM Keith: "I have observed the Mel Meter readings to be 0.7 mG and 80.6°F."

2:17 PM Keith: "The Ovilus IV has given me the word supply which is spelled S-U-P-P-L-Y. The Ovilus IV has pronounced the word supply at a normal conversational level and speed."

2:17 PM Keith: "I have observed the Mel Meter readings to be 0.5 mG and 82.0°F."

2:18 PM Keith: "The Ovilus IV has given me the word page which is spelled P-A-G-E. The Ovilus IV has pronounced the word page at a normal conversational level and speed."

2:19 PM Keith: "The Ovilus IV has given me the word palace which is spelled P-A-L-A-C-E. The Ovilus IV has pronounced the word palace at a normal conversational level and speed."

2:19 PM Keith: "I have observed the Mel Meter readings to be 0.0 mG and 80.9°F."

2:20 PM to 2:25 PM Keith: "I obtained thermal images of the back-porch area. I obtained one thermal image of the rear window on the exterior of the Hays House's and the porch's west wall. I obtained two thermal images of the Sonny Boy electrical equipment on the porch's north wall and is at the upper right-hand corner of the image. I obtained two thermal images of the pink or orange area near the small female's bathroom, located on the back porch's west wall."

2:26 PM Keith: "The Ovilus IV has frozen up again. It is not responding when I tapped the home icon. So, I will turn it off and on one more time, to see if that will help it function properly."

2:28 PM Keith: "The people next door are talking. Case, quiet, real, wicked, supply, page, palace, what are you trying to tell me?"

2:29 PM Keith: "The Ovilus IV has given me two background words family which is spelled F-A-M-I-L-Y and George which is spelled G-E-O-R-G-E. The Ovilus IV has pronounced the words family and George at a normal conversational level and speed."

2:29 PM Keith: "I have observed the Mel Meter readings to be 0.0 mG and 81.8°F."

2:30 PM Keith: "Yes, the George family, I am working on it. If you can convince the owners to let me write about your house. That would be very helpful. George is your last name correct?"

2:31 PM Keith: "The Ovilus IV has given me the word desk which is spelled D-E-S-K. The Ovilus IV has pronounce the word desk at a normal conversational level and speed."

2:31 PM Keith: "I have observed the Mel Meter readings to be 0.0 mG and 80.7°F."

2:32 PM Keith: "The Ovilus IV has given me the word rocket which is spelled R-O-C-K-E-T. The Ovilus IV has pronounced the word rocket at a normal conversational level and speed."

2:32 PM Keith: "I have observed the Mel Meter readings to be 0.0 mG and 79.2°F."

2:36 PM Keith: "How is the George family doing today?"

2:37 PM Keith: "The Ovilus IV has given me the word Jupiter which is spelled J-U-P-I-T-E-R. The Ovilus IV has pronounced the word Jupiter at a normal conversational level and speed."

2:37 PM Keith: "I have observed the Mel Meter readings to be 0.0 mG and 79.5°F."

2:41 PM Keith: "This session 1 ended on Friday, 21st April 2017."

Paranormal Investigation, Session 2, Back Porch, Friday, 21st April 2017, Hays House.

3:45 PM Keith: "Hello, I am Keith Evans. You may use your energy to choose words from the Ovilus IV's Database. This is the Ovilus IV. The Ovilus IV will not hurt you."

3:45 PM Keith: "This is the Mel Meter. The Mel Meter measures temperature and electromagnetic frequencies. The Mel Meter will not harm you."

3:46 PM Keith: "The Ovilus IV has given me two background words: Pound which is spelled P-O-U-N-D, and orb which is spelled O-R-B. The Ovilus IV has pronounced the words pound, and orb at a normal conversational level and speed."

3:46 PM Keith: "I have observed the Mel Meter readings to be 0.0 mG and 79.0°F."

3:46 PM Keith: "I have observed the Mel Meter readings to be 0.0 mG and 79.1°F."

3:47 PM Keith: "The Ovilus IV has given me the word slave which is spelled S-L-A-V-E. The Ovilus IV has pronounced the word slave at a normal conversational level and speed."

3:47 PM Keith: "I have observed the Mel Meter readings to be 0.0 mG and 80.5°F."

3:50 PM Keith: "Pound, orb, and slave, what are you trying to tell me?"

3:51 PM Keith: "It was nice talking to the George family."

3:52 PM Keith: "Are you a slave?"

3:53 PM Keith: "Pat, how often did you set out on the back porch?"

3:54 PM to 3:57 PM Keith: "I obtained seven, thermal images on the back porch. I obtained one thermal image of the rear window which is to the right of the back door, as you're facing the back door. I have obtained two thermal images of the back porch's cemented steps near Frances's hand print. I obtained two thermal images of the small lady's room's door that had an orange area. I obtained two, thermal images of the Sonny Boy electrical equipment on the Back Porch's North wall. The Sonny Boy electrical equipment had an orange or red square at the lower right side of the two thermal images."

3:57 PM Keith: "Okay, the Ovilus IV is frozen up again. I am going to turn it off."

3:58 PM Keith: "I am turning the Ovilus IV on."

3:59 PM Keith: "The Ovilus IV has given me two background words: line which is spelled L-I-N-E, and Chris which is spelled C-H-R-I-S. The Ovilus IV has pronounced the words line and Chris at a normal conversational level and speed."

3:59 PM Keith: "I have observed the Mel Meter readings to be 0.0 mG and 77.6°F."

4 PM Keith: "The Ovilus IV has given me the word solstice which is spelled S-O-L-S-T-I-C-E. The Ovilus IV has pronounced the word solstice at a normal conversational level and speed."

4:01 PM Keith: "I have observed the Mel Meter readings to be 0.0 mG and 80.0°F."

4:01 PM Keith: "The Ovilus IV has given me the word material spelled M-A-T-E-R-I-A-L. The Ovilus IV has pronounced the word material at a normal conversational level and speed."

4:07 PM Keith: "Chris, are you walking the line?"

4:08 PM Keith: "Chris, are you part of the George family?"

4:09 PM Keith: "The Ovilus IV is frozen up again. I'm going to insert new batteries."

4:12 PM Keith: "The Ovilus IV has given me two background words falls which is spelled F-A-L-L-S, and sip which is spelled S-I-P. The Ovilus IV has pronounced the words falls and sip at a normal conversational level and speed."

4:12 PM Keith: "I have observed the Mel Meter readings to be 0.0 mG and 77.0°F."

4:13 PM Keith: "The Ovilus IV has given me the word basement which is spelled B-A-S-E-M-E-N-T. The Ovilus IV has pronounced the word basement at a normal conversational level and speed."

4:13 PM Keith: "I have observed the Mel Meter readings to be 0.0 mG and 79.4°F."

4:16 PM Keith: "Your telling me the words falls, sip, and basement. Are you talking about a water falls, someone sipping on coffee and what is in the basement?"

4:16 PM Keith: "Chris, what do you want to talk about?"

4:19 PM Keith: "You may be talking in sentences. I am only getting bits and pieces of those sentences from my Ovilus IV."

4:20 PM Keith: "So, this makes it hard for me to understand what you are trying to tell me."

4:21 PM Keith: "Chris, are you related to the Buck, Gibson, and or Hays family's?"

4:22 PM Keith: "Sunshine, yes or no did you ever sit out on the back porch of the Hays House?"

4:23 PM Keith: "The Hays House does not have a basement."

4:24 PM Keith: "The Hays House has a crawlspace."

4:25 PM Keith: "Somebody just blew an automobile horn."

4:26 PM Keith: "Annie, are you here today?"

4:27 PM Keith: "I did not feel that you were here today Annie, because my digital camera is not going in and out of focus."

4:28 PM Keith: "Who said the word basement?"

4:29 PM Keith: "Who said the words falls and sip?"

4:30 PM Keith: "Were you trying to choose the word slip instead of the word sip?"

4:30 PM Keith: "I observed the Mel Meter readings to be 0.0 mG and 78.5°F."

4:31 PM Keith: "I noticed that the Mel Meter is not picking up any electromagnetic frequencies."

4:32 PM Keith: "I observed the Mel Meter readings to be 0.0 mG and 79 .5°F."

4:33 PM Keith: "The Ovilus IV has given me the word devil which is spelled D-E-V-I-L. The Ovilus IV has pronounced the word devil with a deep man's voice and very slowly."

4:33 PM Keith: "I have observed the Mel Meter readings to be 0.0 mG and 78.7°F."

4:36 PM Keith: "Devil, I am all about God. So, go away."

4:37 PM Keith: "I wish the Buck, Gibson, and Hays family members would give me more details on the history about the Hays House."

4:38 PM Keith: "I have observed the Mel Meter readings to be 0.0 mG and 79.7°F."

4:39 PM Keith: "Thank you for talking to me. Have a nice day."

4:39 PM Keith: "This session 2 ended on Friday, 21st April 2017."

The Analysis of Session 1, Back Porch, Friday, 21st April 2017, Hays House. Date of analysis was Friday, 29th September 2017.

At 1:50 PM the first and second background words given to me by the Ovilus IV during this session one were own and add. I feel that this was someone from the Hays, or Gibson family asking me to purchase the Hays House and add it to my collection of things that I own. This could be the spirit of Kathleen talking about adding a row to something that she is knitting. Kathleen maybe talking about an item that she owned in the past that she had kitted, such as that Waiter Pulls.

At 1:52 PM the third word given to me by the Ovilus IV during this first session was Molecules. I feel that this is an intellectual response by, a ghost, and or spirit letting me know that they realize that I am a chemist's and they are trying to find common ground.

At 1:55 PM the fourth word given to me by the Ovilus IV during this first session was animal. I do not feel that this word is in response to any of the questions that I've asked so far during this session 1.

At 1:56 PM the fifth letter given to me by the Ovilus IV during this first session was M. I feel that this is an intelligent spirit of Sunshine Gibson and that she is pointing out that her room should not be called the M room. I feel that Sunshine is questioning the naming of her room as M would be incorrect and that I should name her room the Sunshine Room. The present owners had named Sunshine's Room the M room.

At 1:58 PM I Keith Evans, had stated that the electromagnetic frequency on my Mel Meter may be high due to my close proximity to the Sonny Boy electrical equipment. Since the porch is very small. It is hard to not be close to the Sonny Boy electrical equipment as long as I stay on the Back Porch.

At 2:03 PM the sixth word that was given to me by the Ovilus IV during this first session was eggs. I do not feel that this word is responding to any of the questions that I've asked so for during this session number one.

At 2:04 PM the seventh word that was given to me by the Ovilus IV during this first session was slur. Having just recently received the word eggs followed by slur. It occurred to me that may be the ghosts or spirits were saying that they were throwing eggs at me because I was slurring them concerning asking a question about if they were sitting on the back porch instead of asking about the front porch. There may be some negative thoughts concerning choosing to sit on the back porch instead of the front porch. Since this chapter is about my paranormal investigating of the back porch. I have to asked questions only about the back porch.

At 2:13 PM the Ovilus IV stopped working properly. I turned the Ovilus IV off and at 2:14 PM I turned the Ovilus IV back on. At that time, it appeared to be functioning properly.

At 2:14 PM the Ovilus IV gave me the eighth, ninth, 10th, and 11th words for this session 1, which were case, quiet, real, and wicked. I do not feel that any of these words are in response to any of the questions I've asked so far during this session number one. It could be that the ghosts are arguing amongst themselves as to whether I am for real to be working on this paranormal case. One spirit may feel that it's interesting and asked the others to just keep quiet. Wicked is an adjective with many synonyms. Just to name a few of the synonyms: immoral, wrong, bad, corrupt, mean, nasty, harsh, unpleasant, disagreeable, uncomfortable, annoying, irritating, and hateful. There could be a ghost and or spirit that finds me wicked for completing Paranormal Investigations within the Hays House.

Between 1:50 PM and 2:17 PM, I noticed that the electromagnetic frequency range moved between 0.5 mG to as high as 1.3 mG. I had just determined that this was because I was on a small porch and had to sit very close to the Sonny Boy electrical equipment that was mounted on the porch's North wall.

At 2:17 PM the Ovilus IV gave me the 12th word for this session number one, which was supply. I do not believe that this word is in response to any of the questions that I have asked so far during this session number one.

At 2:18 PM the Ovilus IV gave me the 13th word for this session number one, which was page. I feel that this is an intelligent spirit referring to the page that I am writing on as I document the transcript of this session number one, paranormal investigation.

At 2:19 PM the Ovilus IV gave me the 14th word for this session number one which was palace. I feel that this is an intelligent spirit referring to the Hays House is being a palace.

From 2:20 PM to 2:25 PM, I obtained thermal images on the back porch. Most of the thermal images are normal without any anomalies, except for two thermal images that I obtained near the female's bathroom door, which is located on the back porch's west wall. On both images, there are areas of pink or orange color which are too warm to be normal for wooden surfaces. I was unable to identify any reason why this wood should be showing up on the thermal imager as to be warm enough to be the color of pink or orange. I touch the wooden surface near the location where it appeared to be pink or orange on the thermal image and the wooden surface did not feel warm to touch.

At 2:26 PM the Ovilus IV failed to work properly. The Ovilus IV would not respond when I tapped the home icon. So, I turned off the Ovilus IV off and then turned it back on.

At 2:29 PM the Ovilus IV gave me the 15th and 16th background words for this session number one, which was family and George. I feel this was a ghost or spirit from the George family in Apalachicola, Florida, who was responding to my interested in writing a book about where their family at one time resided.

At 2:31 PM the Ovilus IV gave me the 17th word for this session number one, which was desk. I feel that this is an intelligent spirit referring to the double-sided desk, where I sit at, in the Living Room, and save all of the digital pictures, thermal images, and video from my camcorders on to my lap top.

At 2:32 PM the Ovilus IV gave me the 18th word for this session number one, which was rocket. I do not feel that the word rocket is responding to any of the questions that I have asked so far during this session number one.

At 3:37 PM the Ovilus IV gave me the 19th word for this session number one, which was Jupiter. I do not feel that the word Jupiter is responding to any of the questions that I have asked so far during this session number one.

Ovilus IV words: Own, add.

Ovilus IV words: Family, George.

The analysis of the Session 2, Back Porch, Friday, 21st April 2017, Hays House. The analysis was completed on 30th September 2017.

At 3:46 PM the Ovilus IV gave me the first and second background words for session 2, pound and orb. I have not asked any questions yet during this session 2. So, I believe that the words pound, and orb are just spirits and or ghosts talking amongst themselves.

At 3:47 PM the Ovilus IV gave me the third word for session 2, slave. I have not asked any questions yet during session 2. I believe that the word slave is just spirits and or ghosts talking amongst themselves.

From 3:54 PM to 3:57 PM I obtained thermal images on the back porch. I obtained one thermal image of the rear window next to the back door, which appeared to be normal. I obtained two thermal images of the back-porch cement steps which had the hand print of Frances Hays, embossed in to the cement. The thermal images of the back-porch cement steps had no abnormalities. I obtained two thermal images of the lady's bathroom door. These thermal images had an orange stripe that I cannot explain. The wood was not heated and there was nothing to cause a reflected heat signature in that area. I obtained two thermal images of the Sonny Boy electrical equipment on the porch's North wall. There was an orange or red colored square on the lower right-hand side of each of the thermal images of the Sonny Boy electrical equipment.

At 5:57 PM the Ovilus IV failed to function properly. I turned the Ovilus IV off for about one minute. When I turned the Ovilus IV back on, it worked properly.

At 3:59 PM the Ovilus IV gave me the fourth and fifth background words for session 2, line and Chris. I feel that this is an intelligent spirit telling me that their name is Chris and asking me about a certain line within the transcript that I'm documenting concerning session 2. I do not know any Chris that has any association with the history of the Hays House. That does not mean that there is not a Chris who is a member of the Hays, Gibson, and or Buck families. It just means that I have not discovered any connection yet.

At 4 PM the Ovilus IV gave me the sixth word for session 2, solstice. I do not believe that the word solstice is in response to any questions that I have asked so far during this session number two.

At 4:01 PM the Ovilus IV gave me the seventh word for session 2, material. I do not believe that the word material is in response to any questions that I have asked so far during this session number two.

At 4:09 PM the Ovilus IV has stopped functioning properly again. I'm going to put new batteries into the Ovilus IV. I feel that the Spirits are somehow interfering with the Ovilus IV's ability to function properly. Sometimes they will drain the batteries at a very fast rate. On other occasions the ghosts and or spirits will just cause the Ovilus IV to not function properly. Usually when I turned the Ovilus IV off and back on within a minute, then the Ovilus IV will function properly.

At 4:12 PM the Ovilus IV gave me the eighth, and ninth words for this session 2, falls and sip. I do not feel that the words falls and sip are in response to any of the questions that I have asked so far during this session number two.

At 4:13 PM the Ovilus IV gave me the 10th word for this session 2, basement. The Hays House does not have a basement. The Hays House has a crawlspace. I do not feel that the word basement is in response to any of the questions that I have asked so far during this session number two.

At 4:19 PM I explained to the ghosts and or spirits that the Ovilus IV only picks up one or two words of each sentence that they may be trying to relay to me. That is only if one ghost or one spirit is talking at a time. If multiple combinations of ghosts and or spirits are talking at the same time, then I might get two words. The first word may be from the first spirits conversation and the second word might be from the second spirits conversation. That's what makes it so hard to figure out what is being asked or said when you use an Ovilus IV during paranormal investigation.

At 4:33 PM the Ovilus IV gave me the 11th word for this session 2, the devil. I feel that too many ghosts and spirits when they try to communicate with the living get a bad rap by most living human beings. Those who run away, get scared every time a ghost or spirit tries to communicate, are just causing ghosts and or spirits to have a very negative attitude towards the living. Thus, we have a lot of ghosts and spirits who want to say something negative, just to frighten us. But I don't frighten that easy. I don't believe that this ghost or spirit is the devil. I do not believe that this ghost and or spirit is evil and or no more negative than human beings are. That's one reason why we should always treat ghosts and spirits like they are people. Ghosts and spirits are disembodied people who have passed on. Pass on, meaning that they no longer have a physical body, but they definitely can move from heaven to earth. I feel that the things that they cherished and loved like their homes and their possessions, like antiques, cars and homes can actually allow the ghosts and or spirits the ability to travel from heaven to earth. These possessions give the ghosts or spirits an avenue to be able to travel between the state they are now in after death, to our rim which is called life.

From 3:46 PM to 4:38 PM, the Mel Meter's reading for the electromagnetic frequency was 0.0 mG. That totally destroys my theory that sitting close to the Sonny Boy electrical equipment was causing the electromagnetic frequency readings on the Mel Meter to be extra high during Session 1. Throughout today's session 2 paranormal investigation, I was sitting in the exact same location that I was sitting in during session one's paranormal investigation. I was the same distance from the Sonny Boy electrical equipment during both sessions. The only difference was that the Mel Meter readings for the electromagnetic frequency during session 2 was 0.0 mG throughout the entire session.

Digital Pictures, Back Porch, Friday, 11th November 2016, Hays House.

One picture of the entire original back porch.

One picture of the center view of the back porch.

Please see the author's website at www.keithoevans.com to view each digital picture.

Thermal Images, Back Porch, Friday, 11th November 2016, Hays House.

One thermal image of the North side of the original back porch.

One thermal image of the center of the original back porch.

Two thermal images of the South side of the original back porch.

Please see the author's website at www.keithoevans.com to view each thermal image.

CHAPTER 13

1st Floor Wraparound Front Porch, Hays House, Ghosts are People too.

The description of the 1st Floor Wraparound Front Porch, Hays House.

The First Floor Front Porch is a wraparound porch that includes the entire West side of the house which is the front of the house. There is also a section of the wraparound porch which is on the North side of the house. The North side of the wraparound porch ends at the starting of the interior West wall of the dining room. There is also an exterior door that enters the Dining Room. This exterior door is located at the far north side of the First Floor Wraparound Front Porch, right at the location where the four steps go down to the ground.

One may exit the far north side of the wraparound porch by using the four cement steps going down to the ground. The steps have some embossment written on their surface, this had to be there while the cement steps were still wet. The second step from the bottom has Francis Hays, embossed into the surface at the far north side. The third step from the bottom has the name Patsy Ann embossed into the surface, near the far north side. I believe that the four cement steps on the North side of the First Floor Wraparound Front Porch were made on or near to 20 March 1953 because the wet cement has Frances Hays scratched into the soft cement just as it does on the back-porch steps. The back-porch steps have the same name scratched into it, Frances Hays and the date 20th of March 1953. I feel that Pat and Kathleen Hays decided to update the back-porch steps and the steps to the North side of the First Floor Wraparound Front Porch at the same time. I would imagine both porch steps were made out of wood prior to these renovations.

The entire east and south exterior walls of the First Floor Wraparound Front Porch, is covered with ship lap siding that appears to be original from 1908. There are 10 columns on the outer perimeter of the First Floor Wraparound Front Porch, to include the west and north sides. Each column is approximately 11 to 12 inches in diameter. Each column sits above or on top of a 20" x 20" cube shape formed from bricks that are approximately 25 1/2 inches in height above the porch floor. The columns are wood and painted white. The brick cubed shaped stands that the columns are perched on are painted light green. Between the 10 columns at the perimeter of the First Floor Wraparound Front Porch is a white wooden railing that would keep one from falling off the porch. Between the 10 columns is a white, modern, wooden, decorative fencing. This porch has the horizontal railing made from regular 2 x 4 boards that make up the top and bottom railing, with some decorative supporting beams evenly spaced between each column. The exterior of the front door appears to be original. The exterior side of the original front door was last stained sometime after 1996. The glass on the front entrance has only three original glass panes remaining. The fourth panel of the upper section of the front door was broken and replaced sometime after 1996.

The front steps are on the west side of the First Floor Wraparound Front Porch and have three cement steps going down to the sidewalk. The far southwest end of the First Floor Wraparound Front Porch has a natural wooden swing hanging from the ceiling. Located throughout the rest of the First Floor Wraparound Front Porch are six wooden chairs painted green, two wooden white rocking chairs, and a wicker stand which is painted green. There are original tongue and groove ceiling boards, that are approximately 2 1/2 inches wide and are painted white. The floorboards are painted brown, and approximately 5 1/2 inches wide. The porch floor boards may or may not be original. I feel that the columns are original. These columns have probably had some repairs over the years. There are four brown modern ceiling fans mounted evenly across the ceiling of the wraparound porch. This is an excellent porch to relax on in the summertime. Especially, in the early morning and late evening because it is nice and cool. It seems like there's always a breeze coming off of the river.

The description of the First Floor Wraparound Front Porch from pictures dated 1978, Hays House.

In 1978, there was no railing on either side of the steps leading to the front porch. The front porch did have decorative white post and railing between the pillars and the red brick around the perimeter of the porch. The front porch brick under each pillar was not painted. It was just the natural red brick. There was a porch swing, but it was on the Northwest corner of the porch. You can still see the large metal hooks hanging from the ceiling where this porch swing use to be. These hanging hooks are still there, located were the ceiling wood creates a seam that is made from the wood from the west and north sides, that are going in different directions, meet on the ceiling at the Northwest corner of the porch. By the angle that was created by the two large metal hooks that are hanging from the ceiling, the hanging swing faced Avenue D in a southwest direction. Prior to 1978, Kathleen had two hanging flower baskets on the far South end of the porch and near the circular area of the porch. I can still see the metal hooks hanging from the ceiling, but the years have not been good to these hooks. The only thing that is left of these hooks, are the metal shaped pegs sticking out of the porch's ceiling.

The History of the First Floor Wraparound Front Porch, Hays House.

From 1942 until 1964 the Hays Family decorated the screen door at the front entrance. From 1956 to 1964 it was France's project to cover the screen door at the front entrance with a large cardboard box and colorful paper like silver, gold, and red, with a different Christmas theme each year. One-year France decorated the screen door with the Three Wise Men following the North Star. France also decorated the screen door with one large box, as if it was a ramped Christmas gift. Some years France would cover the screen door with multiple Christmas gifts. From 1942 to 1964 most people enjoyed making their know Christmas decorations. The local stores did not carry many

Christmas decorations between 1942 to 1964, like they do in 2017. In 1942 the front porch had no fencing around the edges, and no banister on either side of the steps.

Mel Meter base readings, First Floor Wraparound Front Porch, Hays House.

10:15 AM The electrical outlet on the porch's exterior West side wall of the house. This electrical outlet is not in use.

The electromagnetic frequency range was 0.0 mG to 0.0 mG.

The temperature range was 67.6°F to 67.9°F.

10:16 AM The South side mounted West wall light, located on the exterior of the house. This light is in the off position.

The electromagnetic frequency range was 0.0 mG to 0.0 mG.

The temperature range was 69.4°F to 69.4°F.

10:17 AM the North side mounted West wall light, located on the exterior of the house. This light is in the off position.

The electromagnetic frequency range was 0.7 mG to 1.4 mG.

The temperature range was 69.8°F to 70.0°F.

10:18 AM The electrical out let on the Northern side of the house, located on the exterior West wall. This electrical outlet is in use.

The electrical, magnetic frequency range was 0.0 mG to 0.0 mG.

The temperature range was 68.4°F to 68.6°F.

10:19 AM The white air conditioner unit on the exterior North wall of the house. This air conditioner unit is not in use.

The electromagnetic frequency range was 0.0 mG to 0.0 mG.

The temperature range was 69.4°F to 69.5°F.

10:20 AM The exterior water out let near the North side front porch railing.

The electrical, magnetic frequency range was 0.0 mG to 0.0 mG.

The temperature range was 69.9°F to 70.5°F.

10:21 AM The downstairs doorbell, located on the exterior West wall of the house, near the front entrance.

The electromagnetic frequency range was 0.0 mG to 0.0 mG.

The temperature range was 69.7°F to 69.7°F.

10:22 AM The guest's doorbell, located on the exterior West wall of the house, near the front entrance.

The electromagnetic frequency range was 1.1 mG to 1.1 mG.

The temperature range was 70.2°F to 70.3°F.

10:23 AM The North side of the house, at the steps near where Patsy Ann Hays's name is embossed into the cement.

The electromagnetic frequency range was 0.0 mG to 0.0 mG.

The temperature range was 71.2°F to 71.2°F.

10:24 AM The North side of the house, at the steps near where Frances Hays's name is embossed into the cement.

The electromagnetic frequency range was 0.0 mG to 0.0 mG.

The temperature range was 71.6°F to 71.6°F.

The Paranormal Investigation, Session 1, First Floor Wraparound Front Porch, Saturday, 22nd April 2017, Hays House.

10:35 AM Keith: "Hello, I am Keith Evans. This is the Ovilus IV. You may use your energy to choose words from the Ovilus IV words database. The Ovilus IV will not hurt you." (Hold it up.)

10:35 AM Keith: "This is the Mel Meter. The Mel Meter measures temperature and electromagnetic frequencies. The Mel Meter will not harm you." (Hold it up.)

10:36 AM Keith: "The Ovilus IV has given me two background words; Cast which is spelled C-A-S-T and the letter P. The Ovilus IV has pronounced the word Cast and the letter P in a normal conversational level and speed."

10:36 AM Keith: "I have observed the Mel Meter readings to be 0.0 mG and 77.0°F."

10:36 AM Keith: "I have observed the Mel Meter readings to be 0.0 mG and 76.5°F."

10:38 AM Keith: "That is a squeaky wheel on a trailer pulled by a pickup truck traveling's South bound on Avenue D."

10:39 AM Keith: "The Ovilus IV has given me the word real which is spelled R-E-A-L. The Ovilus IV has pronounced the word real, with a deep male's voice and a normal conversational speed."

10:40 AM Keith: "Two people are walking across the front porch and have entered the front door."

10:41 AM Keith: "I have observed the Mel Meter readings to be 0.0 mG and 76.6°F."

10:43 AM Keith: "I can hear two people exiting through the front door and leaving while walking across the porch."

10:44 AM Keith: "The word cast, the P, and the word real, that does not give me much to go on. Like, what are you trying to tell me?"

10:46 PM Keith: "I feel like you're just jerking me around and given me unassociated words."

10:47 PM Keith: "James Fulion Buck, at one time did you sit out on this front porch?"

10:48 PM Keith: "Lamb Gilland Buck, at one time that you sit out on this front porch?"

10:49 AM Keith: "It is just constant cars and trucks going by on Avenue D."

10:50 AM Keith: "Terryss McBride Buck, at one time did you set out on this front porch?"

10:51 AM Keith: "The Ovilus IV has given me the word calcium which is spelled C-A-L-C-I-U-M. The Ovilus IV has pronounced the word calcium in a normal conversational level and speed."

10:51 AM Keith: "I have observed the Mel Meter readings to be 0.0 mG and 78.4°F."

10:51 AM Keith: "I have observed the Mel Meter readings to be 0.0 mG and 78.7°F."

10:54 AM Keith: "Calcium, I have received a lot of chemistry related words. I am beginning to think that an intellectual alien life form is communicating with me and not a ghost or spirit."

10:56 AM Keith: "The Ovilus IV has given me the word nice which is spelled N-I-C-E. The Ovilus IV has pronounced the word nice like a lude comment but at a normal conversational level and speed."

10:57 AM Keith: "I have observed the Mel Meter readings to be 0.0 mG and 83.4°F."

10:58 AM Keith: "The Ovilus IV has given me the word reveal which is spelled R-E-V-E-A-L. The Ovilus IV has pronounce the word reveal at a normal conversational level and speed."

10:58 AM Keith: "I have observed the Mel Meter readings to be 0.0 mG and 78.2°F."

10:58 AM Keith: "I have observed the Mel Meter readings to be 0.0 mG and 78.5°F."

11:03 AM Keith: "A constant stream of cars are going by on Avenue D and Fourth Street."

11:04 AM Keith: "Pat, Kathleen, Sunshine, and Mary, did you all enjoy sitting out on the porch when you were living here?"

11:05 AM to 11:10 AM: "I obtained thermal readings on the First Floor Wraparound Front Porch. I obtained two images of the rocking chair to the right, with camcorder number one on the center right side arm of the chair. That is as I am facing the chair. I obtained two images of the two rocking chairs with camcorder number one being at the center left position and orange in color. My warm seat is at the center, lower, middle position and colored orange."

11:11 AM Keith: "Two individuals exited the front door. I hear the front door being locked and then two people walking across the wooden front porch."

11:11 AM Keith: "The Ovilus IV gave me the word rocket which is spelled R-0-C-K-E-T. The Ovilus IV has pronounced the word rocket in a normal conversational level and speed."

11:12 AM Keith: "I have observed the Mel Meter readings to be 0.0 mG and 77.1°F."

11:16 AM Keith: "Look, this book is not about aliens, this book is about ghosts and spirits, and people who once lived and have now passed away."

11:18 AM Keith: "I am asking the Buck, Gibson, and Hays families, for some help about the history of the Hays House. So, I may write about this in the book."

11:19 AM Keith: "How well did the Hays House standup during hurricanes and or bad storms?"

11:20 AM Keith: "Give me the name of the storm in which the Hays House received damage?"

11:23 AM Keith: "The Ovilus IV looks like it has frozen up again. No, when I pressed the home icon, the Ovilus IV's program went back to the home position."

11:23 AM Keith: "The Ovilus IV has given me two words; April which is spelled A-P-R-I-L and level which is spelled L-E-V-E-L. The Ovilus IV has pronounced the words April and level at a normal conversational level and speed."

11:24 AM Keith: "I have observed the Mel Meter readings to be 0.0 mG and 77.6°F."

11:24 AM Keith: "The Ovilus IV has given me the word cake which is spelled C-A-K-E. Cake was spoken at a normal conversational level and a normal speed."

11:25 AM Keith: "I have observed the Mel Meter readings to be 0.0 mG and 77.6°F."

11:26 AM Keith: "April, level, and cake are not answering any of my questions."

11:26 AM Keith: "Thank you for talking to me. Have a good day."

11:26 AM Keith: "This session one ended on Saturday, 22nd of April 2017."

The Paranormal Investigation, Session 2, First Floor Wraparound Front Porch, Saturday, 22nd April 2017, Hays House.

12:25 PM Keith: "Hello, I am Keith Evans. This is the Ovilus IV. You may use your energy to choose words from the Ovilus IV's database. The Ovilus IV will not hurt you." (Hold it up.)

12:26 PM Keith: "This is the Mel Meter. The Mel Meter measures temperature and electromagnetic frequencies. The Mel Meter will not harm you." (Hold it up.)

12:26 PM Keith: "The Ovilus IV has given me three background words; Thomas which is spelled T-H-O-M-A-S, bomb which is spelled

B-O-M-B, and Lord which is spelled L-O-R-D. The Ovilus IV has pronounced the words Thomas, bomb, and Lord in a normal conversational level and speed."

12:27 PM Keith: "I have observed the Mel Meter readings to be 0.0 mG and 78.0°F."

12:28 PM Keith: "The Ovilus IV has given me the word Vern which is spelled V-E-R-N. The Ovilus IV has pronounced the word Vern in a normal conversational level and speed."

12:28 PM Keith: "I have observed the Mel Meter readings to be 0.0 mG and 78.2°F."

12:31 PM Keith: "For the last five minutes there has been constant vehicle traffic on North Avenue, I'm wrong, Avenue D."

12:32 PM Keith: "The Ovilus IV has given me the word lie which is spelled L-I-E. The Ovilus IV has pronounced the word lie at a normal conversational level and speed."

12:32 PM Keith: "I have observed the Mel Meter readings to be 0.0 mG and 79.2°F."

12:32 PM Keith: "Lie, yes, good catch."

12:33 PM Keith: "The Ovilus IV has given me the word ashes which is spelled A-S-H-E-S. The Ovilus IV has pronounced the word ashes at a normal conversational level and speed."

12:34 PM Keith: "I have observed the Mel Meter readings to be 0.0 mG and 78.9°F."

12:38 PM Keith: "Thomas and Vern, are you members of the Buck family?"

12:39 PM Keith: "Thomas and Vern, are you members of the Gibson family?"

12:40 PM Keith: "Thomas and Vern, are you members of the Hays family?"

12:41 PM Keith: "Thomas and Vern are you listening?"

12:41 PM Keith: "Is Ashes a name?"

12:42 PM to 12:46 PM Keith: "I conducted a thermal reading of the First Floor Wraparound Front Porch. I obtained two thermal images of the front door. I obtained two thermal images of the two rocking chairs with camcorder one at center left and colored orange and located at lower center is my warm rocking chair, where I had been setting, which is colored orange."

12:46 PM Keith: "Is Ashes a first name or a last name?"

12:47 PM Keith: "There is still constant car traffic on both Fourth Street and Avenue D."

12:48 PM Keith: "Sunshine, what time of day, did you like to sit out on the porch?"

12:49 PM Keith: "Sunshine, was the upkeep on the porch a lot of work?"

12:50 PM Keith: "Pat, how many times did you paint this porch during your lifetime?"

12:51 PM Keith: "Kathleen, how many times did you have this porch painted after Pat passed away?"

12:51 PM Keith: "Kathleen, do you miss living here?"

12:52 PM Keith: "It looks like the Ovilus IV may be frozen up again. No, the Ovilus IV's program went back to its home position. So, if that is the case. It is not frozen up, and the batteries are working fine."

12:54 PM Keith: "I turned the Ovilus IV back on."

12:54 PM Keith: "The Ovilus IV has given me two background words weapon which is spelled W-E-A-P-O-N, and flowers which is spelled

F-L-O-W-E-R-S. The Ovilus IV has pronounced weapon and flowers at a normal conversational level and speed."

12:55 PM Keith: "I have observed the Mel Meter readings to be 0.0 mG and 80.2°F."

12:56 PM Keith: "The Ovilus IV has given me the word apocalypse which is spelled A-P-O-C-A-L-Y-P-S-E. The Ovilus IV has pronounced the word apocalypse at a normal conversational level and speed."

12:56 PM Keith: "I have observed the Mel Meter readings to be 0.0 mG and 78.0°F."

1:01 PM Keith: "Okay, weapons, flowers, and apocalypse, do not answer any of my question."

1:02 PM Keith: "On this front porch, I am getting many random words that are just spirits talking amongst themselves."

1:03 PM Keith: "I guess the Buck, Gibson, and Hays families did not have any good times out here on the front porch."

1:05 PM Keith: "Pat, did you spend more time doing maintenance on the front porch then sitting on the front porch?"

1:06 PM Keith: "The Ovilus IV is frozen up and will not go back to its home position. I am going to turn the Ovilus IV off."

1:07 PM Keith: "I turned the Ovilus IV on."

1:08 PM Keith: "The Ovilus IV has given me two background words woven which is spelled W-O-V-E-N and loss which is spelled L-O-S-S. The Ovilus IV has pronounced the words woven and loss at a normal conversational level and speed."

1:08 PM Keith: "I have observed the Mel Meter readings to be 0.0 mG and 79.5°F."

1:11 PM Keith: "It is just constant vehicle traffic on Avenue D, and Fourth Street."

1:12 PM Keith: "I just heard a horn as a person is securing their car."

1:13 PM Keith: "Does anyone want to talk today?"

1:14 PM Keith: "Maybe all of this vehicular traffic is just too much of a distraction for the ghosts and spirits."

1:14 PM Keith: "I have observed the Mel Meter readings to be 0.0 mG and 79.1°F."

1:15 PM Keith: "I heard two car horns blowing."

1:16 PM Keith: "Thank you for talking to me. Have a good day."

1:16 PM Keith: "This Session 2 ended on Saturday, 22nd day of April 2017."

The analysis of the Paranormal Investigation, Session 1, First Floor Wraparound Front Porch, Saturday, 22nd April 2017, Hays House. The date of this analysis was Tuesday, 11 July 2017.

At 10:36 AM, the first and second background words for this Session 1 were cast and the letter P. Background words given by the Ovilus IV from obtaining the electromagnetic energy within the environment. Since I had not asked any questions yet, I do not feel that the word cast and the letter P are in response to any questions that I have asked in the past.

During this entire Session 1, I spent more time documenting traffic sounds than asking questions. Any noise in the background that is heard while conducting a paranormal investigation must be identified and or tagged as to what it is, this way no one can say well maybe that was something to do with the paranormal. If you know what the noise was created by, and it's not paranormal definitely identify it and say This is truly not a productive way to conduct a paranormal investigation. So, I don't recommend conducting a paranormal investigation during the day and near a busy roadway. I felt that it was important to cover all of the areas that were used by the families two families that lived in the Hays House between 1908 and 1996.

At 10:38 AM I said "That is a squeaky wheel on a trailer pulled by a pickup truck traveling's South bound on Avenue D."

At 10:39 AM I receive the third word for session 1, real. This word real was given to me before I asked my first question. This could be an intelligent spirit or ghost responding to what I had just said at 10:38 AM, about the squeaky wheel on that trailer. The spirit may have responded by saying, "For real", and the Ovilus IV only picked up on the last word real. Now on the other hand, I feel that the word real may have been just the ghosts and spirits in the local area talking amongst themselves. There are those who feel that ghosts have to be called or summons by some special process or method by a living person and that is totally untrue. There is a town hall full of ghosts that just happened to be in the local area. If you are a sensitive or if you take time to notice the small ways that ghosts and spirits attempt to communicate with the living, then you would be able to com-municate with the multitude of ghosts and spirits that happen to be in the area. The ghosts and spirits that are populating different areas are there because they have their own agendas and that has nothing to do with what people do or don't do, or what people want or don't want. Without the specialized equipment like the Ovilus IV that picks up the so-called electromagnetic frequency that is given off by ghosts and or spirits who use their electromagnetic frequencies to choose words from within the Ovilus IV's database. I would only be able to feel certain ghosts and spirits strong emotional feelings. For instance, at the Hays House, I get a very strong emotional feeling, but nothing visual. Nothing audio, but the emotional feelings are that the dearly departed would like someone in the Hays family to purchase and continue to own and maintain and maybe live or work at the present Hays House. This is the extent of my psychic ability that relates to ghosts and or spirits that I have been able to identify.

At 10:44 AM and 10:46 AM my comments in part, such as what are you trying to tell me? Also, my comments as to I feel like you were jerking me around and given me unassociated words. This is just frustration, coming from a paranormal investigator. I too, often for-get that I'm not having a conversation with one spirit or ghost. Also, there are no guarantees with the multitude of ghosts and spirits in the Apalachicola area that I may even hear or talk to any members of the Hays, Gibson, and Buck family's. The probability of speaking to the Hays, Gibson, and Buck family members would be as great as having a town hall meeting with everyone in the town and trying to hear a certain individual shouting out amongst the crowd. There is a far greater possibility of hearing someone who lived in this town that had never lived in the Hays House. That's the same way with the Ovilus IV, the spirits and ghosts whom choose words could be anyone who lived in this town and passed away prior to the day that I actually complete my paranormal session. This could be someone who passed away a minute before I actually asked a question during my paranormal sessions. So, it just shows you that I'm human and my frustrations boil over when so many times the words that I received on the Ovilus IV seen to not be coming from a family member that used to live at the Hays House.

At 10:51 AM I received the fourth word for session 1, which was calcium. I do not feel that calcium is in response to any of the questions I've asked so far during this session 1. Since I have a bachelor's of science in chemistry and do not feel that any of the ghosts or spirits here in Apalachicola would have the need or knowledge to make reference to my chemistry background. I find the only logical explanation could be some form of alien life form that may be trying to communicate. I know it's a wild ideal, but it is the only logical explanation I can come up with.

At 10:56 AM I received the fifth word for this session 1, which was nice. I do feel that this is the intellectual spirit, that is responding to my comment about an alien life form communicating with me about my knowledge of chemistry. The statement nice, could have been sarcasm.

At 10:58 AM I received the sixth word from this session 1, which was revealed. I do not feel that the word reveal is in response to any of the questions that I have asked so far during this session number one.

From 11:05 AM to 11:10 AM, I did a thermal scan of the porch. I obtained two thermal images of the rocking chair to my right to include the camcorder number one which is shown in the image at center, and on the right arm of the chair as you face to chair. Also, I obtain two images of the two rocking chairs, and the camcorder number one, at center left which appears as the orange color. In addition to the two rocking chairs, I obtained an image of the chair that was warmed by me sitting in it. The thermal image of my warm chair is located at lower center frame.

At 11:11 AM I received the seventh word from this session 1, which was rocket. Out of frustration and at 11:16 AM I stated, look, this book is not about aliens, this book is about ghosts and spirits who once lived, and have now passed away.

At 11:23 AM it appeared at the Ovilus IV was not functioning properly and that the batteries were dead. I was surprised. When I attempted to return the Ovilus IV to the home position, the Ovilus IV had no problems returning to the home position. This is a sign that the batteries are not dead.

At 11:23 AM upon turning on the Ovilus IV's, I received the eighth and ninth background words for session 1, which were April and level. I am not familiar with a person by the name of April that had ever lived at the Hays House. The word level may have been an intelligence spirit's observations of me measuring the windows, doorways and the thresholds and maybe stating that my measurements might be off because my ruler was not level. I feel like this is the only way the word level could be used by a spirit who has observed my actions.

At 11:24 AM I received the 10th word for this session number one, which is cake. I do not feel that cake is in response to any of the questions that I have asked during this session number one.

Like many analysis of each paranormal investigation, it is very subjective. Many times, the words I receive seem to have nothing to do with the questions that I am asking. I have found far more ghosts and spirits respond intellectually to situations that are presently taking place.

283

The ghosts and spirits have the fog of death that seems to cloud their memory of the past.

The analysis of the Paranormal Investigation, Session 2, First Floor Wraparound Front Porch, Saturday, 22nd April 2017, Hays House. The date of this analysis was Wednesday, 12th July 2017.

At 12:26 PM the first three background words for session 2 were, Thomas, bomb, and Lord. The background words are the Ovilus IV's evaluation of the electromagnetic frequency within the environment within the first 60 seconds of turning on the program for the Ovilus IV. The name Thomas, I do not feel is associated with anyone who has lived at the Hays House sense 1908.

At 12:28 PM the Ovilus IV gave me the third word of session 2. The name Vern. I am not aware of any person by the name Vern who has any association with the Hays, Gibson, and Buck family's.

At 12:31 PM I made the misstatement by saying the name of the road incorrectly. "There has been constant vehicular traffic on North Avenue, I'm wrong." At 2:31 PM almost as soon as I completed saying incorrectly North Avenue the Ovilus IV gave me the word lie. At 2:32 PM I said lie, yes, good catch. I feel that the spirit was monitoring my statement and was saying that I had lied when I said North Avenue. That spirit would be correct because clearly, I was on the corner of or near the corner of Fourth Street and Avenue D. This denotes an intellectual spirit who is interactive and alert with what is going on in the present.

At 12:33 PM the Ovilus IV gave me the fourth word of this session 2, ashes. Ashes could be a first name or a last name, and or a nickname. I do not know of anyone having the first name, last name, and or nickname ashes who was a member of the Hays, Gibson, and Buck Family.

Between 12:42 PM and 12:46 PM I obtained thermal images of the First Floor Wraparound Front Porch. I obtained two thermal images of the front door. I obtained two thermal images of the two rocking chairs. Camcorder number one was on the left arm of one of the rocking chairs centered within the image and colored orange. Within the same image and at the lower center is the rocking chair that I was setting in, which is warm and colored orange.

At 12:52 PM. it looked like the Ovilus IV may not be functioning properly again. I was able to press the home position and the Ovilus IV when back to the home position. So, the Ovilus IV was not frozen up at all, it's batteries were good.

At 12:54 PM I received the fifth and sixth background words for this session number two, weapon and flowers. I do not feel that the words weapon, and flowers are in response to any of the questions I have asked so far during this session number two.

At 12:56 PM I received the seventh word for this session number two, apocalypse. I do not feel that the word apocalypse is in response to any of the questions I've asked so far during this session number two.

At 1:06 PM the Ovilus IV was frozen up and will not return to the home position. I turned the Ovilus IV off and turn it back on about a minute later to see what would happen. At 1:08 PM the Ovilus IV gave me the eighth and, ninth background words for this session number two, woven and loss. I do not feel that the words woven and lost are in response to any of the questions that I have asked so far during this session number two. This maybe the intelligent spirit of Kathleen who enjoyed knitting. The word woven may be a knitting term that Kathleen might use.

I feel that due to the increase volume of vehicular traffic, this was just too distracting for the ghosts and spirits to respond to many of the questions that I asked during session number two.

Ovilus IV words: Vern, Lie, Ashes.

Digital pictures of the First Floor Wraparound Front Porch, Hays House, Friday, 11th November 2016.

One picture of the East view of the front of the Hays House.

Three pictures of the North side of the wraparound porch with the camera facing the Northeast direction.

One picture of the South side of the Hays House.

One picture of a West view from the wraparound porch.

One picture of the exterior North wall facing the white air conditioner window unit.

Four pictures of a Westview from the wraparound porch.

One picture of a view facing the exterior West wall of the house and the door that leads into the Dining Room.

One picture of a view looking north from the far south side of the wraparound porch.

Please see the author's website at www.keithoevans.com to view each digital picture.

Thermal Images of the First Floor Wraparound Front Porch, Hays House, Friday, 11th November 2016.

Ten images of the ceiling and columns.

Three images of the exterior east wall.

Please see the author's website at www.keithoevans.com to view each digital picture.

CHAPTER 14

Frances Room, Hays House, Ghosts are People too.

A description of the Frances Room, Hays House, Wednesday, 2nd Nov. 2016.

In the Frances Room the East wall has a door way on the room's Northeast corner. This doorway has no door and has the original white wooden trim. A long the room's East wall is a king-sized bed with a white vinyl headboard. This bed has a white bed spread with five pillows, four are white and one pillow is blue and dark blue with a butterfly outlined in lime green. On each side of this king-sized bed are a round, modern, wooden nightstand with the matching cylinder shape silver or white lamps with a white lamp shade. Mounted on the room's East wall is a 4′ x 3.5′ white canvas painting with a blend of blue, green, yellow, and brown colors.

On this room's South wall. There are two original Windows with two glass panes on each section. Both Windows have a tan see-through blind. Both Windows have their original white wooden trim. Located between the two Windows, and, mounted on to the room's South wall is an approximately 1.5′ x 4′ canvas of a painting with a blend of dark blue, and dark green colors. In front of the right side West wall window is a stand-a-lone lamp with a four-sided tetrahedral type shaped white lamp shade.

The room's West wall and near the room's South West corner has an original white, five sunken panels, closet door. This door also has the original brass or metal doorknob and a skeleton key baseplate. This door has the original white wooden door trim. On each side of the of the West wall's fireplace are, chairs with white covers. Each chair has a multi-colored pillow. The fireplace has the original white wooden fireplace mantle with a 6-inch-wide four feet long, top shelf. Resting on this shelf and mounted on to the room's West wall, is an antique dark wooden frame and mirror. The fireproof edge of the fireplace is covered with an olive green, pink and white tiles. The fireplace opening is covered by an antique iron decorative plate. Mounted on the room's West wall and to the right of the fireplace is an approximately 4' x 8' canvas with a painting of different sized horizontal blend of blue, green, and brown colored stripes.

Mounted on the room's North wall and to the left side of the rooms entrance door is a 2-foot-wide 2 1/2-foot white canvas painted with a blend of yellow, gray, and white colors. Located under this painting is a wooden dining room table with two wooden green chairs that have a white and olive green colored textile seat. On top of this table is an olive green colored porcelain lamp, with a white lamp shade. To the right of the table and chairs, and on the room's North wall is a white original five sunken panels door with the original brass or metal doorknob and skeleton key baseplate. This door has the original white wooden trim. To the right side of this door is an antique dark wooden chest of drawers. Above this chest of drawers there is a mirror mounted to the North wall.

This room has the original heart pine, hardwood, tongue and groove flooring. This room also has the original horizontal tongue and groove white wallboards. The ceiling of this room has the original tongue and groove white ceiling boards. This room has its original decorative white wall and ceiling trim. There is a white, modern ceiling fan with four lights located in the center of the room's ceiling.

Description of the Frances Room, Hays House from five pictures taken in 1996.

I am describing the Frances Room from five pictures taken in 1996, starting with the room's East wall and working clockwise around the room.

Near the room's Northeast corner and along the room's East wall is an antique chest of drawers that is sitting in front of the light orange colored original door that leads to Mary Room. On top of the chest of drawers is a wooden framed tombstone shape mirror. There are two red candleholders with decorative clear crystals and an 8-inch candle covered by a clear glass globe on the left and right side of the top of this chest of drawers. Also, on the top of the chest of drawers are; from left to right a single silver candleholder, a round green porcelain covered dish, a small white porcelain dish, and a clear glass dish. To the right of the chest of drawers is a dark wooden antique chair with a tan and brown textile covered seat. On each side of the antique bed are nightstands with a pedestal stand and a square table top with two drawers. On top of each nightstand are matching porcelain multi-colored lamps with white lamp shade. The nightstand on the left side of the bed has a white porcelain dish on its top and in the other picture the same nightstand has a pink Rotary type telephone on its top. The antique bed has a matching decorative wooden head and foot board with four circles inside of each circle, located in the middle of the head and foot boards. This bed has two bedposts at the headboard, that support a decorative covered top partial over the bed.

Both windows on the room's South wall are covered with a white sheer curtain that allows the sunlight to come in to the room. Between the two windows on the room's South wall, and, mounted on the South wall is an oval shaped, golden frame mirror. In front of the window on the right side of the room's South wall is a wooden antique three leg stand that is supporting a central pedestal that supports a decorative round table top. On top of the round table are the following items; a pink and gold glass canister, a pink glass pitcher, a clear glass candy dish, and a pink ashtray. To the right of the round table is an antique decorative wooden rocking chair with an orange or red textile seat and back rest.

Near the room's Southwest corner and on the room's West wall is a light orange door with five sunken panels and a brass or metal doorknob and a skeleton key baseplate. This door has the original light orange wooden door trim. In the center of the West wall is the original fireplace and original white wooden fireplace mantle. Around the fireplace opening are the fireproof green, pink and white tiles. This fireplace has a black iron fireplace cover with a gas heater in front of the fireplace cover. The white original fireplace mantle has a 6-inch-wide top shelf, that is approximately four-foot-long, with two golden colored pitchers that have handles, one is on the left side and the other is on the right side, and two porcelain figurines of a lady sitting and a man sitting. Above the top of the fireplace mantle and mounted on the room's West wall is a golden framed picture of Pat as a child with a calf. In front of the fireplace and on the floor are two items; a wooden suitcase stand, and a dark wooden box with a handle. To the right side of the fireplace and along the room's West wall, is an antique chest of drawers with a white marble top and a decorative wooden framed tombstone shape mirror. The items on top of this chest of drawers are; two porcelain figurines of ladies, two glass bowls, one glass bottle with a ground glass stopper, two white porcelain bowls, one handheld mirror, and one white porcelain figurine. In front of the chest of drawers is an antique wooden chair with a tan and brown textile covered seat.

A long the room's North wall is an antique piece of decorative furniture with dark wood and five shelves. The shelves have multiple items such as; multi-colored plates, cups and saucers, porcelain bowls and porcelain figurines. On the right side of the North wall is the entrance to the room. This entrance leads to the Second Floor Front Stairway Room. This doorway has the original door trim, which is painted light orange and white. The room's lights switch is on the right side of the doorway.

This room has a multi-colored rug on the floor. The room has a mini clear crystal chandelier hanging from the center of the room's ceiling. This room's ceiling boards are the original tongue and groove. These ceiling board are running in an East to West direction. This room has the original light orange horizontal tongue and groove wallboards.

History of the Frances Room, Hays House.

This Chapter and Room within the Hays House is named after Frances Rems Hays, who was born in 1946. Frances spend the first eight years of her life using the Den Room as her bed room. After France turned eight years old she moved up into the center room on the southside of the second floor. It is believed that Carrie Lee Sutton who was employed at Austons Department Store, lived at the Hays House from 1942 until 1959. Carrie Lee Sutton used the center room on the southside of the second floor from 1942 until 1954. It is not clear as to which bed room Carrie used from 1955 to 1959. Sunshine's Room was not being used after Sunshine passed away in 1956. Carrie Lee Sutton left the Hays House and moved to Georgia in 1959.

Frances Hays was a friendly out going student who was involved in many activities at her High School. I counted her picture in the 1964 Chapman High School Shark year book on at least eleven different pages. Frances Hays picture is on page 2 and 25 of the Class of 1964 year book, holding an Apalachicola bander that said "Apalachicola Florida Seniors". On page 10 Frances picture is there under class offices, Frances was the Senior Class Treasurer and President. Frances Reams Hays Senior Class picture is on page 13. It states that Frances was involved in the 4-H club, Class Treasurer, Course, Chapman Science Fair, and Class President during her Freshman year. During her Sophomore year Frances was involved in the Dramatics Club, Chapman Science Fair, Beta Club, and she was a Cheerleader. In Frances' Junior year she participated in the Dramatics Club, Glee Club, Pianist, Junior Play, Beta Club, Cheerleader, Annual Staff, and the Class Vice President. During Frances' Senior year she was involved in the Dramatics Club, Chapman Science Fair, Beta Club, Cheer Leader, Captain, Annual Staff, Home Coming Queen, May Count, Senior Class Treasurer and Senior Class President. On page 51 and page 54, there are pictures of Frances with the May Queen and her Attendants. On page 52 there are two pictures of Frances concerning the Home Coming Queen. On page 56 there is a picture of Frances as the Senior Honors Valedictorian, English Award, Mathematics Award, and the Rouge Award. On page 66 there is a picture of Frances with the Beta Club. On page 72 there is a picture of France as a Cheer Leader. Frances Hays was one of the speakers at her graduation ceremony. Frances Hays graduated from Chapman High School in Apalachicola in 1964.

France used the center room on the southside of the second floor of the Hays House from 1955 until 1968, when she married Nat Toulon and moved away.

In 1968, Nat Toulon and Frances Rems Hays were Married in the Living Room of the Hays House.

On Easter Sunday, 6th April 1969, Mrs. Toulon, formerly Miss Frances Hays played the Organ during the Evening Services at the First United Methodist Church, 75 Fifth Street, Apalachicola, Florida.

On the 25th May 1969, at the First United Methodist Church's 130th Anniversary 1839-1969, Mrs. Frances Toulon was present.

The Mel Meter base readings for the Frances Room, Wednesday, 2nd November 2016.

10:50 AM The electrical cover plate near the rooms entrance, located on the room's North wall.

The electromagnetic frequency range was 0.0 mG to 0.0 mG.

The temperature range was 73.9°F to 74.9°F.

10:50 AM The lamp on the left side of the bed, located on the room's East wall.

The electromagnetic frequency range was 0.0 mG to 0.0 mG.

The temperature range was 74.1°F to 74.5°F.

10:51 AM The lamp on the right side of the bed, located on the room's East wall.

The electromagnetic frequency range was 0.0 mG to 0.0 mG.

The temperature range was 73.1°F to 73.3°F.

10:51 AM The double electrical out let located on the room's South wall. The standalone lamp is plugged into this electrical outlet.

The electromagnetic frequency range was 0.0 mG to 0.0 mG.

The temperature range was 73.1°F to 73.7°F.

10:52 AM The standalone lamp, located along the room's South wall.

The electromagnetic frequency range was 0.0 mG to 0.0 mG.

The temperature range was 73.3°F to 73.6°F.

10:52 AM The lamp on the table along the room's North wall.

The electromagnetic frequency range was 0.0 mG to 0.0 mG.

The temperature range was 73.6°F to 73.6°F.

10:53 AM The room's ceiling fan.

The electromagnetic frequency range was 0.0 mG to 0.0 mG.

The temperature range was 73.8°F to 75.0°F.

The Paranormal Investigation Session 1, Frances Room, Hays House, Tuesday, 30th May 2017.

10:56 AM Keith: "Hello, I am Keith Evans. Today, I wish only to speak with members of the Hays, Gibson, and Buck family's, you may use your energy to choose words from the Ovilus IV's database. This is the Ovilus IV. The Ovilus IV will not hurt you." (Hold it up.)

10:57 AM Keith: "This is the Mel Meter. The Mel Meter measures temperature and electromagnetic frequencies. The Mel meter will not harm you." (Hold it up.)

10:58 AM Keith: "The Ovilus IV has given me three background words: the first back ground word is silent which is spelled S-I-L-E-N-T, class which is spelled C-L-A-S-S, and move which is spelled M-O-V-E. The Ovilus IV has pronounce the background words silent, class, and move all in a normal conversational level and speed."

10:58 AM Keith: "I have observed the Mel Meter readings to be 0.0 mG and 69.7°F."

10:59 AM Keith: "I have observed the Mel Meter readings to be 0.0 mG and 69.5°F."

11 AM Keith: "The Ovilus IV has given me the word timid which is spelled T-I-M-I-D. The Ovilus IV has pronounce the word timid in a normal conversational level and speed."

11:01 AM Keith: "I have observed the Mel Meter readings to be 0.1 mG and 71.9°F."

11:03 AM Keith: "The Ovilus IV has given me the word presidents which is spelled P-R-E-S-I-D-E-N-T-S. The Ovilus IV has pronounced the word presidents in a normal conversational level and speed. It sounds to me like the first four words were spoken by the same person."

11:04 AM Keith: "I have observed the Mel Meter readings to be 0.2 mG and 70.8°F."

11:06 AM Keith: "The Ovilus IV has given me the word reel which is spelled R-E-E-L. The Ovilus IV has pronounced the word reel, at a normal conversational level and speed."

11:10 AM Keith: "The Ovilus IV has given me the word ashes which is spelled A-S-H-E-S. The Ovilus IV has pronounced the word ashes at a normal conversational level and speed."

11:12 AM Keith: "I have observed the Mel Meter readings to be 0.1 mG and 69.4°F."

11:15 AM Keith: "This session started at 10:56 AM and it is 11:15 AM. I have not asked a question yet."

11:16 AM Keith: "Are you upset because the house is up for sale?"

11:17 AM Keith: "Mary, you may talk, also you are grandfathered in with the Hays and Gibson family's as a family member."

11:18 AM Keith: "Mary, what would you like to say?"

11:20 AM Keith: "The first three background words silent, class, and move all sound like something a teacher would say."

11:22 AM Keith: "The words timid, presidents, reel, and ashes are all about different subjects. I have no idea what question, if any, you are asking."

11:23 AM Keith: "The Ovilus IV gave me the word Saliran which is spelled S-A-L-I-R-A-N. I only heard an "S" sound. The letter "S" sound was at a lower than normal conversation level and the speed was faster than normal conversational speed."

11:24 AM Keith: "I have observed the Mel Meter readings to be 0.0 mG and 69.4°F."

11:28 AM Keith: "Is Saliran a name?"

11:29 AM to 11:34 AM Keith: "I completed a thermal imaging of the room. I obtained several thermal images of the Frances Room. I obtained two thermal images of the fireplace on the room's West wall. I obtain two thermal images of dark blue area on the ceiling above the fireplace. I obtained two thermal images of the dark blue area on the room's ceiling in the Southwest corner. I obtained two thermal images of the air conditioner vent opening. I obtained two thermal images of a dark blue square starting at the room's North wall. I obtained two thermal images of the pink area on the floor near the dark stained area. This dark stained area is located between the door on the North wall and the door on the East wall."

11:36 AM Keith: "Whose bedroom was this when the Hays and Gibson families lived here?"

11:38 AM Keith: "I have observed the Mel Meter readings to be 0.1 mG and 69.7°F."

11:39 AM Keith: "Kathleen, how was this room decorated when you lived here?"

11:40 AM Keith: "Pat, did you use this room at all when you lived here?"

11:41 AM Keith: "Pat, which room did you keep your hunting rifles in?"

11:42 AM Keith: "Kathleen, did you have any antiques in this room?"

11:43 AM Keith: "Pat, what was your favorite antique?"

11:44 AM Keith: "Pat, did you have any antique guns?"

11:45 AM Keith: "Kathleen, did you use the gas heater within the fireplace insert when you lived here?"

11:46 AM Keith: "Kathleen, are you happy that I am writing a book about the Hays House?"

11:47 AM Keith: "Kathleen, are you disappointed that the house is going to be sold?"

11:48 AM Keith: "Kathleen, why will you not talk to me?"

11:49 AM Keith: "Pat, who is moving things around in the house like pillows and sheets?"

11:50 AM Keith: "The Ovilus IV gave me the word cement which is spelled C-E-M-E-N-T. I heard an "S" sound spoken at a very low level and a very fast speed."

11:50 AM Keith: "I have observed the Mel Meter readings to be 0.0 mG and 69.2°F."

11:53 AM Keith: "Thank you for talking to me. Have a good day."

11:53 AM Keith: "I have observed the Mel Meter readings to be 0.0 mG and 71.2°F."

11:53 AM Keith: "This session 1 ended on Tuesday, 30th may 2017."

The Paranormal Investigation Session 2, Frances Room, Hays House, Tuesday, 30th May 2017.

2:37 PM Keith: "Hello, I am Keith Evans. Today I wish to speak only to the members of the Buck, Hays, and Gibson family's. You may use your energy to choose words from the Ovilus IV data base. This is the Ovilus IV. The Ovilus IV will not hurt you." (Hold it up.)

2:38 PM Keith: "This is the Mel Meter. The Mel Meter measures temperature and electromagnetic frequencies. The Mel Meter will not hurt you." (Hold it up.)

2:38 PM Keith: "The Ovilus IV has given me no background words."

2:40 PM Keith: "The Ovilus IV gave me the word shot which is spelled S-H-O-T. I only heard an "S" sound. The Ovilus IV has pronounced this word shot at a very low level and at a very fast speed."

2:41 PM Keith: "I have observed the Mel Meter readings to be 0.0 mG and 70.9°F."

2:44 PM Keith: "Sunshine, what do you have to tell me about the history of the Hays House?"

2:46 PM Keith: "The Ovilus IV looks to be frozen up, with five dots in the upper left-hand side of its display."

2:47 PM Keith: "When I touch the home icon, the Ovilus IV will not return to the home position."

2:48 PM Keith: "I will place four new AAA batteries into the Ovilus IV."

2:50 PM Keith: "The Ovilus IV has given me two background words; strange which is spelled S-T-R-A-N-G-E and center which is spelled C-E-N-T-E-R. The Ovilus IV has pronounced the word strange and center at a normal conversational level and speed."

2:51 PM Keith: "I have observed the Mel Meter readings to be 0.0 mG and 71.8°F."

2:53 PM Keith: "The Ovilus IV has given me the word bright which is spelled B-R-I-G-H-T. The Ovilus IV has pronounced the word bright at a normal conversational level and speed."

2:53 PM Keith: "I have observed the Mel Meter readings to be 0.0 mG and 73.7°F."

2:57 PM Keith: "Is this light to my left too bright for you?"

2:58 PM Keith: "Do you want me to turn the bright light over here to my left off? The light that I am pointing to?"

2:58 PM Keith: "I hear talking in the hallway."

2:59 PM Keith: "I hear talking in the hallway."

3 PM Keith: "What is strange and the center?"

3:01 PM Keith: "Are you saying that I am strange for sitting this way in the center of the room? Well, maybe so."

3:02 PM Keith: "What was this room like when you lived here?"

3:03 PM Keith: "What items of antique furniture did you have in this room?"

3:04 PM Keith: "Kathleen, what year did you start to purchase antiques?"

3:04 PM Keith: "I hear talking in the hallway."

3:05 PM to 3:07 PM Keith: "I hear talking in the hallway."

3:06 PM Keith: "Kathleen, did you like the bedroom suit that Annie Gibson Hays had and gave to her son, your husband Pat Hays?"

3:08 PM Keith: "Kathleen, what would you like to talk about when it comes to antiques?"

3:09 PM Keith: "Kathleen, as a ghost, do you no longer like antiques?"

3:13 PM Keith: "James Fulion Buck, born 9th February 1860 and died 28th August 1922. What did you like about the Hays House that you built in 1908?"

3:14 PM Keith: "Okay, that is a no response from James Fulion Buck."

3:16 PM Keith: "Lamb Gilland Buck, born 2 February 1891 and died 7th July 1967. What did you like about this house that your father built in 1908?"

3:18 PM Keith: "No response from Lamb Gilland Buck."

3:21 PM Keith: "Terryess McBride Buck, born 28th, July 1898 and died 2 November 1972. What did you like about this house that your father-in-law built in 1908?"

3:22 PM Keith: "The EDI meter keeps showing a 2.5 mG reading. If you would like to communicate. You have to use the Ovilus IV and choose words from the Ovilus IV's database."

3:25 PM Keith: "I have observed the Mel Meter readings to be 0.1 mG and 69.5°F."

3:25 PM Keith: "I have observed the EDI readings to be 1.0 mG and 69.6°F."

3:26 PM Keith: "I have observed the Mel Meter readings to be 0.1 mG and 69.6°F."

3:26 PM Keith: "I have observed the EDI readings to be 1.0 mG and 69.8°F."

3:27 PM Keith: "I have observed the Mel Meter readings to be 0.1 mG and 69.6°F."

3:27 PM Keith: "I have observed the EDI readings to be 1.5 mG and 69.7°F."

3:28 PM to 3:30 PM Keith: "I obtained the thermal readings within the Frances Room. I obtain four images of the equipment work area that is on top of a chair. I also obtain two images of the small dark blue circle on the South West corner of this room's ceiling. I obtained two images of the dark blue air conditioner vent, that is located on the ceiling. I obtained four images of the dark blue cylinder shape that starts at the North wall, on the ceiling. I obtained five images of my pink footprints located on the stained area of the floor between the north door and the east door."

3:34 PM Keith: "I have observed the Mel Meter readings to be 0.0 mG and 69.9°F."

3:34 PM Keith: "I have observed the EDI readings to be 1.5 mG and 69.7°F."

3:36 PM Keith: "I have observed the Mel Meter readings to be 0.1 mG and 69.8°F."

3:36 PM Keith: "I have observed the EDI readings to be 1.0 mG and 69.8°F."

3:37 PM Keith: "Thank you for talking to me. Have a good day."

3:37 PM Keith: "The EDI refused to turn off. No matter how long I held down the button it still continued to function."

3:37 PM Keith: "This session 2 ended on Tuesday, 30th May 2017."

The analysis of the Paranormal Investigation Session 1, Frances Room, Hays House, Tuesday, 30th May 2017. The date of this analysis was Saturday, 15th of July 2017.

At 10:58 AM the Ovilus IV gave me the first three background words for session 1. Those words were silent, class, and move. These background words could have been coming from a spirit or ghost teacher who is teaching a class. This teacher was asking the class to be silent and to move. Both Sunshine and Kathleen were at one time a Teacher. The last word move could have been a different ghost or spirit talking about the for-sale sign in front of the Hays House, which would indicate a moving of the present owner's. There is no doubt in my mind that the ghosts or spirits are intelligent. These ghosts and spirits may be talking to me or amongst themselves.

At 10:58 AM and 10:59 AM, the Mel Meter readings for the electromagnetic frequency was 0.1 mG. This level of electromagnetic frequency in the atmosphere indicates an active paranormal room.

At 11 AM the Ovilus IV gave me the fourth word for session 1, timid. Family members who remember Sunshine Gibson have told me that they would consider her personality to be timid. For this reason, I feel that this is an intelligent spirit of Sunshine Gibson and she is just reminding me that she is timid.

At 1101, the Mel Meter readings for the electromagnetic frequency was 0.1 mG. This is a continued indication that this room has paranormal activity.

At 11:03 AM the Ovilus IV gave me the fifth word for session 1, presidents. I do not feel that this word presidents have anything to do with questions I have asked during this session one.

At 11:04 AM, the Mel Meter reading for the electromagnetic frequency was 0.2 mG. This is a continued indication that this room has paranormal activity.

At 11:06 AM the Ovilus IV gave me the sixth word for session 1, reel. I do not feel that this word real is in response to any questions that I have asked in this session one.

At 11:10 AM the Ovilus IV gave me the seventh word for this session 1, ashes. Ashes could be a first name, a last name, and or a nickname. I am not aware of anyone connected with the Hays House having the first name, last name, and or nickname Ashes. That doesn't mean that there isn't a connection, just means I haven't found one. If ashes are not being used as a proper name, then I would say that the word ashes are not in response to any questions that I have asked so far during session 1 because I have not asked any questions yet. During the Fire of 1900 in Apalachicola the dwelling that resided on this properly may have brunt. So, this may be an intelligent spirit telling me about the 1900 fire.

At 11:12 AM, the Mel Meter reading for the electromagnetic frequency was 0.1 mG. This is a continued indication that this room has paranormal activity.

At 11:23 AM the Ovilus IV gave me the eighth word of this session 1, Saliran. I can only hear an "S" sound. This word was spoken with at a very low level and a very fast speed. Saliran could be a last name.

I do not know anyone named Saliran that is connected with the Hays House. That doesn't mean that there isn't someone with this name connected with the Hays House, it just means that I am not aware of it yet.

At 11:29 AM to 11:34 AM I obtained thermal images of the Frances room. Two thermal images were taken at the fireplace on the room's West wall. I obtained two thermal images of the dark blue area on the ceiling above the fireplace. I obtained two thermal images of the dark blue area, located on the ceiling's Southwest corner. I obtained two thermal images of the air conditioner vent opening. I obtained two thermal images of the dark blue square starting at the room's North wall. I obtained two thermal images of my pink foot prints in the area on the hardwood floor where there is a dark stain between the door on the room's North wall and the door on the room's East wall. I know that the air conditioner ducts are in the ceiling. I know that heat rises. I know that the ceiling fan should circulate the air in the room. Why it's so much cold air accumulating at the, 10-foot-high ceiling level? Heat should rise and the cold air should settle to the floor. The ceiling fan should move the air throughout the room. So, I do not have an explanation for why the thermal readings are picking up so many areas of cold air near the 10-foot-high ceiling level. These four cold areas could be the spirits or ghosts of Pat, Kathleen, Sunshine, and Annie. As far as my pink foot prints from walking in the area of the hardwood floor between the door on the room's North wall and the door on the room's East wall. I do not feel that my feet are not that hot to transfer enough heat just by walking back and forth. So, it is not my heat that is leaving the pink footprints that are lasting long enough for me to obtained a thermal image. I would have to have some really hot feet. My sandals must not do anything to insulate my hot feet from the wooden floor. I can't explain why my footprints are captured as a pink color by the thermal image on top of the hardwood floor. Unless, there has to be some type of chemical reaction taking place from the force of my weight against the floor causing the wax or resin within the wood to undergo a chemical reaction that gives off enough heat to be seen as pink by the thermal imager.

At 11:38 AM, the Mel Meter reading for the electromagnetic frequency was 0.1 mG. This is an indication that the room has paranormal activity.

At 11:50 AM the Ovilus IV gave me the ninth word of this session 1, cement. I only heard an "S" sound. I had to look at the Ovilus IV's display to see that the word was cement. The Ovilus IV had pronounced the word cement at a very low level and at a very fast speed. From 11:28 AM to 11:49 AM I had asked 13 different questions. I feel that there is only one question that I asked, that would be appropriate for the responding word to be cement. That would be the question I asked at 11:36 AM. Whose bedroom was in this room, when the Hays, and Gibson families lived here? I learned on Tuesday, 11th day of July 2017, that Frances Hays used this room from the time she was eight years old until she married and moved out of her parents' home in 1968. I feel that the word cement was given by Kathleen or Pat as a clue. The cement steps that were made in 1953, at the back porch and at the end of the wraparound porch on the North side of the house, each have Frances name on the surface. Apparently, Frances scratched her name into the wet cement shortly after the steps were poured. One may thing that something you may have done as a child, will not have any significance. Who knows, someday it may end up as part of a chapter in a book.

The analysis of the Paranormal Investigation Session 2, Frances Room, Hays House, Tuesday, 30th May 2017. The date of this analysis was Saturday, 15th of July 2017.

At 2:38 PM the Ovilus IV did not give me any background words. This is rare and unusually.

At 2:40 PM the Ovilus IV gave me the first word of this session number two, shot. The Ovilus IV pronounced the word shot at a very low level and at a very fast speed. The only thing I heard was an "s" sound, until I looked at the Ovilus IV display and saw the word shot. I have not asked any questions yet during this session 2.

At 2:46 PM the Ovilus IV appears to be frozen up, with five solid dots in the upper left-hand side of its display. The Ovilus IV will not return to the home position. I had to place four new AAA batteries into the Ovilus IV.

At 2:50 PM the Ovilus IV gave me two background words. The second and third words for this session 2; strange and center. I feel that this is an intelligent spirit who has sized up the scene. The ghost or spirit see me sitting in the center of the room and think that this is strange. I am talking to ghosts and spirits. I guess to the most unliving friendly ghost, I may appear to be strange and in the center of the room.

At 2:53 PM the Ovilus IV gave me the fourth word for session 2, bright. At the time I was using a bright light to lighten up the area, hoping that it would make for a better videotape. I think this was an intelligent ghost or spirit letting me know that the light I was using was bright. Yes, this light was bright.

At 3:22 PM to 3:36 PM the EDI Meter range was between 0.5 mG and 1.5 mG. This is an indication that there is moderate paranormal activity in the room.

At 3:25 PM to 3:36 PM the Mel Meter range for the electromagnetic frequency was between 0.0 mG and 0.1 mG. This is an indication that there is light paranormal activity in the room.

3:28 PM to 3:30 PM I obtained thermal images of the Frances Room. I obtained four images of the equipment work area and the chair. I obtained two images of a small dark blue circle on the South West corner ceiling. I obtained two images of a dark blue air conditioning vent in the ceiling. I obtained four images of a dark blue cylinder shape object starting from the North wall of the ceiling. I obtained five images of my pink footprints on the stained area of the floor between the door located on the North wall and the room's East wall door. The images that display dark blue areas may be caused by, cold air from the air conditioner vent. I still find these thermally cold areas that are dark blue to be unexplained because the heat should rise and the ceiling fan should circulate the cold air throughout the room. I believe that Kathleen is the small dark blue circle shape near the room's South West corner. I believe that Pat is the dark blue cylinder shape starting at the room's ceiling near the room's north wall. As in session 1, I cannot explain how my feet, warmed up the hardwood floor through my plastic sandals in a short period of time that I stood there. To show a thermally pink image upon obtaining thermal images of the room, the temperature would have to be about 60 degrees. Sometimes I feel like the ghosts and the spirits get the Ovilus IV mixed up with the Mel Meter, and the EDI Meter. The ghosts and the spirits may be working really hard using their energy to choose words from the database, the only problem is the Mel Meter in the EDI Meter only register the ghosts and spirits electromagnetic frequency. The Mel Meter and the EDI Meter do not have any data base for the ghosts or spirits to choose words.

Digital pictures of the Frances Room, Hays House, Wednesday, 2nd November 2016.

Two pictures of the room's North wall.

One picture of the room's ceiling fan.

One picture of the room's East wall.

Three pictures of the room's West wall.

Two pictures of the dark spot on the room's Northeast corner hardwood floor.

Two pictures of the threshold between the Frances Room and the Mary Room.

One picture of the room's South wall.

Four pictures of the room's white wooden wall and ceiling trim.

Three pictures of the room's fireplace, located one the room's West wall.

Two pictures of the mirror over the fireplace, located on the room's West wall.

Please see the author's website at www.keithoevans.com to view each digital picture.

Thermal images of the Frances Room, Hays House, Wednesday, 2nd November 2016.

One image of the exterior door knob.

One image of the North wall entrance door.

One image of the East wall and the bed.

One image of the South wall and two windows.

One image of the West wall and the fireplace.

One image of the room's ceiling fan.

Please see the author's website at www.keithoevans.com to view each thermal image.

The Annie Room, Hays House, Ghosts are People too.

A description of the Annie Room from pictures taken on Friday, 10th, March 2017, Hays House.

The Annie's room's West wall has a modern closet that was created sometime after 1996. There is no door, but there is a blue curtain. The door's white wooden trim is modern. In front of the closet is a tan wicker chair with three multi-colored pillows. In front of the tan wicker chair, is a tan wicker foot stool with a white textile cover. To the right side of the wicker chair is a blue water paddle. This wooden paddle is resting against the wall. In the center of the room's West wall is the original white wooden fireplace mantle. Around the fireplace opening are the fireproof white, pink, and green tiles. The fireplace is covered by an antique decorative iron cover. On the top shelf of the fireplace mantle are 11 white porcelain vases. Above the fireplace mantle is an approximately 3.5' x 3' canvas painting of a white vase with white flowers and green stems. To the right of the fireplace is a modern white wooden open cabinet with six shelves. The three bottom shelves have wicker type baskets and one box. The wicker baskets are light blue and tan in the box is green and white. On the far-right side of the room's West wall and near the room's Northwest corner is a narrow original window with two glass panes within the upper and lower sections. The white wooden window trim appears to be original. This window has a light blue curtain and a shear tan blind that lets in the sunlight.

On the room's North wall is a king size bed with a modern brown headboard. On each side of the king size bed, there are matching a modern wooden nightstand with a matching white porcelain lamp that have a round white lamp shade. The bed is covered with a white and orange bedspread and five pillows, four are white and one pillow has white, violet, light blue, dark blue, and lime green stripes. The North wall has two original windows with two glass panes in the upper and lower sections. These windows have the light blue curtains and a shear tan blind that allows the light to come through. In between these windows and mounted on the room's North wall is a white canvas painting of a forest. In front of the king size bed is a modern multi-colored textile covered bench that is approximately 4.5 feet long, 2-foot-wide, and 18 inches tall.

In this room's Northeast corner and on the room's East wall is an original narrow window with the two glass panes on the upper and lower sections. This window's white wooden trim is original. This window has a light blue curtain and a shear tan blind, that lets in the sunshine. To the right of this window is an antique white wooden cabinet with no backing and three shelves. This cabinet has two doors with glass windows in front. When the cabinet doors are closed one may still see the following items on the three shelves; a light blue toy SUV, two bottles, a book, a candleholder, and two porcelain figurines, one is white and one is gold. Below this white cabinet is a light blue wooden chest. To the right of the white cabinet is the original five sunken panels white wooden closet door with the original white wooden trim. This closet door has the original brass or metal black doorknob and the original black skeleton key baseplate. To the right of the closet door and, mounted on the room's East wall are two paintings on white canvas, with a blend of colors, mainly white, light blue, green, yellow, and having black hand writing throughout each painting. Below these paintings is a green modern wooden decorative table. On top of this table are two candleholders with large square white candles, one metal vase, and a tiny toy deer doe and two fawns. To the far-right side of the room's East wall and near the room's South East corner, there is an original white wooden door with five sunken panels. This door has the original skeleton key baseplate that has been painted white, and a black doorknob that is not original. This door hangs at an opening that was made sometime after 1996. This door has modern white wooden trim. This door leads to the original Second Floor Bathroom. To the top right side of this door is an electrical outlet.

There are eight different sized pictures and paintings, mounted on the room's South wall. Along the room's South wall is a light blue wooden table with a tan wicker chair on each side. Above the light blue table is a modern opening for a fan. This modern opening for a fan, has two white wooden doors. This opening has modern white wooden trim. Near the rooms Southwest corner, and on the room's South wall is an original white wooden five sunken panel door that leads to the Second Floor Front Stairway Room.

A description of the Annie Room from six pictures taken in 1996.

On the West wall is an antique dark wooden stand with shelves at four different levels. There is a mirror behind the back of the top of the fourth shelf and bottom of the second shelf. On the bottom shelf there are two white porcelain figurines and a wooden box with a lid. The second shelf from the bottom has a multi-colored porcelain dish, the third shelf from the bottom has two green porcelain bowls. The top shelf from the left to the right, has a purple cup, a white decorative China plate, and a white porcelain bowl. In the center of the room's West wall is the original white wooden fireplace mantle. Around the fireplace opening are the white, pink, and olive green colored fireproof tiles. The fireplace opening is covered by an antique black decorative iron cover. In front of the fireplace is a brown gas heater. The fireplace mantle has a top shelf that is 6 inches deep and has the following; three dark green glass items, two bowls and one pitcher. Above the fireplace mantle and mounted on the room's West wall is an approximately 2 feet by 2-foot golden frame mirror with a white porcelain face of a lady, mounted on the west wall, on each side of the mirror. There is an antique decorative dark wooden chair in front of the brown, gas heater. To the right of the fireplace mantle is a small gas pipe. The small gas pipe is connected to the gas heater and it is entering the room's West wall to the right side of the fireplace mantle. To the right of the small gas pipe is a small white trashcan with a flower on its front. The trashcan appears to be metal or tin. To the right of the small white trashcan is an antique dark wooden chest of drawers with a dark wooden oval-shaped frame mirror on top of the chest of drawers. On top of the chest of drawers are that following items; a golden vase on each side and a white porcelain bowl with a white lid. There is an antique decorative dark wooden chair in front of the chest of drawers. Near the room's North West corner and on the room's West wall is a narrow window covered with a white curtain.

The room's North wall has two windows that are covered with white curtains. These curtains allow the sunlight to shine through. Mounted on the room's North wall and located between the two windows is a golden frame mirror with a decorative top. This mirror is approximately 13" x 26". Centered in front of the mirror is an antique dark wooden trimmed couch with a blue textile covering on its arms, seat, and back rest areas. In front of this couch is a matching blue textile covered footstool with a decorative red and yellow flower on the center of its top side. To the left side of the couch is an antique dark wooden table with a square white marble top. On top of this table is a lamp with a golden stand and a multi-colored glass lamp shade. To the right side of this couch is an antique dark wooden table with four circular spiral shaped wooden legs. On top of this table are the following items from left to right; a silver vase with two pink flowers with green stems and leaves, a glass candy dish, and a white pitcher. Above this table and mounted on the room's North wall is a golden oval shaped sculpture of may be a person.

Near the room's Northeast corner and on the room's East wall is a narrow window covered with a white curtain. To the right side of this window there is an antique dark wooden desk with a matching mirror and a stool. This desk and its accessories all have the spiral type circular legs and the mirror has spiral type supporting vertical posts. The items on the desk top from left to right are; a clear glass candy dish, a white porcelain dish with matching lid, a black hairbrush, a small white porcelain container with a matching lid, a golden frame picture of Frances Hays, a glass jar with a screw top lid, a white porcelain dish with a matching lid and possibly a hand-held mirror.

There is an antique dark wooden chair in front of the right side of the antique desk. To the right of the antique desk is an original light blue wooden closet door with five sunken panels. The light blue wooden trim around the door is original. To the right side of the original closet door is a dark wooden bed with four 6-foot-tall spiral bedposts. This bed also has a decorative headboard and fencing type footboard. The bed spread is a textured white textile and there are white tonsils on three of its sides. On the top of the bed are four pillows; one pillow is blue and three are white. On each side of the bed, there are matching antique dark wooden small tables with four spiral supporting legs. On the top of the small table that is on the left side of the bed, starting from the left to right are the following items; a light green glass candy dish, a golden lamp stands with decorative clear crystals. This lamp stand supports four white candle looking lights that actually hold four light bulbs, and a white porcelain bowl. On top of the small table that is located on the right side of the bed are the following items; a white porcelain bowl, a black book, a golden lampstand with decorative clear crystals. This lampstand has four white candle looking lights, that hold for light bulbs, and a white porcelain teapot. Above the head of this bed is a golden frame picture of a town. At the foot of the bed is a foldable wooden suitcase stand with three horizontal knitted blue bands.

The South wall of the room has an opening in the wall. This opening has a white electrical fan inserted within. The opening has a modern light blue wooden trim around its edges. The fans black electrical cord is hanging down on the room's North wall and is not plugged in to the electrical outlet that is mounted on to this room's North wall. It looks like one of the lamp's, on one of the small tables is plugged into the electrical outlet on the room's North wall. Near the room's South West corner and on the room's South wall is an original white door with five sunken panels. This door has the original black matching brass or metal doorknob and skeleton key baseplate.

This room has a golden colored chandelier like assembly hanging down from the center of the room's ceiling with four white candle shaped supports that hold light bulbs. All of the walls in this room are covered with the original, light blue, tongue and groove, horizontal wallboards. This room has the original light blue wall trim. The ceiling has the original wooden white tongue and groove boards, and white wooden ceiling trim. The floor is mostly covered with a multicolored rug.

A history of the Annie Room from pictures taken in 1996.

In the late 40s Patsy and Frances step grandfather, Mr. Palmer. Added an opening in the room's South wall, approximately 4' x 4' four and a ventilation fan to coal the room and the rest of the house. Patsy and Frances loved and admired their step grandfather, Mr. Palmer. Mr. Palmer who was employed by Standard Oil and a non-smoker passed away in 1972 due to heart problems.

The Mel Meter base readings for the Annie Room, Friday, 10th March 2017, Hays House.

The electrical out let located halfway up the side of the East wall. This outlet is not in use.

The electromagnetic frequency range was 0.0 mG to 0.0 mG.

The temperature range was 72.4°F to 72.9°F.

The light switch near the rooms entrance, located on the room's South wall. This light switch is in the on position.

The electromagnetic frequency was 0.0 mG to 0.0 mG.

The temperature range was 72.3°F to 72.8°F.

The hardwood floor near the dark area, located near the room's North West corner.

The electromagnetic frequency range was 0.0 mG to 0.0 mG.

The temperature range was 69.5°F to 69.6°F.

The white ceiling fan and ceiling lights. The lights are on, but the ceiling fan is not in use.

The electromagnetic frequency range was 0.0 mG to 0.0 mG.

The temperature range was 71.8°F to 72.6°F.

The Paranormal Investigation, Session 1 of the Annie Room, Wednesday, 31st May 2017, Hays House.

1:38 PM Keith: "Hello, I am Keith Evans. I wish only to speak to members of the Hays, Gibson, and Buck family's. You may use your energy to choose words from the Ovilus IV's database. This is the Ovilus IV and it will not hurt you." (Hold it up.)

1:39 PM Keith: "This is the Mel Meter, and the EDI. Both measure temperature and electromagnetic frequencies. The Mel Meter and the EDI will not harm you." (Hold it up.)

1:40 PM Keith: "The Ovilus IV has given me two background words Amanda which is spelled A-M-A-N-D-A, sugar which is spelled S-U-G-A-R. The Ovilus IV has pronounce the words Amanda and sugar at a normal conversational level and speed."

1:40 PM Keith: "I have observed the Mel Meter readings to be 0.0 mG and 75.9°F."

1:40 PM Keith: "I have observed the EDI readings to be 0.0 mG and 74.8°F."

1:42 PM Keith: "The Ovilus IV has given me the word raid which is spelled R-A-I-D. The Ovilus for has pronounced the word raid at a normal conversational level and speed."

1:42 PM Keith: "I have observed the Mel Meter readings to be 0.0 mG and 75.9°F."

1:42 PM Keith: "I have observed the EDI readings to be 0.0 mG and 74.7°F."

1:46 PM Keith: "Hi Amanda. What is your last name?"

1:47 PM Keith: "Is sugar a nickname?"

1:48 PM Keith: "What type of raid are you referring to?"

1:49 PM Keith: "The Ovilus IV gave me the word find which is spelled F-I-N-D. The Ovilus IV has pronounced the word find at a normal conversational level and speed."

1:50 PM Keith: "I have observed the Mel Meter readings to be 0.0 mG and 75.8°F."

1:50 PM Keith: "I have observed the EDI readings to be 0.0 mG and 75.0°F."

1:52 PM Keith: "What do you want me to find?"

1:53 PM Keith: "Do you want me to find you?"

1:53 PM Keith: "I hear a sliding sound coming from the Third Floor Apartment."

1:54 PM Keith: "I left the FLIR thermal imager downstairs. I going off camera to obtain the thermal imager."

1:57 PM to 2:01 PM Keith: "I'm going to obtain thermal images of this room. I obtained two thermal images of the air conditioning vent on the ceiling. I obtained two thermal images of the long dark blue trail going across the ceiling from the air conditioner vent. I obtained six images of the worn floor area to the left side of the bed, while standing at the foot of the bed. There are some pink footprints within these images."

2:02 PM Keith: "The Ovilus IV has given me the word beg which is spelled B-E-G. The Ovilus IV has pronounced the word beg at a normal conversational level and speed."

2:03 PM Keith: "I have observed the Mel Meter readings to be 0.0 mG and 76.2°F."

2:03 PM Keith: "I have observed the EDI readings to be 0.0 mG and 74.6°F."

2:06 PM Keith: "Why do you need to beg?"

2:07 PM Keith: "You sounded desperate."

2:08 PM Keith: "Amanda, did you live at the Hays House?"

2:09 PM Keith: "So Amanda, with the nickname sugar, are you begging me to find you?"

2:10 PM Keith: "Amanda, what day did you passed away?"

2:11 PM Keith: "Kathleen, what type of antique bedroom suit, did you have in this room?"

2:12 PM Keith: "Kathleen, what was your favorite antique that you had in this room, when you were alive?"

2:13 PM Keith: "Kathleen, did you only collect antique furniture?"

2:14 PM Keith: "Kathleen, what was your favorite type of wood grain furniture, for example oak?"

2:15 PM Keith: "Kathleen, did you ever collect coins?"

2:16 PM Keith: "Pat, did you collect coins?"

2:17 PM Keith: "Pat, what type of furniture was in this room, when you were living here?"

2:18 PM Keith: "Pat, was the closet and the double East wall here in 1942, where the two doors are on the East wall?"

2:19 PM Keith: "Pat, what would you like to tell me about this room?"

2:20 PM Keith: "Pat, do you remember the great depression?"

2:21 PM Keith: "The Ovilus IV gave me the word alone which is spelled A-L-O-N-E. The Ovilus IV pronounced the word alone at a lower level than a normal conversational level and slower speed than, a normal conversational speed."

2:21 PM Keith: "I have observed the Mel Meter readings to be 0.0 mG and 76.2°F."

2:21 PM Keith: "I have observed the EDI readings to be 2.5 mG and 74.4°F."

2:24 PM Keith: "So Pat, does the Great Depression makes you feel alone."

2:25 PM Keith: "What affect did the Great Depression have on the Turpentine business?"

2:26 PM Keith: "What affected the Great Depression have on the Banking business?"

2:27 PM Keith: "James Fulion Buck, did you sleep in this bedroom?"

2:28 PM Keith: "Lamb Gilland Buck, did you sleep in this bedroom?"

2:29 PM Keith: "Terryss McBride Buck, did you sleep in this bedroom?"

2:29 PM Keith: "The Ovilus IV gave me the word shaken which is spelled S-H-A-K-E-N. The Ovilus IV has pronounced the word shaken with a scary the man's voice. The Ovilus IV also pronounced the word shaken at a lower than normal conversational level and slower than normal conversational speed."

2:30 PM Keith: "I have observed the Mel Meter readings to be 0.0 mG and 75.6°F."

2:30 PM Keith: "I have observed the EDI readings to be 2.5 mG and 74.4°F."

2:32 PM Keith: "Why are you shaking?"

2:33 PM Keith: "What is your name?"

2:35 PM Keith: "Thank you for talking to me. Have a good day."

2:35 PM Keith: "I have observed the Mel meter readings to be 0.0 mG and 75.6°F."

2:35 PM Keith: "I have observed the EDI readings to be nothing available for the electromagnetic frequency and 74.4°F."

2:35 PM Keith: "This session 1 has ended on Wednesday, 31st of May 2017."

The Paranormal Investigation, Session 2 of the Annie Room, Wednesday, 31st May 2017, Hays House.

3:34 PM Keith: "Hello, I am Keith Evans. I wish only to speak to members of the Hays, Gibson, and Buck family's. This also includes Mary. You may use your energy to choose words from the Ovilus IV's database. This is the Ovilus IV. The Ovilus IV will not hurt you." (Hold it up.)

3:36 PM Keith: "This is the Mel Meter and the EDI. They measure temperature and electromagnetic frequencies. They will not harm you." (Hold it up.)

3:37 PM Keith: "The Ovilus IV has given me two background words; strep which is spelled S-T-R- E-P and the word digital which is spelled D-I-G-I-T-A-L. The Ovilus IV has pronounced the words strep and digital at a normal conversational level and speed."

3:38 PM Keith: "I have observed the Mel Meter readings to be 0.0 mG and 74.3°F."

3:38 PM Keith: "I have observed the EDI readings to be 0.0 mG and 77.0°F."

3:39 PM Keith: "I have observed the Mel Meter readings to be 0.0 mG and 74.3°F."

3:40 PM Keith: "The Ovilus IV gave me the word Chris which is spelled C-H-R-I-S. The Ovilus IV pronounced the word Chris at a normal conversational level and speed."

3:41 PM Keith: "I have observed the Mel Meter readings to be 0.0 mG and 74.6°F."

3:41 PM Keith: "The Ovilus IV gave me the word England spelled E-N-G-L-A-N-D. The Ovilus IV has pronounced the word England at a normal conversational level and speed."

3:41 PM Keith: "I have observed the Mel Meter readings to be 0.0 mG and 74.7°F."

3:41 PM Keith: "I have observed the EDI readings to be 0.0 mG and 76.7°F."

3:42 PM Keith: "I have observed the Mel Meter readings to be 0.0 mG and 74.4°F."

3:42 PM Keith: "I have observed the EDI readings to be 0.0 mG and 76.6°F."

3:42 PM Keith: "I have observed the Mel Meter readings to be 0.0 mG and 74.2°F."

3:45 PM Keith: "The Ovilus IV gave me the word beer, spelled B-E-E-R. The Ovilus IV has pronounced the word beer with a deep man's voice. The Ovilus IV has pronounced the word beer, at a normal conversational level but at a slow drawn out speed."

3:45 PM Keith: "I have observed the Mel Meter readings to be 0.0 mG and 74.8°F."

3:45 PM Keith: "I have observed the EDI readings to be 0.0 mG and 76.3°F."

3:45 PM Keith: "I have observed the Mel Meter readings to be 0.0 mG and 74.5°F."

3:45 PM Keith: "I have observed the EDI readings to be 0.0 mG and 76.3°F."

3:46 PM Keith: "The spirits and ghosts have a new toy and they will not leave the EDI alone. I have observed the EDI to be off and on between 1 mG to 2.5 mG. It is very hard to get a picture of, EDI, when is not at 0.0 mG."

3:52 PM Keith: "Pat or Kathleen, tell me something about the history of this room."

3:53 PM Keith: "Kathleen, what was your happiest moment here in the Hays House."

3:53 PM Keith: "The Ovilus IV gave me the word basement which is spelled B-A-S-E-M-E-N-T. The Ovilus IV has pronounced the word basement at a normal conversational level and speed."

3:55 PM Keith: "I have observed the Mel Meter readings to be 0.0 mG and 74.5°F."

3:55 PM Keith: "I have observed the EDI readings to be 2.5 mG and 74.5°F."

3:55 PM Keith: "The word basement is not answering any of my one and only question, so far during this session number two, in the Annie Room. The Hays House does not have a basement."

3:58 PM Keith: "Pat, what was your happiest memory from here at the Hays House?"

4 PM to 4:05 PM Keith: "I'm going to obtain thermal readings of the Annie Room. I obtained four images of the long cylinder shape dark blue area along the East wall and South East corner of the room's ceiling. I obtained two images at different angles, of the air conditioner vent on the room's ceiling. I obtained two images of the long cylinder shape dark blue areas across from the air conditioner vents and towards the room's South wall. I obtained two images of the long cylinder shape dark blue areas along the East wall and ceiling. I obtained two images of my pink footprints at the worn-down area of the hardwood floor next to the right side of the bed, as I am standing at the foot of the bed. I obtained four images of my pink footprints on the worn area of the hardwood floor next to the left side of the bed, as I am standing at the foot of the bed."

4:05 PM Keith: "With just short periods of standing next to the left side of the bed where the hardwood floor is worn down, I am able to leave to pink footprints that the FLIR thermal imager is picking up."

4:08 PM Keith: "I have observed the Mel Meter readings to be 0.0 mG and 74.8°F."

4:08 PM Keith: "I have observed the EDI readings to be 2.5 mG and 75.0°F."

4:09 PM Keith: (I sat the EDI up on its side so that it was directly in front of the camcorder number one, and the readings of 2.5 mG stopped.)

4:09 PM Keith: "Oh, I guess since the camcorder number one can see the front of the EDI's display, you want to stop now."

4:10 PM Keith: "I guess you are shy."

4:12 PM Keith: "Sunshine, what is your best memory of the Hays House?"

4:14 PM Keith: "Kathleen, what is your worst memory that you had here at the Hays House?"

4:15 PM Keith: "Pat, what is your worst memory that you had here at the Hays House?"

4:16 PM Keith: "So Sunshine, since you passed away here at the Hays House. I guess I know what your worst memory was."

4:17 PM Keith: "Is there anything that you would like for me to put in the book, that I have not covered, at this point in time?"

4:19 PM Keith: "What should I write about, that I am failing to write about?"

4:20 PM Keith: "The Ovilus IV is frozen up. I touched the home icon button but the Ovilus IV would not return to home position. The batteries are not that old and should have more energy. I am going to turn the Ovilus IV off manually."

4:22 PM Keith: "The Ovilus IV gave me the background word am which is spelled A-M. The Ovilus IV has pronounced the word am at a normal conversational level, but at a very fast speed."

4:22 PM Keith: "I have observed the Mel Meter readings to be 0.0 mG and 75.0°F."

4:22 PM Keith: "I have observed the EDI readings to be 2.5 mG and 74.6°F."

4:24 PM Keith: "Does AM mean in the morning?"

4:26 PM Keith: "I have observed the Mel Meter readings to be 0.0 mG and 74.5°F."

4:26 PM Keith: "I have observed the EDI readings to be 1.0 mG and 74.6°F."

4:26 PM Keith: "A dog is barking in the hallway. I heard some noises downstairs."

4:26 PM Keith: "I have observed the Mel Meter readings to be 0.0 mG and 75.3°F."

4:26 PM Keith: "I have observed the EDI readings to be 1.0 mG and 74.6°F."

4:27 PM Keith: "Thank you for talking to me. Have a nice day."

4:28 PM Keith: "This Session 2 ended on Wednesday, 31st, May 2017."

The analysis of the Paranormal Investigation, Session 1 of the Annie Room, Wednesday, 31st May 2017, Hays House. The date of the analysis was Saturday, 22nd of July 2017.

At 1:40 PM the Ovilus IV gave me two background words Amanda and sugar. I have not asked any questions yet. I do not know anyone by the first name Amanda who has any connection with the Hays House.

THE ANNIE ROOM, HAYS HOUSE, GHOSTS ARE PEOPLE TOO.

At 1:42 PM the Ovilus IV has given me the third word of this Session 1, raid. I had not asked any questions yet.

At 1:49 PM the Ovilus IV has given me the fourth word for this Session 1, find. I had just asked the question to Pat and Kathleen if this was their master bedroom. At the time I did not know that it was Mrs. Annie, Gibson, Hays, Palmer's and her second husband, named Mr. Palmer's, bedroom. I feel that this was an intelligent spirit of either Pat or Kathleen Hays challenging me to find out where their bedroom was. As if for them to say that no, this is not our bedroom.

Between 1:57 PM and 2:01 PM I completed a thermal scan of Annie's room. I obtained two thermal images of the air conditioning vent. I obtained six thermal images of the worn hardwood floor area to the left side of where the present bed sits. The left side is determined while you are standing facing the head of the bed. There are some pink footprints within these last six thermal images.

At 2:02 PM the Ovilus IV gave me the fifth word of this Session 1, beg. I do not feel that the word beg is in response to any of the questions I've asked so far during this Session 1. It could be that the ghost or spirit was trying to choose the word bed. I feel that this may be within reason. I spent the better part of four minutes obtaining six thermal images close to the left side of the bed. If a ghost or spirit is in a hurry to make a quick decision within the Ovilus IV database, they may choose poorly and or they might just be a poor speller.

At 2:21 PM the Ovilus IV gave me the sixth word for this Session 1, alone. I do not believe that the word alone is in response to any of the questions that I have asked so far during this session number one.

At 2:21 PM I did observe that the EDI readings for the electromagnetic frequency was 2.5 mG. This is an indication of paranormal activity. The paranormal activity is so precise that the ghosts and or spirits can be measured on the EDI but not measured at all on the Mel Meter. In fact, the only measurable electromagnetic frequency during this Session number one was at 2:21 PM.

At 2:29 PM the Ovilus IV gave me the seventh word for this Session 1, shaken. At 2:29 PM I had asked Terryss McBride Buck if she had slept in this bedroom? If shaken is her response, then that just leaves more questions. Is she shaking her head up and down for yes or left and right for no. This could be an intelligent response from Terryss McBride Buck. It just isn't a very direct and or helpful response. The Ovilus IV pronounced the word shaken in a scary man's voice. The Ovilus IV also pronounced the word shaken at a very low level and at a slower than normal conversational speed. With that in mind, may be the person shaken has received troubling news. In this case shaken may mean that their emotions have been shaken and or their body is shaking with emotional despair.

Looking at some of the seven words that the Ovilus IV gave me during this Session 1; raid, find, beg, alone, and shaken, this group of words could be understood as a Ghost and or Spirit telling me something about their life. "I was captured in raid. I hope that I will be found. I beg that God to set me free. I feel all alone. I am shaken." It is this type of despair that keeps me going as a Paranormal Investigator. At least this Ghost and or Spirit knows that I cared enough to listen.

The analysis of the Paranormal Investigation, Session 2 of the Annie Room, Wednesday, 31st May 2017, Hays House. The date of the analysis was Saturday, 22nd of July 2017.

At 3:37 PM the Ovilus IV gave me two background words strep and digital. At this point I have not asked any questions. So, I assume that this is just the environmental electromagnetic frequencies that the Ovilus IV is picking up. It is my belief that ghosts and spirits communicating amongst themselves whether a paranormal investigator is asking questions are not.

At 3:40 PM the Ovilus IV gave me the third word of this Session 2, Chris. So far, I have not asked any questions. I do not know anyone with the first name Chris, that is the related to the Hays House in any way.

At 3:41 PM the Ovilus IV gave me the fourth word of this Session 2, England. So far, I have not asked any questions. I do not feel that England is connected with the Hays House in any way.

At 3:45 PM the Ovilus IV gave me the fifth word of this Session 2, beer. So far, I have not asked any questions. I do not feel that beer is connected with the Hays House and anyway.

At 3:46 PM I noticed that the EDI was reading an electromagnetic frequency with the range of 1 mG to 2.5 mG. This is a sign of paranormal activity.

At 3:53 PM the Ovilus IV gave me the sixth word of this Session 2, basement. I do not feel that the word basement is in response to any of the questions I have asked so far during this Session number two.

At 3:55 PM the EDI is measuring an electromagnetic frequency of 2.5 mG. The Mel Meter is measuring an electromagnetic frequency of 0.0 mG. The Mel Meter and EDI are setting just inches apart. It seems that ghosts and spirits can zero in on one small instrument without causing the other instrument to measure any electromagnetic frequency at all.

Between 4 PM and 4:05 PM I scanned the room with my thermal imager. I obtained four images of a long cylinder shape dark blue area along the East wall and near or on the ceiling at the southeast corner of the room. I obtained two images at different angles, of the ceiling near the air conditioner vent. I obtained two images of the long dark blue cylinder shape area across from the air conditioner vent and towards the room's South wall. I obtained two images of a dark blue long cylinder shape area along the East wall and the ceiling. I obtained two images of a pink area on the worn hardwood floor next to the right side of the bed, while standing at the foot of the bed and facing the head of the bed. I obtained four images of the pink area and pink footprints on the worn hardwood floor area next to the left side of the bed, while standing at the foot of the bed and facing the head of the bed. I find it hard to believe that my feet are warm enough, with the installation of the sandals I'm wearing, and the short period of time that I stood on the hardwood floor, that I could leave a heat signature for the thermal imager to see. There may be some type of chemical within the hardwood floor that is reacting to my weight. I feel that my weight is the force causing pressure which has left the heat signature that the FLIR imager is picking up. This is the only thing that I can think of, as a rational cause for there to be a heat signature with the color pink where I have walked on this room's hardwood floor.

At 4:08 PM the EDI is reading 2.5 mG. The Mel Meter is reading 0.0 mG. It seems to me that the ghosts and spirits like the newer, EDI, and they are checking it out. When I tried to film the EDI's readings with camcorder one, each time the EDI readings for the electromagnetic frequency return to zero. It is almost as if the ghosts and spirits do not want me to document proof of their existence.

At 4:20 PM the Ovilus IV appear to be frozen up and it is not functioning properly. Upon touching the home icon, the Ovilus IV would not return to the home position. I do not feel the batteries are that old. And they should have more energy. Sometimes, it seems like the ghosts and spirits are not draining the battery energy, but somehow, they are interfering with or blocking the energy from being used by the Ovilus IV. So, I turned off the Ovilus IV manually. Upon turning the Ovilus IV back on, it worked fine and gave me one back ground word. At 4:22 PM I obtained the seventh word for this Session 2, which is a background word, am. I feel that the ghost and or spirit is trying to say, "I am." Maybe ghost or spirit is saying that they caused the blockage which makes the Ovilus IV not function properly. When the Ovilus IV is not functioning properly, I have coined the phrase that the Ovilus IV is frozen up.

At 4:22 PM the EDI's reading for the electromagnetic frequency was 2.5 mG. The electromagnetic frequency reading for the Mel Meter was zero. Seems like the ghosts and or spirits have the accuracy to pinpoint a response on the EDI while leaving the Mel Meter alone.

At 4:26 PM the EDI's reading for the electromagnetic frequency was 1.0 mG and the Mel Meter's reading for the electromagnetic frequency was zero. These two instruments are designed to measure electromagnetic frequencies and are relatively close together! Maybe 12 inches apart, at the most. When one instrument is measuring an electromagnetic frequency while the other instrument fails to measure anything, that just shows you that the small pocket of energy that the ghost or spirit possesses is very precise and very small.

Digital pictures of the Annie Room, Friday, 10th March 2017, Hays House.

Two pictures of the exterior entrance door.

Two pictures of the left side of the room's West wall.

Two pictures of the center of the room's West wall and the fireplace.

Two pictures of the room's Northwest corner.

Two close-up pictures of the fireplace on the room's West wall.

Two pictures of the room's North wall to include the bed and two windows.

Two pictures of the room's Northeast corner.

Two pictures of the room's center East wall and two doors.

Two pictures of the room's South East corner, and door opening leading to the Second Floor North Side kitchen.

Two close-up pictures of the room's hardwood floor.

Two pictures of the room's South wall and interior entrance door.

Two close-up pictures of the horizontal wallboards.

Two close-up pictures of the closet door's doorknob.

Two close-up pictures of the doorknob on the door leading to the Second Floor North Side kitchen.

Two close-up pictures of the doorknob on the interior side of the entrance door, located on the room's South wall.

Two close-up pictures of the room's ceiling boards and corner trim.

Two close-up pictures of the horizontal wallboards in the corner trim.

Please see the author's website at www.keithoevans.com to view each digital picture.

Thermal images of the Annie Room, Friday, 10th March 2017, Hays House

One thermal image of the room's Southwest corner, near the closet without a door.

One thermal image of the center area of the room's West wall, near the fireplace.

One thermal image of the room's Northwest corner, near the two windows.

One thermal image of the center area of the room's North wall, near the two Windows, and bed.

One thermal image of the room's Northeast corner, near the two windows.

One thermal image of the dark area on the one board on the room's floor board, near the room's Northwest corner.

One thermal image of the room's South East corner, near the door to the Second Floor North Side Kitchen.

One thermal image of the dark blue area on the room's ceiling near the South wall.

One thermal image of the ceiling air conditioner vent, located in the center of the image and the ceiling lights, located at the bottom of the image.

One thermal image of the ceiling fan and lights at the left center of the image, and a dark blue area on the ceiling just south of the ceiling fan.

Please see the author's website at www.keithoevans.com to view each thermal image.

CHAPTER **16**

The Mary Room, Hays House, Ghosts are People too.

A description of The Mary Room, Wednesday, 2nd November 2016, Hays House.

A description of the 2nd Floor South Side Bathroom within the Mary Room from six pictures taken on 2nd November 2016, Hays House.

On the room's West wall and in the room's Southwest corner is a modern white vinyl shower covering part of the South and West wall's. This shower has a partial glass enclosure with a glass door. To the right of this shower and on the room's West wall are two wooden frame pictures of flowers.

Near the room's Northwest corner and on the room's North wall is a modern door way that was built sometime after 1996. This doorway has an original white five sunken panel door. In the center of the North wall is a modern sink with a square wooden framed mirror above the sink that is mounted on the North wall. To the left side of this modern white sink is a silver round towel rack. To the right side of the white, modern, sink is a light blue cabinet that is approximately 3 feet wide, 3 feet tall, and 6 inches deep, with three shelves and a door with a glass front. This cabinet is mounted on the room's North wall. The middle shelf has a white toy a pickup truck. On the top of this cabinet is a large Conkle type seashell and a can of spray deodorizer.

Near the room's Northeast corner and mounted on the room's East wall is a covered electrical outlet. In the center of the room's East wall is a modern white toilet that is sitting on a rectangular shaped white marble slab. This white marble slab was originally on the floor, beneath the toilet that was in the original bathroom that is located at the Northeast corner of the second floor. Above the modern white toilet is a 3' x 5' group of four triangular white canvases. These canvases are covered with a painting of pink and red flowers with green stems, green leaves, and a light blue background. Mounted on the room's South wall is a 4-foot-long, 6-inch-deep shelf, with two tan and light blue wicker basket, and some extra white towels on top. To the right side of this mounted shelf and on the room's South wall is an original window with two glass panes on the upper and lower sections. This window has the original white wooden trim. This window is covered by a sheer tan shade that that lets in the sunlight.

The room has a light mounted on the center of the room's ceiling. The room's ceiling has the original light blue tongue and groove ceiling boards that are running in an East to West direction. On this room's East, South, and West walls are the original white horizontal tongue and groove wallboards. On this room's ceiling are the original light blue and white wooden trim. The room's floor has the original heart pine, tongue and groove, hardwood flooring that is running in an East to West direction. The room's North wall and trim boards are white and modern. The North wall was added sometime after 1996.

A description of the 2nd Floor South Side Kitchen within the Mary Room from 17 pictures taken on 2nd November 2016, Hays House.

Near the rooms Southwest corner, and on the room's West wall is an electrical outlet with the black electrical cord plugged into this electrical outlet. The microwave oven is plugged into this electrical outlet. To the right of the electrical outlet is the silver microwave. To the right of the microwave oven is a silver toaster oven. Both appliances are sitting on top of a stainless-steel table that has three shelves. There is a light blue wicker basket on the top shelf and a gray wicker basket on the second shelf. To the right of the stainless-steel table is an opening to the Frances Room. This opening does not have a door. This doorway has the original white wooden trim. Above the doorway and on the room's West wall is a painting of a sign that says. "Is anything all right?" This signed has a light blue background, and white and red letters, and is outlined in red.

On the room's North wall and near the room's Northwest corner is a stainless-steel rack. Above the stainless-steel rack is a 1.5' x 2.5' cork note board. To the right of the cork note board is an original white wooden five sunken panel door. This door has the original white wooden trim. This door does not have the original brass or metal door knob but has an antique smooth oval-shaped brass or metal door-knob. This door has the original brass or metal skeleton key baseplate that is painted white. To the right side of this original door way, that leads to the Second Floor Back Stairway Room, is a white double light switch. To the right side of the white double light switch is a white Kenmore refrigerator with a light blue, wooden tray on top.

Mounted on the East wall is a 3' x 2.5' white canvas with a painting of an olive green, framed window with white vinyl blinds. On the inside of the window are white flowers in a clear glass vase. On the outside of the window are pink and white flowers on a green Bush, with the light blue sky in the background. To the right side of this painting and on the room's East wall, is an original window with two glass panes on the upper and lower sections. This window is covered by a tan sheer blini that allows the sunlight to enter the room.

On the room's South wall and near the room's South East corner is a dark wooden frame under glass, picture of a painting. This is a picture of a painting of pink and red flowers in a green pot, sitting on a light green table, with a pink wall in the background. Below the painting and within the frame are the words, "Amy Friedman Apalachicola, Florida." Below the painting and on the room's South wall are knives and other utensils that are mounted on to the wall by stainless steel brackets. To the right of the painting are two, 6-foot-long, 10 inches deep, stainless steel shelves, with different type of dishes. The lower shelf is lined with hooks that has hanging pots and pans. Below the stainless-steel shelves is a modern green speckled colored countertop, with a double stainless-steel sink on the far-right side. To the right of the double stainless-steel sink, and near the room's Southwest corner is a modern door way to the Second Floor South Side Bathroom, which is within the Mary Room. This doorway has a modern white wooden trim, but an original white wooden, five sunken panel door, with the original black brass or metal doorknob and skeleton key baseplate.

This room's West, North, and East wall's all have the original tongue and groove, horizontal, white wall boards. This room's South wall is modern, white, wooden, and was created sometime after 1996. This room's ceiling trim is original, white and wooden. The room's ceiling has the original, green, tongue and groove, wooden boards that is approximately 2 1/2 inches to 3 inches wide. This room has the original heart pine, hardwood, tongue and groove flooring. The room has a combination white light with four bulbs, and a ceiling fan hanging from the center of the room's ceiling.

A description of The Mary Room from two pictures taken in 1996, Hays House.

From a photo taken of the North West corner within The Mary Room. Starting from the left and going to the right on the room's West wall is a white wooden antique table with a matching high backboard. This table has the following items on top, I am starting from the left and going to the right; a pink and red flowered covered glass or porcelain lamp, a porcelain figurine of a bald eagle, a clear crystal vase, a multicolored porcelain picture, a golden colored porcelain dish. In front of this table is a light wooden antique chair. Mounted on this room's West wall and above the antique table is a modern black wooden framed under glass, picture or drawling of a man and a woman in Victorian style clothing. To the right of the antique table, is an 8-foot-tall light wooden antique armoire. This armoire has two full length doors in front.

From a photo taken of this room's South wall. On the room's South wall and near the room's South East corner is an antique dark wooden twin bed with a possibly hand carved, with a high decorative headboard and footboard. This twin bed is covered with a white textured, with a geometrical design, bedspread with tassels on its sides. This bed has two pillows, one pillow is under the bedspread and the other pillow has multiple colors. To the right of the twin bed is an antique wooden nightstand with a red marble top. This nightstand has wheels on its four legs. On top of this nightstand, from left to right is an antique lamp with a golden supporting stand and two white porcelain or glass globes. At this lamp's base is a porcelain figurine of a man. On the left side of the nightstand is some type of wooden jewelry box or container. Above this nightstand is a window with its original white wooden trim. This window is covered with a white curtain. On the left side of this room's South wall and in this room's Southwest corner is a white wooden crib with a white mattress. Above this crib and mounted on the room's South wall is a 10" x 15" rectangular dark wooden framed mirror. There are two small golden framed pictures on the left and right sides of this mirror. In front of the crib is an antique dark wooden chair.

All of the walls in this room are covered with the light green, original, tongue and groove, horizontal, wallboards. This room has the original, tongue and groove, heart pine, hardwood flooring. There is a small multi-colored rug in the middle of this room's floor. This room has the original light green ceiling trim.

The history of The Mary Room, Hays House.

In 1942 Mary occupied this room until her dead, from Heart related problems, in the early 1960's. Mary's Room never had a fire place and or an oil heater. It is believed that Mary's Room had an electrical heater during the cold weather. After Mary passed away, it is not known if this bedroom was ever used by anyone. Prior to the Hays family living at the Hays House, the Buck family lived at the Hays House from 1908 to 1923. The Buck family had six children, two boys and four girls. So, it is believed that one of James Buck's children use this bedroom from 1908 until 1923. When the Buck family gave the house back to the bank in the early 1920's. It is believed that the Apalachicola State Bank had the Hays House until 1942 and used it as a boarding home. So many individuals may have used Mary's room from early 1920's up until 1942 when the Hays family bought the house. I have not been able to find any pictures of Mary and or find out Mary's last name.

Mel Meter base readings of The Mary Room, to include the 2017 Second Floor Southside Bathroom and Kitchen, Wednesday, 2nd November 2016, Hays House.

11:05 AM The double switch on the South Side Kitchen Room's North wall.

The Electromagnetic frequency range was 0.0 mG to 0.0 mG.

The temperature range was 75.2°F to 75.5°F.

11:05 AM The Kenmore refrigerator located along the South Side Kitchen Room's North wall.

The electromagnetic frequency range was 0.0 mG to 0.0 mG.

The temperature range was 75.5°F to 75.5°F.

11:06 AM The electrical outlet on the South Side Kitchen Room's North wall.

The electromagnetic frequency range was 0.0 mG to 0.0 mG.

The temperature range was 75.1°F to 75.2°F.

11:06 AM The Osley microwave oven on the South Side Kitchen Room's West wall.

The electromagnetic frequency range was 0.0 mG to 0.0 mG.

The temperature range was 74.8°F to 74.9°F.

11:07 AM The micro wave oven on the South Side Kitchen Room's West wall.

The electromagnetic frequency range was 0.0 mG to 0.0 mG.

The temperature range was 74.6°F to 75.1°F.

11:07 AM The double switch on the Bathroom's North wall.

The electromagnetic frequency range was 0.0 mG to 0.0 mG.

The temperature range was 74.4°F to 74.6°F.

11:08 AM The electrical cover plate on the Bathroom's East wall.

The electromagnetic frequency range was 0.0 mG to 0.0 mG.

The temperature range was 74.8°F to 75.1°F.

11:08 AM The electrical cover plate on the Bathroom's West wall.

The electromagnetic frequency range was 0.0 mG to 0.0 mG.

The temperature range was 74.9°F to 74.9°F.

Paranormal Investigation, Session 1 of The Mary Room, to include the present day Second Floor Southside Bathroom and Kitchen, Thursday, 1st June 2017, Hays House.

Prior to the Paranormal Investigation Session 1, I noticed that Mary's original bedroom, is now divided into two parts. Now, the Mary Room has a bathroom on one half of the original room and a kitchen on the second half of the original bedroom. The kitchen half of The Mary Room always feels thermally the coolest room in the house. No matter what the temperature is outside and no matter if the air conditioning is on or off, this room feels cold to me. I've always found Mary's room, to be a comfortable cool temperature room. Although I felt hurry to complete all my paranormal sessions within the Hays House just in case the house sold. The house was put up for sale in early March 2017 prior to my starting the second group of Paranormal Investigations. I felt at ease throughout the Paranormal Investigation, Session 1. I felt like this was going to be a good Paranormal Investigation, and that Mary would communicate.

10:39 AM Keith: (The ceiling fan and the air conditioner are on.) "Hello, I am Keith Evans. I wish only to speak with members of the Hays, Gibson, and Buck family's. That includes you to Mary. You may use your energy to choose words from the Ovilus IV's database. This is the Ovilus IV and it will not hurt you." (Hold it up.)

10:40 AM Keith: "This is the Mel Meter and the EDI. They measure temperature and electromagnetic frequencies. They will not harm you." (Hold it up.)

10:41 AM Keith: "The Ovilus IV has given me three background words; violence which is spelled V-I-O-L-E-N-C-E, tragic which is spelled T-R-A-G-I-C, and you which is spelled Y-O-U. The Ovilus IV has pronounced all three words, at a normal conversational level and speed."

10:41 AM Keith: "I have observed the Mel Meter readings to be 0.0 mG and 74.6°F."

10:42 AM Keith: "I have observed the EDT readings to be 2.5 mG and 73.9°F."

10:42 AM Keith: "The Ovilus IV has given me the word tremor which is spelled T-R-E-M-O-R. The Ovilus IV has pronounced the word tremor in a normal conversational level and speed."

10:43 AM Keith: "I have observed the Mel Meter readings to be 0.0 mG and 74.4°F."

10:43 AM Keith: "I have observed the EDI readings to be 2.5 mG and 74.0°F."

10:48 AM Keith: "Pat and Kathleen, what was this room used for when you lived here?"

10:49 AM Keith: "Kathleen, how was this room furnished when you lived here?"

10:51 AM Keith: "Kathleen, name one piece of antique furniture that you had in this room?"

10:52 AM Keith: "Violence, tragedy, you, and tremor, seems to be a very negative theme we do not need to be negative today."

10:53 AM Keith: "On a positive note, let's talk about history."

10:54 AM Keith: "Pat, how often did you buff and shine the hardwood floors in the Hays House?"

10:55 AM Keith: "Kathleen, how often did you buff and shine the hardwood floors in the Hays House?"

10:56 AM Keith: "Sunshine, how often did you buff and shine the hardwood floors in the Hays House?"

10:57 AM Keith: "Mary, how often did you buff and shine the hardwood floors in the Hays House?"

10:58 AM Keith: "Kathleen, was this room, a bedroom in the 1940's."

10:59 AM Keith: "Kathleen, did this room ever have a TV in it when you were living here?"

11 AM to 11:05 AM Keith: "I'm going to completed a thermal scan of this room. I have obtained two thermal images of my pink footprints on the floor near the North wall and door. I have obtained two thermal images of my pink footprints on the floor where I was standing near the table. I have obtained two thermal images of my 1 footprint and the chair where I was sitting at the table. I have obtained two thermal images of three pink squares on the bathroom ceiling. I have obtained two thermal images of my two pink footprints on the bathroom floor. I have obtained five thermal images of the room's ceiling, near the air conditioner vent and the cold air moving towards the North wall."

11:06 AM Keith: "Kathleen, what would you like to tell me about the Hays House?"

11:07 AM Keith: "Kathleen, what was your favorite moment in this room?"

11:08 AM Keith: "I can hear talking in the hallway."

11:09 AM Keith: "Pat, what can you tell me about this room?"

11:10 AM Keith: "Pat, how was this room furnished in the 1940's?"

11:11 AM Keith: "Pat, did you paint this room's floor with Brown paint?"

11:13 AM Keith: "I have observed the Mel Meter readings to be 0.0 mG and 73.6°F."

11:14 AM Keith: "I have observed the EDI readings to be 2.5 mG and 73.3°F."

11:15 AM Keith: "The Ovilus IV gave me the word total which is spelled T-O-T-A-L. The Ovilus IV has pronounce total at a normal conversational level and speed."

11:15 AM Keith: "I have observed the Mel Meter readings to be 0.0 mG and 73.1°F."

11:16 AM Keith: "I have observed the EDI readings to be 2.5 mG and 73.3°F."

11:16 AM Keith: "Something is causing the EDI to have an electro-magnetic frequency reading between 1.0 mG to 2.5 mG."

11:20 AM Keith: "What is the total? You may be speaking in a sentence, but I only hear the word total."

11:21 AM Keith: "Do I have three guesses. Total loss? Total amount of money? Total amount of time?"

11:22 AM Keith: "Am I right?"

11:23 AM Keith: "I did not receive a response."

11:24 AM Keith: "Sunshine, give me some words of wisdom?"

11:25 AM Keith: "Sunshine, give a Paranormal Investigator some advice?"

11:26 AM Keith: "Sunshine, I have criticized your family. Let me have it?"

11:29 AM Keith: "I can hear some strange sounds coming from the Ovilus IV." (I held the Ovilus IV close to the camcorder one.)

11:30 AM Keith: "The Ovilus IV has given me the word thought which is spelled T-H-O-U-G-H-T. The Ovilus IV has pronounced the word thought at a normal conversational level and speed."

11:30 AM Keith: "I have observed the Mel Meter readings to be 0.1 mG and 75.3°F."

11:30 AM Keith: "I have observed the EDI readings to be 2.5 mG and 73.0°F."

11:33 AM Keith: "Thought-provoking?"

11:34 AM Keith: "Thank you for talking to me. Have a good day."

11:34 AM Keith: "This Session 1 ended on Thursday, 1st June 2017."

Paranormal Investigation, Session 2 of The Mary Room, to include the present day Second Floor Southside Bathroom and Kitchen, Thursday, 1st June 2017, Hays House.

1:41 PM Keith: "Hello, I am Keith Evans. I wish only to speak with members of the Hays, Gibson, and Buck family's. Mary, you may talk too. You may use your energy to choose words from the Ovilus IV's database. This is the Ovilus IV. The Ovilus IV will not hurt you." (Hold it up.)

1:42 PM Keith: "This is the Mel Meter, and the EDI. They measure temperature and the electromagnetic frequency. They will not harm you." (Hold it up.)

1:43 PM Keith: "The Ovilus IV has given me three background words; way which is spelled W-A-Y, Oremus which is spelled O-R-E-M-U-S, and picture which is spelled P-I-C-T-U-R-E. The Ovilus IV has pronounced the words way, Oremus, and picture at a normal conversational level and speed."

1:43 PM Keith: "I have observed the Mel Meter readings to be 0.0 mG and 71.7°F."

1:44 PM Keith: "I have observed the EDI readings to be 2.5 mG and 75.6°F."

1:45 PM Keith: "I have observed the Mel Meter readings to be 0.0 mG and 72.0°F."

1:45 PM Keith: "The Ovilus IV has given me the word haunting which is spelled H-A-U-N-T-I-N-G. The Ovilus IV has pronounced the word haunting at a normal conversational level and speed."

1:49 PM Keith: "Oremus, picture, and haunting, I do not know what type of question that you may be asking me there."

1:50 PM Keith: "Oremus what picture are you talking about?"

1:51 PM Keith: "Is Oremus your first or last name?"

1:51 PM Keith: "I hear talking in the hallway."

1:52 PM Keith: "Sunshine, who is Oremus?"

1:53 PM Keith: "Oremus, is there a picture of you in the Hays House today?"

1:54 PM Keith: "The Ovilus IV gave me the word design which is spelled D-E-S-I-G-N. The Ovilus IV pronounce the word design at a normal conversational level and speed."

1:55 PM Keith: "I have observed the Mel Meter readings to be 0.0 mG and 72.7°F."

1:55 PM Keith: "I have observed the EDI readings to be 2.5 mG and 74.5°F."

1:58 PM Keith: "Who said the word design?"

1:59 PM Keith: "Oremus, did you design something in the Hays House?"

2 PM Keith: "What did you design?"

2 PM Keith: "I hear talking in the hallway."

2:01 PM to 2:05 PM Keith: "I'm going to take some thermal images of the room. I have obtained two thermal images of my two pink foot prints and yellow seat of the chair that I was sitting in. I have obtained one thermal image of the ceiling's air conditioner vent near the room's interior South wall. This image is light blue, possibly resulting from the cool air distribution. I have obtained two images of the ceiling with the cool air moving towards the North wall. I have obtained two images of the bathroom ceiling with dark blue areas near the ceiling light and the ceiling vent."

2:06 PM Keith: "The Ovilus IV gave me the word fuzzy which is spelled F-U-Z-Z-Y. The Ovilus IV has pronounced the word fuzzy at a normal conversational level and speed."

2:07 PM Keith: "I have observed the Mel Meter readings to be 0.0 mG and 72.6°F."

2:07 PM Keith: "I have observed the EDI readings to be 2.5 mG and 73.5°F."

2:08 PM Keith: "I have observed the Mel Meter readings to be 2.5 mG and 73.5°F."

2:11 PM Keith: "I was looking at a picture of two chickens mounted on the West wall near the South West corner of the Kitchen Room, when the Ovilus IV gave me the word fuzzy. I guess the chickens do look fuzzy."

2:12 PM Keith: "Oremus, did you paint the chickens."

2:14 PM Keith: "Did you design this room? This room is rectangular in shape, with the original heart pine hardwood floor, the original horizontal wall boards, the original ceiling boards, and possibly the original ceiling trim boards and floor trim boards."

2:18 PM Keith: "Sunshine, what part of this room is not original?"

2:19 PM Keith: "Kathleen, was there ever a radio in this room?"

2:20 PM Keith: "Kathleen, were you a coin collector?"

2:21 PM Keith: "Kathleen, if you could, what changes would you make to the Hays House?"

2:22 PM Keith: "Yes my vision has been fuzzy since I have been doing the hyper barometric chamber treatments."

2:25 PM Keith: "Pat, can you tell me more about the Great Depression?"

2:26 PM Keith: "Pat, did your property value go down, during the Great Depression?"

2:26 PM Keith: "The Ovilus IV gave me the word Ameline which is spelled A-M-E-L-I-N-E. The Ovilus IV has pronounced the word Ameline at a normal conversational level and speed."

2:26 PM Keith: "I have observed the Mel Meter readings to be 0.0 mG and 72.5°F."

2:27 PM Keith: "The Ovilus IV gave me the word crayon which is spelled C-R-A-Y-O-N. The Ovilus IV pronounced the word crayon at a normal conversational level and speed."

2:27 PM Keith: "I have observed the Mel Meter readings to be 0.0 mG and 72.5°F."

2:28 PM Keith: "I have observed the EDI readings to be 2.5 mG and 72.6°F."

2:32 PM Keith: "Mary, do you like playing with the crayons?"

2:33 PM Keith: "Ameline, do you like playing with the crayons?"

3:34 PM Keith: "Sunshine, do you like playing with the crayons?"

2:35 PM Keith: "Ameline, what year were you here at the Hays House?"

2:36 PM Keith: "Is there an old water well, located on the property here?"

2:37 PM Keith: "Please, I need more history from the spirits and ghosts."

2:38 PM Keith: "I have observed the Mel Meter readings to be 0.3 mG and 72.2°F."

2:39 PM Keith: "I have observed the Mel Meter readings to be 0.3 mG and 72.5°F."

2:39 PM Keith: "I have observed the EDI readings to be 2.5 mG and 72.4°F."

2:40 PM Keith: "Thank you for talking to me. Have a nice day."

2:40 PM Keith: "This Session 2 ended on Thursday, 1st June 2017."

The analysis of the Paranormal Investigation, Session 1, The Mary Room, to include the present day 2nd Floor Southside Bathroom and Kitchen. Date of the analysis was Saturday, 30th July 2017, Hays House.

At 10:41 AM the Ovilus IV gave me the first three background words for session 1, violence, tragic, and you. Since I have not asked any questions during this Session 1. These words were given by the Ovilus IV within one minute of turning on the Ovilus IV. These words are an evaluates the electromagnetic energy within the environment. So, some ghost or spirit within the environment is sharing these words with me; violence, tragic, and you. It appears that they are saying that I will have had or may have, violence and or tragedy. Now these ghosts and spirits may be talking to me or maybe talking to each other, or they may be talking to another living person within the environment. Ghosts and spirits are people too. I'm sure that they may have tough skin and ignore people who think or feel that they are demonic and are here to cause harm. I feel that it is my duty to listen to a ghost ventilate and tell me how they feel. Maybe their words are not directed towards me. This shows me that this ghost and or spirit, was at one time a living being with emotions and feelings and at times they have to express themselves. These ghosts and spirits are expressing themselves by using their energy to manipulate and choose words from the Ovilus IV's data base.? Hearing, the words violence, tragic, and you, does not alarm me and should not alarm you.

At 10:42 AM the Ovilus IV gave me the fourth word for session 1, tremor. Since I have not asked any questions yet during this session 1, I do not feel that the word tremor is directed towards me. I can only assume that a ghost is tremoring in fear and or this ghost is telling me that I should be tremoring in fear.

At 10:42 AM and 10:43 AM the EDI had a strong electromagnetic frequency of 2.5 mG. At the same time. The Mel Meters readings for the electromagnetic frequency was 0.0 mG. So, this is an indication that ghosts and spirits can zero in on a small target and manipulate precisely what they wish to manipulate.

Between 11 AM and 11:06 AM I obtained thermal images from this room. The images involving my pink foot prints are the most intriguing to me. My sandals should act as an insulator to keep the floor from being warmed by my feet. I do not feel that my body temperature is causing the pink footprints on the hardwood floor. I feel that it is my pressure from my weight is cause a chemical reaction with some type of wax or oil that has been applied to the wood. So, my weight is applying pressure to activate a chemical and that is the heat signature which allows us to see my two pink footprints.

At 11:15 AM the Ovilus IV gave me the fifth word for session 1, total. The word total maybe the intelligent Spirit of Pat Hays telling that he totally painted the floor in this room brown. This word total is in response to the question that I had asked Pat at 11:11 AM. Pat, did you paint this room's floor brown?

At 12:30 AM the Ovilus IV gave me the sixth word for session 1, thought. This may be an intelligent response from a ghost or spirit that wants me that they had thought about things.

At 11:14 AM, 11:16 AM, and 11:30 AM the EDI is reading for the electromagnetic frequency to be 2.5 mG. This is an indication of a highly active small area within the room. At 11:30 AM, the Mel Meter readings for the electromagnetic frequency was 0.1 mG. This shows how a ghost or spirit may choose one piece of equipment to register a higher electromagnetic frequency while ignoring another piece of equipment sitting less than a foot away.

I had a good feeling that Mary would communicate with me during this paranormal session. I cannot say that any of the words given to me by the Ovilus IV, are connected to Mary.

The analysis of the Paranormal Investigation, Session 2, The Mary Room, to include the present day 2nd Floor Southside Bathroom and Kitchen. Date of the analysis was Saturday, 30th July 2017, Hays House.

1:43 PM the Ovilus IV gave me the first three background words for Session 2, way, Oremus, and picture. I have not asked any questions yet during this Session 2. I do not feel that the evaluation of the environment by the Ovilus IV, has given me any words that are talking to me. I do not know anyone by the name of Oremus, that is connected to the Hays House. I have spent several minutes looking at the fuzzy Chicken painting on the 2nd Floor, South Side, Kitchen Room's West wall. I have made some verbal remarks about this painting. The word picture maybe in respondence to those actions.

At, 1:45 PM the Ovilus IV gave me the fourth word for session 2, haunting. I have not asked any questions yet during this session 2. I do not feel that the word haunting is responding to me. This may be an intelligent ghost who is aware of their surroundings and naming their communications with me as a haunting.

At 1:44 PM, 1:46 PM, and 1:55 PM the EDI measured an electromagnetic frequency of 2.5 mG. This is an indication of a highly paranormal active area near the EDI.

At 1:54 PM the Ovilus IV gave me the fifth word for this session 2, design. I feel that this is an intelligent spirit or ghost that is asking me to pay attention to the design within a painting of the chicken that was on the West wall on the 2nd Floor, South Side, Kitchen Room. I was distracted by the painting of the chicken, mounted on the room's West wall because the chicken looks like it has hair not feathers.

Between 2:01 PM and 2:06 PM I obtained thermal images of the Mary Room. As in session 1, I am still obtaining pink footprints on the tongue and groove, heart pine, hardwood floor. I do not feel that the floors being warmed up by my feet. My sandals should insulate my warm feet from warming up the hardwood floor. I think the pressure from my weight is causing chemicals within the hardwood floor to give off a heat signature that is observed by the FLIR imager. I touched the hardwood floors and it did not feel to be warm at all in the areas where my footprints were located.

At 2:06 PM the Ovilus IV gave me the sixth word for this session 2, fuzzy. I feel that this is an intelligent spirit or ghost that is pointing out that the painting of the chicken is absent from having a feather texture and just looks fuzzy. I was standing there looking at the picture of the chicken on the room's West wall when the word fuzzy was given to me by the Ovilus IV. This spirit or ghost is watching me and responding to what I am doing in real time. I agree with the ghost. The chicken looks to have fuzzy hair and no feather.

At 2:07 PM, 2:08 PM, and 2:39 PM the EDI readings for the electromagnetic frequency was 2.5 mG. This indicates Paranormal activity, but it is just very close to the EDI. For the most part, the Mel Meter readings for the electromagnetic frequency have been 0.0 mG, except for a 0.3 mG reading at 2:38 PM.

At 2:26 PM the Ovilus IV gave me the seventh word for this session 2, Ameline. I did not know anyone by the name of Ameline, that is connected with the Hay House at the time of during this Paranormal Investigation, Session 2. Since that time, I have discovered that James F. Buck had six children, four girls and two boys and one of the girls was named Emoline. There's a strong possibility that this room was used by Emoline during the time that the Buck family lived in the Hays House. There is a possibility that the spelling that I was giving is incorrect. This lady's name may have been spelled, Ameline.

At 2:27 PM the Ovilus IV gave me the eighth word for this session 2, crayon. I feel that this could be the intelligent spirit of Mary who I have been told had an intellectual level of an eight-year-old. This may be Mary's way of saying that she would like to play with a crayon. This was Mary's Room from 1942 and until Mary passed away sometime in the early 1960's.

Ovilus IV words: Picture, Haunting, Design.

Ovilus IV words: Fuzzy, Ameline, Crayon.

Digital pictures of The Mary Room, to include the present day Second Floor Southside Bathroom and Kitchen, Wednesday, 2nd November 2016, Hays House.

The Second Floor, South Side, Bathroom's digital pictures.

One picture of the room's East wall.

One picture of the room's South wall and ceiling.

One picture of the room's Northeast corner.

One close-up picture of the light blue cabinet mounted on the room's North wall.

One picture of the room's West wall and ceiling.

One picture of the room's West wall.

The Second Floor, South Side, Kitchen's digital pictures.

One picture of the room's Northeast corner.

One picture of the room's West wall.

One picture of the top part of the room's West wall and ceiling.

One picture of the room's Northwest corner and ceiling.

One close-up picture of the left side of the room's South wall.

One close-up picture of the right side of the room's South wall.

Two pictures of the entrance door's original doorknob and skeleton key baseplate.

Two pictures of the Second Floor Southside Bathroom door's doorknob and skeleton key baseplate.

Two close-up pictures of the original black brass or metal skeleton key baseplate.

Two close-up pictures of the original black brass or metal doorknob.

Two pictures of the original, white, five sunken panels door, located on the room's North wall.

Please see the author's website at www.keithoevans.com to view each digital picture.

Thermal images of The Mary Room, to include the present day Second Floor, South Side, Bathroom and Kitchen, Wednesday, 2nd November 2016, Hays House.

One thermal image of the Bathroom's ceiling's exhaust fan. The exhaust fan is in the off position.

One thermal image of the sink on the Bathroom's North wall.

One thermal image of the toilet on the Bathroom's East wall.

One thermal image of the window on the Bathroom's South wall.

One thermal image of the shower glass area, located on the Bathroom's Southwest corner.

One thermal image of the South Side Kitchen Room's ceiling fan.

One thermal image of the South Side Kitchen Room's door, located on the room's North wall.

One thermal image of the South Side Kitchen Room's window, located on the room's East wall.

One thermal image of the South Side Kitchen Room's kitchen area, located on the room's South wall.

One thermal image of the South Side Kitchen Room's two microwave ovens, located on the room's West wall.

Please see the author's website at www.keithoevans.com to view each thermal image.

CHAPTER 17

Second Floor Front Porch, Hays House, Ghosts are People too.

A brief description of the Second Floor Front Porch, Hays House.

On the porch's East wall and to the left side of the door are two groups of painted boards that are mounted on the East wall. The top group of boards are painted light blue with black letters that say. "Camp Friedman." Below the group of boards that says camp Friedman, there is a group of boards with a painting of a man who has caught and is holding a large green fish. Below the bottom painting is a modern iron shelf that is mounted on to the East wall. On top of this modern shelf is an olive green square candle. In the middle of the porch's East wall is an original light green exterior door with two sunken panels, on the lower half and a large window on the upper half. This door has the original brass or metal doorknob and skeleton key baseplate. Both the doorknob and the skeleton key baseplate are painted light green. This doorway has the original doorway trim that is painted white. This doorway has a light green wooden screen door, that may be original. On the porch's East wall and to the right side of the door, is a piece of plywood with a light green background and different areas of green, blue, and white paint.

On the porch's South side and in the porch's South East corner is a 2' x 2' brown iron table with a potted plant on top. To the right side of the brown iron table is a light green wicker couch with four pillows. One pillow is white, two pillows have white and light green stripes and one pillow has white and blue stripes. In front of this couch is a small metal table. On top of this metal table is a glass bowl that has a square yellow candle.

In the porch's Southwest corner is a green column with white trim at the top and bottom. This column supports the roof over the porch. The porch's West side wall is approximately 2 foot tall. This wall has a row of Christmas lights across its top. From left to right, along the porches West side is a blue and white textile footstool, a small black metal stand, and a porch chair with a green cushion and a green pillow. In the porches Northwest corner is a light green column with white trim at the top and the bottom that supports the porch's roof.

The porches North side wall is approximately 2-foot-tall at the far-left side of this wall. As this wall gets closer to the house, it increases to about 2 1/2-foot-tall as it reaches the porch's East wall. Along the top of the North side wall is a row of Christmas lights with clear light bulbs. There is a 2' x 2' square table centered on this porch's North side. This table has a clear plastic chair, on each side.

This porch has the original light green tongue and groove ceiling boards. This porch has a floor that is modern and made out of outdoor deck boards. These deck boards were added to this porch sometime after 1996. The porch's East side exterior wall has the original ship lap boards that are painted light green.

The history of the Second Floor Front Porch, Hays House.

Prior to 1996, the Second Floor Front Porch did not have a wooden floor. This porch was mounted on top of the down sloping shingles, that are located on top of the roof over the First Floor Wraparound Front Porch, which lies below the Second Floor Front Porch. Sometime after 1996, the Second Floor Front Porch was given a level wooden deck type floor. The rest of the Second Floor Front Porch seems to be unchanged and original.

Mel Meter base readings, Second Floor Front Porch, Wednesday, 2nd November 2016, Hays House.

The electrical outlet on the porch's exterior East wall located on the right side of the door. This electrical outlet is not in use.

The electromagnetic frequency range was 0.0 mG to 0.0 mG.

The temperature range was 81.3°F to 81.9°F.

Paranormal Investigation, Session 1, Second Floor Front Porch, Friday, 2nd June 2017, Hays House.

10:58 AM Keith: "Hello, I am Keith Evans. I wish only to speak with members of the Hays, Gibson, and Buck family's. To include anyone who has lived at the Hays House. You may use your energy to choose words from the Ovilus IV database. This is the Ovilus IV and it will not hurt you." (Hold it up.)

10:59 AM Keith: "This is the Mel Meter and the EDI. The Mel Meter and EDI measure temperature and electromagnetic frequencies. The Mel Meter and the EDI will not harm ghosts, and or spirits." (Hold it up.)

11 AM Keith: "The Ovilus IV has given me two background words; Nona which is spelled N-O-N-A, and Vern which is spelled V-E-R-N. The Ovilus IV has pronounced the words Nona and Vern, at a normal conversational level and speed."

11:01 AM Keith: "The housekeeper has walked into the frame of both video recorders."

11:02 AM Keith: "I have observed the Mel Meter readings to be 0.0 mG and 83.4°F."

11:02 AM Keith: "I have observed the, EDI readings to be 1.0 mG and 84.3°F."

11:02 AM Keith: "I hear the vacuum cleaner, running."

11:03 AM Keith: "The Ovilus IV gave me the word stop which is spelled S-T-O-P. The Ovilus IV has pronounced the words stop at a normal conversational level and speed."

11:04 AM Keith: "I have observed the Mel Meter readings to be 0.0 mG and 83.8°F."

11:04 AM Keith: "I have observed the EDI readings to be 2.5 mG and 84.3°F."

11:06 AM Keith: "The housekeeper is taking a cigarette break and talking to me."

11:09 AM Keith: "The Ovilus IV has given me the word worry, which is spelled W-O-R-R-Y. The Ovilus IV has pronounced the word worry at a lower than conversational level and at a normal conversational speed."

11:10 AM Keith: "I have observed the Mel Meter readings to be 0.0 mG and 84.5°F."

11:10 AM Keith: "I have observed the EDI readings to be 2.5 mG and 84.4°F."

11:13 AM Keith: "Nice to meet you Nona and Vern."

11:14 AM Keith: "What year did you live in the Hays House?"

11:15 AM Keith: "Nona, what can you tell me about the history of the Hays House?"

11:16 AM Keith: "Vern, what can you tell me about the history of the Hays House?"

11:17 AM Keith: "The Ovilus IV gave me the words before time which is spelled B-E-F-O-R-E, T-I-M-E. The Ovilus IV room has pronounce the words before time at a normal conversational level and speed."

11:18 AM Keith: "I have observed the Mel Meter readings to be 0.0 mG and 85.5°F."

11:18 AM Keith: "I have observed the ED I readings to be 2.5 mG and 85.4°F."

11:22 AM Keith: "Nona and Vern, do you want me to stop worrying?"

11:23 AM Keith: "What would you like me to stop?"

11:24 AM Keith: "Nona, are you related to the Hays family?"

11:25 AM Keith: "Nona, are you related to the Gibson family?"

11:26 AM Keith: "Nona, are you related to the Buck family?"

11:27 AM Keith: "Vern, are you related to the Hays family?"

11:27 AM Keith: "The Ovilus IV gave me the word writing which is spelled W-R-I-T-I-N-G. The Ovilus IV has pronounced the word writing at a normal conversational level and speed."

11:28 AM Keith: "I have observed the Mel Meter readings to be 0.0 mG and 86.9°F."

11:28 AM Keith: "I have observed the EDI readings to be 1.0 mG and 87.3°F."

11:32 AM Keith: "Yes, I am writing. I always document a transcript of everything that takes place during a Paranormal Investigation."

11:34 AM Keith: "Do you want to go inside. I will let you go inside." (Open the door so that Jody the dog could go inside the Hays House.)

11:35 AM Keith: "Vern, are you related to the Gibson family?"

11:36 AM Keith: "Vern, are you related to the Buck family?"

11:37 AM Keith: "Vern, what is your last name?"

11:38 AM Keith: "Nona, what is your last name?"

11:39 AM Keith: "Nona and Vern, did you live and Westminster, Maryland?"

11:39 AM Keith: "It appears that the Ovilus IV is frozen up again. No, it went back to the home position."

11:41 AM Keith: "The Ovilus IV gave me the word trouble which is spelled T-R-O-U-B-L-E. The Ovilus IV pronounced the word trouble at a normal conversational level and speed."

11:41 AM Keith: "I have observed the Mel Meter readings to be 0.0 mG and 88.3°F."

11:42 AM Keith: "The Ovilus IV gave me the word view which is spelled V-I-E-W. The Ovilus IV has pronounced the word view at a normal conversational level and speed."

11:42 AM Keith: "I have observed the EDI readings to be 0.0 mG and 88.3°F."

11:43 AM Keith: "I have observed the Mel Meter readings to be 0.0 mG and 88.4°F."

11:43 AM Keith: "I have observed the EDI readings to be 2.5 mG and 88.4°F."

11:48 AM Keith: "So, you want me to see the view because there is trouble?"

11:49 AM Keith: "What type of trouble are you talking about?"

11:50 AM Keith: "Do you know the name of the person that seems to be staring at me?"

11:51 AM Keith: "Nona, did you know Sunshine Gibson?"

11:52 AM Keith: "Nona, did you know anyone that lived in the Hays House?"

11:53 AM Keith: "Nona, were you ever in the Hays House?"

11:54 AM Keith: "Pat, did you ever enjoy sitting out on the Second Floor Front Porch?"

11:55 AM Keith: "Kathleen, what time of the day would you sit out on the Second Floor Front Porch?"

1:56 AM Keith: "Thank you for talking to me and have a good day."

11:56 AM Keith: "I have observed the Mel Meter readings to be 0.0 mG and 87.8°F."

11:56 AM Keith: "I have observed the EDI readings to be 1.0 mG and 88.4°F."

11:56 AM Keith: "This Session 1 ended on Friday, 2nd June 2017."

11:57 AM to 11:59 AM Keith: "I obtained thermal images of the Second Floor Front Porch. I obtained two images of the North view from the Second Floor Front Porch. I obtained two images of the porch's South East corner."

Paranormal Investigation, Session 2, Second Floor Front Porch, Friday, 2nd, June 2017, Hays House.

2:37 PM Keith: "Hello, I am Keith Evans. I only wish to speak with the members of the Hays, Gibson, and Buck family's. You may use your energy to choose words from the Ovilus IV's data base. This is the Ovilus IV and it will not hurt you." (Hold it up.)

2:38 PM Keith: "This is the Mel Meter and the EDI. They measure the temperature and the electromagnetic frequencies. They are not harmful to people, ghosts, and or spirits." (Hold them up.)

2:40 PM Keith: "The Ovilus IV has given me no background words."

2:40 PM Keith: "I have observed the Mel Meter readings to be 0.0 mG and 77.9°F."

2:41 PM Keith: "I have observed the EDI readings to be 0.0 mG and 77.9°F."

2:42 PM Keith: "The Ovilus IV gave me the word oxygen which is spelled O-X-Y-G-E-N. The Ovilus IV has pronounced the word oxygen at a normal conversational level and speed."

2:42 PM Keith: "The Ovilus IV gave me the word matter which is spelled M-A-T-T-E-R. The Ovilus IV has pronounced the word matter at a normal conversational level and speed."

2:46 PM Keith: "The Ovilus IV gave me the word date which is spelled D-A-T-E. The Ovilus IV has pronounced the word date at a normal conversational level and speed."

2:47 PM Keith: "I have observed the Mel Meter readings to be 0.0 mG and 80.1°F."

2:47 PM Keith: "I have observed the EDI readings to be 2.5 mG and 79.8°F."

2:51 PM Keith: "Pat, did you use to smoke on this porch?"

2:52 PM Keith: "Pat, what type of cigarettes did you smoke?"

2:53 PM Keith: "Pat, what was the last year that you played on the Apalachicola City Baseball team?"

2:54 PM Keith: "Pat, what was the name of your baseball team?"

2:55 PM Keith: "Pat, what was the color of your baseball teams uniforms?"

2:56 PM Keith: "Pat, as a member of the board of directors of the Apalachicola State Bank, did you work more than one half of a day each month approving loans?"

2:58 PM Keith: "The Ovilus IV gave me the name Alice which is spelled A-L-I-C-E. The Ovilus IV pronounced the name Alice at a normal conversational level and speed."

2:59 PM Keith: "I observed the Mel Meter readings to be 0.0 mG and 82.6°F."

2:59 PM Keith: "I observed the EDI readings to be 0.0 mG and 82.3°F."

3:02 PM Keith: "It is nice to meet you Alice. My name is Keith."

3:03 PM Keith: "My last name is Evans. What is your last name?"

3:04 PM Keith: "Alice, did you live at the Hays House?"

3:05 PM Keith: "What would you like to talk about Alice?"

3:06 PM Keith: "You will tell me your first name, but you will not tell me anything else. Why?"

3:07 PM Keith: "Alice, have you run out of energy to choose words from the Ovilus IV's database?"

3:08 PM Keith: "If you are really Alice knock on the table."

3:09 PM Keith: "Sunshine, is it you just saying names?"

3:10 PM Keith: "Sunshine, yes or no, did you like being a School Teacher?"

3:11 PM Keith: "Sunshine, yes or no, did you like working at the Gibson Inn?"

3:12 PM Keith: "Pat, do you know Alice?"

3:13 PM Keith: "Kathleen, do you know Alice?"

3:13 PM Keith: "The Ovilus IV gave me the word near which is spelled N-E-A-R. The Ovilus IV has pronounced the word near in a normal conversational level and speed."

3:14 PM Keith: "I have observed the Mel Meter readings to be 0.0 mG and 82.5°F."

3:14 PM Keith: "I have observed the Mel Meter readings to be 0.0 mG and 82.1°F."

3:14 PM Keith: "I have observed the EDI readings to be 0.0 mG and 83.8°F."

3:15 PM Keith: "Who is here?"

3:18 PM Keith: "Alice, are you here?"

3:19 PM Keith: "Knock on the table if you are Alice."

3:20 PM Keith: "My hearing is not very good, if you knocked, I did not hear it."

3:21 PM to 3:23 PM Keith: "I am going to get some thermal readings on the porch. I obtained two thermal images of the North East corner of the porch. I obtained two thermal images of the South East corner of the porch. All areas of the porch looked normal."

3:26 PM Keith: "I open the Ovilus IV's battery case to look at the position of the four AAA batteries. The batteries look to be in their normal positions."

3:28 PM Keith: "The Ovilus IV is frozen up and will not return to the home position."

3:29 PM Keith: "I am going to turn the Ovilus IV off manually and turn it back on in about one minute. Let us see if that will help."

3:30 PM Keith: "The Ovilus IV has given me two background words before which is spelled B-E-F-O-R-E and both which is spelled B-O-T-H. The Ovilus IV has pronounced the word before and the word both in a normal conversational level and speed."

3:31 PM Keith: "I have observed the Mel Meter readings to be 0.0 mG and 84.3°F."

3:34 PM Keith: "I have observed the EDI readings to be 0.0 mG and 84.3°F."

3:34 PM Keith: "The words before and both, I'm not sure what type of question you are asking me."

3:36 PM Keith: "Thank you for talking to me. Have a good day."

3:36 PM Keith: "This session 2 ended on Friday, 2nd June 2017."

The analysis of the Second Floor Front Porch, Session 1, Friday, 2nd June 2017, Hays House. The date of the analysis was Monday, 9th October 2017.

At 11 AM the Ovilus IV gave me the first and second background words for this session number one. This background words were Nona and Vern. Since, I have not asked any questions yet, I will consider that this is just Ghosts and or Spirits talking within the environment. They may or may not be talking to me. Nona and Vern are not names that I am aware of. Nona and Vern are not connected to any members of the Hays, Gibson, and Buck family members who once lived at the Hays House. Nona and Vern maybe a couple who lived at the Hays House between 1923 and 1942. During this time period, the Apalachicola State Bank owned the Hays House and used it as a boarding house. A boarding house was a place where a person could rent a room and have access to use a common bathroom. Nora and Vern may have share enjoyable moments together on this 2nd Floor Front Porch.

At 11:01 AM the housekeeper walked on to the Second Floor Front Porch.

At 11:03 AM the Ovilus IV gave me the third word for this session number one, which was stop. We feel that the word stop is from an intelligent Ghost or Spirit who is asking the housekeeper to stop interfering with the paranormal investigation.

At 11:06 AM the housekeeper walked out onto the Second Floor Front Porch to take a cigarette break and we talked for three minutes.

At 11:09 AM the Ovilus IV gave me the word worry. The Ovilus IV pronounced the word worry at a lower than normal conversational level but at a normal conversational speed. I feel that this was an intelligent spirit or ghost whispering to me that they knew that I was worried. I was worried that the housekeeper would continue to come out onto the Second Floor Front Porch and that my paranormal investigation was going to be continuously interrupted. In the pasted, frequent interruption will cause the Ghosts and Spirits to stop communicating. It is if they want to only talk in private. From my years of paranormal investigating. I feel that ghosts and spirits are for far more able to communicate about what is happened in the present, more so than what has happened in the past.

At 11:17 AM the Ovilus IV gave me the words before time. At 11:16 AM I had asked Vern a question. That question was, "what can you tell me about the history of the Hays House?" This response is an intelligent Spirit or Ghost that is asking me what year or what time I want to know about.

At 11:27 AM I asked Vern if he was related to the Hays family. At 12:27 AM exactly after I completed my question. The Ovilus IV gave me the word writing. I feel that Vern was asking me if my question was related to what I was writing. Vern may have been asking if question was related to the book I was writing and or if my question was related to what I am presently writing, a transcript of what took place and what was said during this Paranormal Investigation.

At 11:34 AM I asked Jody the dog if she wanted to go inside the Hays House. Jody was standing near the door. I opened the door so Jody could go inside.

At 11:39 AM the Ovilus IV has failed to function properly. The Ovilus IV went back to the home position. So, the batteries are not dead. I turned the Ovilus IV back on. It seems to me that the Ghosts and Spirits have a blocking effect, that keeps the energy in the battery from reaching the Ovilus IV.

At 11:41 AM the Ovilus IV gave me the background word trouble. I feel that this is an intelligent Spirit or Ghost, who is acknowledging to me that the Ovilus IV is not functioning properly. This intelligent Spirit or Ghost may be the one that is intentionally or unintentionally causing my trouble or problems with the Ovilus IV.

At 11:42 AM the Ovilus IV gave me the word view. I feel that this is an intelligent Spirit or Ghost who is asking me if I am enjoying the view from the Second Floor Front Porch. I am more concerned with making contact with the Ghosts and Spirits, than I am about enjoying the view. Though I must say, it is a good view. I wish I had more free time to enjoy the view.

At 11:50 AM I asked the question; do you know the name of the person that seems to be staring at me? I felt that there was a person intensely looking at me. This was just a feeling there was no one that I can see looking at me. It is my opinion that a Ghost or a Spirit was staring me down. Maybe because I was not catching onto what they were saying. I certainly didn't explore the view from the Second Floor Front Porch. After I have had time to think about it that's probably what the Ghosts wanted, to talk about the view that could be seen from the Second Floor Front Porch. I don't feel that the staring was threatening. It was just a Ghost or Spirit feeling frustrated because it is very hard to communicate with the living.

From 11:02 AM to 11:56 AM I noticed that the EDI readings for the electromagnetic frequencies ranged from 0.0 mG to 2.5 mG. The Mel Meter readings between 11:02 AM and 11:56 AM, maintained a constant 0.0 mG. The EDI meter and the Mel Meter were only inches apart. This proves that an intelligent Ghost or Spirit can be very precise in how they guide their electromagnetic frequency. Their electromagnetic frequency can be pinpointed and be registered by one piece of equipment while another piece of equipment, maybe 5 inches at the most, away from the other piece of equipment will not register any electromagnetic frequency at all.

At 11:57 AM to 11:59 AM I obtained thermal images of the Second Floor Front Porch. I obtained two thermal images of the North view from the Second Floor Front Porch. I did not see anything unusual, unexplained, and or paranormal on the thermal images from this view of the front porch. I obtained two thermal images of the porch's South East corner. I did not see anything unusual, unexplained and or paranormal on these thermal images.

The analysis of the Second Floor Front Porch, Session 2, Friday, 2nd June 2017, Hays House. The date of the analysis was Saturday, 16th December 2017.

At 2:40 PM the Ovilus IV did not give me any background words. Usually, I get one or two back ground words.

At 2:41 PM the Ovilus IV gave me the first word for this session number two, oxygen. I have not asked any questions yet during this session number two.

At 2:42 PM the Ovilus IV gave me the second word for this session number two, matter. I have not asked any questions yet during this session number two.

At 2:46 PM the Ovilus IV gave me the third word for this session number two, date. I have not asked any questions yet during this session number two. I always document my transcript of the paranormal investigation simultaneously as I conduct the paranormal investigation. I always document the date of the paranormal investigation. I believe that this is an intelligent Spirit letting me know that they have observed that I am documenting the date within my transcript.

At 2:47 PM I observed that the Mel Meter reading for the electromagnetic frequency is 0.0 mG.

At 2:47 PM I observed that the EDI readings for the electromagnetic frequency is 2.5 mG. The Mel Meter and the EDI are at the most 8 inches apart. So, a Ghost or Spirit is accurately pinpointing their energy towards the EDI while avoiding contact with the Mel Meter. I feel that this denotes an intelligent Spirit's and or ghost's, who has and electromagnetic signature. If this electromagnetic frequency was caused by something within the environment and or the electrical current from the nearby electrical outlet, then both the Mel Meter and the EDI would be picking up the same readings for the electromagnetic frequency.

At 3:09 PM I said, "Sunshine, is it you just saying names?" I felt like it may be Sunshine just playing with me and speaking names just to keep me busy. At times I do not feel that the Ghosts and or Spirits of Pat, Kathleen, Sunshine, and Annie are taking my Paranormal Sessions seriously at all. I feel like they may play along with me in hopes that the Book will assure that the home that they loved, the Hays House, will be loved by future owners and will live on for a long, time to come.

At 3:13 PM the Ovilus IV gave me the fourth word for this session number two, near. At 3:13 PM I had just asked Kathleen if she knew Alice. In less than 60 seconds I received the word near from the Ovilus IV. I feel that this is Kathleen stating that as a Spirit, she is close in proximity to Alice. I do not know who Alice is. I do not believe that Alice is a family member. I have not determined yet, if Alice may be a close friend to Kathleen.

Between 3:21 PM and 3:23 PM I obtained thermal images on the Second Floor Front Porch. I obtained four thermal images and did not notice any unexplained and or paranormal events.

At 3:26 PM because I had not received any words from the Ovilus IV since 3:13 PM, I decided to take the back off of the Ovilus IV without turning the Ovilus IV off and check to make sure that the batteries were in the proper position. I observed that all four of the AAA batteries were in the proper position.

At 3:28 PM I observed that the Ovilus IV was frozen up and is not functioning properly. I was able to return the Ovilus IV to the home position.

At 3:29 PM I manually turn the Ovilus IV off for about one minute and then turned it back on.

At 3:30 PM the Ovilus IV gave me the fifth and sixth background words for this session number two, before and both. I cannot say with any degree of accuracy that either the word before or the word both are answering any of the questions that I've asked so far during this session number two. On the other hand, at 3:18 PM I asked the question, "Alice, are you here?" At 3:19 PM I asked another question, "Knock on the table if you are Alice." The words before and both may be Alice saying that before the Ovilus IV failed to function properly, Alice did both of those things. Alice was here on the 2nd Floor Front Porch and Alice knocked on the table. I was not able to see Alice and or hear Alice knocking on the table.

Digital pictures, Second Floor Front Porch, Wednesday, 2nd November 2016, Hays House.

Two pictures of the Northeast corner of the porch.

Two pictures of the porch's ceiling.

Four pictures of the porch's East wall.

Two pictures of the porch's Northwest corner.

Two pictures of the porch's North wall.

Four pictures of the porch's South East corner.

Two pictures of the porch's South wall.

Two pictures of the porch's Southwest corner.

Two pictures of the porch's West wall.

Two pictures of the exterior side of the doorknob.

Please see the author's website at www.keithoevans.com to view each digital picture.

Thermal images, Second Floor Front Porch, Wednesday, 2nd November 2016, Hays House.

One thermal image of the East exterior wall of the porch.

One thermal image of the porch's South wall.

One thermal image of the porch's West wall.

One thermal image of the porch's North wall with a dark area in the center of the image. This dark area is located near the tin roof or the trailer next door. This tin roof should be hot with the color of red, orange, or yellow. I not sure what is inside of the trailer or what temperature the trailer should be. I am leaning towards the trailer next door being the dark triangular shaped object in the thermal image. The trailer is not on the Hays House Property, so I cannot pursue that line of questioning.

Please see the author's website at www.keithoevans.com to view each thermal image.

CHAPTER **18**

Second Floor Front Stairway Room, Hays House, Ghosts are People too.

A description of the Second Floor Front Stairway Room, Wednesday, 2nd November 2016.

This is a description of the Second Floor Front Stairway Room obtained from 20 pictures. Starting from the left side of the room's West wall and working in a clockwise direction around the room, on the left side of the door on the West wall there is a modern white wooden table. Above this table is a 2.5' x 3' canvas painting of possibly a wooden post supporting a roof, that is overlooking the ocean. To the right of this painting is an original white wooden door with two sunken panels, on its lower half and a large window on its upper half. This door has the original brass or metal doorknob and the original brass or metal skeleton key baseplate. To the right of this door is a 2.5' x 3' canvas painting of the same described painting that is on the left side of this door on the West wall. Below this painting is a white wooden table with one clear plastic chair.

The North wall has the original doorway, that led to the Patsy Room. This doorway has the original white wooden trim. To the right side of this doorway is an antique looking entertainment center that stands about 5-foot-tall, 4-foot-long, and 2 feet deep. This piece of furniture has two full length doors on its front side. On top of this entertainment center are the following items; three small framed pictures, three porcelain figurines, one large glass jar and a 2' x 3' canvas painting of pink and orange flowers. To the right side of the entertainment center is an original white five sunken panel door that leads to the Annie Room. To the right of this door is a 3' x 3' modern opening, on the room's North wall, with modern white trim around the opening that has two modern hinged doors. Below and to the left corner of this opening is a painting with black letters that are outlined in white that say, "Love you more." This painting has a light orange background with pink hearts and an orange outline along the edge of its 18" x 2' canvas. In this room's North East corner, there is a stairway coming up from the first floor. The steps of the stairway were stripped sometime after 1996 and has a lighter looking wood then the dark looking wooden handrailing's and post tops along this stairway that have never been stripped.

On the East side of the room and against the front stairway railing is a modern, white textile, chair with a blue pillow. There is a multi-colored footstool in front of the white chair. To the right of this white chair is a modern light blue nightstand. On top of this nightstand is a white porcelain lamp with a round white and gold lamp shade. On the room's East wall is a 4' x 4' canvas with a painting of a house, and the number 54. To the right of the painting is an original doorway with the original white wooden trim. There is a light switch to the left of this doorway. Above this doorway is a 1 foot by 3-foot canvas painting of a green and blue fish with the words in black, "Go fish."

A long the room's South wall is a light green wooden bookshelf. Above the bookshelf is a wooden frame picture. There is a white, modern couch along this room's South wall with several multi-colored pillows. In front of this white, modern couch is a modern wooden coffee table. The room's South wall has many framed under glass pictures and canvas paintings.

All the walls in this room have the original horizontal, tongue and groove, wallboards. The ceiling has the original, light blue, tongue and groove, ceiling boards that are running in an East to West direction. The floor in this room has the original, tongue and groove, heart pine, hardwood flooring, that is running in an East to West direction.

A description of the Second Floor Front Stairway Room from seven pictures taken in 1996.

On the South West corner of this room, there is an antique dark wooden triangular stand that fits into the corner. The top of this stand has two built in decorative wooden frame mirror approximately 5" x 8". One mirror is on the room's South wall and the other mirror is on the room's West wall. This triangular piece of furniture has a shelf located level with the bottom of the two mirrors and a second shelf at the level above the two mirrors. On the bottom shelf is a porcelain bowl. On the top shelf is a china cup. In front of the triangular piece of furniture is a white large China bowl decorated with red roses. The picture is too dark to be able to see what the China bowl is sitting on. It may be sitting on the floor. Also, in front and to the right side of this triangular piece of furniture is an antique wooden round table with the following items from left to right; a large decorative multi-colored vase, a white porcelain candy dish, a silver framed picture of Patsy and a silver candleholder with one white candle. To the right side of this antique roundtable is an antique decorative dark wooden table with Annie's favorite possession on top. This possession is an 1880's wooden music box that was given to Annie by a Riverboat Captain that she once dated. Behind the music box is the original white wooden door with two sunken panels on its lower half and a large window on its top half. The store has the original black brass or metal doorknob and skeleton key baseplate. This door's window that is covered by a shear white curtain. To the right of the door is an antique wooden cabinet that stands approximately 6-foot-tall, 18 inches wide and 10 inches deep, with glass doors on its front side. This antique wooden cabinet has five glass shelves. On the top shelf is a china plate, on the second shelf is a white square serving tray leading on a stand, on the third shelf is a white porcelain teapot, on the fourth shelf is a golden vase and on the fifth shelf is a white porcelain bowl with yellow flowers.

On the North wall and near the room's Northwest corner is an antique roundtable with an upper and lower section. On the top section is a round table with a large white china plate with a pink rose leaning within a black stand and a pink, green and white glass, or porcelain lamp with two globes. On the lower table is a white candy dish. Above this antique roundtable is a wooden framed under glass, picture of Annie. To the right of the antique roundtable there is an antique dark wooden chair with a textile seat that has an alternating pattern of gold and red diamonds. To the right of the antique chair is an original doorway to Patsy's room with the original white wooden trim. A long the North wall and between the doorways to the Patsy Room and the Annie Room, is an antique couch with dark wooden legs, arms, and trim. This couch has a textile seat and a back rest with a tan background and yellow and red flower pattern alternating throughout. On each end of this couch is a square yellow pillow. Above the couch is an antique dark wooden framed round mirror. This mirror is mounted to the North wall and has three different shelves. Two of the shelves have some type of a porcelain figurine. The bottom shelf has a multi-colored coffee cup. Mounted on the North wall, and on each side of the dark wooden frame rounded mirror are golden decorative shelves with a porcelain lady on each shelf. The doorway to the Annie Room has the original white wooden trim. To the right of the door way that leads to the Annie Room is a 3' x 3' modern white wooden trim that is around two modern white wooden hinged doors. These doors cover the opening for the fan.

On the room's East side and in front of the stairway railing is an antique table with an irregular white marble top. On top of the antique table and from left to right are the following items; a lamp with a square marble base and a gold colored supporting stand with two purple globes, a dark purple candy dish and two golden candle holders with one white candle each. On the left and right sides of the antique table are an antique dark wooden chair with a tan textile seat and back rest. In front of the antique table is a 2' x 5' multi-colored drop drug with white tassels on each side.

There is a multi-colored drop drug in front of the entrance to the Frances Room on the room's South wall. The entrance to the Frances Room is on the South wall and this entrance has the original white wooden door trim. To the right of the doorway to the Frances Room is an antique dark wooden entry way table with a rectangular white marble top. Below the table top, and to the rear of the table is a square mirror that is approximately 3 feet by 3 feet. On top of this entry way table are from left to right the following items; a golden counterbalance with a pan on each side that has grapes on a vine, and a lamp with a golden supporting stand with a glass globe. On the entry way table's bottom shelf there is an orange porcelain bowl. Above this entry way table and mounted on the room's south wall is an approximately 4' x 4' square golden frame mirror. To the left and right side of the golden frame mirror are a golden candle holder that are mounted on the room's South wall. These candleholders do not have any candles. On each side of this entry way table are the antique dark wooden chair with a light green textile seat. To the right side of the entry way table is an antique light wooden decorative stand-a-loan shelf with four levels. On the bottom level is a china cup and saucer and a porcelain vase, on the second shelf from the bottom there are two branches with birds perched on them, on the third shelf from the bottom are a porcelain white teapot and a matching coffee cup and saucer on each side of the tea pot and on the top shelf is a white porcelain figurine.

This room's floor has the original brown paint, heart pine, hardwood, tongue, and groove flooring that is running in an East to West direction. In the middle of this room is a multi-colored 8' x 8' square rug with tonsils on its east and west sides. This room's walls all have the original, tongue and groove, horizontal, white wallboards. This room's ceiling has the original white wooden tongue and groove ceiling boards that are all orientated in an East to West direction. On the wooden cross beam in the center of the room's ceiling is an interesting chandelier, with seven rows of clear crystal beads.

The history of the Second Floor Front Stairway Room.

In the early 1950's Mr. and Mrs. C. Bryan Palmer had an approximately 3 feet by 3 feet opening made between The Annie Room and the Second Floor Front Stairway Room. This opening would house a fan to circulate air and keep the second-floor cooler during hot weather. This opening had modern white wooden trim and two hinged doors on the north wall of the Second Floor Front Stairway Room side. Mrs. C. Bryan Palmer's first name is Annie.

Mel Meter base readings, Second Floor Front Stairway Room, Wednesday, 2nd November 2016, Hays House.

1:30 PM The electrical outlet on the room's North wall. One item is plugged into this electrical outlet.

The electromagnetic frequency range was 0.0 mG to 0.0 mG.

The temperature range was 75.8°F to 77.1°F.

1:31 PM The lamp hanging from the ceiling. This lamp is on.

The electromagnetic frequency range was 0.0 mG to 0.0 mG.

The temperature range was 75.4°F to 76.7°F.

1:32 PM The thermostat mounted on the room's South wall. This thermostat is in use.

The electromagnetic frequency range was 0.0 mG to 0.1 mG.

The temperature range was 75.8°F to 76.8°F.

1:33 PM The cable and wire leading to the TV within the wooden entertainment center, located along the room's North wall. The TV is in the off position.

The electromagnetic frequency range was 0.0 mG to 0.0 mG.

The temperature range was 75.8°F to 76.4°F.

1:34 PM The lamp on the table near the stairs, located on the room's East side near the stairway railing. This lamp is off.

The electromagnetic frequency range was 0.0 mG to 0.0 mG.

The temperature range was 76.5°F to 76.7°F.

1:35 PM The light switch near the interior side of the door that leads to the Second Floor Back Stairway Room, located on the room's South wall.

The electromagnetic frequency range was 10.1 mG to 10.2 mG.

The temperature range was 76.5°F to 76.8°F.

1:36 PM The speaker on the room's South wall, near the interior side of the door that leads to the Second Floor Back Stairway Room.

The electromagnetic frequency range was 0.0 mG to 0.0 mG.

The temperature range was 76.4°F to 76.9°F.

Paranormal Investigation, Session 1, Second Floor Front Stairway Room, Wednesday, 7th June 2017, Hays House.

11:21 AM Keith: "Hello, I am Keith Evans. I only wish to speak with the members of the Hays, Gibson, and Buck family's today. That includes you too Mary. You may use your energy to choose words from the Ovilus IV's data base. This is the Ovilus IV will not hurt you." (Hold it up.)

11:22 AM Keith: "This is the Mel Meter, and the EDI. They measure temperature and electromagnetic frequencies. The Mel Meter and the EDI will not cause you any harm." (Hold it up.)

11:23 AM Keith: "The Ovilus IV has given me two background words equator which is spelled E-Q-U-A-T-O-R and seek which is spelled S-E-E-K. The Ovilus IV has pronounced the words equator and seek at a normal conversational level and speed."

11:23 AM Keith: "I did not obtain any pictures of the Mel Meter and EDI readings."

11:25 AM Keith: "It looks like the Ovilus IV is frozen up again."

11:26 AM Keith: "I tried tapping the home icon, but the Ovilus IV will not return to the home position."

11:28 AM Keith: "I am going to change the batteries."

11:28 AM Keith: "There is talking in the other room."

11:30 AM Keith: "The Ovilus IV has given me two background words. Monica which is spelled M-O-N-I-C-A, and move which is spelled

M-O-V-E. The Ovilus IV has pronounced the words Monica and move at a normal conversational level and speed."

11:31 AM Keith: "I have observed the Mel Meter readings to be 0.0 mG and 76.4°F."

11:31 AM Keith: "I have observed the EDI readings to be 0.0 mG and 74.7°F."

11:32 AM Keith: "The Ovilus IV has given me the word call which is spelled C-A-L-L. The Ovilus IV has pronounced the word call at a louder than normal conversational level and at a faster than normal conversational speed."

11:33 AM Keith: "I have observed the Mel Meter readings to be 0.0 mG and 76.6°F."

11:33 AM Keith: "I have observed the EDI readings to be 0.0 mG and 74.7°F."

11:35 AM to 11:36 AM Keith: "I was talking to the owner for two minutes."

11:40 AM Keith: "Hello Monica. It is nice to meet you."

11:41 AM Keith: "Monica, what family are you related to?"

11:42 AM Keith: "Monica, is your last name Hays, Gibson, and or Buck?"

11:43 AM Keith: "The Ovilus IV gave me the word soul which is spelled S-O-U-L. The Ovilus IV has pronounced the word soul with a deep man's voice, at a lower than normal conversational level, and at a slower than normal conversational speed."

11:43 AM Keith: "I have observed the Mel Meter readings to be 0.0 mG and 75.9°F."

11:44 AM Keith: "I have observed the EDI readings to be 0.0 mG and 74.5°F."

11:46 AM Keith: "Monica, do you want me to move and then call you?"

11:47 AM Keith: "Where should I moved to?"

11:48 AM Keith: "How will I call you? I do not have your phone number. Should I just call your name aloud?"

11:49 AM Keith: "Monica, I need some type of response?"

11:50 AM Keith: "I'm going to obtain thermal images of the room."

11:51 AM to 11:55 AM Keith: "I have obtained the following thermal images of the Second Floor Front Stairway Room. I obtained two thermal images of the ceiling's air conditioning vent near the room's South West corner. I obtained two thermal images of the blue cool air trail going along the ceiling near the northwest corner of the room. I obtained two thermal images of the vent on the room's ceiling near the room's East wall. I obtained two thermal images of the yellow light switch on the room's East wall just to the left side of the door way that leads to the Second Floor Back Stairway Room."

11:56 AM Keith: "Mary, are you here today? If you are here, tell me how old you are?"

11:57 AM Keith: "Mary, what is your birth date?"

11:59 AM Keith: "Kathleen, what type of furniture did you have in this room?"

12 noon Keith: "Kathleen, can you tell me the name of any antiques that you had in this room?"

12:01 PM Keith: "Pat, what type of antiques and furniture was in this room, when you lived here?"

12:02 PM Keith: "This room by itself is larger than most of the apartments that I have lived in."

12:03 PM Keith: "Who said the word soul?"

12:05 PM Keith: "Are you calling me a soul?"

12:06 PM Keith: "Do you like soul food?"

12:07 PM Keith: "Name some of the soul food that you like to eat?"

12:08 PM Keith: "I like porkchops, mashed potatoes, cornbread, fried squash, fried cabbage, and succotash."

12:09 PM Keith: "Choose one item from the Ovilus IV's database that would be your favorite soul food to eat."

12:10 PM Keith: "Do ghosts and spirits get hungry?"

12:11 PM Keith: "Do ghosts and spirits get thirsty?"

12:12 PM Keith: "The Ovilus IV has four AAA brand-new batteries that are fully charged."

12:13 PM Keith: "I have observed the Mel Meter readings to be 0.0 mG and 75.5°F."

12:14 PM Keith: "I have observed the EDI readings to be 0.0 mG and 73.9°F."

12:14 PM Keith: "The Ovilus IV gave me the word diction which is spelled D-I-C-T-I-O-N. The Ovilus IV pronounced the word diction at a normal conversational level and speed."

12:14 PM Keith: "I have observed the Mel Meter readings to be 0.0 mG and 75 .8°F."

12:15 PM Keith: "The Ovilus IV has given me the words Creek which is spelled C-R-E-E-K and chills which is spelled C-H-I-L-L-S. The Ovilus IV has pronounced the words Creek and chills at a normal conversational level and speed."

12:15 PM Keith: "I have observed the Mel Meter readings to be 0.0 mG and 75.7°F."

12:15 PM Keith: "I have observed the EDI readings to be 0.0 mG and 74.0°F."

12:20 PM Keith: "The Ovilus IV has given me the word pounds which is spelled P-O-U-N-D-S, and the word shaken which is spelled S-H-A-K-E-N. The Ovilus IV has pronounced the words pounds and shaken at a normal conversational level and speed."

12:20 PM Keith: " I have observed the Mel Meter readings to be0.0 mG and 77.0°F."

12:21 PM Keith: "The Ovilus IV has given me the word coat which is spelled C-O-A-T. The Ovilus IV has pronounced the word coat at a normal conversational level and speed."

12:21 PM Keith: "I have observed the Mel Meter readings to be 0.0 mG and 77.1°F."

12:21 PM Keith: "I have observed the EDI readings to be 0.0 mG and 74.1°F."

12:21 PM Keith: "I have observed the Mel Meter readings to be 0.0 mG and 77.0°F."

12:22 PM Keith: "I have observed the EDI readings to be 0.0 mG and 74.1°F."

12:22 PM Keith: "No more words. This session number one is over. Thank you for talking to me. Have a good day."

12:22 PM Keith: "This session number one ended on Wednesday, 7th June 2017."

Paranormal Investigation, Session 2, Second Floor Front Stairway Room, Wednesday 7th, June 2017, Hays House.

2:45 PM Keith: "Hello, I am Keith Evans. I wish only to speak to the Hays and Gibson family during this session 2. You may use your energy to choose words from the Ovilus IV database. This is the Ovilus IV and it will not hurt you." (Hold it up.)

2:46 PM Keith: "This is the Mel Meter and the EDI. They measure temperature and electromagnetic frequencies and they will not harm ghost or spirits." (Hold it up.)

2:47 PM Keith: "The Ovilus IV has given me four background words fast and back to back: done which is spelled D-O-N-E, fell which is spelled F-E-L-L, tilde which is spelled T-I-L-D-E, and index which is spelled I-N-D-E-X. The Ovilus IV has pronounced the words done, fell, tilde, and index, at a normal conversational level and speed."

2:47 PM Keith: "I did not obtain any pictures of the words done, fell, tilde, and index."

2:48 PM Keith: "I have observed the Mel Meter readings to be 0.0 mG and 77.1°F."

2:48 PM Keith: "I have observed the EDI readings to be 0.0 mG and 75.8°F."

2:48 PM Keith: "I have observed the Mel Meter readings to be 0.0 mG and 76.8°F."

2:48 PM Keith: "The Ovilus IV has given me four words fast and back to back: iron which is spelled I-R-O-N, farmers which is spelled F-A-R-M-E-R-S, crash which is spelled C-R-A-S-H, Edison which is spelled, E-D-I-S-O-N. The Ovilus IV has pronounced the words iron, farmers, crash, and Edison at a normal conversational level and speed. I did not obtain a picture of iron. I did not see iron on the Ovilus IV display. I only heard the word iron."

2:49 PM Keith: "I have observed the Mel Meter readings to be 0.0 mG and 76.5°F."

2:49 PM Keith: "I have observed the EDI readings to be 0.0 mG and 75.8°F."

2:50 PM Keith: "The Ovilus IV gave me the word paint which is spelled P-A-I-N-T. The Ovilus IV pronounced the word paint at a normal conversational level and speed."

2:50 PM Keith: "I have observed the Mel Meter readings to be 0.0 mG and 76.9°F."

2:50 PM Keith: "I have observed the EDI readings to be 0.0 mG and 75.7°F."

2:52 PM Keith: "The Ovilus IV gave me the word synn which is spelled S-Y-N-N. The Ovilus IV has pronounced the word synn at a normal conversational level and speed."

2:52 PM Keith: "I have observed the Mel Meter readings to be 0.0 mG and 76.5°F."

2:53 PM Keith: "I have observed the EDI readings to be 0.0 mG and 75.7°F."

2:53 PM Keith: "I have not asked my first question yet for this Session 2. I had been receiving rapid-fire words from the Ovilus IV."

2:55 PM Keith: "That was a person walking down the steps from the third floor, to the second floor."

2:56 PM Keith: "I was just talking to the lady in charge of the Bed and Breakfast. Now a person is walking down the steps from the second to the first floor."

2:57 PM Keith: "Why do you Ghosts, and Spirits wait until the Session is just about over, to start to talk?"

2:57 PM Keith: "The Ovilus IV has given me the word dug which is spelled D-U-G. Dug is the past tense for dig. The Ovilus IV has pronounced the word dug at a normal conversational level and speed."

2:58 PM Keith: "I have observed the Mel Meter readings to be 0.0 mG and 76.6°F."

2:59 PM Keith: "I have observed the EDI readings to be 0.0 mG and 75.5°F."

3:02 PM Keith: "Okay, I'm going to do the thermal imaging of this room."

3:03 PM to 3:08 PM Keith: "I obtained thermal images of the Second Floor Front Stairway Room. I obtained four images of the room's West wall and ceiling which had a dark blue area trailing off from the air conditioner in a cylinder shape. I obtained two thermal images of my two pink footprints on the floor where I had been sitting. I obtained two thermal images of the air conditioner vent, and the dark blue cool area that was trailing off from the air conditioner vent on the room's East wall, ceiling, and South East corner. I obtained two thermal images of where I had been standing. This area shows two pink footprints on the room's hardwood floor."

3:08 PM Keith: "Okay Sunshine, since you do not know any history, what can you tell me?"

3:09 PM Keith: "None, iron, paint, synn, and dug, what are you trying to tell me. The owner is an artist and she like to paint."

3:11 PM Keith: "What type of art do you like Sunshine?"

3:12 PM Keith: "Pat and Kathleen, did you have any artwork in the Hays House when you lived here?"

3:13 PM Keith: "Pat, do you feel like you still own the Hays House?"

3:14 PM Keith: "Pat, one knock if you feel like you still own the Hays House or two Knocks if you feel like you do not own the Hays House."

3:15 PM Keith: "Pat, if the Great Depression makes you angry give me one knock. If the Great Depression does not make you angry give me two knocks."

3:16 PM Keith: "That may have been one knock sound, but it was very soft."

3:18 PM Keith: "Okay, Kathleen, I got one for you. Are you ready for a question? If you like antiques, give me one knock. If you do not like antiques, give me two knocks."

3:19 PM Keith: "I may have heard one knock sound, but it was very light and soft coming from the room's West wall." (I turned at that point and looked at the West wall.)

3:22 PM Keith: "When you said the word iron, were you referring to the metal iron or were you talking about ironing clothes?"

3:24 PM Keith: "This was a poor Paranormal Investigation, and nothing to write about in a book."

3:29 PM Keith: "I could buy this place and do Paranormal Investigations every day. How would you like that?"

3:30 PM Keith: "I have observed the Mel Meter readings to be 0.0 mG and 76.4°F."

3:31 PM Keith: "Thank you for talking to me. Have a good day."

3:31 PM Keith: "This Session 2 ended on Wednesday, 7th June 2017."

The Paranormal Investigation, Session 1, 2nd Floor Front Stairway Room, Wednesday, 7th June 2017, Hays House. The date of analysis was Thursday, 19th October 2017.

At 11:23 AM the Ovilus IV gave me the first two background words of Session 1, equator and seek. I have not asked any questions yet, during this Session 1. These words seem to be an intelligent Ghost and or Spirit asking me for directions to the Earth's equator.

At 11:30 AM the Ovilus IV gave me the third and fourth background words for this Session number one, Monica and move. I do not know any Monica associated with the Hays house. I have not asked any questions yet, during this Session 1. I feel that this is an intelligent Ghost or Spirit that is asking Monica to move. I do not know if Monica is a living lady or a lady who has passed on.

At 11:32 AM the Ovilus IV gave me the fifth word for this session 1, call. The Ovilus IV pronounced the word call loud and fast. The Ghost or Spirit was desperate to get the information to me or to someone. So far during this Session I, I have not had time to ask any questions. It would be wrong of me to feel that somehow this Ghost or Spirit was asking me a question, because I have not asked any questions yet. We live in a world that treat Ghosts and Spirits as if they are not there. Most individuals feel that we can control everything. That is not true. Ghosts and Spirits are within the atmosphere communicating amongst themselves all the time. They're not just magically communicating with me. My Ovilus IV is picking up their electromagnetic energy and their electromagnetic energy is automatically choosing a word. I would say that on any given day, A Ghost or Spirit may try to communicate with people who were just too uninformed to realize it or have a belief system that will not allow them to understand what is happening. When I do an hour-long Paranormal Investigation. I sit in the same place, just as if I would be having a conversation with a living person. I feel that the Ghost's and Spirit's find this action is profoundly respectful. So, all the Ghosts and Spirits in the area want to talk to me all at the same time.

At 11:43 AM the Ovilus IV gave me the fifth word for this Session 1, soul. The Ovilus IV pronounced the word soul with a man's deep voice. The Ovilus IV pronounced the word soul at a lower than normal conversational level and a slower than normal conversational speed. I've had the chance to asked three questions prior to the fifth word soul being given to me by the Ovilus IV. I do not feel that the word soul is answering any of my questions. This may be an intelligent Spirit or Ghost telling me that they have just their soul. This could be an Intelligent Spirit or Ghost telling me that they are no longer within a biological body.

From 11:51 AM to 11:55 AM. I obtained thermal images of the Second Floor Front Stairway Room. I obtain two thermal images of the room's ceiling air conditioner vent, located near the room's Southwest corner. I obtained two thermal images of the blue cold air trail extending from the ceiling's Northwest corner of this room. I obtained two thermal images of the vent on the ceiling located near the room's East wall. I obtained two thermal images of the yellow light switch, located on the room's East wall just left of the door. I did not find anything, paranormal, during my thermal image scan of this room. It does appear that the light switch wiring is producing an increase amount of heat. At the same time the light switch is not hot to touch. This is unexplained but, I can't say for sure that this is being caused by the Paranormal.

At 12:14 PM the Ovilus IV gave me the sixth word for this Session 1, diction. I feel that this is an intelligent spirit. I feel that this is the spirit of Sunshine Gibson. Sunshine was a school teacher. Sunshine likes to be very remindful that an author should use good grammar and or good diction. I may not be meeting Sunshine Gibson's standards.

At 12:15 PM the Ovilus IV gave me the seventh and eighth words for this Session 1, Creek, and chills. This may be Sunshine Gibson referring to me as a Creek and maybe my poor diction sends chills down her spine. I will thank Sunshine Gibson for honoring the percentage of my genes that are Native American. I am thinking in a positive matter and I hope that Sunshine Gibson has chills going down her back because she finds me to be rather exciting and helpful to the Ghosts and Spirits in our community.

At 12:20 PM the Ovilus IV gave me the ninth and 10th words for this Session 1, pounds and shaken. I do not feel that the words pounds and shaken are in response to any of the questions that I've asked so far during this Session 1. Maybe this is an intelligent Ghost or Spirit who is telling me that I have lowered my pounds and that they are shaken by this.

At 12:21 PM the Ovilus IV gave me the 11th word for this Session 1, coat. It could be that a ghost is telling me that they are cold. They are shaking with the chills and they need or want to coat. I'm sorry to say that these words are not in response to any of the questions that I've asked so far during this Session 1. When I am analyzing each word with in a Paranormal Session, sometimes it is important to look at the last three or four words that the Ovilus IV has given me, as a group. Then the meaning of what a Ghost or Spirit may have said, may change.

Analysis of the Paranormal Investigation, Session 2, Second Floor Front Stairway Room, Wednesday, 7th June 2017, Hays House. The analysis date was completed on Thursday, 19th October 2017.

At 2:47 PM the Ovilus IV gave me four background words: done, fell, tilde, and index. I have not asked any questions yet, and do not believe that any of these words are answering questions from the Paranormal Investigation Session 1. This could be an intelligent Ghost and or Spirt that is asking me if I am done with the Paranormal Investigations. I have two more room's in the Hays House to complete Paranormal Investigation within. So, I am almost done. This could be an intelligent Ghost and or Spirit who is asking me if I am indexing the Paranormal Investigation, because they see be constantly writing information into my note book.

At 2:48 PM the Ovilus IV gave me the fifth through ninth words for this Session 2, Iron, Farmers, Crash, Edison. I have not asked any questions yet during this session number two. I do not believe that any of the words are in response to questions that I asked during Session 1. I feel that the Ovilus IV is just picking up the Ghosts and Spirits electromagnetic energy, as they talk to each other within the environment. I feel that Ghosts are communicating to one another all the time. There doesn't have to be someone having a Paranormal Investigation for ghosts to be communicating between one another. I have previously asked the Ghosts and Spirits for history, so maybe these are a group of Ghosts and Spirits who have interjected these historical subject; Iron, Farmers, Crash, and Edison.

At 2:50 PM the Ovilus IV gave me the 10th word for this Session 2, paint. Upon finishing my paranormal investigation on the second floor, I met and spoke with the owner on the second floor and told her that I was given the word paint by the Ovilus IV. I told her that I was not aware of anyone painting with in the house and was not aware of what the ghost could be talking about. She just smiled and said that the painter had started painting the dining room that very morning, after I had started my Paranormal Investigation. I have learned that Ghosts and Spirits are far better at telling you what is going on now, and in the moment, then what has happened in the past while they were still alive.

At 2:52 PM the Ovilus IV gave me the 11th word for this session number two, synn. The word synn is not responding to any of the questions I've asked so for during this Session 2.

Between 2:55 PM and 2:57 PM there was a person walking down the steps who I spoke to briefly.

At 2:57 PM I asked why the Ghosts and Spirits wait until my Paranormal Sessions are just about over before they start to utilize the Ovilus IV to talk to me?

Right after I asked that question at 2:57 PM the Ovilus IV gave me the 12th word for this Session 2, dug. Dug which is the past tense of dig is a word that is not answering any of the questions that I've asked so for during this Session 2.

Between 3:03 PM and 3:08 PM I obtained thermal images of the Second Floor Front Stairway Room. I obtained four thermal images of the room's West wall and ceiling where there is a dark blue trail caused by the cold air coming from the air conditioner vent. This dark blue trail was in a cylinder shape. I obtained two pictures of my two pink footprints on the floor where I was sitting. I obtained two pictures of the vent where the cold air that is coming from the air conditioner is causing a dark blue cold air trail which extends towards the room's South and East wall, ceiling and towards the room's South East corner. I obtained two pictures of where the air conditioner vent and the dark blue cold air trail is located along the room's East wall, ceiling, and near the Northeast corner. I obtained two pictures of where I had been standing and left two pink footprints on the room's hardwood floor.

At 3:15 PM I asked Pat if the Great Depression made him angry, to knock one time.

At 3:16 PM I heard one very soft sound tap. I feel that this was the Ghost of Pat Hays confirming that the Great Depression made him angry.

At 3:18 PM I asked Kathleen Hays to knock ones if she liked antiques.

At 3:19 PM I heard one very soft tap coming from near the room's West wall. I feel that this was the Ghost of Kathleen Hays confirming that she likes antiques.

By the end of this Paranormal Investigation Session 2, I was beginning to become frustrated and I thought that the Paranormal Evidence should be better then what Paranormal Evidence that I was receiving. I wanted the Ghosts and Spirits here at the Hays House to respond to every question that I ask during a Paranormal Investigation, and not just one or two questions per each hour long Paranormal Investigation Session.

Ovilus IV words: Crash, Farmers, Paint.

Digital pictures, Second Floor Front Stairway Room, Wednesday, 2nd November 2016, Hays House.

Two pictures of the room's North wall.

Two pictures of the room's North wall and the fan opening.

Two pictures of the room's South wall.

Two pictures of the room's tongue and groove ceiling boards.

Two close-up pictures of the interior side of the door leading to the Second Floor Front Porch.

One close-up picture of the lower part of the interior side of the door leading to the Second Floor Front Porch.

Two close-up pictures of the room's tongue and groove heart pine, hardwood floor.

One picture of the room's Northeast corner.

One picture of the room's South East corner.

Two pictures of the Second Floor Front Porch door's threshold board.

Please see the author's website at www.keithoevans.com to view each digital picture.

Thermal images, Second Floor Front Stairway Room, Wednesday, 2nd, November 2016, Hays House.

One image of the room's West wall. At the top of the image are the five mounted ceiling lights. At the lower center of the image is the Second Floor Front Porch door.

One image of the North wall. On the center left side of the image is one of the mounted ceiling lights. On the lower right side of the image is the top of the lamp.

One image of the South wall and the entrances to the Frances Room and The Sunshine Room.

Two images of the East wall. On the lower left side of the image is the door way that leads to the 2nd Floor Back Stairway Room. At the bottom of the image is the stairway and the lamp, which is in the on position.

Please see the author's website at www.keithoevans.com to view each thermal image.

CHAPTER **19**

Second Floor Back Stairway Room, Hays House, Ghosts are People too.

A brief description of the Second Floor Back Stairway Room, Wednesday, 2nd November 2016, Hays House.

This room has the back stairway in its north-west corner. On the room's north wall is the original door way, minus the door, to the original second floor bathroom. Today this door way leads to the small second floor North-side kitchen. On the east wall of this room is a countertop with a coffee pot maker and a microwave oven. There is a window on the east wall with the original widow and the decorative stained-glass window insert on the interior side of the window. There is some damage to the lower left side of the stained-glass. In the room's south-east corner is a white refrigerator. On the room's south wall is the original door and door way to Mary's Room, which today this door way leads to the small second floor South-side kitchen. On this room's west wall is the original door way and original door that leads to the Second Floor Front Stairway Room.

A description of the Second Floor Back Stairway Room from two pictures taken in 1996.

In a photo of the Second Floor Back Stairway Room's East wall, and starting from left to right, in the rooms Northeast corner and against the room's North wall is a dark wooden bookshelf standing approximately 4-foot-tall, with books on the top shelf and a clear glass pitcher on top of the bookshelf. On the East wall and to the left of the window, is an 18" x 18" glass covered door that is built into the wall. In 2017 this wooden box contains four screw type electrical fuses. This wooden box that is built into the wall, originally held the city water meter and possibly the city electrical meter. In the center of the room's East wall is an original window with the original white wooden trim. This window has two panes on the top and bottom sides. Each of the window's panes are covered with an internal stained-glass insert. These inserts have 14 pink squares outlined with black lines all around the perimeter of each window pane. In the center of each window pane, are decorative pink flowers with green leaves. Below the window is an orange or red textile antique couch with dark wooden trim. To the far-right side of this photo and along the room's East wall is the top of a white lamp shade.

The next photo shows the room's South East corner. This photo also shows the items that are on, and along the room's East wall, which I have already mentioned in the above paragraph within the first photo. This photo also includes two white round pillows in each corner of the orange and red antique couch that sits along the room's East wall. On the room's South wall is an antique piece of furniture with a white and gray marble top. This top has an irregular shape. On top of this piece of furniture are the following items; a blue and gold porcelain lamp with a white lamp shade, a book, possibly a Bible on a light-colored wooden pedestal, a porcelain three Leaf dish, and two golden candle stick holders, each with 6-inch white candles. This room's walls are covered with white horizontal tongue and groove wooden boards. The room's floor has an oval shaped pink rug which is situated in front of the antique couch.

The history surrounding the Second Floor Back Stairway Room, Hays House.

There is still one historical feature that remains in this second-floor back stairway room and that is a 18″ x 18″ wooden box that is built into the room's East wall near the Northeast corner. This wooden box has a glass window within its door. At one time within this box was the city water gauge. Apparently, this gauge showed how much water the family or house had used. The city paid a man to go house to house on a monthly basis to check the gauge, so that the city would know how much to charge the homeowner for water usage. It is also believed that the city gas meter may have been within this wooden box.

In the early 1950s Counsil Bryan Palmer, who was married to Patsy and Frances' Grandmother Annie Gibson Hays Palmer, installed a ventilation system to keep the Second and Third floors cool. This involved taking the wooden door off of the entrance which led from the Second Floor Back Stairway Room to the what is today the third-floor apartment and installing a screen door. Back in the 1950's, the third floor was used just for storage.

The Mel Meter base readings for the Second Floor Back Stairway Room, Wednesday, 2nd November 2016, Hays House.

1 PM the white whirlpool refrigerator located along the room's East wall.

The electromagnetic frequency range was 2.1 mG to 2.3 mG.

The temperature range was 76.2°F to 76.9°F.

1 PM the double electrical out let located on the room's South wall. Two items are plugged into this electrical outlet, one is a nightlight.

The electromagnetic frequency range was 3.2 mG to 3.8 mG.

The temperature range was 76.9°F to 77.5°F.

1:01 PM the white microwave oven on the countertop, located along the room's East wall.

The electromagnetic frequency range was 0.0 mG to 0.0 mG.

The temperature range was 76.6°F to 76.8°F.

1:01 PM the black coffee pot maker on the countertop, located along the room's East wall.

The electromagnetic frequency range was 0.0 mG to 0.0 mG.

The temperature range was 76.8°F to 76.9°F.

1:02 PM the white toaster on the countertop, along the room's East wall.

The electromagnetic frequency range was 0.0 mG to 0.0 mG.

The temperature range was 76.5°F to 76.7°F.

Paranormal Investigation, Session 1, Second Floor Back Stairway Room, Friday, 9th June 2017, Hays House.

Prior to this paranormal investigation, session 1, I did not sense any emotions from the ghosts and or spirits. I thought that this room probably would not be an important room because it was just a hallway for each of the five second floor bedrooms to reach the only bathroom on the second floor prior to 1996. I felt that today's paranormal investigation would probably not be very interesting.

11:12 AM Keith: "Hello, I am Keith Evans. I wish only to speak to the Hays, Gibson, and Buck family's that lived here at the Hays House. You may use your energy to choose words from the Ovilus IV database. This is the Ovilus IV and it is harmless." (Hold it up.)

11:13 AM Keith: "This is the Mel Meter, and the EDI. They measure temperature and electromagnetic frequencies. They will not hurt ghosts and or spirits." (Hold it up.)

11:14 AM Keith: "The Ovilus IV has given me two background words; add which is spelled A-D-D, and equate which is spelled E-Q-U-A-T-E. The Ovilus IV has pronounced the words, add and equate at a normal conversational level and speed."

11:14 AM Keith: "I have observed the Mel Meter readings to be 0.0 mG and 77.8°F."

11:15 AM Keith: "I have observed the EDI readings to be 0.0 mG and 76.3°F."

11:15 AM Keith: "I have observed the Mel Meter readings to be 0.0 mG and 78.0°F."

11:15 AM Keith: "I have observed the Mel Meter readings to be 0.0 mG and 78.2°F."

11:15 AM Keith: "I have observed the EDI readings to be 0.0 mG and 76.4°F."

11:16 AM Keith: "I have observed the EDI readings to be 0.0 mG and 76.5°F."

11:16 AM Keith: "The Ovilus IV has given me the word Twenty, which is spelled T-W-E-N-T-Y. The Ovilus IV has pronounced the word 20, at a normal conversational level and speed."

11:16 AM Keith: "I have observed the Mel Meter readings to be 0.0 mG and 78.0°F."

11:16 AM Keith: "I have observed the Mel Meter readings to be 0.0 mG and 77.5°F."

11:17 AM Keith: "The Ovilus IV has given me the words heard which is spelled H E-A-R-D the and roadway, which is spelled R-O-A-D-W-A-Y. The Ovilus IV has pronounced the words heard and roadway, at a normal conversational level and speed."

11:17 AM Keith: "I have observed the Mel Meter readings to be 0.0 mG and 77.9°F."

11:17 AM Keith: "I have observed the EDI readings to be 0.0 mG and 76.6°F."

11:17 AM Keith: "The Ovilus IV gave me the words slain which is spelled S-L-A-I-N, and continued which is spelled C-O-N-T-I-N-U-E-D. The Ovilus IV has pronounced the words slain and continued at a normal conversational level and speed."

11:18 AM Keith: "I have observed the Mel Meter readings to be 0.0 mG and 77.6°F."

11:18 AM Keith: "I have observed the EDI readings to be 0.0 mG and 76.7°F."

11:18 AM Keith: "Amy is talking and walked by twice."

11:19 AM Keith: "Amy is talking. I moved from video camera frame. I am trying to keep the door closed."

11:21 AM Keith: "Amy is talking."

11:25 AM Keith: "Kathleen, was there any antique furniture in this room, when you were living here?"

11:26 AM Keith: "The Ovilus IV gave me the word devil which is spelled D-E-V-I-L. The Ovilus IV has pronounced the word devil with a man's deep voice, at a lower than normal conversational level and a slower than normal conversational speed."

11:26 AM Keith: "I have observed the Mel Meter readings to be 0.0 mG and 77.7°F."

11:26 AM Keith: "I have observed the EDI readings to be 0.0 mG and 76.8°F."

11:26 AM Keith: "I like devil eggs."

11:29 AM Keith: "Come on Sunshine, stop being Mrs. angry britches. Stop giving me all of these negative words. I do not know what 20 means. Because I had not asked a question yet, when the Ovilus for gave me the word 20. The Ovilus IV did not give me the symbol 20."

11:35 AM Keith: "Sunshine, name one piece of antique furniture that was in this room during the time that you lived here?"

11:36 AM Keith: "Kathleen, is it true that there was no furniture in this room, when you lived here?"

11:38 AM Keith: "Pat, what is underneath the 3-foot space under the first-floor stairway landing?"

11:39 AM Keith: "Kathleen, what is underneath the 3-foot space under the first-floor stairway landing?"

11:39 AM Keith: "That was the door being closed by someone in the house."

11:40 AM Keith: "Sunshine, what is underneath the 3-foot space under the first-floor stairway landing?"

11:41 AM Keith: "Sunshine, when was the back stairway remodeled?"

11:42 AM Keith: "Pat, what year was the back stairway remodeled?"

11:43 AM Keith: "Amy asked if her phone was in the Second-Floor Back Stairway room. I told her that I did not see her phone in this room."

11:45 AM Keith: "Kathleen, what year was the back stairway remodeled?"

11:46 AM Keith: "Pat, did you keep your baseball bat, baseball glove, and baseball in this room, when you were alive?"

11:47 AM Keith: "Pat, what year did you play on the Apalachicola baseball team?"

11:48 AM Keith: "I heard that you were a good first baseman."

11:49 AM Keith: "Pat, did Kathleen, and Sunshine ever play baseball?"

11:52 AM Keith: "Amy cannot find her phone, she asked me to call her phone so she could pinpoint where the phone is located. I said that I would."

11:53 AM Keith: "Amy walked by both camcorder's one and two, as she was looking for her phone in the Second Floor South Side Kitchen Room."

11:54 AM Keith: "Amy thanked me for calling her cell phone number."

11:57 AM Keith: "The Ovilus IV gave me three words farmers which is spelled F-A-R-M-E-R-S, 13 which is spelled T-H-I-R-T-E-E-N, and walk which is spelled W-A-L-K. The Ovilus IV has pronounced the words farmers, 13, and walk all at a lower than normal conversational level and at a normal conversational speed."

11:57 AM Keith: "I have observed the Mel Meter readings to be 0.0 mG and 78.4°F."

11:58 AM Keith: "I have observed the EDI readings to be 0.0 mG and 76.5°F."

12:01 PM Keith: "The kitchen dishes are rattling."

12:02 PM Keith: "Farmers, 13, walk are all words that I do not feel that are in response to any questions that I've asked so far during this session number one."

12:02 PM to 12:04 PM Keith: "I obtained thermal images of the Second-floor Back Stairway room. I obtained two images of the pink area, as you go down the stairs from the back-stair way. I obtained two images of the ceiling air conditioner vent. I obtained two images of my three pink footprints and the yellow chair where I have been sitting during the paranormal investigation."

12:04 PM Keith: "Thank you for talking to me. Have a nice day."

12:04 PM Keith: "This session 1 ended on Friday, 9th June 2017."

Paranormal Investigation, Session 2, Second Floor Back Stairway Room, Friday, 9th June 2017, Hays House.

2:39 PM Keith: "Hello, I am Keith Evans. I wish only to speak to the Hays, Gibson, and Buck family members who actually lived at the Hays House. You may use your energy to choose words from the Ovilus IV database. This is the Ovilus IV and it will not hurt ghost, and or spirits." (Hold it up.)

2:40 PM Keith: "This is the Mel Meter and the EDI. They measure temperature and electromagnetic frequencies. The Mel Meter and the EDI will not harm ghosts, and or spirits." (Hold it up.)

2:41 PM Keith: "The Ovilus IV has given me two background words; Monday which is spelled M-O-N-D-A-Y and reservation which is spelled R-E-S-E-R-V-AT-I-O-N. The Ovilus IV has pronounced the words Monday and reservation at a normal conversational level and speed."

2:42 PM Keith: "I have observed the Mel Meter readings to be 0.0 mG and 76.4°F."

2:42 PM Keith: "I have observed the EDI readings to be 0.0 mG and 75.3°F."

2:44 PM Keith: "Are you asking about my reservations to stay here at the Hays House on the 1 July 2017? That may be a Monday. I am not sure. I would have to look at a calendar."

2:45 PM Keith: "Sunshine, do you mind if I stay here for a month?"

2:47 PM Keith: "The Ovilus IV looks to be frozen up again and not functioning properly. There are seven dots in the Ovilus IV's" upper left side of the its display. I do not feel that these batteries have been in use long enough, to be totally without energy."

2:49 PM Keith: "I'm going to try to tap the home icon."

2:50 PM Keith: "The Ovilus IV is not responding to my touching of the icon."

2:51 PM Keith: "I'm going to manually turn the Ovilus IV off. I'm going to adjust the four AAA batteries in the back compartment of the Ovilus IV and then I'm going to turn the Ovilus IV on."

2:54 PM Keith: "The Ovilus IV has given me two background words trouble which is spelled T-R-O-U-B-L-E a demand which is spelled D-E-M-A-N-D. The Ovilus IV has pronounced the words trouble and demand at a very low level and at a very fast speed. I cannot understand what the Ovilus IV had said."

2:54 PM Keith: "I have observed the Mel Meter readings to be 0.0 mG and 76.4°F."

2:54 PM Keith: "I have observed the EDI readings to be 0.0 mG and 75.0°F."

2:59 PM Keith: "Am I going to be in trouble if I do not meet your demands? What are your demands?"

3 PM Keith: "It looks like the Ovilus IV is frozen up again. Not functioning properly. I can see six solid non-moving dots in the Ovilus IV's upper left side of its display."

3:01 PM Keith: "I am going to try to adjust the four AAA batteries without turning the Ovilus IV off."

3:03 PM Keith: "The Ovilus IV is not responding to my adjusting the batteries. I am touching the home icon and nothing is happening. I am going to turn the Ovilus IV off manually."

3:05 PM Keith: "The Ovilus IV gave me the number six as a symbol. The Ovilus IV has pronounced the symbol six at a normal conversational level, but at a very fast speed. I was only able to hear a S sound."

3:06 PM Keith: "I have observed the Mel Meter readings to be 0.0 mG and 78.7°F."

3:06 PM Keith: "I have observed the EDI readings to be 0.0 mG and 75.0°F."

3:10 PM Keith: "So, Sunshine are you demanding the number six?"

3:11 PM Keith: "I am not sure if I know what your demand is!"

3:12 PM Keith: "I am going to take some thermal images of this room."

3:13 PM to 3:18 PM Keith: "I obtained thermal images of the second-floor back stairway room. I obtained four images of the dark blue area on the room's ceiling. I obtained four images of the air conditioner vent on the room's ceiling. I obtained two images of my two pink footprints and my yellow and orange area on the chair where I was setting. I obtained four images of the pink shape, located down the back stairway near the middle landing. In each of these pictures, the pink shape changes."

3:19 PM Keith: "Sunshine, are you just making my Ovilus IV freeze up so you do not have to talk?"

3:20 PM Keith: "The Ovilus IV will not function properly. The Ovilus IV will not return to its home position. I am going to manually turn the Ovilus IV off."

3:21 PM Keith: "I am going to adjust the batteries in the back of the Ovilus IV and then turned the Ovilus IV on."

3:24 PM Keith: "The Ovilus IV gave me two background words; button which is spelled B-U-T-T-O-N, and stood which is spelled S-T-O-O-D. The Ovilus IV pronounced the words button and stood at a lower than normal conversational level and at a faster than normal conversational speed." (I did not obtain a picture of button and stood.)

3:26 PM Keith: "Are you ordering me to button my mouth? Are you asking me if I understand?"

3:27 PM Keith: "I know one thing, you quickly draining all of the energy from my batteries."

3:29 PM Keith: "I will say this much, if you care about history, you do not share that with me."

3:30 PM Keith: "Thank you for talking to me. Have a nice day."

3:30 PM Keith: "I have observed the Mel Meter readings to be 0.0 mG and 76.6°F."

3:30 PM Keith: "I have observed the EDI readings to be 0.0 mG and 74.9°F."

3:31 PM Keith: "This session 2 has ended on Friday, 9th, June 2017."

The analysis of the Paranormal Investigation, Session 1, Second Floor Back Stairway Room, Friday, 9th June 2017, Hays House. The date of analysis was Tuesday, 24th October 2017.

At 11:14 AM the Ovilus IV gave me the first and second background words for this session 1, add, and equate. I had not yet asked any questions during this session number one. I feel that this is an intelligent spirit who is observing me and letting me know that they are aware that I am adding to my documents the information concerning the paranormal research and that I am evaluating this research. An intelligent ghost or spirit maybe pointing out my recurring use of ghost and spirit by saying add and equate. I feel that a ghost is a spirit of a deceased person who at least has partially materialized so that one may see the ghost. On the other hand, a spirit makes themselves know without materializing. To add something together will increase the total number, but to equate just means two equations are of equal value to each other.

At 11:16 AM the Ovilus IV gave me the third word for this session 1, 20. I had not asked any questions yet during this session number one. I feel that this is an intelligent spirit who feels that 20 is a significant amount. I cannot think of any questions that I have asked during the previous session that may be answered by the number 20. Maybe there is such a question that I have asked in the past that I'm failing to remember at this point in time. I know that I am planning about 20 chapters for the Hays house book. So maybe that is what the intelligent ghost and or spirit is referring to.

At 11:17 AM the Ovilus IV gave me the fourth and fifth words for this session number one, heard and roadway. I have not asked any questions yet during this session number one. I do not believe that the words heard and roadway are in response to any questions that I have asked in previous sessions. I feel that there are always ghosts and spirits in the environment and that their energy may be automatically picked up by the Ovilus IV, without the ghost and or spirit making any decision to choose a word from the Ovilus IV's database. These intelligent ghosts or spirits may be talking about how noisy the traffic on the road is today.

At 11:17 AM the Ovilus IV gave me the sixth and seventh words for this session number one, slain and continued. I have not asked any questions yet during this session number one. I do not believe that the words slain and continued are in response to any questions that I have asked in previous sessions.

From 11:18 AM to 11:21 AM the investigation experienced some interruptions from the owner and then after that the responses from the Ovilus IV were less than before the interruptions. It seems to me that ghosts and spirits like to have private conversations and if there is an interruption they seem to just give up on the conversation and leave. If they do not leave they just stop communicating and or communicate at a much less frequency.

At 11:26 AM the Ovilus IV gave me the eighth word for this session number one, devil. This word was spoken by the Ovilus IV in a low level deep man's voice, and at a slow speed. As if the spirit or ghost was trying to be Halloween scary. I blamed the word devil on Sunshine Gibson, just to see if I could get a response out of her. There was no response from sunshine Gibson. So, that does not prove or disprove that it was Sunshine that said the word devil.

From 11:43 AM to 11:54 AM the investigation experienced some interruptions from the owner.

At 11:57 AM the Ovilus IV gave me the ninth through 11th words for this session number one, farmers, 13, and walk. I do not feel that the words farmers, 13, and walk are answering any of the questions I have asked so far during this session number one. The word walk may be an intelligent spirit pointing out that someone is walking around in the Hays House.

At 12:01 PM the kitchen, dishes rattled loud enough for me to hear them. I find this to be unexplained. There is no mechanism of force that could have caused anything in the kitchen to rattle. I was the only one in this area and there was no one there to cause the dishes to rattle. I have walk around in all of the rooms and when I do it does not cause the dishes to rattle.

From 12:02 PM to 12:04 PM I obtained thermal images of the Second Floor Back Stairway Room. I obtained two images of the area down towards the first landing of the Back Stairway. In each image, I saw a pink area that I cannot explain. The pink areas seem to change on its own as if it was morphing into a different irregular shape of a person standing on the first landing as you are walking up the Back Stairway. There is no source of heat in this area of the wall that could produce a pink thermal image. A ghost or spirit would cause a cold, dark blue, and or black thermal image. A pink thermal image is about 50 to 60 degrees Fahrenheit.

The analysis of the Paranormal Investigation, Session 2, Second Floor Back Stairway Room, Friday, 9th June 2017, Hays House. The date of the analysis was Wednesday, 25th October 2017.

At 2:41 PM the Ovilus IV gave me the first and second background words for session 2, Monday, and reservation. I had not asked any questions yet for this session 2, and I do not believe that the words Monday and reservation are in response to any of the questions that I asked during session number one. This may be an intelligent spirit asking me what day of the week my reservations start and or ends at the Hays House. Upon looking at a calendar, I have seen that my check day at the Hays House was a Saturday, 1st July 2017 and my check out day was Monday, the 31st July 2017. I think I made the reservations in advance sometime in March of 2017. So, a Ghost and or Spirit may be telling me that my reservations will be ending on Monday. On Friday, 9th June 2017, I had already made the Reservations to stay at the Hays House in July 2017.

At 2:47 PM it appears that the Ovilus IV Is not functioning properly again. These batteries are not very old, and still should have energy.

It is almost like a spirit or ghost is blocking the flow of energy from the batteries to the Ovilus IV. Touch the home icon and not having it respond is a good indication that the batteries are fully drained of energy. Upon manually turning the Ovilus IV off and then back on, I obtained two more background words. If the Ovilus IV's batteries were totally drained, this would not happen.

At 2:54 PM the Ovilus IV gave me the third and fourth background words for this session number two, trouble and demand. I do not believe that the words trouble and demand are in response to any questions that I've asked so far during this session number two. The word trouble may be an intelligent spirit stating that they know that I am having trouble with the Ovilus IV functioning properly. It could be that a ghost and or spirit is telling me that I am too much trouble and too demanding. I have had living people tell me that before.

At 3 PM the Ovilus IV failed to function properly again. I'm having the same problems that I had earlier during this session, the Ovilus IV will not respond to my pressing the home icon. I have decided to manually turn off the Ovilus IV. I am going to wait about a minute and turned the Ovilus IV back on.

At 3:05 PM the Ovilus IV gave me the fifth background word for this session 2, the number as a symbol six. The Ovilus IV pronounced the number six at a normal conversational level but at a very fast speed. I only heard a "S" sound. I do not believe that the word six is in response to any questions that I have asked so far during session number two. I cannot imagine what any ghost and or spirit would be talking about by stating the number six.

From 3:13 PM to 3:18 PM I obtained thermal images of the second-floor back stairway room. I obtained four images of the pink shape, located at the middle landing as you are going down the back stairway. In each picture the pink shape seems to change its shape. In two of the images the pink shape seems to be a full-bodied image standing near the mid-landing, as you're going down the back stairway. In two other images the pink shape seems to be closer to the camera and a view of the outline of a person from the waist up. I am not sure who this image may be of, but it may be Annie. Annie's granddaughter said that she loved to have her picture taken. Annie and her husband, Counsil Bryan Palmer use to visit the Hays House nearly every weekend from 1942 until Annie Gibson Palmer passed away in 1960.

From 3:19 PM to 3:23 PM the Ovilus IV was failing to function properly again. I'm still having the same problems that I had earlier during this session when the Ovilus IV continuously freezes up. The Ovilus IV will not respond to my pressing of the home icon. I have decided to manually turn the Ovilus IV off. Even though the instructions say you should return it to the home position before you turn it off. But if it will not return to the home position and you have no choice but to manually turn the Ovilus IV off. Now guess what upon turning the Ovilus IV back on, it has enough energy to give me two more background words during this session number two. If that is not paranormal, I don't know what is.

At 3:24 PM the Ovilus IV gave me the sixth and seventh word background words for this session 2, button and stood. The Ovilus IV pronounce the words button and stood at a lower level than normal conversational level and at a faster than normal conversational speed. I felt like I was being scolded by a lady that was telling me to button my lips more or less keep quiet and following that with a, do you understand me. That is totally subjective, but that's the way I felt at the time this was happening. I will say this much, I always take pictures of the words that I obtained on the Ovilus IV. After completing this session 2, I was unable to find where I had obtained any pictures at 3:24 PM of the words button and stood. It is very important as a legitimate Paranormal Investigator to document your evidence. Anyone can make something up and write a book about a fantasy story. By failing to document and obtain pictures of my evidence, I am shooting myself in the foot. I guess with my emotional response to being told to shut up and being asked if I understood that somehow allowed my brain to malfunction, to the point that I did not obtain any pictures of the words button and stood at 3:24 PM. I'm not happy with myself for failing to obtain pictures of the words button and stood at 3:24 PM.

This is the first session where all the words were background words. A background word is the word that the Ovilus IV obtains from evaluating the environment within 60 seconds after you turn the Ovilus IV on. The seven words given to me during this session number two from the Ovilus IV were all background words. This is the first session, that I ever remember where I did not get a response on the Ovilus IV that was something other than a background word.

Digital pictures of the Second Floor Back Stairway Room, Wednesday, 2nd November 2016, Hays House.

One picture of the room's West wall.

Three pictures of the room's Northwest corner.

Two close-up pictures of the doorknob and skeleton key base plate of the door leading to the third-floor apartment.

Two pictures of the door opening leading from the second-floor back stairway room to the stairway to the first floor.

Two pictures of the door that leads to the second-floor front stairway room.

Two pictures of the exterior side of the door leading to Mary's room.

Two pictures of the door's threshold board, leading to Mary's room.

Two pictures of the room's tongue and groove hardwood floor.

One picture of the interior stained-glass window on the room's East wall.

Two pictures of the room's tongue and groove ceiling boards.

Two pictures of the door's threshold board, located between the Second Floor Back Stairway Room and the Second Floor Front Stairway Room.

Two close-up pictures of the door hinges on the door between the Second Floor Back Stairway Room and the Second Floor Front Stairway Room.

Please see the author's website at www.keithoevans.com to view each digital picture.

Thermal Images of the Second Floor Back Stairway Room, Wednesday, 2nd November 2016, Hays House.

One thermal image of the room's East wall and window.

One thermal image of the room's North wall showing in the center is the open bathroom door.

One thermal image of the room's West wall showing the open door on the left, three ceiling lights on the Second Floor Front Stairway Room and in the center, bottom is the Second Floor Front Porch door.

One thermal image of the room's South wall door that leads to Mary's room.

Please see the author's website at www.keithoevans.com to view each thermal image.

CHAPTER **20**

The Patsy Room, Hays House,
Ghosts are People too.

A description of the Patsy Room from pictures taken on Friday, 10th March 2017, Hays House.

The west wall has two original white wooden frame windows with two glass panes on the upper and lower sections. Each window has a shear tan blind and a pink curtain. Mounted on the wall between the two windows is a decorative golden round metal disc. This disc has gray rays coming out from its perimeter. Each ray has a round disc near its distal point. Along the West wall and centered under the golden round metal disc is a king size bed with four pillows and a white bedspread. On each side of this bed is a modern nightstand with a light blue lamp that has a round white lamp shade. Mounted on the room's West wall and to the right of the right-side window there is eight inches by 10 inches white canvas. This canvas has a painting of a lady with a light green background.

A long the room's North wall is a light blue, modern chest of drawers with three framed pictures on top. Above the chest of drawers is approximately 18″ x 28″, white canvas painting of a lady in a white dress with a light green background. To the right side of the chest of drawers is an electrical outlet. To the right side of the electrical outlet is an original white wooden window with two glass panes in the upper and lower sections. This window has the original white wooden trim. This window has a shear tan blind. On the floor in front of the window and along the room's North wall is a modern white wooden bench with a brown top. There is a white and blue pillow on top of this bench and to the far-right side of this bench. To the right side of the window is an electrical outlet. To the right of this electrical outlet and mounted on the room's North wall is a light blue, antique wooden door.

On the room's East wall and near the rooms Northeast corner is a modern light green wooden table with a brown top. On top of this table and from left to right are the following items; a light blue porcelain lamp with a round, brown, lamp shade, a black wooden box, a light blue small box, and an approximately 3' x 4' cork note board. In front of the light green table is a clear plastic chair. Above the light green table is a black metal shelf that is mounted on to the room's East wall. This shelf is about 12 inches deep and has three tan wicker baskets on top. To the right of the light green table, is an original white wooden fireplace mantle. Around the opening of the fireplace are the brown and tan fireproof tiles. The floor area in front of the fireplace is covered with cement that is painted red. The fireplace opening is covered with an antique black iron decorative cover with a sculpture of a lady climbing a tree. To the left of the fireplace is a red basket, and a tan wicker basket. To the right of the fireplace is a large clear glass jar. On the fireplace mantel's shelf are eight different light green pots and pitchers. To the right of the large clear glass jar is an antique white wooden chair with a light green seat cushion and a golden colored pillow. On the room's East wall and near the room's South East corner is original white wooden five sunken panels closet door. This door way has the original white wooden trim. Mounted on this closet door is approximately 2' x 2' white canvas painting of an oyster shell with a light blue background.

Along the room's South wall and near the room's South East corner is an approximately 6-foot-tall, modern, silver rack with shelves and bars for hanging clothes. To the right of the silver rack is the original white wooden door with five sunken panels. This door has the original black brass or metal doorknob and skeleton key baseplate. This doorway has the original white wooden door trim. This door way is the entrance to this room and it leads to the 2nd Floor Front Stairway

Room. To the right of this door is a light switch. To the right of the light switch is a light green, modern table with two light blue porcelain bowls on top. Above the table is an approximately 4 feet by 4-foot wooden framed mirror mounted on the room's South wall. The frame around this mirror has alternating white, light blue, and light green blocks of antique wooden trim boards. To the right of the mirror is an electrical outlet. The South wall is covered by many framed pictures and decorative items. On the room's South wall and near the room's Southwest corner is a carving of hippopotamus.

All the walls in this room have light blue paint and are the original tongue and groove, horizontal, wallboards. The ceiling has the original white ceiling boards and trim. The ceiling boards are orientated in an East to West direction. This room has the original, tongue and groove, heart pine, hardwood flooring that is orientated in an East to West direction.

A description of the Patsy Room from pictures taken in 1996, Hays House.

Starting with the West wall and going clockwise round the room. The first picture includes the room's South wall and part of the room's West wall. Going from left to right on the room's South wall, is the entrance that leads to the Second Floor Front Stairway Room. This door has the light blue original wooden trim. To the right of this doorway is a light switch. Under the light switch is an antique dark wooden table with the following items on top and going from left to right; a porcelain figurine, a lamp with a golden supporting stand with a pink decorative glass or porcelain globe. To the right of this table is an antique light wooden decorative bed with a hand carved headboard and matching footboard. This bed is covered with a white bedspread and two blue pillows and one white pillow. To the right of the bed is an antique square table with a white marble top. On top of the antique square table is a multi-colored porcelain vase and a dark wooden hand carved figurine. On the room's West wall is a window with the white original wooden trim. This window has a white curtain.

The second picture shows part of the room's North wall. From left to right and along the room's North wall is an antique decorative chest of drawers with a square marble top. This chest of drawers has an antique matching wooden framed squared mirror. On top of the chest of drawers are the following items, going from left to right; a white porcelain plate, four blue bottles, a clear glass dish, and two white porcelain figurines. The South wall and the ceiling trim are painted light blue and they have the original wooden trim and tongue and groove, horizontal, wallboards. To the right of the antique chest of drawers, is a white and blue metal trashcan. In front of this trashcan is an antique dark wooden chair. To the right of the wooden chair is an antique table with the following items, starting from left to right; two small framed pictures, a white porcelain dish with the lead, a porcelain candy dish, and a large light blue vase. Behind this antique wooden table is a window that is covered with a white curtain. There is an air conditioner within this window. To the right of this window there is an electrical outlet that has the air conditioner plugged into this electrical outlet. To the right of this electrical outlet is an antique white wooden table with a rectangle, white marble top. On the top of the rectangular wooden table are the following items; six matching white porcelain items, two of which are pitchers, two are bowls, one is a vase and one is a candy dish with a lead. One of the six matching pieces is a bowl, located on the bottom shelf of this rectangular wooden table. Above this rectangular wooden table and mounted on the North wall, is a decorative wooden framed mirror that has two shelves. On each shelf there is a small golden and white porcelain pitcher. Mounted on the left and right side of this wooden frame mirror are the oval wooden framed pictures of Patsy on the right side and Frances is on the left side. The North wall has the light blue, original, tongue and groove, horizontal, wallboards. The floor in this room is painted dark brown and has a 6' x 8' multi-colored rug with tassels on the North side. This rug is in the middle of this room's floor.

The history of the Patsy Room, Hays House.

This room was named after Patsy Hays Phillyaw who was born in 1938. Patsy was born at the Archbold Hospital in Thomasville, Georgia.

From 1946 to 1959, this was Patsy's room. Patsy is the daughter of Pat and Kathleen Hays. Patsy's family were the owners of the Hays house during the period from 1942 to 1996.

As a child Patsy would travel during some Holidays with her parents, her paternal grandparents, and her Aunt Sunshine to visit relatives in Tallahassee, Florida and Tarpon Springs, Florida.

Patsy graduated from the Chapman High School in Apalachicola, Florida in 1956.

Patsy attended the University of Missouri during her freshmen year and sophomore years.

Patsy attended the University of Florida for her Junior year.

Patsy was married in 1959 to James Phillyaw. They were married at the Methodist Church at the corner of Fifth Avenue and E Street in Apalachicola Florida. James and Patsy had their wedding reception at the Hays House. I was able to see pictures of their wedding reception.

Pictures that were taken of Patsy wedding reception in the Living Room in 1959 showed that the external parts of the gas heater fire-place insert are the same as the external parts of that gas heater that exists in the living room in 2017. Pictures of the wedding reception taken in 1959, in the Dining Room, also show the decorative plates that Kathleen had displayed on the 5-inch ledge bordering the top of the wainscoting which still exist in the dining room at the Hays House in 2017.

Patsy taught as a substitute teacher at the Chapman High School in Apalachicola, Florida from September 1961 to June 1962. Patsy was filling in for a teacher who was on Parental leave. Patsy taught; Math for the 7th and 8th graders, English for the 8th graders, Science for the 7th graders, and Geography for the 7th graders.

In the 1970's when Pat and Kathleen Hays purchased a new king-size bed for their bedroom on the first-floor level of the Hays House, they moved their old bedroom suit to the Sunshine Room. The furniture that was in the Sunshine Room was moved to the Patsy Room and stayed there until 1996.

On Easter Sunday, 6th April 1969 Mr., and Mrs. James Philyaw, (James and Patsy), attended the Church services at the First United Methodist Church located at 75th Fifth Street, Apalachicola, Florida.

Patsy and James Philyaw attended the First United Methodist Church's, 1839-1969, 130th Anniversary, on the 25th May 1969, at the Church on 75th Fifth Street, Apalachicola, Florida.

Patsy Hays Philyaw has been a lifelong member of the First United Methodist Church, located at 75th Fifth Street, Apalachicola, Florida.

Mrs. James Philyaw, (Patsy), helped at the First United Methodist Church's nursey from 1965 to 1975.

Mrs. James Philyaw, (Patsy), was a Sunday School Teacher at the First United Methodist Church's from 1970 to 1978.

Mel Meter Base Readings for the Patsy Room, Friday, 10th March 2017, Hays House.

The blue lamp on the left side, located on the room's West wall. This lamp is not in use.

The electromagnetic frequency range was 0.0 mG to 0.0 mG.

The temperature range was 71.2°F to 71.3°F.

The blue lamp on the right side, located on the room's West wall. This lamp is not in use.

The electromagnetic frequency range was 0.0 mG to 0.0 mG.

The temperature range was 71.3°F to 71.4°F.

The electrical outlet located on the room's North wall. This outlet is in use, with a nightlight plugged into this outlet.

The electromagnetic frequency range was 0.0 mG to 0.0 mG.

The temperature range was 71.4°F to 72.1°F.

The electrical outlet on the room's North wall. This outlet is not in use.

The electromagnetic frequency range was 0.0 mG to 0.0 mG.

The temperature range was 70.8°F to 70.8°.

The lamp located on the room's Northeast corner. This lamp is in use.

The electromagnetic frequency range was 0.0 mG to 0.0 mG.

The temperature range was 71.3°F to 71.4°F.

The black iron decorative fireplace cover located on the room's East wall.

The electromagnetic frequency range was 0.0 mG to 0.0 mG.

The temperature range was 71.9°F to 72.1°F.

The light switch near the room's entrance, located on the room's South wall. The light is in use.

The electromagnetic frequency range was 0.0 mG to 0.0 mG.

The temperature range was 71.9°F to 72.4°F.

The electrical outlet on the room's South wall. This electrical outlet is in use.

The electromagnetic frequency range was 0.0 mG to 0.0 mG.

The temperature range was 71.3°F to 71.5°F.

The white ceiling fan and light. The fan is off, and the light is in use.

The electromagnetic frequency range was 0.0 mG to 0.0 mG.

The temperature range was 72.8°F to 73.5°F.

Paranormal Investigation, Session 1, the Patsy Room, Wednesday, 14th June 2017, Hays House.

11:11 AM Keith: "Hello, I am Keith Evans. I wish only to speak to Pat, Kathleen, Sunshine, and Mary, today. You may use your energy to choose words from the Ovilus IV's database. This is the Ovilus IV and it will not hurt ghost and or spirits." (Hold it up.)

11:12 AM Keith: "This is the Mel Meter and the EDI. They are used to measure temperature and electromagnetic frequencies. The Mel Meter and EDI will not harm Ghosts, and or Spirits." (Hold it up.)

11:14 AM Keith: "The Ovilus IV gave me four background words; I did not hear, see, and or obtain a picture of the first word, felt which is spelled F-E-L-T, there which is spelled T-H-E-R-E, and happy which is spelled H-A-P-P-Y. The second through fourth words were pronounced by the Ovilus IV at a lower than normal conversational level and faster than normal conversational speed."

11:14 AM Keith: "I have observed the Mel Meter readings to be 0.0 mG and 74.9°F."

11:14 AM Keith: "I have observed the EDI readings to be 0.0 mG and 75.3°F."

11:16 AM Keith: "It is great to get four words, but Sunshine, if I do not know what the first word is, then it is a word that is unknown and a failure in communications."

11:19 AM Keith: "Sunshine, did you rattle off four words fast and back to back? Did you cause my Ovilus IV to stop functioning properly? All these actions are not good communication skills. When the Ghosts and or Spirits drain my AAA batteries, this action is costing me a lot of money."

11:21 AM Keith: "The Ovilus IV will not return to the home position. I am still trying to press the home icon. I will have no choice but to manually turn off the Ovilus IV and then place four new AAA batteries into the Ovilus IV."

11:22 AM Keith: "I hear talking in the hallway."

11:25 AM Keith: "I change the batteries in the Ovilus IV. I have turned the Ovilus IV back on."

11:26 PM Keith: "The Ovilus IV has given me three background words; rail which is spelled R-A-I-L, while which is spelled W-H-I-L-E, and question which is spelled Q-E-S-T-I-O-N. The Ovilus IV pronounced the words rail, while, and question at a normal conversational level and speed."

11:26 AM Keith: "I have observed the Mel Meter readings to be 0.0 mG and 73.9°F."

11:26 AM Keith: "I have observed the EDI readings to be 0.0 mG and 74.0°F."

11:27 AM Keith: "The Ovilus IV has given me the word quiet, which is spelled Q-U-I-E-T. The Ovilus IV has pronounced the word quiet at a lower than normal conversational level, but at a normal conversational speed."

11:28 AM Keith: "The Ovilus IV has given me the word psychic which is spelled P-S-Y-C-H-I-C. The Ovilus IV has pronounced the word psychic at a normal conversational level and speed."

11:28 AM Keith: "I have observed the Mel Meter readings to be 0.0 mG and 74.6°F."

11:29 AM Keith: "I have observed the EDI readings to be 0.0 mG and 73.8°F."

11:30 PM Keith: "I have been having problems with the digital camera going in and out of focus."

11:35 AM Keith: "No, I have not traveled on a train in a while. If that is the question that you were asking me from today at 11:26 AM."

11:36 AM Keith: "Did that answer your question that you asked me today at 11:26 AM?"

11:37 AM Keith: "No I do not feel that I am psychic."

11:38 AM Keith: "Does that answer your question from today at 11:28 AM?"

11:39 AM Keith: "I am going to take a look at Patsy's Room with a thermal imager."

11:40 AM to 11:42 AM Keith: "I obtained six thermal images of Patsy's Room. I obtained two images of my two pink foot prints and the yellow chair that I was setting on. I obtained two thermal images of the ceiling air conditioner vent near the center of the North wall. This vent had a dark blue square area extending from the air conditioner vent. I obtained two thermal images of the air conditioner, cold air trail, which was a dark blue cylinder shape, near the South side of the ceiling."

11:42 AM Keith: "I did not see anything unusual, unexplained, and or paranormal about any of the six thermal images."

11:44 AM Keith: "Pat, Kathleen, Sunshine, and Mary, do you have any more questions that you would like me to answer?"

11:45 AM Keith: "Pat, when you played for the Apalachicola baseball team, how many games did you play each season?"

11:47 AM Keith: "Pat, what year did your baseball team have its best season?"

11:48 AM Keith: "Pat, what were some of the other baseball teams that you use to play?"

11:50 AM Keith: "The Ovilus IV gave me the letter M. The Ovilus IV pronounced the letter M, at a normal conversational level and speed."

11:50 AM Keith: "I observed the Mel Meter readings to be 0.0 mG and 73.5°F."

11:50 AM Keith: "I observed the EDI readings to be 0.0 mG and 72.9°F."

11:53 AM Keith: "What does the letter M, mean?"

11:54 AM Keith: "The Ovilus IV gave me the word paint which is spelled P-A-I-N-T. The Ovilus IV pronounced the word paint at a normal conversational level and speed."

11:54 AM Keith: "I have observed the Mel Meter readings to be 0.0 mG and 74.3°F."

11:55 AM Keith: "I have observed the EDI readings to be 0.0 mG and 72.8°F."

11:56 AM Keith: "Do you like what has recently been painted?"

11:57 AM Keith: "You know what room that painting took place in?"

11:58 AM Keith: "Are you a painter?"

11:59 AM Keith: "Thank you for talking to me. Have a nice day."

11:59 AM Keith: "This session 1 ended on Wednesday, 14 June 2017."

Ovilus IV words: Psychic, M, Paint.

Paranormal Investigation, Session 2, the Patsy Room, Wednesday, 14th June 2017, Hays House.

1:54 PM Keith: "Hello, I am Keith Evans. Today, I only wish to talk to Pat, Kathleen, Sunshine, and Mary. You may use your energy to choose words from the Ovilus IV's data base. This is the Ovilus IV and it will not hurt ghosts and or spirits." (Hold it up.)

1:55 PM Keith: "This is the Mel Meter and the EDI. They measure temperature and electromagnetic frequencies and they will not harm ghosts, and or spirits." (Hold it up.)

1:56 PM Keith: "The Ovilus IV has given me two background words; fun which is spelled F-U-N, and wonder which is spelled W-O-N-D-E-R. The Ovilus IV has pronounced the words fun and wonder at a normal conversational level and speed."

1:56 PM Keith: "I have observed the Mel Meter readings to be 0.0 mG and 76.9°F."

1:57 PM Keith: "I have observed the EDI readings to be 0.0 mG and 75.6°F."

1:57 PM Keith: "Do you wonder if I am having fun? Yes, I guess I am having a little fun."

1:58 PM Keith: "The Ovilus IV has given me the word felt which is spelled F-E-L-T. The Ovilus IV has pronounced the word felt at a normal conversational level and speed."

1:59 PM Keith: "I have observed the Mel Meter readings to be 0.0 mG and 78.2°F."

1:59 PM Keith: "I have observed the EDI readings to be 0.0 mG and 75.7°F."

2:02 PM Keith: "A paranormal investigation can be a lot of hard work."

2:03 PM Keith: "Do you like the color that the owner has painted the Dining Room down on the first floor?"

2:04 PM Keith: "Pat, Kathleen, Sunshine, and Mary, do you like what the owner has done with the house so far?"

2:07 PM Keith: "It is a lot of work writing this book."

2:08 PM Keith: "It is very hard and time-consuming trying to find history concerning the Hays House, and those who lived here. I always try to cross reference, what a person tells me during an interview with what I can find in the library and in the old newspapers."

2:11 PM Keith: "Do you have any advice as to how or where to look for history concerning the Hays House, and those who lived here?"

2:11 PM Keith: "The Ovilus IV gave me the word ah which is spelled A-H. The Ovilus IV has pronounced the word ah at a normal conversational level, but at a slower than normal conversational speed."

2:11 PM Keith: "You said ah, like that was a really good question."

2:11 PM Keith: "I have observed the Mel Meter readings to be 0.0 mG and 78.7°F."

2:12 PM Keith: "I have observed the EDI readings to be 0.0 mG and 75.8°F."

2:12 PM Keith: "The Ovilus IV gave me the word animal which is spelled A-N-I-M-A-L. The Ovilus IV has pronounced the word animal at a normal conversational level and speed."

2:13 PM Keith: "I have observed the Mel Meter readings to be 0.0 mG and 78.8°F."

2:14 PM Keith: "I have observed the EDI readings to be 0.0 mG and 75.8°F."

2:18 PM Keith: "What animal are you talking about?"

2:19 PM Keith: "Pat, Kathleen, Sunshine, and Mary, do you like what the owner is doing with the house?"

2:20 PM Keith: "I hear a noise, and vibrations near the foot of the bed."

2:22 PM Keith: "So, you have no advice for me, as far as obtaining history about the Hays House and the people who lived here?"

2:23 PM Keith: "Mary, do you like the new color that the dining room?"

2:24 PM Keith: "The Ovilus IV gave me the word dark, which is spelled D-A-R-K. The Ovilus IV has pronounced the word dark in a deep man's voice, at a lower than normal conversational level and at a slower than normal conversational speed."

2:24 PM Keith: "I have observed the Mel Meter readings to be 0.0 mG and 78.9°F."

2:24 PM Keith: "Yes, the Dining Room is being painted a dark color. I have not yet seen the dining room, sense the color change. I am going to look at Dining Room later today."

2:25 PM Keith: "I have observed the EDI readings to be 0.0 mG and 76.4°F."

2:30 PM Keith: "I'm going to do some thermal imaging of the Patsy Room."

2:32 PM to 2:34 PM Keith: "I have obtained six thermal images within the Patsy Room today. Two images were of my one pink footprints, one yellow footprint, and my yellow seat where I had been sitting. I obtained two images of the ceiling air conditioner vent which had a dark blue trail. I obtained two images of the air conditioner's dark blue cool air area on the room's South side ceiling."

2:35 PM Keith: "I did not see anything, paranormal and or unexplained within the images I obtained from the Patsy Room today."

2:36 PM Keith: "So, Pat, Kathleen, Sunshine, and Mary, do you like the dark paint in the Dining Room?"

2:38 PM Keith: "Pat, what color would you have painted the Dining Room?"

2:39 PM Keith: "Kathleen, what color would you have painted the Dining Room?"

2:39 PM Keith: "I heard a knock sound towards the Northwest corner of the Patsy Room."

2:40 PM Keith: "There is a man painting downstairs, so he may be causing the sounds that I am hearing."

2:41 PM Keith: "Sunshine Gibson, do you like the color that the Dining Room is being painted today?"

2:43 PM Keith: "I have observed the Mel Meter readings to be 0.0 mG and 77.6°F."

2:43 PM Keith: "I have observed the EDI readings to be 0.0 mG and 76.4°F."

2:45 PM Keith: "Thank you for talking to me. Have a nice day."

2:45 PM Keith: "This Session 2 ended on Wednesday, 14th June 2017."

Analysis of the Paranormal Investigation, Session 1, the Patsy Room, Wednesday, 14th June 2017, Hays House. The analysis was completed on Saturday, 27th October 2017.

At 11:14 AM the Ovilus IV gave me the first through fourth background words for this session number one, first word is unknown, felt, there, happy. I have not asked any questions yet during this Session 1. It is sad that I did not hear, see, and or obtain a picture of the first background word. I feel that these words are an intelligent spirit saying that they felt happiness there. In the past I've always felt that when there are four or more words fast and back to back, that this is a trademark of Sunshine Gibson. This assumption is subjective.

At 11:16 AM I observed that the Ovilus IV is not functioning properly. I use the term freezing up which is denoted by the eight dots that start at the upper left-hand side of the Ovilus IV's display, freeze in some combination and from 1 to 8 dots. When these dots don't fluctuate the Ovilus IV is not functioning properly and will not give you any words. It's almost like the ghosts or spirits are jamming up my Ovilus IV, so that the Ghosts and or Spirits cannot communicate with me through the Ovilus IV.

At 11:21 AM I have determined that the Ovilus IV will not return to its home position. I decided to place four new AAA batteries into the Ovilus IV.

At 1122. I could hear talking in the hallway from individuals that are in the Hays House. This is not paranormal.

At 11:26 AM the Ovilus IV gave me the fifth through seventh background words for this Session 1, rail, while, and question. I have not asked any questions yet during this Session 1. I do not believe that the words rail, while, and question are in response to any questions that I had asked previously in other Paranormal Investigations within the Hays House.

At 11:27 AM the Ovilus IV gave me the eighth word for this Session 1, quiet. Apparently, this is an intelligent spirit, that is asking me or someone else to be quiet.

At 11:28 AM the Ovilus IV gave me the ninth word for this Session 1, psychic. This Paranormal Investigation has been going on for 17 minutes and I have not asked one question yet. This is an intelligent spirit asking me if I'm psychic. I deny being psychic during this Paranormal Investigation. I have looked up on the definition of psychic. I do have the ability to feel the emotions of our dearly departed, ghosts and spirits, therefore, I am somewhat psychic.

From 11:40 AM to 11:42 AM I obtained six thermal images of the Patsy Room. I have determined that all six thermal images are free from any unexplained and or paranormal situations.

At 11:48 AM I heard a door squeak in the hallway. I do not feel that this was related to the paranormal.

At 11:50 AM the Ovilus IV gave me 10th response for Session 1, the letter M. It is a possibility that the M is Mary's way of communicating her name to me. I've been told that Mary had the abilities of a younger child. So, quite possibly, M is her way of saying hello, I am Mary.

At 11:54 AM the Ovilus IV gave me the 11th word for this Session 1, paint. The Ghost and or Spirit, that gave me the word paint, knew that the Dining Room was being painted before I knew that the Dining Room was being painted. That shows me that the Ghost or Spirit is intelligent and is willing to let me know what is going right on now. It seems like Ghosts and Spirits have a hard time remember what has happened in the past.

Analysis of the Paranormal Investigation, Session 2, the Patsy Room, Wednesday, 14th June 2017, Hays House. The analysis was completed on Sunday, 28th October 2017.

At 1:56 PM the Ovilus IV gave me the first and second background words for this Session 2, fun, and wonder. Since I have not asked any questions yet during this Session 2, I will assume that this is an intelligent Spirit or Ghost that is given me an independent analysis of what they think. This Spirits and or Ghosts feels that I am having fun and that I am full of wonder concerning the Paranormal Investigations that I am completing.

At 1:58 PM the Ovilus IV gave me the third word for this Session 2, felt. At 1:57 PM I had asked the question; do you wonder if I am having fun? This is an intelligent Spirit telling me that they felt that I was having fun.

At 2:11 PM I had asked the question, do you have any advice as to how or where to look for history concerning the Hays House, and those who lived here? At 2:11 PM the Ovilus IV gave me the fourth word for this Session 2, ah. I feel this was an intelligent response to my question. A Ghost was saying good question! I am sad to say that the ghosts are not answering more of my history driven questions.

The Ovilus IV had pronounced the word ah at a normal level, but at a slow and drawn out speed like aaaahhhhhh. It was almost as if the Ghost or Spirit was thinking about how to answer my question that I asked at 2:11 PM.

At 2:12 PM the Ovilus IV gave me the fifth word during this Session 2, animal. I do not believe that the word animal is in response to any of the questions I've asked so for during this Session 2.

At 2:20 PM I heard a noise's and or vibration near the foot of the bed. This may have been caused by the painter working on the first level. This noise and or vibration may be a cell phone that some-one lost with in the covers of this bed. I do not feel that this noise is Paranormal.

At 2:24 PM the Ovilus IV gave me the sixth word during this Session 2, dark. The Ovilus IV pronounced the word dark in a man's deep voice, at a lower than normal conversational level and at a slower than normal conversational speed. At 2:23 PM I had just asked the question, Mary, do you like the color that the Dining Room is being painted? I feel that this is the intelligent Spirit of Mary responding that the colors are dark.

Between 2:30 PM and 2:34 PM I obtained six thermal images of the Patsy Room. I did not see anything unexplained and or paranormal within the six thermal images that I obtained.

At 2:39 PM I asked Kathleen the question, what color would you paint, the Dining Room? At 2:39 PM I heard a knock sound coming from the room's Northwest corner. I do not feel that the painter on the first level is working, near the Northwest corner of the Hays House on the first level. The painter is working in the Dining Room on the first level which is closer to the Patsy Room's East wall. This knock may be cause by the Paranormal. I have no idea what one knock may mean. My question at 2:39 PM was, what color would you paint the Dining Room, is not a yes or no question.

Digital pictures of the Patsy Room, Friday, 10th March 2017, Hays House.

One picture of the two windows on the room's West wall.

One picture of the room's Northwest corner.

One picture of the room's North East corner.

One picture of the center of the East wall to include the fireplace.

One picture of the room's South East corner.

One picture of the center of the room's South wall to include the left side of the entrance door.

Two pictures of the room's Southwest corner.

One picture of the room's white tongue and groove ceiling boards.

One picture of the room's white ceiling boards and the white ceiling trim boards.

One picture of the room's horizontal wall boards.

Two pictures of the room's hardwood floor.

Four pictures of the decorative black iron fireplace cover located on the room's East wall.

Four pictures of the fireplace located on the room's East wall.

Two pictures of the black doorknob on the closet door, located on the room's East wall.

Two pictures of the black doorknob on the entrance door, located on the room's South wall.

Please see the author's website at www.keithoevans.com to view each digital picture.

Thermal images of the Patsy Room, Friday, 10th March 2017, Hays House.

One image of the Southwest corner of the room.

One image of the center of the room's West wall to include the two windows.

One image of the room's Northeast corner.

One image of the center of the room's North wall to include one window.

One image of the room's Northwest corner.

One image of the center of the room's East wall, to include the fireplace.

One image of the room's South East corner.

One image of the room's South wall, to include the entrance door.

Four images of the room's ceiling, and the room's air conditioner ceiling vent.

Please see the author's website at www.keithoevans.com to view each thermal image.

CHAPTER **21**

Third Floor Apartment, Hays House, Ghosts are People too.

Description of the Third Floor Apartment, Thursday, 15th June 2017, Hays House.

The Third Floor Apartment is occupied, so I will only mention the room's description as if it was empty. I will not mention any personal items.

The Third Floor Apartment's East wall has the narrow back stairway that comes up from the Second Floor Back Stairway Room. The East wall in part is a kitchen with a stove, over, and sink. The Southeast corner of the room has a walk-in closet. Near the South wall but standing separate from the south wall is a narrow stairway that leads to the widows walk. The West wall has an opening that leads to a small window. Within this opening on the West wall is another A-frame shaped, smaller crawlspace, that leads to the small window, located on the south side of the Hays House. The room's North wall has a small window. In the room's Northeast corner is a bathroom. Other than the bathroom and the walk-in closet, the Third Floor Apartment is a wide-open space. The floor of the Third Floor Apartment is modern.

The history concerning the Third Floor Apartment.

The Third Floor Apartment did not exist until after 1996. Prior to 1996 this Third-Floor area was just used for storage. It is believed that the Third Floor just had open rafters with installation in between. The modern steep stairway near the South wall that leads to the Widows

426

Walk was built sometime after 1996. Before, 1996 there was just a wooden ladder to climb up to the Widows Walk. When the Hays and Buck families owned the Hays House, the third-floor area was just used for storage. In the early 1950's Counsil Bryan Palmer, Annie's second husband, had a venting system placed into the floor of the widows walk and ceiling of the Third-Floor storage area. From the outside, this rectangular shape, coffin looking object allowed hot air to vertically remove through the top of the Hays House. As of June 2017, the chain system to open the vent is still functioning and you can still see the vent in the ceiling of the Third Floor Apartment that allows horizontal air circulation. It has been reported to me that a busload of students on a field trip had knocked on Kathleen's door and asked if her husband Pat was buried on the roof. Kathleen did not like that at all. As of June 2017, there is a wooden box over the coffin shaped vent. So, from the roadway this vent system looks more like a rectangular table or bar on top of the Widows Walk.

I did not obtain any Mel Meter base readings because someone was living in this apartment and my time within the Third Floor Apartment was limited.

Paranormal Investigation, Session 1, Third Floor Apartment, Thursday, 15th, June 2017, Hays House.

11:15 AM Keith: "Hello, I am Keith Evans. I wish only to speak to the members of the Buck, Gibson, and Hays families. That includes you too, Mary. You may use your energy to choose words from the Ovilus IV's database. The Ovilus IV will not hurt ghost's and or spirits." (Hold it up.)

11:16 AM Keith: "This is the Mel Meter and EDI. The Mel Meter and EDI measure temperature and electromagnetic frequencies. The Mel Meter and EDI will not harm Ghosts, and or Spirits." (Hold it up.)

11:17 AM Keith: "The Ovilus IV has given me two background words; sky which is spelled S-K-Y, and Lynn which is spelled L-Y-N-N. The Ovilus IV has pronounced the words sky and Lynn at a normal conversational level and speed."

11:17 AM Keith: "Hi Lynn. It is nice to meet you. Which family are you a member of?"

11:17 AM Keith: "I have observed the Mel Meter readings to be 0.0 mG and 74.5°F."

11:17 AM Keith: "I have observed the EDI readings to be 0.0 mG and 73.5°F."

11:18 AM Keith: "The Ovilus IV has given me the words: cut which is spelled C-U-T, communication which is spelled COM-M-U-N-I-C-AT-I-O-N, and focus which is spelled F-O-C-U-S. The Ovilus IV has pronounce the words cut, communicate, and focus at a normal conversational level and speed."

11:18 AM Keith: "My digital camera is out of focus."

11:18 AM Keith: "I have observed the Mel Meter readings to be 0.0 mG and 74.7°F."

11:18 AM Keith: "I have observed the EDI readings to be 0.0 mG and 73.3°F."

11:21 AM Keith: "The Ovilus IV gave me the word fate which is spelled F-A-T-E. The Ovilus IV pronounced the word fate at a normal conversational level and speed."

11:21 AM Keith: "I have observed the Mel Meter readings to be 0.0 mG and 73.9°F."

11:22 AM Keith: "I have observed the EDI readings to be 0.0 mG and 73.5°F."

11:25 AM Keith: "Lynn, are you back?"

11:26 AM Keith: "Lynn, are you married to a Buck?"

11:27 AM Keith: "Lynn, are you a Hays or a Gibson?"

11:28 AM Keith: "Frequently my camera seems to take forever to focus."

11:34 AM Keith: "Sunshine, when you lived in Apalachicola, how old were you?"

11:36 AM Keith: "Sunshine, did you like that school you went to an Atlanta?"

11:37 AM Keith: "What was the name of the school you went to in Atlanta?"

11:38 AM Keith: "Sunshine, do you not remember any history about your life?"

11:39 AM Keith: "Sunshine, I am disappointed that you have not been more forthcoming with information about the history of the Hays House."

11:40 AM Keith: "The Ovilus IV gave me the word immersion which is spelled I-M-M-E-R-S-I-O-N. The Ovilus IV has pronounced the word immersion at a normal conversational level and speed."

11:41 AM Keith: "I have observed the Mel Meter readings to be 0.0 mG and 73.9°F."

11:41 AM Keith: "I have observed the EDI readings to be 0.0 mG and 72.6°F."

11:41 AM Keith: "I could snap the picture, right away, but the picture would be so blurry that you could not make out what was in the picture."

11:44 AM Keith: "Are you immerged in water?"

11:46 AM Keith: "Lynn, what do you have to say today?"

11:47 AM Keith: "Do you like the color that the Dining Room?"

11:48 AM Keith: "Mary, do you like the color of the paint in the Dining Room?"

11:49 AM Keith: "Pat, Kathleen, and Sunshine, do you like the color of the new Dining Room paint?"

11:50 AM Keith: "Sunshine, did you ever paint, the Dining Room?"

11:51 AM Keith: "I'm going to obtain thermal images of the Third Floor Apartment."

11:52 AM to 11:57 AM Keith: "I obtained 10 thermal images of the Third Floor Apartment. Two images of my body's pink reflection in the mirror. Two images of the air conditioning vent on the room's West wall. Two images of the air conditioner vent on the room's South wall. Two images of the air conditioning vent on the room's East wall. One image of the steep stairway leading from the Third Floor Apartment to the Widows Walk."

11:58 AM Keith: "Pat, what was stored in this third-floor area when you were living here?"

11:59 AM Keith: "James Buck, what was stored in the third-floor area when you were living here?"

12:01 PM Keith: "L. G. Buck, what was stored in this third-floor area when you lived here?"

12:02 PM to 12:05 PM Keith: "I obtained digital pictures of the Third Floor Apartment."

12:05 PM Keith: "I am away from the Ovilus IV. It sounded like an S sound. It was either the Ovilus IV and or a disembodied voice. We will see."

12:05 PM Keith: "It was the Ovilus IV."

12:05 PM Keith: "The Ovilus IV gave me the word sail which is spelled S-A-I-L. The Ovilus IV pronounced the word sail at a lower than normal conversational level and at a faster than normal conversational speed. I only heard and S sound."

12:05 PM Keith: "I have observed the Mel Meter readings to be 0.0 mG and 73.9°F."

12:06 PM Keith: "I have observed the EDI readings to be 0.0 mG and 72.3°F."

12:11 PM Keith: "Thank you for talking to me. Have a nice day."

12:11 PM Keith: "This Session 1 ended on Thursday, 15th June 2017."

Paranormal Investigation, Session 2, Third floor Apartment, Thursday, 15th, June 2017, Hays House.

1:23 PM Keith: "Hello, I am Keith Evans. I wish only to speak to members of the Buck, Gibson, and Hays families today. That includes you too Mary. You may use your energy to choose words from the Ovilus IV's database. The Ovilus IV will not hurt ghosts and or spirits." (Hold it up.)

1:24 PM Keith: "This is the Mel Meter and the EDI. They measure temperature and electromagnetic frequencies. The Mel Meter and the EDI will not harm ghosts, and or spirits." (Hold it up.)

1:24 PM Keith: "The Ovilus IV has given me one background word scare which is spelled S-C-A-R-E. The Ovilus IV has pronounced the word scare at a normal conversational level and speed."

1:24 PM Keith: "No, I do not feel that I scare easily."

1:25 PM Keith: "I have observed the Mel Meter readings to be 0.0 mG and 75.8°F."

1:25 PM Keith: "I have observed the EDI readings to be 0.0 mG and 73.8°F."

1:25 PM Keith: "My digital camera is going in and out of focus again."

1:28 PM Keith: "Annie is that you that is causing my digital camera to go in and out of focus?"

1:29 PM Keith: "Hello, Annie. I know you are here. What do you have to say? Use the Ovilus IV to talk to me."

1:30 PM Keith: "I am going to take some more digital pictures of the room."

1:35 PM Keith: "I'm going to do a thermal scan of the Third Floor Apartment."

1:35 PM to 1:40 PM Keith: "I obtained 18 thermal images of the Third Floor Apartment. I obtained two images of my pink footprints. I obtained two images of my pink footprints and the yellow seat of the chair where I had been sitting. I obtained eight, thermal images of the air conditioner vent on the wall near the Third Floor Apartment's Southwest corner. I obtained two thermal images of the pink area of the wall at the bottom of the narrow and steep back stairway that lead down from the third-floor apartment. I obtained two images to the left side of the air conditioner vent on the room's South wall. I obtained two images of the ceiling door that leads to the Widows Walk."

1:41 PM Keith: "I do not see anything unexplained and or paranormal, during my thermal scanning of the Third Floor Apartment."

1:42 PM Keith: "This question is for anyone who has lived here at the Hays House, how did you use the third floor?"

1:43 PM Keith: "Mary, did you ever play up here on the third floor when you lived here?"

1:44 PM Keith: "James Buck, how did you use this third floor?"

1:45 PM Keith: "James Buck, how often did you use the Widows Walk?"

1:46 PM Keith: "Pat, Kathleen, Sunshine, and Mary, how often did you use the Widows Walk?"

1:47 PM Keith: "It looks like the Ovilus IV is frozen up again. I tried to press the home icon, and the Ovilus IV would not go back to the home position. The Ovilus IV's batteries should not be dead yet. I am going to turn the Ovilus IV off. I am going to place four new AAA batteries in the Ovilus IV."

1:49 PM Keith: "I turned the Ovilus IV on."

1:50 PM Keith: "The Ovilus IV gave me the word sex which is spelled S-E-X. The Ovilus IV pronounced the word sex at a lower than normal conversational level, but at a normal conversational speed."

1:50 PM Keith: "I have observed the Mel Meter readings to be 0.0 mG and 74.4°F."

1:51 PM Keith: "I have observed the EDI readings to be 0.0 mG and 73.2°F."

1:51 PM Keith: "So Sunshine, by saying the word sex you know what I'm thinking. I'm going to ask that question and it is going into the book. Sunshine, did you ever sunbathe nude on the Widows Walk?"

1:56 PM Keith: "It looks like the Ovilus IV has frozen up again."

1:57 PM Keith: "Sunshine, it seems that if you're not happy with me just drain the batteries in the Ovilus IV. See the batteries are dead in the Ovilus IV is frozen up."

1:59 PM Keith: "The Ovilus IV will not go back to the home position. You can see me pressing the home icon with my pen and nothing is happening."

2 PM Keith: "I am going to turn the Ovilus IV off manually. I am going to adjust the batteries, because I know the four AAA batteries cannot be dead yet."

2:02 PM Keith: "The Ovilus IV has given me two background words hung which is spelled H-U-N-G and plant which is spelled P-L-A-N-T. The Ovilus IV has pronounced the words hung and plant at a normal conversational level and speed."

2:02 PM Keith: "I have observed the Mel Meter readings to be 0.0 mG and 75.1°F."

2:02 PM Keith: "I have observed the Mel Meter readings to be 0.0 mG and 74.9°F."

2:03 PM Keith: "I have observed the EDI readings to be 0.0 mG and 72.9°F."

2:05 PM Keith: "The Ovilus IV gave me the word memory which is spelled M-E-M-O-R-Y. The Ovilus IV pronounced the word memory at a normal conversational level and speed."

2:05 PM Keith: "I have observed the Mel Meter readings to be 0.0 mG and 74.1°F."

2:05 PM Keith: "I have observed the EDI readings to be 0.0 mG and 72.9°F."

2:06 PM Keith: "The Ovilus IV gave me the word crops which is spelled C-R-O-P-S. The Ovilus IV has pronounced the word crops at a normal conversational level and speed."

2:06 PM Keith: "I have observed the EDI readings to be 0.0 mG and 72.8°F."

2:07 PM Keith: "It is like the Ghosts and Spirits know when this Session 2 is coming to an end. Every Ghost and Spirit in town wants to choose words from the Ovilus IV. These words are not answering any of the questions that I have asked during this Session 2."

2:07 PM Keith: "Thank you for talking to me. Have a good day."

2:07 PM Keith: "This session 2 has ended on Thursday, 15th June 2017."

The analysis of the Paranormal Investigation, Session 1, Third Floor Apartment, Thursday, 15th June 2017, Hays House. Date of the analysis was Tuesday, 31st October 2017.

At 11:17 AM the Ovilus IV gave me the first and second background words for this Session 1, sky and Lynn. I have not asked any questions yet during this Session 1. I do not feel that the words sky and Lynn are in response to any questions that I've asked in the past. I do not know anyone named Lynn that is associated with the Hays House. J. F. Buck had a daughter that was named after his wife, Lillian Maude, maybe her nick name with Lynn. Maybe J. F. Buck, (Jeff), called his daughter

Lynn to avoid the confusion of calling the name Lillian and having his wife and daughter respond.

At 11:18 AM the OvilusIV gave me the third through fifth words for this Session 1, cut, communicate, and focus. I do feel that this is an intelligent Ghost and Spirit and it could be Annie. Annie seems to be saying that she is going to cut communications with me and cause my camera to go out of focus. In the past, I've always thought that Annie's trademark to let me know that she is present is to cause my camera to go in and out of focus. Annie always liked having her picture taken. I imagine that the automatic focus on my camera may have a hard time focusing on a Spirit and or Ghost that is not a solid image. I think that Annie is in front of my camera saying take my picture.

At 11:18 AM I stated that my digital camera is going out of focus most of the time.

At 11:21 AM the Ovilus IV gave me the sixth word for this Session 1, fate. I have only asked one question during this Session 1, and the word fate does not answer that question. Maybe this is Annie saying that my fate is to have a camera that keeps going in and out of focus.

At 11:28 AM I state that my camera is frequently not in focus.

At 11:40 AM the Ovilus IV gave me the seventh word for this Session 1, emmersion.

At 11:41 AM I state that I could snap a picture right away, but it would be so blurry that no one would be able to see it.

From 11:52 AM to 11:57 AM I obtained 10, thermal images of the third-floor apartment. I did not find any thermal images with unexplained and or paranormal situations.

At 12:05 PM the Ovilus IV gave me the eighth word for this Session 1, sail. I had asked three questions about what was stored on the third-floor level in the past. This could be an intelligent Spirit or Ghost saying that at one time, a sail to a sailboat was stored on this third-floor level.

The analysis of the Paranormal Investigation, Session 2, Third Floor Apartment, Thursday, 15th June 2017, Hays House. Date of the analysis was Tuesday, 31st October 2017.

At 1:24 PM the OvilusIV gave me the first back ground word for Session 2, scare. I have not asked any questions yet during this Session 2. I do not feel that the words scare is responding to any of the questions that I have asked so for today. Maybe this was an intelligent Ghost or Spirit that was surprised that I was not afraid of Ghosts and Spirits.

At 1:25 PM I state that my digital camera is going in and out of focus. As before I feel this is the spirit of Annie Gibson Palmer. This is Annie's signature move to let me know that she is here. I feel that Annie liked to have her picture taken and as her Spirit is posing for the picture. My digital camera's automatic focus has a difficult time zeroing in on a spirit that the camera can sense, but not see.

From 1:35 PM to 1:40 PM I obtained 18 thermal images of the Third Floor Apartment. I did find two thermal images with an unexplained pink area on the wall at the bottom of the narrow and steep back stairway going from the third floor to the second floor, looking down from the top of the steps. I could not identify any reason for this area to be warm enough, to give a pink area. There are no hot water pipes and or drainage pipes in this area of the wall. There is a refrigerator and freezer on the opposite side, but I don't feel that it would get that warm to heat up the wall. I cannot say that it is paranormal but this pink area is definitely unexplained.

At 1:47 PM I noticed that the Ovilus IV was frozen up and not functioning properly. The Ovilus IV would not return to the home position. I turned the Ovilus IV off.

At 1:49 PM I turned the Ovilus IV back on.

At 1:50 PM the Ovilus IV gave me the second back ground word for this session 2, sex. I had asked three questions concerning what the third floor was used for. Looks like one Ghost and or Spirit felt that someone may have had sex on the third floor. The Ovilus IV pronounced the word sex at a lower than normal conversational level, but at a normal conversational speed. Almost as if the Ghost or Spirit was whispering the word sex to me, so no one else would hear.

At 1:56 PM the Ovilus IV has stop functioning properly again.

At 1:57 PM I said to Sunshine Gibson, if this is what it looks like when you're unhappy with me. Is it you that is draining the batteries in the Ovilus IV.

At 1:59 PM I state that the Ovilus IV will not go to its home position.

At 2 PM I state that I'm going to turn the Ovilus IV off manually. I also state that the batteries could not be dead and I'm going to adjust the four AAA batteries within the Ovilus IV.

At 2:02 PM I turned the Ovilus IV on and obtain the third and fourth background words for this Session 2, hung and plant. I do not feel that the words hung and plant are in response to any of the questions that I have asked during this Session 2. This could be the intelligent Spirit or Ghost of Kathleen talking about the hanging potted plants that she had on the Wraparound Front Porch prior to 1996. On the other hand, when Kathleen lived at the Hays House, she may have keep her potted plants hanging in the Third Floor Storage Area in the winter time.

At 2:05 PM the Ovilus IV gave me the fifth word for this Session 2, memory. It seems like an intelligent spirit is referring to their memory, like they are trying to remember.

At 2:06 PM the Ovilus IV gave me the sixth word for this Session 2, crops. I do not feel that the word crops are in response to any of the questions that I've asked so far during this Session 2.

At 2:07 PM I am letting off steam and blaming Sunshine and or Annie, for just spouting off words right at the end of the hour-long session. Sometimes I feel like the Ghost or Spirits are wasting my time by choosing words from the Ovilus IV that are not answering my questions. I want every word chosen on the Ovilus IV to count and have meaning.

437

Digital Pictures, Third Floor Apartment, Thursday, 15th June 2017, Hays House.

One picture of the room's Southwest corner.

Three pictures of the room's West wall.

Two pictures of the room's Northwest corner.

Two pictures of the room's North wall.

Two pictures of the room's Northeast corner.

Three pictures of the room's East wall.

Four pictures of the room's South East corner.

Two pictures of the room's South wall.

Two close-up pictures of the stairway leading to the widows walk.

Two pictures of the stairway going from the Third Floor Apartment to the Second Floor Back Stairway Room.

Two pictures of the ceiling's door that open into the Widow's Walk.

Four pictures of the room's ceiling.

Please see the author's website at www.keithoevans.com to view each digital picture.

I did not obtain any background thermal images, because someone is living in this apartment and my time within the Third Floor Apartment was limited.

Throughout my journey of completing at least two, one-hour Paranormal Sessions in each room of the Hays House. I always sensed that the prior owners and residents who loved their home never valued a man who would be conducting a Paranormal Investigation, when they were alive. I do not feel that Ghosts and Spirits personality's change that much from went they were living. So, I sensed that;

Pat, Kathleen, Sunshine, Annie, Mary, Jeff, and L. G. were just tolerating me, in the hopes that the Book, "The Hays House, Ghosts are People too", would be a best selling and this would produce several generations of new people, to become the owners, caretakers, and guardian angles for the Hays House for the next two hundred years.

I feel that keeping the original tough & groove, heart pine, hard wood flooring, the original tough & groove, horizontal, wall boards, and the original tough & groove ceiling is the connection that the Ghosts and Spirits need to be able to travel back and forth from heaven, to look after the home that they loved. The things that Ghosts and Spirits love can be anything; such as; a house, a car, an antique, a cat, a dog, and a person.

In closing, from my completing the historical research and Paranormal Investigations within the Hays House, I have felt like I have known; Pat, Kathleen, Sunshine, Annie, Mary, Jeff, and L. G. They all were outstanding citizens within their community. I feel that they love their families and Apalachicola. I know my life has been enriched by having known each and every one that has lived in the Hays House. Thank you. Keith O. Evans

CPSIA information can be obtained
at www.ICGtesting.com
Printed in the USA
BVHW031935170419
545826BV00001B/84/P